QUARTERBACK SNEAK

ANITA BARNEY
AS TOLD TO **DEANNA C. STEVENS**

Cover Design: FORT

ISBN: 0–692–58239–8
ISBN-13: 978–0–692–58239–8

CONTENTS

ACKNOWLEDGMENTS

When I was first contacted about helping Anita tell her story, I had no idea who she was, and precious little awareness of Art Schlichter and his feats on the football field—or his criminal activity off of it. Approaching this story without prejudice was at the same time exhilarating and risky. The opportunity to shape a memoir from so many unbelievable experiences was a delight. Tracking down accurate details regarding a hometown hero's widely publicized misconduct was, at times, complicated.

Nearly everyone I spoke with had developed an opinion regarding Art, as his woes are well known. However, most people did not have a clear understanding how his ticket schemes operated or how Anita became involved to such a degree. *Quarterback Sneak* will answer those questions. I assembled the information by conducting untold hours of personal interviews with Anita and others, poring over police reports, reading through news articles, reviewing interrogations, and listening to hundreds of recorded phone conversations. I discovered Art is a chameleon—he plays whatever role is required at that moment in order to get what he wants. He can be a helpless victim or a charming romantic, a beguiling friend or an abusive tormenter. Time and again the authorities talked about Art's charisma and uncanny ability to persuade his victims to take action according to his whims—even to the point of personal ruin.

Quarterback Sneak is a true story. Whenever possible, details have been confirmed through public documents, court filings, personal interviews, and police reports. However, many names have been changed, identifying information has been altered, and some events summarized to provide clarity to the reader, protect innocent victims, and shield the family members of individuals involved in nefarious activities.

This story would not have been possible without the generous assistance of various law enforcement agencies and community leaders—many who prefer to remain anonymous due to the nature of their work. I would also like to acknowledge the kind contribution of individuals who made themselves available to take my calls, answer my questions, and provide background for the story: Angela Genereux, Alan Valko, Carol Jean Moone, Trish Newkirk, Nora Hanley, Ruth Joseph, Vincent J. Margello Jr., Karen Butler, Mary Bernardo, Sue Noe, and Sheriff Vernon P. Stanforth.

My heart overflows with gratitude for Karen Kaiser, who invested countless hours editing, proofreading, and polishing this story. Debbie Schierholt and Dawn Stephens also provided valuable editorial assistance. James Gebhart, Ph.D., explained the ways childhood trauma can affect adult decisions, as well as provided insight into the behavior of victims of abuse. Attorney William Loveland has stood by Anita as a fierce defender, and graciously made time for my questions regarding her case, and legal procedures in general.

I am grateful for my husband, Greg, who gave me the space and support I needed to develop this story.

Of course, Anita was the driving force behind this project. She provided an unvarnished view of her life, sharing the unbelievable experiences and the tragic events. We traveled many roads together—some more difficult than others—and shed many tears during our sessions. By the end of the journey we had ventured further than anyone could have imagined. I appreciate the trust she placed in me.

Finally, if you suspect elder abuse in Ohio, I encourage you to contact the Ohio Attorney General's Elder Justice Initiative at 800-282-0515 and your local authorities.

Deanna C. Stevens

ANITA'S MESSAGE

November 2015

Over the years, when people would hear me recount my life's experiences and suggest I write a book, I would laugh it off asking, "Who would care to read about me?" Later, when authorities mentioned they had never come across a case like mine, and with so many compelling components it would make a fascinating story, I entertained their suggestions even though the idea was inconceivable. I was just trying to survive Art, his abuse, and the subsequent fallout; I didn't have the energy or inspiration to talk about what had happened. I couldn't envision having to relive such a desperate time in my life in order to be able to describe events and emotions that depleted me of the will to live.

After a while I found myself in a place of relative peace and safety and the idea of a book didn't seem so overwhelming. My plan was to give readers a glimpse into how a compulsive gambler operates, explain my role in the events that took place between 2009 and 2012, and perhaps, generate some income to help repay the friends who, due to my association with Art, were unknowingly caught up in his terrible schemes.

And then, as sometimes occurs with a project such as this, the content of the book expanded to include not only my involvement with Art, but my entire life so you might be able to understand how I became the woman Art targeted, financially decimated, and personally destroyed. As you will read, my life has been one wild ride after another with extreme highs and unbelievable lows. But in the end, it was a compassionate God who heard my cries of distress, His love that saved me, and His strength that now carries me from day to day.

While my past still remains a haunting reminder of a scandalous time, I try not to spend too much time looking back. I've learned that if I entertain regret and shame, they have a way of tightly wrapping their tentacles around my mind in an attempt to squeeze the life right out of me. Instead, I prefer to use my past as a signpost of how far I've come. There is a newfound hope in my life as I acknowledge God's mercies and give Him the glory.

I hope my story sparks hope in your life. If God was willing to bring me through the valley of the shadow of death, I know He will bring you through your circumstance, too!

Fondly,
Anita

VOLUME I

1 | LATE SUMMER 2010

He flipped a page. "What about her?" he asked as he pointed to yet another entry and held my address book up so I could see. He had been at this for hours.

I could rattle off a hundred stories about "her." She was a dear friend who kept my confidences and eagerly agreed to join me in any escapade. When my forties rolled around and I noticed a little belly forming, she was my co-conspirator as I scheduled a liposuction procedure without Bob knowing. Well, I mean, I didn't tell him until I was unable to get out of bed the next morning without his help. I was sore and bruised for days.

She was always ready for any of my adventures. When I wanted to go soaring near King's Island, off we went. We stopped for some sliders at White Castle on the way down to Cincinnati, which we discovered later wasn't the best idea. As we got into the plane, which was designed for only one passenger and a pilot but we both squeezed in, it was hot and uncomfortable. We spent most of the flight desperately wishing there was a window to open for some fresh air, and barely noticed the view as we circled above the amusement park.

I can't begin to count the number of times she would help me prepare for the parties Bob and I hosted, before rushing home to shower and change and returning with her husband as our guests.

We could laugh and talk for hours about everything and anything or nothing at all.

"What about HER?!" he demanded as he shoved the book my way again and broke my concentration.

"Oh, Art!" I pleaded. "Don't make me call Joyce. I really don't like asking people for money. It doesn't feel right."

He was getting angry with me. I could see it in his face. When we met in the parking lot earlier he was disheveled, and I could tell he had not showered that morning. Bed head. That's what he had.

"We've talked about this!" he exploded. "I can GET THE TICKETS! I got the OSU tickets, didn't I?"

It's true. He had come through with the OSU football tickets. Everyone who wanted them got them. But it was such a mess. So weird how that worked out. I didn't like it. Not one bit. Meeting in parking lots late on Fridays or early Saturday mornings. Boxes of tickets in the backseat of his car. Rushing to make deliveries before kickoff.

"Well, I have a similar deal with the Colts. I've got a guy and the tickets are guaranteed. And I've got people willing to pay a premium for 'em. And with the money we can make on the mark-up, I'll be able to pay you, and you can pay back your friends. You know that's the goal."

"You're *sure* you can get the tickets?" I asked before my voice dropped and I looked away. "You're not gambling," I sighed, "are you?"

"Damn it, Anita! How many times do I have to tell you? I haven't gambled in five years! NO, I'M NOT GAMBLING!"

I couldn't wrap my head around how all the money had disappeared. Nearly everything I owned was gone in exchange for hollow promises. My bank accounts were empty, as was my resolve. Bob had warned me about this: a man coming to take all of my money. How did I not recognize it before now? I was so stupid.

"Anita! If we don't do this right now—RIGHT NOW!—the deal will be off and it will be ALL OVER! AND IT WILL BE YOUR FAULT! You crazy b**ch!! You're going to ruin EVERYTHING!"

He was screaming now. I could feel his breath and the spittle flying from his mouth as his face turned red. My heart started racing and I began trembling in fear.

"And then you will NEVER be able to repay your friends. NEVER! And all those checks you wrote won't be any good and YOU'LL go to jail. And let me tell you, that's one place you don't want to be, trust me! If this all blows up, you won't have anyone to blame but YOURSELF!"

It was true; it was all on me. No one knew—really knew—Art was involved. It was always at his direction that I made the calls, borrowed the money, and wrote the checks. Often I didn't even know the payee or the purpose of the check. I was the puppet as he pulled the strings behind the scenes. He had positioned himself to avoid any blowback while I stood alone in the line of fire. I was so tired. And afraid. I wanted it all to stop.

Sensing I was shutting down, he tried a gentler approach.

"Anita, honey, look, we're in this together. I never imagined things would be like this. I'm just trying to help us out of it. And I know you want to pay your friends back. That's what I want, too. You know that. Let's work this out together. Everything will be OK."

Would it? Would anything *ever* be OK? If I turned my back on him at this moment I was doomed and my friends would never be repaid. I couldn't fix this, *any of this*, by myself. The only glimmer of hope I had was that Art would be able to make good on this new set of promises. And the money really was coming in.

"Come on, Anita, *please* make the call. Please do this."

Out of options. I took a deep breath and dialed the number I knew by heart.

2 | THE BEGINNING

Where does one start to tell the story of a life? I guess it would be easy to jump right in the middle, where headlines shouted half-truths for the world to read. I think I know what people are expecting. My family is looking for answers and a return to what had been. My accusers are demanding justice. My enemies are hoping for revenge. My co-conspirators are praying for my silence. My friends are rooting for my redemption. And even from his prison cell, Art is scheming for a shorter sentence.

The assumptions and charges, the testimony and sentences have been splashed across newspapers, discussed on talk shows, and written about on websites too numerous to list. If you want to hear any version of the truth, you can find what you're seeking.

But what am I searching for?

You may wonder why would I agree to write about my failings and misjudgments. I suppose it's because my story has not been told. I've never had the opportunity to share what really happened or explain things in a meaningful way—to dissect the events that occurred and caused me to become caught up in the lies and schemes and loss that affected so many.

When I had wanted to speak out in the past, I was silenced by Art's threats and cautioned by authorities. More often than not, I was too weak to find my voice after suffering at the hands of an abuser. Thankfully, that past is behind me and as I seek to understand what happened and the part I played, I have found courage to face the horror of it all.

And I've also discovered something else.

Courage is not the same as bravado, which I had in spades. I'm not trying to impress you with a life well-lived or solicit your pity by playing the victim. I want to share with you what can happen when a debt of gratitude turns into legal charges. When well-meaning actions evolve into ripples of lies and deceit. When things go horribly wrong and a reputation of generosity and kindness is erased through a tidal wave of manipulation, fear, and abuse.

My story, like all the stories that have been told before, is best started at the beginning. It doesn't start in 1980 when my ten-year-old son Alan nearly died in a horrific plane crash, or in November 2009 when I connected with former OSU star quarterback Art Schlichter to thank him for changing the course of my son's life. And, it certainly doesn't end with my pleading guilty to extracting more than $400,000 from friends and employees in 2012. There are many events to examine before we can talk about how I became the woman who called the authorities in 2010 to plead for protection from a publicly heralded, well-known predator, and eventually became the catalyst that finally put an end to the path of destruction caused by Art's gambling addiction.

I wasn't the first person Art victimized but, hopefully, I will be the last. Unbeknownst to me there were countless others over many years who had fallen prey to Art and his dazzling charisma before he set his sights on me. Wealthy men bought into his lies. Business owners gave him money repeatedly. Community leaders praised Art's wondrous turnaround since being released from prison. Respected publications splashed Art's face on their covers and told his story on their pages. Television and radio personalities sought interviews, invited him to participate in weekly sports broadcasts, and celebrated his return as the hometown hero who won big, lost it all, and returned to seek redemption for past sins.

I knew Art as a popular and kind-hearted OSU quarterback who was dating our neighbor's daughter, and who took an hour out of his afternoon one day to visit my son. At the time, Alan was a broken child, struggling to heal from the physical and mental wounds he suffered in a plane crash that nearly killed him and claimed the life of his father. That one and only encounter changed Alan's outlook from sad and despondent to hopeful and happy. The transformation was evident to everyone. I even received a call from the teacher at Alan's school the week after Art visited, to discuss the incredible and visible change in my son:

> *It's the first time since the accident Alan hasn't been focused on what happened to him. He's talking about football again. The change is amazing.*

I was beyond grateful. However, my days were consumed attending to Alan's physical recovery and managing multiple appointments with physicians, therapists, and counselors, and I never genuinely thanked Art or told him about the difference his visit had made in Alan's life.

In fact, I was out when Art stopped by our home on Stoney Bridge Lane to visit. As I came into the house that day after running errands, my daughter Angela told me Art had just left and called after him to return and meet me. I thanked Art for his time and the OSU memorabilia he had brought. That was the first and last interaction I had with him until we spoke at Genoa Church in 2009—nearly thirty years later—when he was campaigning against a state issue to permit the legalization of casinos in Ohio.

News articles later reported that even while Art was speaking about his freedom from gambling addiction and peddling his memoir that day, he was selling and reselling the financial rights to his book and harassing people to buy into his ticket schemes. Obviously, he couldn't stop the raging desire to gamble and would take whatever actions necessary to feed his habit. Gambling addiction is not that different from a drug addict looking to score the next fix or an alcoholic desperate for a drink. Addiction, whatever form it takes, is ugly and heartbreaking.

Sadly, I've witnessed first-hand the damage gambling addicts inflict. Nothing is too much. No action crosses the line. Asking, begging, lying, scheming, demanding, threatening—

anything is acceptable if it means scoring some cash. So focused on his overwhelming desire to gamble, Art couldn't help himself even as he lived a frenzied life at the brink of impending destruction.

I was as naïve as he was cunning. My willingness to help a man who had changed the course of my son's life, along with an ignorance of how addicts behave, blinded me to the fact that he was swindling me out of everything I owned.

After Art was arrested in February 2011, I learned the authorities were aware of his new round of gambling and money laundering schemes in early 2010 but didn't have enough evidence to arrest him. However, after Art had depleted my accounts of everything I owned and deceived me to act as his accomplice, authorities had enlisted my assistance and with my help were able to obtain more than enough evidence for a conviction. I was the catalyst for their case against him, and played a vital role in Art being convicted on three federal counts of fraud and one state count of theft.

I was in the Gallery the day Art learned his sentence in Franklin County Court. There are two memories I recall vividly. The first is when I saw him enter the courtroom in an inmate uniform. I was shocked to see visible evidence of his crime. Here was the man who had dramatically affected my life on two separate occasions. The first encounter resulted in hope and recovery for my son, the last culminated in my personal despair and ruin. To see the man who had asserted so much control over my actions—the person who verbally and emotionally abused me—diminished to a thug in a prison jumpsuit was astounding. It was only at that point that I truly realized the extent of his actions and I finally felt the excruciating weight of his control lifted from my shoulders. It's impossible to explain why I couldn't see it before.

People have asked why I simply didn't deny Art's continual requests for more money or his demands that I solicit funds from friends. The relationship between an abuser and his victim is complicated. Art positioned himself in such a way that I couldn't see him for what he was—an addict and a predator. And as he seductively led me down the path of abuse, I unwittingly handed over my power to stop him. His panicked phone calls, threats of physical abuse, paranoid ramblings, promises of big payoffs, and sporadic payments kept me locked into believing that if I ever knocked over his house of cards, I would never be able to reclaim the money to pay back my friends. Until the day he was arrested, I clung to a misguided hope that Art would be true to his word, the money would come in, and I would be able to settle all accounts. As unbelievable as it sounds, I believed him until the very last moment.

The second memory from that day in court was a private one. At the conclusion of the proceedings, Franklin County Prosecutor Ron O'Brien walked over and thanked me for assisting with his case:

"We couldn't have done it without you."

I'm sure there are many reasons he was unable to thank me publicly as his office had implied he would, but I wish he had gone on record to say something about my involvement in bringing Art to justice. It would have helped offset the price I had paid, served to answer my accusers, and provided the press with a different perspective to consider. Although I was bitterly disappointed at his public silence on the matter, I appreciated his personal acknowledgement.

I've learned many lessons in the past five years. I discovered how previous personal experiences set the stage for my victimization. I witnessed how quickly people will abandon relationships to preserve their reputations. I confronted the dark side of addiction and came face-to-face with a community willing to protect an abuser and punish the victim. I've also benefitted from true friendships with people who were willing to believe the best in me and, in the process, open doors of opportunities for my redemption.

I learned that obtaining justice often extracts a high cost, and doing the right thing can bring its own misery.

I've suffered privately and lost publicly. Even now, it appears there are more questions—and certainly more accusations—than answers or explanations.

And here's something else I've learned along the way: While the truth may be elusive, it is worth the effort to find.

3 | FAMILY

1942—1956

"When it was good, it was very good. *When it was bad, it was horrid."*	*Anita Barney*

I came from a typical working class family. My mother worked as a secretary for the Ohio State Life Insurance Company at Broad and Grant (where she was introduced to future championship golfer Jack Nicklaus, who was working his way through college) before moving on to the Columbus Defense Supply Center and then to the Columbus City School District for many years. She was always volunteering to coordinate office socials and covered-dish dinners, and kept a drawer filled with "last-minute gifts" for friends. I can trace my joy of entertaining and organizing social events to her. I often wonder if her desire to find ways to make people happy came from the impossible life she had with my father. My dad spent many long hours away from us at the bars, and a fight was always waiting for him when he returned. I think his drinking was the way he coped with his horrific childhood. When things would get to be too much for him he would shut down, walk out on us, and walk into a bar where he could drink his troubles away.

I can recall going with my mother from bar to bar looking for my dad a lot of late nights. We'd find him nearly passed out at one of his haunts, drag him into the car, and take him home to sleep it off. He had a well-paying job working with my uncles on the line at the General Motors Turnstead Automotive Plant on West Broad, where the Hollywood Casino is now located. He earned a solid living, but his constant drinking was the reason my mom worked. She was fearful that his drunkenness would cause him to lose his job and without a second income, our family would become destitute. This pattern of irresponsible behavior was also rampant among my uncles. Drinking, cards, and gambling were the bane of the women in the family.

The story of my father's childhood always left me in tears. My dad, Raymond Franklin Long, was one of seven children who grew up near Lilly Chapel, which is not far from West Jefferson, Ohio. When he was ten, his mother Rebecca and a sister died when their house caught fire. My dad was able to save his sister Jenny, who bore the scars of the fire for the rest of her life. It was a tragedy that the family would never escape. Five years after his wife's death, my grandfather shot himself while his surviving children were attending a church service. Six children were now orphans. They were distributed to area foster families, who were happy to welcome the cheap labor on their farms. Dad told me stories of how cruel people were to him. He was provided with meager rations and few, if any, comforts. He was forced to milk cows in the cold mornings without appropriate shoes or clothing, and would seek out the warm hay where the cows had been lying and stand in those spots to alleviate the chilling numbness in his feet. Eventually, Bill McGiner, a local man, took my father in and created a safe haven for him.

When he was sober, my dad was a kind and thoughtful father; he just couldn't stop drinking. Alcohol often turned him into an uncontrollable and angry person my young brain couldn't reconcile with the man who was otherwise fun and generous. When my dad was drunk, I did everything I could to avoid confrontation or set him off. I was careful to maintain a peaceful demeanor, and I went out of my way to be obedient.

After sleeping off his drunken stupor, my dad would awaken the next morning with no recollection of the fear and destruction he had caused. Even from my bedroom I could clearly hear my mother's harsh tone and detect her frustration toward him. His memory impaired by alcohol, he didn't have a clue what transpired just hours before. *Why are you angry with me? What did I do?* If he could summon an apology (which was rare), it was empty of meaningful intent to change or an ability to rectify the situation. My dad was a textbook alcoholic.

***

My parents celebrated me in grand style, and my birthdays always consisted of a party filled with friends and family. However, my mother's plans for my seventh birthday were especially exciting. We invited six of my friends to see Snow White at the Ohio Theater, and then we enjoyed lunch at Mill's Cafeteria on State Street. When I was a little girl it was a big deal to dress up and go "downtown," and it made quite the impression for my friends who had never been to a theater. At my mother's funeral years later, my friend Betty Gabor, recalled how much fun we had and reminded me that outing had been the first time she had attended a theater.

Because both of my parents worked and I was an only child, they had a considerable amount of disposable income. When I was about seven, my parents surprised me at Christmas with my very own black and white television for my bedroom. I was over the moon; none of my friends had something so extravagant. While I had a multitude of other gifts under the tree, and my mom had purchased several items for my dad, there were no gifts for my mom to open that morning. Once again Dad had spent Christmas Eve playing cards and drinking and had neglected to purchase the only item she had requested—an electric typewriter from Kay's Jewelers. When Dad realized his error, he looked my way and asked if I had purchased the typewriter for my mother. I was horrified that the look of sadness on Mom's face was somehow my fault. It took only a minute for her disappointment at being forgotten once again to fade into anger and my parents were embroiled in another fight. After that, my dad did his best to make up for his blunder. He would buy presents for my mom for any and every holiday. Even on Independence Day my mom would receive a gift.

Sunday dinners consisted of fried chicken and mashed potatoes with little variation, and then came our traditional Sunday afternoon outing. I looked forward to driving to Plain City to count the Amish buggies. Content and settled, with the effects of the previous night's alcohol a distant memory, Dad would often sing *Cotton Fields* to me as we drove through the countryside. This has continued to be one of my personal "theme songs," a favorite selection to share when I have a microphone in my hand.

My dad was always looking for ways to delight me. He was quite spontaneous and a simple errand could turn into an hours-long adventure as we might visit the hardware to purchase a new bike, run in Isaly's Dairy for lunch and ice cream, or stop at a roadside carnival we had come upon. Rarely guided by an agenda, we would be off and running toward anything that looked fun or tickled his fancy at that moment.

My parents ensured I was kept busy with interesting and challenging activities. In grade school I took ballet lessons at the Jimmy Rawlins Studio at West Broad and Hague Avenue. As I got older, my days were filled with ballet and piano lessons. I took accordion lessons in the Larrimer Building above The Clock Restaurant on North High Street. My mom enrolled me in the prestigious Lazarus Charm School for modeling lessons when I was about twelve. Students were instructed in appropriate makeup application, wardrobe considerations, proper social and dining manners, and techniques for engaging in polite conversation. Our final exam consisted of walking the runway and modeling the latest fashions while ladies were enjoying tea at the Lazarus Chintz Tea Room. My ensemble involved carrying a hat box. I felt so proud and grown–up . . . and charming!

While I did enjoy an enchanted childhood, there were many dark times, too. I endured a variety of physical maladies. I was treated for blepharitis and suffered with whooping cough. At one point I developed an uncontrollable facial tic. I also had painful recurring infections in my left ear that doctors were unable to successfully treat. With the threat of the infection spreading to my skull, I underwent a radical mastoidectomy when I was in fourth grade. The surgery resulted in full hearing loss in that ear and I missed school for a quite a while. When I was able to return, I wore a large bandage on the left side of my head until the incision healed. It was quite humiliating.

Family was everything to my mom and dad, and the weekend typically signaled family time. The guys would clock out of work on Friday nights, and the weekends were spent playing cards or football, or sitting at the bar drinking. The women spent their time together cooking in the kitchen preparing barbeque and other favorites, tending the children, and cleaning up. One year a makeshift baseball diamond was created in the backyard and we played until it was too dark to see. There were unlimited outdoor activities for the children and when the weather turned sour, we could ride mattresses down the stairs for hours.

The whole mess of us might pack up for a cook–out at Darby Park or head to Fairfield Beach at Buckeye Lake for a weekend filled with camping and fishing. Other Saturday mornings the moms and kids would drive to Scioto Park to prepare breakfast, while the dads, who had started fishing up river before dawn, would slowly make their way down to meet us. If one of us was going, we all were going. We probably looked like a band of gypsies with kids hanging out the windows of the car and gear strapped on top. Often the fun didn't stop until Sunday night rolled around and we dispersed to our individual homes, falling asleep with the memories of a great weekend and counting the hours until the next adventure

4 | RELATIONSHIPS WITH MEN

"I was driven to make people happy because their validation quieted my greatest fear of being abandoned."	*Anita Barney*

When I was a child, I was raped by a family friend.

Before I mustered the courage to write this sentence and stare at the words on the page, I had shared this with just two other people, neither family members, both within the past five years.

When I was young there wasn't the permission to talk about violations against women, much less against children. I was powerless. No voice to accuse. No proof to punish. Only me. Alone with my memory and without any understanding of the influence this single event might wield over the rest of my life.

I didn't mention the attack until more than sixty years after it occurred, and then only as a footnote to the story of my life. A casual aside. Oh, by the way, this *thing* happened to me. It was a horrible afternoon . . . but life goes on.

Then I was asked to stop and reconsider the experience. My responses were quick and sharp.

> *What did that rape mean to you?* Nothing.
> *Do you think it influenced your life in any way?* No.

Really? Not even subconsciously? I can't see it.

As we dug a little deeper into cause and possible effect, I thought about my attitudes and actions toward men over the course of my life. I was able to uncover connections that had been previously hidden from me. I learned that our history influences how we act and respond whether we realize it or not. I also discovered some events—like my rape—never allow life to continue unaltered. There are invisible effects and repetitive cycles of choice and consequence, many of which are unidentifiable for the victim.

I was told when I was still in high school I would never be able to have children. Although I was eventually blessed with two beautiful babies, during my life I suffered nine miscarriages, faced numerous health issues, endured an emergency hysterectomy, battled cancer, and was never able to connect with men on a sexual level.

Psychologically, there were other undesirable behaviors that resulted. It has been only recently that I could trace these back to my early sexual assault:

• An understanding that being attractive could be used to open doors and create opportunities, and a willingness to play that card.

• A delight in being associated with wealthy, famous, and influential men and an ability to form an intimate bond with them very quickly.

• A blurring of the acceptable boundaries when it came to relationships with men, and a determination to pursue what I wanted.

• Putting my needs and desires secondary to those of the men in my life—including accepting inappropriate and abusive behavior—in an anomalous desire to please.

When I look back over my relationships with men, I discover that many times I was seeking more than just companionship or financial stability. At the core, what caused a man to be desirable was his ability and willingness to validate me. To confirm that I was worthwhile and deserved him and the life he could provide.

I wasn't searching for someone to build up my public self-confidence, and I had never lacked for courage. It was something more complicated. I lived with a deficiency born out of a sexual assault I suffered at the hands of a family friend when I was about eight years old. This man, Ruben Katz, was a member of my grandmother's church. A successful business owner. A neighbor. A person I knew.

He called out to me as I rode by his business that warm afternoon, asking if I wanted something to drink. High on the adrenaline of being allowed to take my shiny new bike to the larger and more-desirable corner grocery—which was further from my house—I agreed.

While my battered and bruised body eventually healed and the bleeding ended, unbeknownst to me the damage inflicted on that little girl has influenced my attitude, behavior, and response toward men to this very day. Unable to make sense of the violence and afraid to "tell" on a grown-up, I raced to my grandmother's home after the rape, quietly tore off my bloody panties, and secretly burned them in a barrel in the back yard.

Unaware of the attack, my parents continued their regular Saturday evening socials at Mr. Katz's home, and didn't think twice when I clung to them throughout the evening. I was too fearful to leave their side for even a minute, as my attacker sat across the table, smoking cigarettes, drinking beer, and dealing cards.

There were other times when men took advantage of me. As a child, close friends and family members would corner me to fondle my breasts. Other times I barely escaped as they chased me around the house while my parents were right outside, unaware of what was happening. Instead of enjoying a safe and carefree childhood, I was constantly on guard. The idea that men desired my young body was reinforced repeatedly in frightening and unexpected ways and shaped my response toward them in ways I couldn't foretell.

Out of those assaults a void developed within my soul that felt vast and empty. It created an inconsolable fear that I would be isolated, without a protector. I had recurring nightmares that a headless man hid behind our family's garage, waiting to kill my parents. As an only child, I constantly worried about what would happen to me if my parents died. For several years, our family took in foster children. In particular, I can remember Mark and Rosalie, distant cousins whose own parents were going through an especially trying time and couldn't care for them. I would sit and hold Rosalie at night and just cry for her because she was separated from her mom and dad.

These fears reappeared with a vengeance when my second husband, Dick, was killed in a plane crash and our son was left fatherless. What I had so greatly feared had been visited on my own child, and was the impetus to ensure Alan had whatever treatment or counseling he needed, including daily sessions with a therapist. I held him close and watched over him with the vengeance of a mother grizzly protecting her cub. His loss was nearly too much for me to bear.

As a wife, the worry of losing my husband was constant. The idea of being abandoned terrified me. Social status, financial freedom, exotic travel, and all the trappings of being married to a successful man were meaningless without the intimacy of a safe relationship. Foremost, the goal was to make my husband's life pleasant and enjoyable and tend to his needs. However, beyond the reach of the public spotlight it was of utmost importance that my husband was pleased with me as his partner.

I didn't question Marcel, my first husband, when he refused to allow me to drive the car, earn my own money, or accept gifts from my parents. I kept the house pristine to his exacting standards and overlooked his physical roughness and sexual abuse for years. Believing our marriage was supposed to be forever, I made so many excuses for him that my parents were not only surprised at the state of our relationship, but initially angry with me when we separated and eventually divorced.

Dick, a physician, would schedule late appointments at the office for the convenience of his patients. Regardless of the hour of his arrival home, I greeted him at the door in an attractive robe and pajama ensemble with flawless hair and makeup. Dinner was ready at his convenience, and with the children tucked away in their rooms, we would enjoy adult conversation together before retiring for the evening.

At the end of the day, Bob (my third husband) craved quiet time after tending to the demands of his high-pressure job as CEO of Wendy's. I ensured Alan had been fed and was quietly occupied before my husband's arrival. I would have a Crown Royal ready for Bob while he relaxed and I either finished dinner or we prepared to head out to a restaurant of his choosing. It was very important to Bob that I always look my best. Even while on our African safari I styled my hair, applied makeup, and dressed in outfits better suited for a resort than a savanna in an effort to please him. When we were out in the bush observing the magnificent animals, I would ensure he had the best view even if it meant I couldn't see a thing.

By today's standards, it probably seems archaic that I endorse the traditional view of the man being the head of the family. By celebrating my "second place" position, I was protected and provided for, while happily accepting the task of tending to all other responsibility concerning the children and the household. There was this unspoken contract of respect and fidelity required from both sides, and hell to pay when the terms of that contract were shattered. What broke my heart was the infidelity, and it didn't always involve my man jumping into the bed of another woman. Sometimes, it was simply a flirtatious exchange with a pretty young thing at a nearby table. Other times it was a sexy comment to a friend in our home. This type of behavior could set me off in a fit of anger. *How dare he disrespect me that way after all I do for him?*

Yes, sometimes it felt uncomfortable to submit to requests that weren't what I preferred. Often I was forced to ignore my own interests and abandon friendships to maintain a peaceful relationship, but outside of repeated physical abuse or marital unfaithfulness, there were few actions I wouldn't overlook or requests I was unwilling to fulfill. I was never regretful, always obedient and devoted, because the fear of abandonment was constantly chattering in the recesses of my mind.

To calm this fear of being discarded, I learned to keep a lot of things private: secrets of sexual and physical abuse, emotional torment, open-marriage requests, stalking, harassment, sexual predilections, gambling, covert travel, marriages and divorces, clandestine meetings, destructive drunken rages. It didn't matter how outrageous the act; I would stand faithfully by my man and do whatever it took to pacify the situation, regardless if his actions justified keeping his confidences.

I was introduced to such behavior by observing my own mother. She worked because my father's drinking and gambling caused him to be unreliable. His addictions created a lot of uncertainty in our family, and she never knew if he would make it to work after a night of drinking or get fired because he couldn't perform his job duties. She could not rely on him to predictably provide for his family on a financial or emotional level. Yet she stood by him until his death. I was groomed to be an obedient spouse and became an attractive accessory who eagerly stood in the shadow of successful men.

This overwhelming need to be liked and accepted carried over into my social life. I was driven with a desire to ensure all of our friends were happy and the smallest detail of every interaction was considered. I couldn't just plan a party. It had to be the most grandiose affair I could imagine with animals from the zoo and hot air balloons and celebrities. Hosting houseguests meant I went into overdrive preparing itineraries that kept friends busy from morning until night and begging for some down time to recuperate. A simple spaghetti dinner included coordinating fresh flower arrangements and formal place settings with linen napkins and chargers. Christmas celebrations meant valet parking and bartenders and DJs.

Laughter and food and entertainment . . . nothing was too much money or too much work to make happen. And it wasn't so that I could flaunt my financial success. No, nothing like that. I was driven to create memorable events to make people happy because their validation quieted my greatest fear of being abandoned.

It was never about the money or prestige or position. It was always about making people happy. In the end, it didn't matter.

Despite years of feasting on my generosity, when the world came crashing down around me and I turned to my friends to explain, my fears were realized, as most of them turned their backs and walked out.

I was left standing alone.

5 | COMING OF AGE IN LINCOLN VILLAGE
1956—1958

"Among others, I met Ricky Nelson, Tennessee Ernie Ford, Molly Bee, and The Four Preps—exciting times for an otherwise routine life of a young teen."	*Anita Barney*

We moved from our tiny bungalow in the New Rome area to our delightful little house at 358 Yarmouth Lane in 1956. My parents had one of the first homes built in Lincoln Village. It was a small Cape Cod with two bedrooms and one bath consisting of less than 850 square feet. It was cozy and perfect. Our house may have been small compared to others, but for me it provided all the space a girl would ever need. In subsequent years, several family members built or purchased homes nearby. Most everyone I knew and loved was within walking or biking distance.

Lincoln Village was an amazingly awesome place to grow up, and I was quite proud to live there. It was the landing pad for national celebrities and the launching point for new ideas. We could count many local celebrities and community leaders among our neighbors: Tom Ryan, a newscaster at WBNS Channel 10, and Joe Holbrook who was the weatherman at the same station, Jerry Poston, Press Secretary for Governor DiSalle, and Gene Fullen who had a popular television show on Channel 6. (Years later, when I was a guest on Gene's show to promote Model of the Year, I met Adam West, the first actor to play Batman on TV.)

But what made Lincoln Village especially exciting were the celebrities who would often stay at Lincoln Lodge when they were in the area to perform. My neighbor worked the front desk, and I babysat for the manager, Mr. Anderson. Between the two of them I usually had advance notice when a big act was scheduled to arrive. Among others, I met Ricky Nelson, Tennessee Ernie Ford, Molly Bee, and The Four Preps—exciting times for an otherwise routine life of a young teen.

I babysat for several neighbors including Joe Holbrook, who remained a friend through the years. I enjoyed working and earning my own money, and I was diligent at saving. When I was about thirteen, I treated my parents to a special anniversary dinner at the Clarmont Restaurant on South High Street. I'm not even sure how I would know about such an elegant location, but they were impressed with the white linens and attentive service. It was a memorable evening for all of us. (Yes, I attended dinner with them; we did most everything together!)

Throughout my teen years, I suffered with female issues and by the time I was in high school doctors told me I would never be able to have children. Although I was sad, my parents were devastated for me. I accepted the diagnosis for what it was—a reality I couldn't change.

Were my problems inherited? Or were these reproductive issues caused or accelerated by the trauma I suffered during the sexual assault I experienced as a child? I'll never know.

6 | MARRIAGE & MOTHERHOOD
1960—1964

"Nothing was good enough, clean enough, or straight enough. His words sparked terror in my heart and his actions resulted in damage to my body."	*Anita Barney*

I was about fifteen when I spied a handsome, albeit slightly older, guy visiting the family next door. I quickly found out the visitor, Marcel Genereux, was their nephew and his parents lived nearby in Columbus. He seemed exotic and worldly with a mother from Montreal and a father from Boston. I was enthralled with this man who had graduated high school, drove a handsome car, and had a steady job as a lineman for Columbus Southern Power electric company. We began going steady shortly before he left to serve two years in Korea.

Upon his return, we rekindled our relationship. I had enrolled at The Ohio State School of Cosmetology and, before long, he delighted me with a marriage proposal and an engagement ring from Roger's Jewelers.

In order to marry Marcel, who was Catholic, I agreed to convert to Catholicism. This wasn't a difficult decision as our family had never committed to any religion. I enjoyed my catechism classes at St. Agnes Parish on West Mound Street with

Father Lavelle. My mother was impressed with my new-found faith and also converted. Father Lavelle baptized her, as well, and in July 1960 he officiated my Marriage Mass at St. Agnes. The ceremony took place in the morning and I was thrilled when the priest introduced me to the congregation as "Mrs. Marcel Genereux." Everyone went to our house to kill a few hours before returning to the church for our evening reception. The men wanted to celebrate the happy occasion by drinking. My mom, in a fit of anger, tried to stop them to no avail. Hours later my dad showed up at the reception hall drunk. It was a terrible scene and remains a haunting memory to this day.

By early afternoon the following day Marcel and I were heading to Wildwood, New Jersey in his 1958 Chevy convertible. My father's drunkenness and my mother's anger from the night before were fading fast in the rearview mirror as I started my new life.

After a day of driving we arrived at our destination near Atlantic City but couldn't find any hotel with a vacancy. It was getting really late; I was tired and willing to take whatever we could find. Eventually, Marcel convinced a motel manager to rent us a tiny non-descript room behind his office. We quickly discovered our bedsprings were very squeaky and I was quite embarrassed that people would overhear our newlywed activities. Hoping to be more discreet, I convinced Marcel to move the mattress to the floor. Not quite the picture of romance I had in mind when planning our honeymoon.

After Marcel and I returned from our honeymoon, we moved into an apartment on Wicklow Road, in the Westgate Park area. My husband became strict with me very quickly. Our first fight was over his demand that I use a paring knife to peel potatoes, like his mother always did. I preferred the ease of using a vegetable peeler. It started as a difference of opinion and, when I wouldn't give in to his demand, it quickly escalated into a violent argument. I was so blindsided by his behavior I could barely breathe. There had been times in the past when Marcel had been sarcastic and unkind toward me, but this was the first time he was ruthless. Little did I know this was the beginning of sorrows.

Believing I could never have children, I was shocked when I quickly became pregnant. I hoped a baby would soften my husband's attitude toward me. Once I completed cosmetology training, I worked at various locations around Great Western Shopping Center including Joe Florio's salon. I enjoyed talking with all the clients and utilizing my new skills to create hairstyles they loved. My pregnancy was quite difficult; however, and I was sick so often that when I delivered our baby I weighed only ninety-eight pounds. Angela's arrival was a happy event—my parents were bursting with pride—and I was eager to settle into the routine of a stay-at-home mom with my new daughter.

Marcel and I were anxious to purchase a home, and by the summer of 1961 we had placed an offer on 4871 Palmetto in Lincoln Village South. It was a small three-bedroom house with little rooms, but we couldn't have been happier with a place to call our own. Once the house was ours, we got right to work expanding the space by adding a family room with a fireplace and a garage. In the evenings Marcel would prepare the walls and while he was at work the next day, I would sand them smooth. Our neighbors were so impressed with Marcel's construction skills, they hired him to add garages and family rooms and extend living spaces in their homes. We didn't know it at the time, but those projects marked the beginning of his successful building career, and the eventual end of his job at the electric company.

Although I cooked most meals at home, for Sunday dinner I would often purchase chicken dinners at the Kentucky Fried Chicken just up the street at the corner of South Murray Hill and Redmond Road. Unbeknownst to me, the manager of this restaurant was Bob Barney, the man who would eventually become Chairman and CEO of The Wendy's Corporation, and whom I would marry twenty years later.

I loved our little house and stayed busy morning until evening cutting the grass, tending the flowers, and keeping occupied with general cleaning and maintenance inside and out. Between the house and caring for Angela, my days were full and happy as I overlooked the many freedoms Marcel withheld from me. Even with a newborn on an erratic sleep schedule, I wasn't permitted to take naps. I didn't have access to any money except what he gave me for specific expenses—and I had to account for every cent. I didn't dare go shopping alone; Marcel always accompanied me to the grocery store. My parents were forbidden from giving me any gifts except on holidays. They worked around this silly rule by turning every national observance—even Groundhog Day—into a giftable occasion. To earn a little spending money, I would invite women to our house for a cut and style. Of course, I couldn't charge them since I wasn't allowed to work, but was always happy to accept whatever "donation" they could afford.

Neither was I permitted to drive the car that sat in our garage every day while Marcel rode with a colleague to work. He would purchase a new Pontiac most every year, but when the guys at the Haydocy dealership saw him coming they would scatter. Marcel was so condescending and rude to the employees that the effort to deal with him simply wasn't worth the sale. I was so embarrassed by his treatment of the salesmen, I wouldn't have accompanied him if he hadn't forced me.

In the evenings when Marcel returned from work, dread and fear permeated my life. Nothing was good enough, clean enough, or straight enough. His words sparked terror in my heart and his actions resulted in damage to my body. His anger would flare up without warning and his responses were unpredictable. Once he put his arm through a wall because I had called his mother to discuss his behavior. Another time I was several months pregnant when he held my arms behind my back as he angrily slammed my swollen belly against the doorframe, resulting in the loss of our baby. He didn't care. Sadly, it would be the first of nine miscarriages I would suffer throughout my life; eight which occurred while I was married to Marcel.

It was during one of these high-risk pregnancies when I met my future husband—Dr. Albert (Dick) Valko. The physician who had treated our family for years had retired and sold his practice to Dick. I was struggling through yet another problematic pregnancy when my mother suggested I make an appointment to see the new physician, which I did. But there was nothing he could do and yet another pregnancy ended prematurely. This one at 25 weeks. To cope with each loss, I would convince myself that things happened for the greater good. God, Who was all-knowing, was watching out for my unborn child and, for reasons unknown to me, the baby was better off in heaven with Him, instead of brought into the world to face an uncertain future filled with untreatable health issues or other insurmountable challenges.

Honestly, what else could I tell myself in the face of such misery?

One year I was able to convince Marcel to allow me to take a part-time seasonal job during the holidays, and I was hired as a cashier at the Great Western JCPenney. It was fantastic to get out of the house and taste a bit of freedom. I earned enough money that year to purchase a blazer, shirt, and slacks for Marcel to wear to Sunday Mass at St. Cecilia, our parish. I was incredibly proud of being able to do that for him.

A week after Christmas Marcel and I stopped by Mom and Dad's house on New Year's Eve and, of course, Dad had been drinking. Marcel was agitated with me for some reason and he and I engaged in a mean-spirited exchange in front of my parents. The next thing I knew Dad had grabbed a gun, returned to the kitchen, and threatened to kill everyone. I quickly exited the house with Angela in my arms while Mom and Marcel wrestled the gun away. My dad's escalation of violence was frightening. However, with his drinking continuing to cause blackouts, which erased his memory of events, it was impossible to convince him to stop drinking or seek treatment. He did, however, agree to sell his gun and never purchased another. As his drinking intensified, we were always under the threat of an unprovoked rampage, and this was the primary reason I was hesitant to reveal that Marcel was abusing me. There was no telling what action my father would take against my husband.

With Marcel's construction business taking off, he decided to build a house for us. We scouted available properties until we found a lovely wooded lot on Hardwood Court near Thorn Apple Golf Course. We purchased it and put our house up for sale; it sold three weeks later. To save money for our new home, we moved into a small one-bedroom basement apartment near Doctors West

Hospital. Again, I was able to convince Marcel to allow me to secure a job with the promise that I could save all of my earnings and put the money toward new furniture. I took a secretarial job at the Janitrol office near Phillipi Road. We still owned just one car, which I still wasn't allowed to drive. Fortunately, several of my neighbors were employed at Janitrol and I was able to join their carpool.

I don't know if it was my working or living in a small apartment or the stress of building our home, but Marcel's violence increased. He started becoming rough with Angela, and one Saturday he became so angry he broke my arm. His battering was becoming worse and when I suggested we go for counseling, I was surprised that he agreed. We met several times with Father Lavelle and another priest, whose name I no longer recall. During the first session, I stated that I was willing to do whatever they suggested to improve the situation. I was shocked when, after weeks of counseling, both priests recommended we divorce.

I was devastated when I heard their advice. Was there really nothing I could do to heal this relationship? When I married Marcel it was with the intention that it would be forever: *for better or for worse, for richer, for poorer, in sickness and health . . . until death do us part.* Had I failed? Looking back, I realize the priests had the benefit of seeing our family for what it truly was: a husband suffering with uncontrollable rage expressed through physical violence, a wife whose very life was dependent on the impossible task of managing her husband's moods, and an innocent little girl who was in immediate danger of becoming a victim of physical abuse.

I struggled with the decision to divorce Marcel. In my heart it didn't feel right. But logically I knew I had to leave. Every day it was becoming increasingly evident neither Angela nor I was safe. On a Saturday afternoon in the summer of 1964, after I had finished all of my chores around the apartment and put Angela down for a nap, I lay down on the sofa and closed my eyes. Before I realized it, I had fallen asleep. I didn't hear Marcel open the front door, but awoke with a jolt of pain as he forcibly ground his knuckle into my jaw, his words exploding in my ear:

"GET UP, B**CH! WHAT ARE YOU DOING TAKING A NAP?
THERE'S WORK TO BE DONE! YOU LAZY SACK OF SH**!"

The pain was so intense I could barely respond with an apology, explaining all my work was complete. I silently berated myself: *How could I have been so careless to actually fall asleep in the middle of the day?*

He pulled a bag out of the cabinet, opened it and began throwing flour all over the kitchen and living room. In a matter of seconds the floor and counter and furniture and every other visible surface were covered in a fine white coating.

"THERE! Now you have something to do. GET BUSY!"

Even with signs of his abuse on my body, it was very difficult to make the decision to leave Marcel. I knew he would be furious, and looking at myself in the mirror provided undeniable proof of what happened when his anger became uncontrollable. For a multitude of reasons, I had not told my parents about the abuse I suffered, so they were unaware of our marital problems. And now, when the situation was desperate, I had no one to consult as I contemplated my options.

How was I supposed to know when *enough* was enough? That *this* round of abuse signaled the time I needed to leave the man I had loved not that long ago? How could I be certain that he *wouldn't* change? What if the last time really was the *last* time he would hit me?

As I looked around the apartment, past indecision evaporated as something snapped inside. The time for considering and reconsidering was over. I had finally reached the end of the line with him. With the advice of Father Lavelle echoing in my ear and my daughter's safety in jeopardy, I knew our marriage was over.

I cleaned up the mess Marcel had created and started making plans. I realized that my decision would need to be a permanent relocation. If after leaving I changed my mind and gave him a second chance, I would pay dearly for my disobedience with my life, and I wanted to live long enough to watch my little girl grow up. As Marcel was preparing to leave for work on Monday I told him I was filing for divorce. "You don't have the guts, b**ch!" he growled as he slammed the door shut behind him. I packed up

Angela's things and my clothes. I dropped Angela off at Aunt Lil's before heading to the bank and withdrawing half of the balance in our joint account. I called my parents and never looked back.

I didn't know what the future held for me. But I did know that if I ever wanted to get out alive, I had to act immediately.

7 | SINGLE IN THE SIXTIES
1965—1967

"It was 1965, I was a Catholic wife one court decree from being divorced, sharing a bedroom with my four-year-old daughter in my parents' home."	*Anita Barney*

After I separated from Marcel, Angela and I moved in with my parents. I was back to my childhood home, only now with a daughter in tow. I painted the small, unfinished second story, put down carpet, added two cots and created a sitting area at one end. It was a short-term solution and my parents weren't thrilled. Neither was Marcel, who continued his harassment whenever he would find me alone.

I had always portrayed Marcel in a positive way, and never revealed his abuse. With an array of stories at the ready to explain away the cuts and bruises, and even the broken bones, I encouraged Mom and Dad to accept and like my husband in spite of his actions. And now, Marcel frequently stopped by, claiming all my allegations of ill treatment were fabricated. Mom and Dad simply didn't believe my "new" version of our marriage, and were certain I was just being hysterical over a disagreement that didn't go my way.

For the first time in my life, with my parents on one side of the issue and me standing on the other side facing them, I felt utterly alone. But in a strange way, I also felt quite proud that I had summoned the courage to leave my abusive husband. It took a lot of convincing on my part, but as Marcel finally began revealing his true self and they eventually caught him in lies, Mom and Dad came to understand why I left my husband, and I was finally back in their good graces.

A week later I received a layoff notice from Janitrol.

Stress doesn't even begin to describe how I felt. It was 1965, I was a Catholic wife one court decree from being divorced, sharing a bedroom with my four-year-old daughter in my parents' home. With half of a savings account that just last week had represented the seed money for a new house and a future any young mother would dream about, I wasn't sure what my next step should be. Thankfully, Marcel agreed to provide twenty dollars a week to help cover Angela's living expenses, as well as pay for her health and dental insurance.

During this time I continued to suffer with female issues, which eventually required surgery at Doctors West Hospital. Mom and Dad were in my room when Dr. Frank Dono entered to share devastating news. "There is just no way you can ever have any more children." I started crying, and I could see tears in the eyes of my parents before they hurriedly left the room. They couldn't bear to see me cry and didn't want to make it worse by crying in front of me. The sadness engulfed all of us for quite some time.

Feeling cramped in my parents' attic, I found a third-floor apartment in a building on Sturbridge Road. As an adult I had never handled money, as my parents paid my bills until I was married and Marcel doled out money only if absolutely necessary. To keep things simple, I opened my first individual savings account and had the bank process my rent and utility payments. I withdrew small amounts of cash for groceries and other expenses, as needed. It would be nearly forty years later, a few weeks prior to Bob's death, before I would write my first check or manage money in any significant way.

I quickly became friends with one of my new neighbors, who was a night supervisor at Doctors West Hospital. We fell into the routine of having dinner together a few nights a week. We'd meet in the cafeteria during her break, share the events of the day, and gossip about what was going on around Lincoln Village. It was a welcome respite from the newly discovered pressure of being a single parent. As luck would have it, I repeatedly crossed paths with Dr. Birrer, who was finishing his residency and preparing to open his own practice. One night he approached me during dinner and mentioned that he was looking to hire an assistant to support patient care in the new practice he would be sharing with Dr. Seipel. He explained the office would be located on Cleveland Avenue, in a building they were sharing with the *Linden Newspaper*.

Although I didn't have a car and I would need a babysitter for Angela, I jumped at the chance to secure employment and much-needed income. I quickly worked out a plan with my Aunt Lil to watch Angela during the day, and she also agreed to provide transportation to the bus stop at Great Western each morning and pick me up each evening. There wasn't a direct route from Lincoln Village to my new office on Cleveland Avenue, so I had to transfer buses downtown. This was hassle for sure—especially in inclement weather—but nothing could dampen my enthusiasm for this amazing turn of events.

Now that I had a regular paycheck, I didn't waste any time searching for a larger apartment. I found a charming bi-level to rent on Beacon Hill. It was just few blocks from my parents and around the corner from Aunt Lil.

Dr. Birrer and Dr. Seipel were quite generous toward me. After I had been with them for a short time, they paid for my medical assistant training at Bliss College in Clintonville. And when they discovered I was taking public transportation to and from work and school, they co-signed a loan for my very first car: a dark green Volkswagen Beetle and I loved it! It was spunky and fun, and now I really did have freedom.

To show my appreciation for my family's support while I was working and going to school, I purchased tickets for my mom and grandmother and several other family members to attend The Stamps Quartet Gospel Concert at Veteran's Memorial auditorium downtown. During intermission, Mom and I headed toward the product tables, where I ran into one of the singers, Mylon Le Fevre. A couple of years earlier, while still married to Marcel, I had seen The Stamps perform at my alma mater, Franklin Heights High School. I had been sitting down front with my family when Mylon came off stage and asked me out. I was flattered by his attention but rebuffed his request by informing him I was married. This time, however, when Mylon asked me out I responded, "If you can find my name in the phone book, you can call me. My last name is Genereux." I laughed it off, never thinking he would put any effort into finding my number, and if he did, wouldn't know how to spell it. A short while later during the performance he spied me in the audience. He jumped off stage, came up to me, correctly recited my number from a piece of paper in his hand, and ran back up on stage to finish the performance.

Mylon did call and we went out a few times. I drove to Cincinnati once to meet up with him when The Stamps were performing there. When the group was traveling through Columbus, it was not unusual to wake up to see their tour bus parked outside my apartment. Mylon called one day to say they were passing through and asked me to meet them for breakfast at the Howard Johnson's on Route 161. After we ate he proudly gave me a tour of their new bus, pointing out each singer's bunk. I enjoyed my brief romance with Mylon, but refused his proposal of marriage even though the ring he offered was beautiful and my uncle encouraged me to accept it. Eventually, Mylon stopped calling and we drifted apart before The Stamps became back-up singers for Elvis.

8 | FLYING WITH EXECUTIVE JET
1967—1969

"We were backstage at The Ed Sullivan Theater one night when Elvis performed. The energy and sex appeal he exuded were palpable."	*Anita Barney*

I had been working at the medical office for about two years when I started feeling rumblings of discontent. I wanted an adventure. I was weary of Marcel and his ongoing harassment. I needed to put some distance between us.

In the spring of 1967 I put on my best suit and, with a dream of becoming a TWA stewardess, headed for the Columbus Airport where I was promptly informed they didn't have any openings. Before disappointment could set in, the TWA representative suggested I check in at Executive Jet Aviation (EJA, now known as NetJets) as he thought they were filling some positions.

I drove over to the EJA offices where I filled out an application and was immediately interviewed for a stewardess position by Paul Tibbets, who I later learned was a former Brigadier General in the U.S. Air Force and pilot of the first aircraft to drop an atomic bomb. At the conclusion of the interview he announced I was hired. "Follow me," he said. I want you to meet the General." I didn't know it then, but the General he was referring to was General Dick Lassiter (also a retired Air Force Brigadier General), the President and Chairman of the Board of EJA.

My offer letter, dated May 10, 1967, confirmed my training would begin on June 15, my salary would be $400 a month plus expenses with projected raises, and I would be expected to repay EJA at the rate of $20 per month for my uniform.

I was excited to begin my new job, but it was a sad day when I turned in my notice to Dr. Birrer and Dr. Sieple. How could I ever adequately thank the men who had taken a chance on me when I was in a desperate situation and as a result, provided me with the means to dream and the confidence to follow those dreams? I was eternally grateful for the opportunity, and for the generosity they showed me.

I was one of eight or so stewardesses who were hired around the same time at EJA. Our training took place in an actual jet at the airport, but because none of us had actually flown before, I suggested one class be conducted in the air. The instructors agreed and within a few days we were flying to Cleveland. When I became nauseated mid-flight and couldn't stop vomiting, I began to panic. *What if I'm unable to continue with the program? What if I get sick on every flight?* I could see my new life evaporating right before my eyes. Fortunately, my concerns were unfounded. As embarrassing as it was at the time, that was the one and only time I've ever experienced airsickness.

My schedule with EJA was to be on call for seven days, and then I would be off seven days. I had my attorney ensure the job wouldn't create a conflict with Angela's custody agreement. At the beginning, there were periods of time when I might not have an assignment and be home two or three weeks in a row. For a single mom, it worked out great as I often had long stretches of time to be home with my daughter. When I was flying, my mom and Aunt Lil cared for Angela.

With a better-paying job, I was able to move into a nicer place. I found a townhouse to rent at 455 Tarryton Court West in Lincoln Village. It was a great location near Angela's school. Our new home had two bedrooms and a bath upstairs; a kitchen, dining, living, and a powder room on the main floor, and a basement. There was a pool and party room on the property. Even though it was part of an apartment community, it felt like we were living in a real house.

Shortly after I started training, General Lassiter and I started dating and began a relationship that lasted for several years. I had strong feelings for the General, but I couldn't see myself married to a pilot—you could never be sure where they were or what they were doing. Nonetheless, I enjoyed his company and admired his professional success, as well as his kindness and generosity. My relationship with General Lassiter created many opportunities to travel and rub shoulders with interesting people all over the world.

Lassiter's personal Lear jet had his name emblazoned on the side and he enjoyed flying us all over the country. A frequent destination was New York City. Upon arrival, we would take a limo to El Moraco's for dinner and then head to 21 Club, where we would often meet up with Ed Sullivan for cocktails. For a small-town girl from Ohio, it was flattering when the paparazzi snapped photos and called out to us as we departed, asking the General to identify who was on his arm. Ron Galella, the photographer who later had a restraining order issued against him by Jackie Onassis, was often there and his voice would ring out over the crowd, "Who is with you tonight, General? What is her name?" Lassiter would humor him by rattling off the name of some well-known actress, and everyone knew the joke was on them. For me, it was a big ego trip.

As friends of the host, we had an open invitation to attend The Ed Sullivan Show. During one especially memorable evening we were backstage when the Beatles were the guests. I will never forget standing in the wings and watching them perform. I wasn't a huge fan of their music, so I didn't press to meet them, but the significance of the event did not escape me. What a night! We were also in the wings once when Elvis performed. The energy and sex appeal he exuded were palpable. While I didn't meet Elvis, if Pat Boone had been the guest, I would have almost lost my mind and insisted on an introduction. Pat's singing could cause me to swoon like no other.

Another evening Lassiter and I were in New York and planned to stop by his friend's home for cocktails before going to dinner. The limo pulled up in front of a beautiful apartment building on Fifth Avenue across from Central Park. The elevator opened directly into the grand living room, and beyond the open terrace I could see the lights of the city. Small groups of glamorous people, with drinks in hand, were standing around the most luxurious home I had ever seen. We made our way across the room and before long Lassiter and I found ourselves on the balcony overlooking the park. He cautioned me against getting too close to the railing, confessing he was afraid of heights. I thought this was so funny—a decorated war hero who piloted countless missions being afraid of heights. Our host for the evening? Stanley Rumbough Jr., heir to the Colgate-Palmolive fortune and former husband of Dina Merrill, actress and heir to Post Cereals.

Later, I accompanied Lassiter and Curtis LeMay on an unforgettable trip to Switzerland where we met up with a number of retired military personnel who were on vacation. Lassiter always made the travel plans and organized the itinerary; I was literally just along for the ride (and the fun). We stayed at the Hotel Gstaad Palace where the views of the Alps were breathtaking. However, the weather was much colder than I had anticipated, and I headed toward nearby shops to find warmer clothes than I had packed. Among other items, I purchased a pair of bearskin boots for $150. They were the warmest boots I've ever owned and, in fact, still sit in my closet.

One evening our dining companions were actress Brigitte Bardot and her husband, Gunter Sachs, as well as several other retired military personnel and guests I didn't know. I was seated at one end of the long table and enjoyed a very pleasant conversation with a male dining companion seated near me. After the meal had concluded, I learned I had spent the evening dining with Mohammad Reza Shah Pahlavi, the Shah of Iran.

***

During an assignment with EJA, the pilots and I were eating at a hotel bar in Syracuse, New York, when we engaged the people next to us in conversation. They were friends of Frankie Laine, who was performing that evening in the hotel. They invited us to attend the concert as their guests and seated us at a table incredibly close to the stage. I could see Frankie was wearing the prettiest black velvet slippers with gold trim. Backstage, he graciously signed an album for me.

**

Leonard Tose, EJA client and owner of the Philadelphia Eagles, scheduled a flight to Notre Dame to attend a football game at his alma mater. He invited the pilots and me to accompany him to the stadium but we didn't have the proper attire to sit outside in the cold weather. Instead, we hung out in the pilot's lounge at the terminal until the game ended and Tose was ready to return home. On the return flight he attempted to hand me a $100 bill as a tip. I explained that while I appreciated his generosity, company policy prohibited accepting gratuities. Later, while I was cleaning the plane, I discovered he had placed the $100 bill in the galley. This was the only time I ever received a tip and it was a doozy, equal to a week's pay. Tose then began calling me for dates; I would take his calls and we would chat, but I always had an excuse ready to explain my being unavailable. Finally, he invited me to go to the Dominican Republic with him and, before I could protest, assured me I would have my own room. Because Ed McMahon and his wife would be accompanying us, I agreed. We had a splendid time, and I eagerly accepted his next invitation to the Dominican Republic, which again came with my own room. Thinking his patience had to be wearing thin and he would soon insist on sharing a room, I declined his third invitation.

Years later Bob and I were watching a football game on television when a clip of Tose entering the stadium flashed across the screen. A stunning woman wearing an impressive fur coat clung to his arm. Aware of my previous interaction with Tose, Bob said, "If you had stayed with him, you could have that coat and be there with him." As I snuggled a little closer to my husband, I responded, "I have a coat just like that in my closet, and I'm right where I want to be."

**

During one flight for the president of Bristol Meyers, our client asked if I had ever done any commercials or modeling. I talked about my work with famous model Ivola Nonenmaker, who owned an agency in Columbus. After my divorce, she had booked me on a number of modeling and talent jobs for Byer & Bowman Advertising Agency. My first job was a television commercial shot at Plank's Pizza for Gambrinus beer. I enjoyed the work and appeared in more than 100 television commercials and print ads for Lazarus Department Store (working closely with Ron Foth, as the Lazarus account executive), Gold Circle, and other local brands.

The Bristol Meyers executive gave me his card and said I should call him. Later I did call him, and was booked for a Clairol commercial that shot at the top of the Pan Am Building in New York City.

**

One of my longest assignments with EJA was servicing the flights for Henry "Hank" Mancini and Andy Williams while they were on tour. When I arrived at the hangar on the first day of the assignment, I prepared the plane with the many items our clients had requested, and then we flew to Miami to pick up the guys. Mancini arrived on time with several other members of the band. I noted he was quite handsome, but I didn't really have an awareness of who he was. We patiently waited and waited for Andy to arrive. Finally, his car pulled up right next to the plane and he exited wearing oversized purple sunglasses. Once onboard, his immediate request was for oxygen, saying he had been doing drugs and needed to sober up. After everyone was settled, we headed toward the first tour stop. En route, Hank and Andy asked me to go to dinner with them that evening. I protested, insisting I would need the permission of my pilots (who I hoped wouldn't approve the request). Things didn't work out like I planned. The pilots readily agreed and I found myself with dinner plans.

When we landed, I followed the pilots to our assigned hotel. For safety purposes, EJA typically reserved three adjoining rooms, with the stewardess in the middle and pilots in rooms on either side. The front desk clerk at our hotel explained she had rooms for the pilots, but no reservation, nor an available room for me. It was quite perplexing until someone mentioned I had a reservation at the hotel where the performers were staying—oh, and my room just happened to be located between Henry and Andy. No explanation was offered for the change in protocol and no one ever confessed to making the switch.

I accompanied Henry and Andy to dinner in the main floor dining room where we were constantly interrupted by people asking for their autographs. They graciously greeted each fan. After the meal and a few more autographs, the limo arrived and the police escorted us to the venue. I watched the performances from backstage and was entertained by all the activity occurring behind the curtains. When the show concluded, we took a limo back to the hotel and then the RCA party kicked into high gear. Hours later Hank escorted me back to my room before retiring to his own for the night. I slept like a rock.

The three of us had a good deal of fun for the rest of the week, until I advised them that my assignment was coming to a close and a new stewardess would be dispatched. The guys were insistent I stay on. "I'm running out of clothes. I've got to go home." I pleaded. They protested my departure and decided that taking me shopping would change my mind. Henry ordered a rental car and in no time we were headed toward the nicest department store in town, where they encouraged me to select whatever I wanted, as they were paying. While I was shopping, they were busy signing autographs. New cities, additional concerts, and I was out of clean clothes again. Rental car. Department store. Autographs. Bags filled with new outfits. Back to the hotel. The cycle repeated numerous times. It was so much fun!

A relationship began developing between Hank and me, but it was casual. I was still dating Lassiter and back in Columbus, Dr. Dick Valko had just entered my life as a suitor. Between flight assignments, I made an appointment to see him for a severe sunburn. During the office visit, he asked me for a date. I was flattered. I agreed, and he called a few days later. Dick and I would go out for dinner occasionally when I was in town, and before long a budding romance began. There was nothing unusual about my dating situation. During the late sixties, it was common for a single woman to date several men simultaneously, until one relationship or the other became serious with the potential of marriage.

Meanwhile, when I was on the road with Hank and Andy, I had a standing invitation to attend their concerts each night and then a group of us would go out afterward. Even though it was the same show every night I would always go, because the alternative was sitting alone in a hotel room. The night they played in Wichita, they didn't want me to accompany them to the concert, and they weren't interested in providing a plausible reason for the change in routine. I was peeved! *"And I'll tell you one thing,"* I said to myself as I returned to my room, *"I'm not going to suffer through a miserably boring evening in this hotel!"*

I placed a call to Lassiter in Columbus. When he picked up I began speaking immediately. "Hey, are you doing anything? I'm out here in Wichita and I'm so bored. Do you think you could come and pick me up? I'm thinking La Scala in Beverly Hills sounds divine for dinner." Before we disconnected, plans were set for his arrival in less than three hours. I called for a shuttle to the airport, reduced the ring volume on the phone, shoved it between the mattress and box spring, and grabbed my suitcase. Lassiter and I flew to California, enjoyed an excellent dinner at La Scala and spent the night in Beverly Hills. We returned to Wichita early the next morning before he continued toward Columbus.

When Hank and Andy boarded the plane a few hours later, I cheerfully greeted them. They were full of questions: "Where did you go last night? Where have you been? We've been trying to call you. Why didn't you answer?" I glibly responded, "Well, who wants to know?" I never did reveal what transpired the night they refused to invite me to their concert.

My friendship with Hank was developing into a loving relationship even though I was still regularly dating Lassiter and also spending time with Dick. Between tour dates, Hank invited me to his home in California. I accepted and ended up spending a good deal of time with him on the West Coast. Ours was an easy relationship rooted in friendship and developed on the road. We laughed a lot, enjoyed many of the same interests, and rarely disagreed on anything. When Hank was tapped to conduct the orchestra for the Academy Awards, he invited me to attend as his guest. I had a seat right in front of the orchestra pit with Warren Beatty, Elizabeth Taylor, and Kim Novak sitting around me. It was such a glamorous evening, and unexpectedly long due to our early call time.

Hank and I remained close and he became friends with my second husband Dick and then my third husband, Bob. Nearly every time we chatted, either in person or on the phone, he would ask about that night in Wichita, "Where *did* you go that night?" I always responded, "Well, who wants to know?" And we would share a laugh as we recalled carefree days of long ago. During one of our final conversations in late 1993, Hank talked about the music he had been composing for the musical *Victor/Victoria* and promised to send Bob and me tickets for the premier. Sadly, he passed away in June 1994 before his work was complete.

***

I had been with EJA for about 18 months when I discovered my mother had been taking Angela with her to the bars at night to search for my dad. With visions of my own childhood midnight bar trips flooding my memory, I was determined not to allow my daughter to relive my troubled history.

Suddenly I was very tired of living out of a suitcase and realized how much I craved a normal life. At home. With Angela. I submitted my resignation and began looking for another job.

My grandmother was selling ads for the *Hilltop-West Spectator* and she suggested I come in and see about applying to join her department. The day I stopped by Robert Ryder, the owner, handed me an application with instructions to "Fill this out." I did and he promptly hired me as his secretary. The work wasn't difficult and the pay was adequate. One day Mr. Ryder requested that I run an errand for him. I asked if he was planning on answering his own phone and taking his own messages while I was out of the office. He chuckled and said he would do just fine.

When I returned a short while later, Mr. Ryder announced that *he* had not received any calls, but he had taken four calls on my behalf: one from General Lassiter, one from Henry Mancini, a third from Dr. Valko, and a final one from Tom Weiskopf, who happened to be my golf instructor at the time. With a grin spread across his face, Mr. Ryder said he was quite impressed by the caliber of my callers.

9 | BEGINNINGS & ENDINGS AT STONEY BRIDGE

1969—1980

"You must let everyone know, Anita saved us."	*Nora Joseph* *Neighbor*

When Dr. Dick Valko proposed marriage he was offering me so much more than simply an engagement ring. He provided me with a lovely home in a wonderful neighborhood and a life far beyond anything I could have imagined. Our union produced a beloved son—a child I was able to carry to term after so many heartbreaking miscarriages. Dick provided a stable home and family environment, stature within the community, and financial security after years of uncertainty following an abusive marriage. Here was the opportunity where I could excel as a wife.

It would probably take you less than fifteen minutes to drive from Lincoln Village where I was living in a two-bedroom townhouse with Angela, to the lovely prairie-style home on Stoney Bridge Lane, my new address as Mrs. Dick Valko. But for me, the distance was measured less in mileage and more by the opportunities and memories this new neighborhood signified.

A new beginning. A breath of fresh air. This was going to be a good life!

Our marriage ceremony was so low-key, if you blinked you would have missed it. Dick frequently golfed with his minister and one day asked him to come to the house we had rented on Ongaro Drive to officiate. We had not invited any relatives to attend and Angela, who was nine, was asleep. I'm sure we had a witness present, but for the life of me I cannot recall who that might have been. There was no reception for friends to congratulate us and with Dick's schedule, no opportunity to leave town for a honeymoon.

Alan's arrival in November 1969 was a happy surprise for everyone. After suffering so many miscarriages, I had never expected to become pregnant again, much less carry a baby to term and deliver a healthy son. Although Alan weighed eight pounds at birth, I didn't gain any weight during my pregnancy because I was sick all the time. Despite this, it was such a joyful time, and my dad was ecstatic there was finally a boy in the family.

Dick and I loved to entertain and quickly discovered our rental home was much too small to accommodate my family and our friends. In December 1970, we bought the house at 3150 Stoney Bridge Lane. I had resisted the purchase. With more than 6,000 square feet of living and entertaining space on a three-acre lot, I didn't view it as a status symbol. I could only see the additional hours Dick would need to be away from us, working to finance this purchase. I wasn't aware of what he earned or what we spent as Dick's nurse and secretary, Leona Lundgren, took care of our personal finances. Nonetheless, I pictured my future filled with many lonely hours in this extravagant home that had caught my husband's eye. But he was adamant and persuasive, selling me on the extra space we would have to welcome guests, and he eventually won me over. Although I endured many depressing days at Stoney Bridge Lane—our marriage would end just months before he tragically died, and my son Alan suffered a great deal as a result of the accident—there were, without a doubt, many happy memories created as well.

On a daily basis, Dick's time was consumed with the needs of his patients. He had appointments at his office on the Doctors West Hospital campus during the day and I regularly joined him for evening appointments at his Parsons Avenue location. If a minor surgery was on the schedule, we might not arrive home until midnight. Our neighbor Susan or my parents would regularly sit with the children on the evenings I worked. When he opened a third office with Saturday hours at 5212 West Broad Street, I expanded my work schedule to include Saturday mornings. I was a working mom in every sense of the word, but not that I had to be. Dick was a successful physician who was able to provide financially for us. But if I wanted to spend any time with my husband, I went to work with him.

When I wasn't assisting Dick with patients, I was busy around our house cutting grass, painting, tending to whatever needed done. I didn't have time to enjoy glamorous lunches with the wives of other physicians or plan daylong shopping trips. My free time was reserved for my children. Before Alan started school I might pack a lunch for us to enjoy on the banks of the Scioto River. We would catch turtles, feed ducks, go fishing, and fill our days with whatever schemes a young child can imagine.

One Saturday morning when Alan was three, I woke up feeling quite dreadful. I placed him in front of the television to keep him busy watching Popeye while I reclined on the sofa. I was experiencing terrible pain in my abdomen and started sweating profusely. Before I realized what I was doing I had removed most of my clothing in an attempt to cool off. Alan rushed over to me with a blanket and started covering me up because he was concerned, "Popeye seed you, mommy!" The pain was increasing and I asked Alan to bring me the phone. I called Dick's office and Leona answered. When I told her what was going on she put Dick on right away. He immediately came home and took me to the hospital for an evaluation. Even though the intense pain continued, the doctors were unable to determine the cause.

The following Monday I underwent exploratory surgery and the surgeon discovered I had a tubal pregnancy that had ruptured, and I was bleeding internally; I was prepped for an immediate D&C. In the recovery room following the procedure my blood pressure dropped to thirty-six and I was in cardiac arrest. They had to use the defibrillation paddles to restart my heart two separate times. Along with the complications of the tubal pregnancy, no one could have known I also was allergic to the anesthesia they had administered. Either event could have killed me. I cheated death twice that weekend.

***

Our home on Stoney Bridge was situated off Dublin Road, with Carriage Lane and Old Poste Road to the north and the Scioto River to the west. We had unwittingly become members of a neighborhood populated with Columbus notables including Senator John Glenn, the Coughlin family (founders of JEGS Performance), Bill Davis (businessman and OSU alumnus whose accomplishments were honored with the OSU Bill Davis Stadium), Peter White (President of Ohio Power, now AEP), Jack Frost (construction company owner), The Hill Family (owners of Scioto Downs), Al Savill (owner of the Columbus Owls and later the Pittsburgh Penguins), real estate developer Jim Casto, a judge, and several doctors. And, in the house directly behind ours was the Joseph Family: Norman and Effie (Boots), and their children, Trisha, Nora, Martha, Mary, Mike, and Ruthie.

Angela and Martha were the same age, and only a year separated Alan and Ruthie. The children were always together playing, riding their horses, sledding, ice skating, driving the Honda 50 trail bikes all over the neighborhood long past sundown, and occasionally climbing onto the roof at John Glenn's house. If John was in town, they would receive an angry scolding from him. *YOU KIDS GET OFF MY ROOF!* To the children's defense, his roof dipped down to just a few feet from the ground and sat there as a constant temptation to run around on it and sneak a glimpse of the river from the amazing vantage point it offered.

Even with the happiness of my new life, I continued to struggle under the weight of my dad's alcoholism. It took a fatal accident, while Alan was still a toddler, for Dad to give up drinking and gambling. He was pulling out from a parking area at Lane Avenue and Riverside Drive when the back wheels on his car started spinning in the loose gravel. Unable to find traction, he was blocking the road and unable to move forward. The driver of an oncoming car failed to see what was happening in time to avoid a collision and crashed into my father. Unfortunately, the other driver died from the impact. Although the accident wasn't caused by my father's drinking, he was at fault. The experience affected my father deeply; he stopped drinking and gambling cold turkey and never picked up another drink or bet another dollar.

Through my dad's experience, I witnessed a conversion that was instantaneous and permanent. And I came to understand the power an individual possesses to dramatically change the course of his own life. It didn't matter how long my father had been gambling or abusing alcohol. Once he turned away from those reckless habits, he never looked back.

My willingness to give others a second, third, or even fourth chance to get it right originated from watching the revolution in my dad's life. If there is even a flicker of hope for a better future, I am willing to wait for the moment of awakening and transformation. Having seen the miracle of new life in my own family, it has been impossible to walk away from that hope for others.

***

On Saturdays, Angela and the older Joseph girls attended the Noni Agency Charm & Modeling School on Long Street downtown, owned by Ivola Nonemaker, who had booked me for many ads before and after I married Dick.

Closer to home, I knew the Joseph family situation was desperate as Boots, who struggled with alcohol, was often "too sick to get out of bed." I loved Boots and when she was well, we would laugh and have a good time. Her husband, Norman, owned a successful telephone refurbishing business. He worked long hours and was prone to violence toward his wife and unpredictable anger toward his children.

Growing up with an alcoholic father myself, I felt a measure of camaraderie with the children and tenderness toward the girls. I made a point to include them in whatever activity was on my agenda: garage sales, shopping trips, errands, visits to my parents, anything at all—and planned special activities, like a day trip to King's Island amusement park, to allow them to escape the unpleasantness of their lives. They became an extension of my family and could often be found in our yard playing or stopping by when the situation at their home became unbearable.

***

In 1972 Dick decided to run for Franklin County Coroner. To support the campaign effort, he rented an RV from Dr. Santangelo. The children covered it with bumper stickers and signs and I drove it around downtown Columbus at noon, with the horn blaring as we approached the intersection of Broad and High. We spent long hours putting up posters and distributing yard signs. We would pull up to an intersection and the kids would jump out and plaster the adverts on all four corners. We put so many stickers on the RV that when we pulled them off, the paint came off, too. It cost Dick a lot of money to have it repainted before we returned it.

While I supported him in every way imaginable, I didn't plan on voting for my husband, because I didn't want Dick to become coroner. He already spent so much time working and away from his family, I knew this would take him away even more. I told him from the beginning that I would support him, but it was my right to vote any way I wanted.

With the campaign underway, I wanted to get away for a few days so I talked my friend, Bonnie Yinger, into heading to California and going to Universal Studios. I called Henry Mancini and he made all the arrangements for our brief getaway. While we were waiting to board the plane in Columbus, we spied OSU Basketball Coach Fred Taylor milling about and encouraged Bonnie's son, Eddie, to ask for his autograph. A short while later we learned the plane was overbooked and we didn't have seats. Before we had a chance to make alternate plans, a stewardess approached and said that she found seats for us in first class. We ended up right behind Coach Taylor.

The flight was uneventful and once we landed at LAX we started toward the rental car area. On the escalators we could see Coach Taylor standing ahead of us. Feeling quite anxious about the idea of driving in LA traffic, something came over me and I approached him. "You don't know us, but we just left Columbus with you where my friend's son got your autograph. I'm really nervous about driving on California highways. If I get the rental car and pay for it, will you be our driver?" After a brief back and forth we discovered his hotel was near ours. He agreed and drove us to his hotel, with the intention that I would be able to drive surface streets to our hotel. During the ride from the airport, we enjoyed pleasant conversation and as he grabbed his bag from the trunk of the rental, he invited us to dinner with friends that night at Lawry's the Prime Rib in Beverly Hills. Neither Bonnie nor I could think of a reason to decline his offer, as we didn't have any other plans for the evening.

When we walked into the restaurant several hours later, it felt like we had crashed a college basketball convention; coaches were everywhere. We enjoyed dinner that night with Coach Taylor and Coach Bobby Knight. When asked if she wanted a shrimp cocktail, my friend Bonnie, who was very religious replied, "No, thank you. I don't drink," and everyone at the table laughed at her naiveté. It was a fun evening for sure, and out of that happenstance meeting a friendship developed between Coach Taylor and his wife and Dick and me. In fact, Coach even agreed to take several of Dick's campaign posters and did a little campaigning for him.

Back home, I was pressed into service as Dick's representative on Candidate Nights. These events provided an opportunity for the local candidates to introduce themselves to voters, and briefly discuss their platform. I met John Glenn when he was the keynote speaker during one of these events.

I saw John again on election night when I was able to introduce him to my husband. John mentioned that he and his wife Annie were building a home along the Scioto River on Old Poste Road, and I was delighted to learn they were moving into our neighborhood. When he said he was planning to run for a seat in the United States Senate, I told him to call me if he needed volunteers. Dick lost the race that night (and not just by my vote).

John did call me, taking me up on my offer to volunteer in his office at 88 East Broad. I jumped at the chance for a new adventure, but my availability was limited as I continued to assist my husband with patients and Alan was still quite young. At first, my job was to support John's secretary, Kathy Prosser. I would show up whenever my schedule allowed, usually a couple of days a week for a few hours, and performed light office duties including covering the phones when Kathy was out of the office. I was a volunteer without specific tasks and if John wasn't busy with appointments, we would fill the time sharing stories and talking, and a friendship soon developed.

I was tasked with organizing a fundraising fashion show for John's election at the Neil House Hotel on High Street across from the Ohio Statehouse. I contacted Nick Clooney, a popular television variety and talk-show host from Cincinnati, to emcee; his fee for the evening was $125. I had previously met Nick when he was working for Channel 4 in Columbus and I was promoting Model of the Year on his program. I met Nick's son George Clooney, then a pre-teen and now a renowned actor, who happened to be in studio that day. Another successful fundraising event I coordinated was at the Sheraton Hotel downtown with Rosey Grier as a guest of honor. To support my fundraising efforts, someone gave me Jackie Kennedy's private phone number, which I never had an occasion to call, though not for a lack of trying to come up with a legitimate reason to contact her.

Things were moving fast and furious as Election Day loomed. I took calls from big names in Ohio and Washington, including several calls from Ted Kennedy. Ted was always pleasant to me on the phone, but initially refused to endorse John due to a Kennedy family loyalty, and this resulted in many heated exchanges between the two of them. Nonetheless, John prevailed over his rival and won the senate seat. Election night November 1974 was one huge celebration! Dick and I were invited to the January reception in Washington D.C., following John's swearing-in ceremony. Among the guests, Ethel Kennedy made an appearance that night, as did Rosey Grier and Rafer Johnson.

I discontinued volunteering after John's first campaign, but we remained friends for years. When he was in town, John had an open invitation to our parties and cookouts on Stoney Bridge.

***

Dick was a generous host and our home was always filled with guests as we organized Christmas parties, cookouts in the summer, and some sort of get-together whenever we could. He was also a considerate husband, a loving father, and a generous provider. He liked nice cars and purchased a Porsche for himself, a Mercedes convertible for me, and a Mercedes sedan to accommodate carpooling the children. I preferred tooling around in my plain VW station wagon, which annoyed him to no end.

He didn't place any restraints on my spending; I could purchase anything I desired for the children or myself, and he lavished gifts on Angela and Alan, as well. Angela had her own horse, and our garage was filled with trail bikes, fishing and hunting gear, sports equipment, and anything else that a young boy might enjoy.

It was evident to everyone that Dick and Alan enjoyed a special bond. Alan was all boy and quite a hyper child. He was constantly climbing and jumping and running and falling and sported his cuts and scrapes and bruises as badges of honor of his wild adventures. In kindergarten, he talked so much in class his exasperated teacher finally put his desk in the hall so she could teach without interruption. Alan would not be silenced! He simply opened the door and, while remaining in the hall as instructed, continued talking to his friends seated at their desks inside the classroom. He was not only a fun child, but also funny and his antics were continually entertaining us.

Alan and his father spent countless hours together and when Dick was serving as the doctor for the West High School football team, he would regularly take Alan with him to their Friday night games. Dick was also very kind to my parents, and continued to treat them for minor aches and pains at his office while we were married. Mom loved having a doctor in the family.

***

Dick loved to fly and had encouraged me to obtain my pilot's license. I enrolled, and successfully completed the Private Pilot Ground Course at The Ohio State University, Department of Aviation. He purchased a little Cessna, justifying the purchase by convincing me it was cheaper for us to buy a plane than to rent one all the time. The plane was perfect; it was simple to learn and operate. I loved the thrill of flying and I practiced "touch and goes" frequently.

Just as I became comfortable in the Cessna, Dick brought in a plane from Canada. With its larger size, retractable gear, and high-tech instruments I thought it was too aggressive for my new skills, and I was intimidated. As I continued to inspect it, my husband asked if I wanted the plane. I told him I couldn't fly it. *It's too much for me,* I thought. But then I reconsidered. It wasn't that long ago that I thought I couldn't learn to fly at all because the process looked much too complicated for a simple housewife like me. However, with Dick's encouragement, not only did I learn to fly, I loved it. "I want it!" I told him. I would get in that plane, take it to a certain speed, lift those gears, and off I'd go. Although I wasn't licensed to carry passengers without my instructor onboard, I enjoyed taking the plane to West Virginia or Cincinnati or any landing field where I could have lunch and return home before Alan's school let out for the day.

Dick would regularly fly Alan and me all around and we would often travel to Lake Erie for dinner before returning home the same evening. Flying became such a hobby for us that Dick eventually helped incorporate and served as president of Air Columbus, a private flight school and service located at Bolton Field. After that, I had the choice to fly any plane I wanted.

Angela was maturing into a beautiful young lady, but at every opportunity she enjoyed stretching the boundaries I set. One afternoon her principal notified me that she and her friend Susan had set off fireworks in the girl's bathroom at their high school. They were suspended for two weeks. Of course, I gave her a stern lecture about actions and responsibilities, and warned her that she absolutely must never do anything like that again! Not knowing what to do with her for two weeks, I cobbled together a plan. I called Hank Mancini, told him we were coming out to Hollywood, and asked him to make arrangements for our visit. Angela and I toured Universal Studios and Disneyland, visited Hank's offices, and even watched as he worked on scoring the soundtrack for a movie. I'm sure it was not the type of punishment school officials may have hoped for, but it was valuable bonding time for a mom who had been much too busy and a daughter seeking attention.

Not long after our trip to California, Hank was scheduled to appear at the Veteran's Memorial. He called to invite Dick and me to his concert and also asked us to come backstage to his dressing room during intermission. We took Dick's secretary, Leona, and her husband Roy with us as our guests that night. It was an amazing show, as always. After the first set concluded and Hank left the stage I said, "Come on, you guys, let's go say hello to Hank." Dick didn't think we'd get backstage and decided to stay put in his seat. I wasn't about to be deterred and marched right up to the guard at the gate and gave him my name, which he confirmed was on the list, and let us pass. Backstage I saw John Glenn and we both were surprised to learn we had a mutual friend in Mancini. We spent a few minutes with Hank before heading back to our seats. "You didn't get in, did you?" Dick asked sarcastically. Leona quickly retorted, "What do you mean? We met Henry, and we just met John Glenn, too!"

***

I had the opportunity to meet Hollywood makeup artist George Masters during a special event at The Union department store on South High Street. At the time, George was famous for working with starlets such as Marilyn Monroe and Ann-Margret. The store was offering complimentary consultations and makeovers by George and so many women made reservations that his schedule was overbooked. Late in the evening, after my appointment time had come and gone and I was still waiting to be called, an assistant finally came for me. Masters and I engaged in an enjoyable conversation and before the next patron took my spot in the chair, he handed me his business card. Over the next several years I hired him to do my makeup for special events. One occasion in particular was the Snowflake Ball, sponsored by Doctors North and West hospitals. It was a special and glamorous evening held every year at the Neil House Hotel. I would pay for Masters' airfare from Hollywood to Columbus and he only charged me 50% of his consultation fee, since he had friends in town he would visit. George would come to our house on Stoney Bridge and it would take him about an hour to work his magic. It was so much fun!

***

Life was wonderful until, somewhere along the way, Dick's habits shifted a bit and I felt the foundation of our marriage tremble under my feet.

Dick and I would see patients at his office on Parsons Avenue every Thursday and at the end of the day it was customary that we would join Dick's business partner, Dr. John Adams, at the Clarmont Restaurant for dinner. After a while, Dick asked that I no longer attend these dinners, explaining that Dr. Adams felt uncomfortable discussing business with me at the table. I found the request off-putting and was suspicious Dick had orchestrated my absence.

Fears of my husband's unfaithfulness were reinforced one evening when I received a phone call from Dick's Wednesday night poker partner, Dr. Urse. "Tell Valko that if he isn't going to show up anymore, to let us know so we can fill his seat." And that's how I discovered my husband wasn't playing poker on Wednesday evenings, as he had led me to believe. *Where was he? What was he doing? Was he having an affair?* My mind went wild with imagined scenarios. When Dick arrived home well after midnight, I was livid! A screaming match ensued as my emotions reached a boiling point. "I work hard to keep a clean house, care for the children, cook, keep myself up, help you at work! I DON'T DESERVE TO BE TREATED THIS WAY!!"

Shortly thereafter, while preparing Dick's clothing for the cleaners, I discovered a receipt from Red Roof Inn. I immediately called the front desk where I learned Dick had checked in with a companion, a woman. With proof of his philandering in my hand, I was furious.

Sadly, our relationship continued to deteriorate. No longer compelled to disguise his actions, Dick began arriving home after midnight, taking a shower, and crawling into bed. He explained he wanted to remain married to me, but have the freedom to date others; in return he was willing to grant me the same freedom. *What was he thinking? How could he even make that request out loud?*

The next day I stashed a blanket, pillow, and alarm clock in my car. I went to bed that night just like always, waiting for Dick to arrive home after spending time with his girlfriend. As he got into bed I threw off my covers, and began changing out of my bedclothes and into street clothes. "Where do you think you're going?" he demanded. I responded, "You said we both had freedom. I'm exercising mine. No questions. Remember?" I spent the evening in my car parked in a nearby lot, and set my alarm clock to wake me in time to return home before Dick left for work. Although I was stiff from my uncomfortable sleeping position, I didn't let it show. I desperately hoped my charade would cause my husband to see things from my perspective, but it had the opposite effect. He misinterpreted it as my acceptance of our new lifestyle.

It was clear Dick wanted to retain his standing in the community as a respected family guy by remaining married to me, while discreetly entertaining women on the side. I begged and pleaded and promised. He didn't care. He wanted what he wanted. After one especially nasty fight I gave in. "Fine! You go your way and I'll go mine!" I thought he would be pleased but his response perplexed me. "That's not a relationship!" *What was up with this guy?* His creative approach to marriage was stupefying.

Well, here I was again with a broken marriage and a husband who was selfish and unwilling to respect me. I was humiliated. I considered divorce, but having already traveled down that road with Marcel, I knew the costs and this time, with two children depending on me, they were too high. I thought if I filed for divorce I would be forced to move out of the house and find a job to support the three of us. Dick was willing to stay married (if that's what he wanted to call it), and continue to provide for the children and me. I was willing to let him play, and wait for his return . . . for a while.

***

In 1974, when Alan was five, Dick and I had joined the Muirfield Golf Club. We were one of the first members, I had my own locker, and this was the only course Alan played throughout his childhood. He and Gary Nicklaus were good friends and Alan regularly hung out at his house and would even go to the driving range with Gary's dad, Jack. Dick and I golfed many rounds on this beautiful course.

Through the years, Alan had become quite involved with golfing and was spending a lot of time at Muirfield where he became friends with Head Pro Jim Gerring and Keith Schneider, who managed the Junior Players program (and whose parents owned Schneider's Bakery in Westerville). The entire team involved with the junior players was a tight-knit group and we came to know them quite well. To show our appreciation for their support of Alan and work with other young athletes, Dick and I hosted Jim, Keith, and several of their colleagues at our home for a cookout. It was an enjoyable evening, and would influence future events in a way I would never imagine.

The following spring we were looking forward to attending the Memorial Tournament at Muirfield. On Friday I attended alone and at the end of the day, as I was standing in the parking lot waiting for the tram to transport me back to my car, I struck up a conversation with the woman standing next to me. When I introduced myself, she repeated, "Anita Valko? Are you married to

Dr. Valko? Didn't you host a dinner at your home for several members of the Muirfield staff?" When I confirmed that I was *that* Anita Valko, she introduced herself as Keith Schneider's mom, Jane. She was quite impressed that Dick and I would host the "staff" from Muirfield at our home. She then introduced me to the woman standing nearby who happened to be her best friend, Carol Barney. We continued chatting until the tram delivered us to the parking area and we parted ways.

The following day I was headed back to the tournament while Dick had planned to spend the morning golfing with his father at The Riveria Golf Club in Dublin. We had agreed to meet at Muirfield at a certain spot at a particular time later in the day. When the appointed time arrived, Dick was nowhere to be found. I continued to wait for quite a while. Suddenly a golf cart pulled up and stopped abruptly in front of me in an attempt to avoid running through a water puddle. In the cart were sportscasters Pat Summerall and Ben Wright, along with PGA golfer Ben Crenshaw. I asked if they happened to know Charlie, an acquaintance of mine who worked in the CBS control booth. One of the guys in the cart responded, "We know Charlie! He's back that way." I mentioned I was going to head over that way to say hello. "Oh, you don't want to talk with Charlie! Come and go with us, we're going to Nicklaus' villa." I told them I didn't have a pass to get in. "You can go as our guest. Come on! You'll have a good time and we'll introduce you to a lot of people." I checked my watch. So much time had passed I wasn't sure Dick was going to show up, so I accepted their invitation.

I did meet a lot of people that day and had an enjoyable time chatting with various community leaders, broadcast personalities, and golfers who were milling around Jack's villa. At one point I was sitting on the patio talking with the CBS staff when I saw Jane and Carol walk by, with Jim and Nancy Near. (Jim would later become CEO of Wendy's.) Carol approached me a short while later and introduced me to her husband, Bob, who was President of the Wendy's Corporation. We exchanged pleasantries before they returned to their friends. When our paths crossed later, Carol asked if I would introduce them to Pat Summerall and Jack Whitaker, also a CBS sportscaster, which I gladly did.

Later, Carol came over asked if I wanted to join her and Bob, and Chip and Jane Schneider for dinner at the Fifth Dimension on Henderson. I didn't feel comfortable making plans without touching base with Dick, so I found a phone and called Stoney Bridge. Dick was at home. Unable to find me among the crowds at Muirfield, he had headed home to wait my arrival. I explained about the dinner invitation and he agreed to meet us at the restaurant. I rode with Bob and Carol to dinner, and Dick arrived soon thereafter.

Shortly after The Memorial Tournament ended I began experiencing a lot of pain and Dick took me to the hospital, where I was diagnosed with meningitis. I remained in isolation in the intensive care unit for several weeks. The pain never abated. Later my doctor told me that several times I was within twenty-four hours of dying. For whatever reason, God had His hand on me and I survived.

It would be many more months before I realized my marriage to Dick was broken beyond repair. He was unwilling to change from his philandering ways, and I was feeling more and more despondent that I wasn't the wife he needed. He would apologize but I couldn't trust him. We decided that he would move out of Stoney Bridge to give us some space and see if our marriage could be restored. But it was too late for reconciliation. Our separation confirmed what I already knew: our marriage was over. I filed for divorce and it was granted in March 1980.

By this time, Angela had married her high school sweetheart, Steve Martin, and was living in Hilliard. I remained in the Stoney Bridge house, attempting to maintain a normal schedule for Alan. Dick moved into an apartment across from Westland Mall with Paul, a fellow pilot. He continued to provide financially for us, and I had a settlement from the divorce. Two marriages, two divorces. I was thirty-eight years old and battling feelings of failure and low self-esteem. *What was wrong with me? Why wasn't I enough? What would it take to find a partner who would remain true to his marriage vows?*

One afternoon, Bob Barney called from his office at Wendy's and invited me to lunch. At first, I rebuffed his invitation, thinking he was still married. He told me he had moved into an apartment owned by Wendy's at The Continent, and divorce proceedings had been initiated between him and Carol. I recalled our enjoyable conversation during The Memorial Tournament and couldn't think of a reason to refuse his invitation. Throughout our first date we learned we had a lot in common and a relationship began to develop.

Bob shared that he started his restaurant career at the Bobcat restaurant in Athens, Ohio, and then in 1962 opened a Kentucky Fried Chicken franchise in the city. In 1964 Colonel Sanders, as he was known to do, was delivering supplies to the restaurant out of the trunk of his Cadillac when Bob mentioned he wanted to expand but lacked the capital. Sanders suggested he make an appointment to meet up with Dave Thomas in Columbus, who was working with Kentucky Fried Chicken at their manufacturing facility, and ask for a loan. Bob took the Colonel's advice and before long he and Dave were collaborating on business deals involving Kentucky Fried Chicken and Arthur Treacher's Fish and Chips. Shortly after, in 1969, Dave started Wendy's restaurants with the original location on East Broad Street in downtown Columbus. He hired Bob and then quickly asked him to serve on the board as President.

Bob began working at Wendy's second location on Henderson Road to learn about the business. He soon realized the potential of the drive-thru window and made it his goal to refine this new service option that was awkward for customers, and inefficient for the staff. His efforts were rewarded and sales ballooned. In 1972, the company had expanded to four locations and Dave was content with keeping Wendy's a Central Ohio brand. Bob, on the other hand, envisioned what franchising could mean to the organization and embarked on a mission to expand Wendy's market and the bottom line. Over the next several years, Bob's success executing Dave's vision throughout the country and internationally resulted in massive growth. His achievements were widely heralded, and he was rewarded for his efforts by being named CEO in 1980 and Chairman of the Board in 1982.

When Bob and I started dating, my former husband became jealous. Before Bob entered the picture, Dick had been interested in playing the field and keeping me conveniently on the side; now that another man had expressed interest he began to constantly pursue me. He called continually and stopped by without notice. He became intimidating and annoying.

Five months after our divorce, Dick stopped by the house around midnight to pick up Alan for a fishing trip. They had made plans to fly to Northern Michigan, spend the day salmon fishing near Lake Huron, and return home later that night. I had been invited, but at the last minute thought it would be more fun for Dick and Alan if it were just a "guys trip." Before I could awaken Alan, Dick stopped me and asked if we could talk for a minute. He wanted us to get back together. He had made a big mistake. He was sorry for his actions. Was I willing to give him another chance?

Taken completely by surprise, I was speechless. He removed a small jewelry box from his pocket and opened it to reveal a beautiful engagement ring. Even though I still had feelings for him, his gift felt more like a bribe than a promise. I told him I had a lot to think about before I could answer. He insisted I take the ring. That night we connected in a way that had been missing throughout the last several years of our marriage. During the fleeting moments we had together, we were affectionate and intimate.

Later, as I watched Dick and Alan drive away toward their big fishing adventure, I held the ring in my hand. I knew in my heart of hearts that even if I loved Dick, there was no way I would be able to trust him. And without trust, what kind of marriage could exist?

Back in the quiet and dark house, I was feeling unsettled. I returned the ring to the jewelry box and placed it in a drawer before making my way to bed. The guys would return in less than twenty-four hours and I would have to find a way to tell Dick the time for second chances had expired. It would not be an easy conversation to have with him but there was no other choice for me. With so many thoughts swirling through my mind, I fell into a fitful sleep before they were wheels up to Michigan.

10 | THE CRASH
1980

"When are we going to bury Dad?"	*Alan Valko*

Suddenly, I was awake and I could feel my heart beating through my nightgown as I gasped for air. *What was it?*

As my thoughts came into focus I glanced toward the clock on the nightstand. It was still dark outside, but morning was on its way and I was engulfed by panic. Then the crushing memory of the nightmare that had just ended flooded my consciousness. Dick and Alan's plane had crashed and both had died. I gulped several times before common sense took over and I realized the adrenalin rushing through me was caused by a ridiculous dream. No cause for concern, I assured myself. Dick and Alan would have no doubt already landed in Michigan on their eagerly anticipated fishing trip. I closed my eyes, attempting to return to sleep.

The next time I would recall this dream was more than a month later, when Joanne Williams, a reporter for the *Columbus Messenger,* interviewed me about the plane crash that killed my former husband and nearly claimed the life of my son that night.

***

Dick, Alan, two pilots and a guide had organized an end of summer trip to catch salmon in Michigan. Leaving after midnight would allow them to begin fishing at first light, put in a full day, and return to Columbus the same evening. Although the school year had started the day before, we agreed to let Alan miss a day of fifth grade leading into the Labor Day weekend.

Dick selected the twin-engine, six-passenger Piper PA-23 Aztec they flew that trip.

On August 27, 1980, at approximately 2:30 a.m., a twin-engined Piper aircraft departed Columbus, Ohio, for the purpose of transporting (Dr. Albert Valko) and three other individuals to northern Michigan for a fishing trip. After stopping in Utica, Michigan, to pick up the final passenger, the aircraft headed for its destination at the Iosco County Airport. At approximately 4:01 a.m., with a professional pilot at the controls, the ill-fated craft began its approach to the airport. At approximately 4:18 a.m., the pilot, now experiencing very limited visibility due to a lingering fog, advised Approach Control that he had missed the approach, i.e., he did not visually sight the airport. He was then cleared to climb to 3,500 feet and repeat his approach. During his climb and return to approach position, the pilot indicated that the problem was that the passengers' ground transportation was waiting for them at the Iosco County Airport. The pilot then advised Approach Control, "OK, we'll give it one more try." While maneuvering for his final approach the pilot was again given the weather conditions, and at 4:33:10 was advised that his descent on approach had now taken him below radar service. At 4:33:20 the pilot acknowledged the termination of radar service. There were no further communications.

While continuing its descent, the aircraft apparently struck the top of a stand of trees, flipped over and crashed. Due to the fog, search efforts were delayed until late morning. The wreckage was located approximately

1.25 miles from the end of the runway. All but one of the
occupants died as a result of the crash.[1]

I learned later that because the landing strip at Iosco County
was unmanned late at night, it took more than an hour after the
plane crashed before anyone realized it had not landed safely. And
then dense fog nearly paralyzed search efforts until later in the
morning. Except for Alan, everyone was killed instantly due to
severe head trauma. Alan had been so tired as they boarded the
plane, Dick had not required that he fasten his safety belt, and
permitted him to lie across the seat. This probably saved his life, as
he was thrown in the back luggage compartment upon impact and
avoided the fatal injuries that killed everyone around him.

Alan was stranded in the plane for nearly seven hours before
rescuers were airdropped into the forest and discovered he was
alive at 11:00 a.m. His left leg had been broken in three places and
nearly severed from his body. He had burns and lacerations all
over, and had been in and out of consciousness the entire time. He
had no awareness of what had happened. Alan didn't realize the
other passengers, including his father, were dead, hanging upside
down and held in place by their safety belts just feet away from
where he was hanging onto life by a miracle. He was so delirious
he kept thinking Paul, the pilot, was walking around watching
him. He couldn't understand why his dad wouldn't help him, even
after calling for him repeatedly. Once he was found, he kept asking
for his grandfather who he erroneously recalled had been traveling
with them on the plane. The rescuers did spend time looking for a
fifth victim.

The National Guardsmen who were first to arrive on the scene
by air rescue told me once they saw the bodies upside down, they
didn't expect any survivors. And they were shocked when they
rapped on the window and Alan turned his head and said, "Yeah, I
hear you," and then "I'm awake!" before he started to cry. Alan
doesn't remember much of the accident, but he does recall he was
really hot and felt the cool wind across his face as the rescue

---

1 Bank One Trust., Co., N.A. v. County of Iosco, CIV NO 82–10238

helicopter blades chopped the air. They were able to airlift Alan out, but it took a bulldozer to clear the area in order to recover the bodies several hours later.

Meanwhile, back in Columbus I was going about my normal Wednesday routine, oblivious to the fact that my son's life was in danger until Kay, the secretary from the flight school, called and asked if I had spoken to anyone about what happened. Her tone caused my pulse to quicken and dread to fill my stomach even though I didn't have any idea what she was talking about.

She explained what she knew. Dick's plane had crashed overnight, and she had just received a call from St. Joseph's Hospital in Tawas, Michigan. I needed to contact them right away. She didn't have any other details. I wrote down the number and got in touch with the hospital immediately. They had been calling about Alan who had suffered a compound leg fracture; I needed to come up and sign him into surgery. I asked about Alan's father, Dick. The voice on the end of the line didn't have any information about other victims, and I assumed Dick had probably been taken to a different hospital for treatment.

As I finished the call, Jim King, a friend who owned a plane at Bolton, appeared at the door to take me to the airport where Mike Certa was waiting to fly me to Michigan. I had tried to reach my cousin Carol Jean repeatedly without success. Angela and Steve met me at the Air Columbus office and offered to travel with me. I told them to stay put in Columbus, thinking it would be a quick trip up and back. Honestly, I wasn't thinking clearly. I had no idea what I would find in Michigan. The only thing I *knew* was that I needed to see Alan as soon as possible.

On the flight up, we flew over the crash site. I could plainly see where the trees had been sheared off and it was unreal to glimpse the crumpled plane on its roof with wheels in the air. Twisted wreckage was lying haphazardly on the forest floor. I still was not aware that Alan was the only survivor and I vowed that no matter what injuries Dick had suffered, I would bring him home and care for him. Members of the Highway Patrol met us at the airport and escorted me to the hospital with their sirens screaming the entire way.

The doctor was waiting for me as I entered the hospital and we quickly made our way the Intensive Care, where Alan was listed in guarded condition. As I walked into the room I heard him cry weakly, "Mommy!" I answered, "I'm here!" And then everything went into slow motion. I saw the burns and lacerations and his small body in the large hospital bed. I heard the doctor recount his injuries and surgical options, and I noticed the new school clothes Alan was so proud of the day before discarded into a careless pile in the corner. Understanding that Alan's survival was a miracle, the seriousness of the situation hit me like a boulder and I went into shock. I had no control of my response; my hands started curling into tight fists and I began retching. I could barely control my physical reaction enough to be able to hold the pen to sign my son into surgery. As they wheeled Alan toward the operating room, a doctor suggested I take a sedative. I refused. I wanted to be aware and available for my son when he came out of anesthesia.

Shortly thereafter I was approached by two patrolmen and informed of the deaths of the other passengers and the pilot. I was asked to go to the morgue to identify Paul Rinaldi the pilot, and Bob Johnson who was Vice-President of Arjay Construction, as well as my former husband. It was beyond dreadful. I was numb, simply going through the motions. I didn't know the fourth passenger who was killed that day. I had never met Bill Walter, the professional fishing guide they had picked up in Michigan.

Back in Columbus my family was quickly making plans to leave for Michigan. My mom, my cousin Carol Jean, Angela, and Steve loaded into my dad's van. Taking turns driving they made the 350-mile trip to Tawas in record time, arriving late Wednesday evening.

The local media, both in Michigan and Columbus, were reporting heavily on the crash and several distant members of Dick's family, who lived in the Tawas area, reached out to my family. They invited us to their home for some rest and a meal. There was no way I would even consider leaving Alan alone—not after knowing he endured nearly seven hours alone in the plane after the crash. I was prepared to send my regrets when Carol

Jean, sensing I needed a break, encouraged me to accept their invitation while she remained at Alan's bedside.

When I returned to the hospital a few hours later, the relief on Carol Jean's face when she saw me was obvious. Alan's condition was precarious and his little body was so mangled from the crash, she was fearful he would pass away on her watch, and couldn't bear the thought of it.

The nurses had placed a cot for me to sleep just outside the intensive care unit. When Alan was moved to a private room, I moved my cot right beside him and when he would awaken between doses of pain killers, he would often ask for his dad. Because he was heavily medicated, he would accept any vague answer I provided, and then I would quickly find some reason to leave his room. I couldn't face the reality of Dick's death any more than I could give such devastating news to my son. I was heartbroken for him and his injuries, as well as for the loss of his father.

This was the very fear—the loss of a parent—that had haunted me from childhood. Now, I was a front row witness to the devastating effects of this situation in my son's life. I couldn't look away or pretend this wasn't happening. I just didn't know how to deal with it. Finally, not being able to put it off any longer, I asked Alan's doctor to tell him about his father. I held Alan's hand in mine as he learned his father had died in the crash. Tears washed down our faces as sadness surrounded us.

Working in the Channel 10 weather station, long time friend Joe Holbrook learned of the accident right away. As luck would have it, he had just finished two weeks of National Guard training in Michigan as part of the 107th Attack Helicopter Troop. Their medical helicopter was still in Michigan and preparing to return to Columbus when Joe reached me. He coordinated with Dr. Peter Johnston, our friend and orthopedic surgeon at Doctors West Hospital, and made arrangements to fly Alan from St. Joseph's Hospital aboard the National Guard medical helicopter. This was a welcome turn of events, as we had never considered the possibility of returning to Columbus so quickly. My family left Michigan for Columbus Friday morning. With Alan stabilized, sedated, and in temporary traction, we departed just after noon. After making two stops, Alan and I arrived in Columbus around 7:00 p.m.

Immediately after landing in the parking lot at Doctor's West Hospital, Alan was prepped for surgery with Dr. Johnston. My parents had brought a change of clothes to the hospital for me so I could freshen up before driving to Schoedinger Funeral Home on West Broad to make preliminary arrangements for Dick's services. After the urgent details had been discussed, I returned to the hospital to be with Alan.

Alan began inquiring about the funeral service for his dad the very next morning. "When are we going to bury Dad?" he would ask. With nothing else to occupy his mind, he naturally focused on the events surrounding his father's death. In traction following surgery, Alan was unable to leave his bed and there wasn't any way he was well enough to leave the hospital to attend the funeral. Every time he would ask, I would gently respond, "Not today, Alan," and that would quiet his questions for the moment.

Early the following morning my parents accompanied me as I returned to the funeral home. I told the attendant I wanted to see Dr. Valko. The director escorted me into a back room, where a body was visible in a casket. He said, "Here is Dr. Valko." The man was completely unrecognizable to me. The only way I was finally able to identify my former husband was by the ridges on his fingernails. While I had been able to identify Dick in Michigan shortly after the crash occurred, the head trauma and other injuries that damaged his body had resulted in significant disfigurement in the ensuing days. Without a question, his casket would be closed during calling hours.

When Dick's parents arrived in Columbus that evening, they assumed responsibility of the funeral services and his final affairs. It was incredibly sad to witness the grief over the loss of their only child, and to see the two of them sitting side by side at the gravesite was nearly unbearable.

11 | ART'S VISIT CHANGES EVERYTHING
1980—1982

"To say the change I saw in Alan after Art Schlichter's visit was miraculous does a disservice to the word miracle."	*Anita Barney*

When I returned to the hospital from the cemetery, Alan again asked when we were going to bury Daddy. I didn't know how I was going to explain things to a ten-year-old boy in a way he would understand. I breathed a quick prayer and began. I told him how if Daddy had lived he would have been in a wheelchair, and be unable to play sports or do many things with him like they used to do together, and this would make Daddy very sad. We reminisced about the fun times the three of us had enjoyed together in the past. Then I told Alan that God needed the very best doctor he could find to come to heaven and take care of all the sick angels, and that Daddy had been the chosen one. I said Daddy was sitting on a cloud watching over us and if we did things that were naughty, Daddy might even yell at us sometimes. But with Daddy and God watching over us, we would be fine.

I hoped Alan believed me because I was speaking with a confidence I didn't feel. My life had spun out of control in a big way and I wasn't sure what I should be doing. Dick, whom I still relied upon for guidance and financial support, was gone. I was immediately and utterly alone, facing an overwhelming situation I couldn't fix. The only thing I knew to do, and was committed to doing, was be present for Alan.

There were two beds in Alan's room, and the hospital kept the second bed vacant for me. Generally, I spent every night with him, but my parents, Angela, and other family members would relieve me occasionally. We were determined that Alan wouldn't be alone in the hospital. With images of Alan feeling abandoned after the crash haunting me, I was desperate to ensure he wouldn't relive even a minute of that horrible ordeal.

For the next month Alan was in traction, which caused him a lot of pain. Combined with the absence of his father and the frustration of not being able to get out of bed, my formerly good-natured, active son became depressed. He started complaining and whining about everything all the time. I hired a tutor to keep Alan from falling too far behind in school, and a child psychologist to help Alan work through the terrible turn his life had taken. He met with both of them five days a week.

My attention on Alan's physical and emotional recovery was interrupted when the hospital's billing department contacted me. I was shocked to learn the expenses we were incurring were not covered by health insurance. It seems Dick, who had responsibility for Alan's insurance, had been in the process of changing policies right before the crash. The previous coverage had lapsed and enrollment forms for the new policy had yet to be signed. Without Dick's financial support, I was already beginning to feel pressure to cover the expenses of daily life and I couldn't imagine how I would begin to pay for the extraordinary medical costs that were piling up.

After multiple conversations with the insurance company, the hospital, and Dick's secretary, I was relieved to hear they were able to find a solution to keep Alan on the original policy. With that crises averted, I focused on the more immediate need of paying for our general living expenses. By this time Bob and I had been dating for a while, and when he generously offered to cover whatever I needed, I felt an enormous weight lift from my shoulders.

As the days turned into weeks and Alan's impatience at being confined in a hospital bed increased, we did whatever we could to divert his attention in the hope of making him as happy as possible. He quickly tired of hospital food so we would bring his favorite burritos from Zantigo's and there was pizza—lots of pizza. Whenever Alan mentioned he wanted something, we were on a mission to make it happen. The nurses were kind and also went out of their way to make Alan comfortable and keep his mind busy. A young nurse named Cindy became a good friend to Alan. She worked the three-to-eleven shift, but would arrive an hour early to play checkers with him or teach him to draw using grid paper. Cindy also regularly visited Alan during her breaks to help him pass the time. She was an angel!

Meanwhile, Bob contacted his friend Allen Bernstein, who at the time owned a number of Wendy's restaurants on Long Island, in Queens and Manhattan, and would go on to acquire Morton's of Chicago steakhouses. Bernstein had access to a number of professional football and basketball players and, at Bob's request, asked them to send greetings to Alan. Before long Alan's hospital room was filled with signed pictures and memorabilia from well-known athletes including Reggie Jackson with the New York Yankees, Dr. J with the Philadelphia 76ers, and Franco Harris with the Pittsburgh Steelers.

I was regularly contacted by reporters from Columbus and Michigan eager for information about Alan as the "lone survivor" of the crash that claimed the life of his father and three other men. I made myself available as often as I could to answer questions and, when possible, included Alan in the interviews as a distraction from the miserable routine that had become his life. Time and again, people were very kind and encouraging. When columnist Neal R. Miller from the *Iosco County News* discovered Alan had started a baseball card collection, he asked readers to mail old baseball cards they no longer wanted to Alan at the hospital. Everyone was pulling for my son.

Alan was in traction at Doctors West Hospital for a month before he came home to Stoney Bridge in a body cast that encompassed both legs. Thankfully, Steve and Angela offered to move in to help attend to Alan. While Alan was glad to be home, it was a difficult transition. Steve was the only one with the strength to move him from room to room, but he worked during the day. The hustle and bustle of the hospital, with nurses and doctors around all the time to distract and entertain, was replaced with periods of boredom watching television from the sofa. He was embarrassed for me to attend to his personal hygiene needs. Reporters had moved on to the next story; athletes were no longer sending greetings. Even though the school tutor and the psychologist continued daily visits, it was a dark time for Alan.

To lift his spirits, I invited his friends over and we would play football in the yard. Alan was quarterback from his hospital bed, devising plays and shouting commands, while I pushed him around as fast as those wheels could move. Other days when the weather cooperated, I would wheel his bed down to the bridge over the creek where we would fondly recall fishing trips with his dad. For Halloween, I hosted a costume party for his classmates. Alan had so much fun selecting a white wig and face paint to wear. Everyone had a grand time, even though Alan was still confined to his bed.

In late November the cast came off and Alan was able to begin using a wheelchair, which meant he was able to return to school at Ridgewood Elementary. Another step toward progress, another painful transition. The children at school were inquisitive about his injury and the accident. He received many questions and his explanations reopened painful wounds as he described the crash that took the life of his father. Nothing was easy for him. I drove him to school because he couldn't take the bus, but getting in and out of the car and the building was a challenge. Moving a wheelchair down the hallway, through the doorways, and in the classroom was difficult and frustrating.

Alan was still suffering from depression and crying a lot. Although his physical pain was subsiding, emotionally he was a wreck. He no longer needed a tutor, but I still had the psychologist meeting with Alan regularly. One afternoon his doctor pulled me aside and suggested I consider putting Alan on medication to help him deal with the depression. I was vehemently opposed. I could easily recall the hyper, fun-loving, active child from just a few months ago and was certain medication wasn't the answer. What I wanted for my son was a return to his joyful childhood. I had seen children on medication; sure, their pain was diluted, but so was their zest for life. I demanded more time before we revisited the option of medication. He agreed to wait.

On a Sunday afternoon a few weeks later I was out running errands when my neighbor Kim Cassady stopped over with her boyfriend, who happened to be highly celebrated OSU quarterback Art Schlichter. Art brought a few football items he had signed and engaged Alan in conversation for a couple minutes. I arrived just as Art was leaving, but did have the chance to quickly meet him and thank him for his visit.

As I entered the house with bags of groceries in my arms, Alan was talking nonstop about Art and the OSU items he left behind. The smile plastered across my son's face lit up the room. To say the change I saw in Alan was miraculous does a disservice to the word miracle. I was astounded at what I saw in my son and hoped the glow of the encounter would stay around for a few days. We could use a little happiness around here.

Alan woke up the next morning still talking about Art Schlichter. Gone were the sadness and grief that had accompanied him every day since the crash. He didn't grumble when I helped dress him. He was excited and couldn't wait to get to school to tell everyone about Art's visit. At the breakfast table, in the car and, as I learned later, all day at school it was non-stop Art Schlichter and OSU football. When I picked him up that afternoon, he was still talking about Art's visit. Later that week Alan's teacher gave me an update on his progress. It was the first time since his return Alan wasn't focused on the crash or his physical limitations or losing his dad. His sadness had evaporated. He was interacting with his friends and participating in class. And, yes, he was enthusiastically talking about Art Schlichter and football. Alan's teacher was amazed at the transformation. I was elated.

The effects of Art visiting our home and meeting with Alan lasted beyond a few days. In fact, it was the catalyst Alan needed to break out of his depression and stop focusing on the past. With this newfound energy, Alan's recovery accelerated and before long he was able to discard the wheelchair and begin using crutches before quickly graduating to a cane. And a few weeks later the cane was relegated to a corner in the closet, as Alan was able to walk unassisted. The following June I was so proud when Alan limped toward the car, clutching a fist full of papers on his last day of school. My son had not only survived a fatal plane crash nine months previous, but his joyful zest for life was back in a big way. And even though the time out of the classroom necessitated his repeating fifth grade, that was but a tiny challenge compared to the progress he had been able to make following Art's visit. My heart was full and overflowing.

That summer Bob began suggesting that we get married, but I wasn't sure I was ready to commit at that level. While Bob was a kind and financially generous man, and I enjoyed spending time with him and accompanying him to various Wendy's events locally and internationally, I wasn't ready to give up my single lifestyle. My two divorces and round-the-clock care for Alan since the crash had left me physically exhausted and emotionally depleted. I had found little time to think about the future and I really wasn't sure what my next step should be. Besides, it was easy to recall that the most satisfying times of my life occurred during the freedom I experienced as a single woman.

While we continued traveling and discussing marriage, Bob purchased a lovely house at 5566 Dublin Road. It was a large family home with a pool overlooking the Scioto River; he was certain I would eventually accept his proposal of marriage. A successful business executive, Bob was accustomed to getting what he wanted. He was politely relentless in his pursuit. I remained steadfast in my refusal.

One morning Bob announced he wanted to take me to Lazarus to select a bracelet. He was always surprising me with gifts and I was delighted by this unexpected offer. Before I knew it, we were in his Cadillac heading downtown. In the jewelry department we were met by Bob's favorite salesperson, Flo, who began pulling out beautiful diamond tennis bracelets for me to try on. Before I could make a selection, Bob tugged at my sleeve, "Hey, look at these diamonds over here! Let's get you one of these and it will be your engagement ring." His ploy was so endearing and in the moment, all of my silly excuses melted away. I happily accepted his proposal and we began shopping for the perfect setting for the diamond of my choice. I walked out of the store that afternoon with a stunning diamond bracelet on my wrist, a promise of marriage in my future, and a prayer that the third time would be the charm.

***

Alan was very bright and inquisitive but had always struggled with reading comprehension, so I hired reading tutors each summer to help him overcome his challenges in this area. After the crash I noticed a marked improvement in his overall learning while he worked with a tutor full–time. I considered sending him to a private school, which would be able to offer the individual attention he needed. Dave Thomas, Len Immke, Dave Swaddling, Jack Ruscilli, and several area entrepreneurs had just founded The Wellington School on Reed Road with a mission to allow every student who attended to become a champion. It sounded like a perfect environment for Alan and he was excited about the opportunity to transfer to a private school. He enjoyed the small class size and quickly made many friends, including the son of Headmaster Walter Ebmeyer.

Several months into the new school year, I received a call from Mr. Ebmeyer asking me to meet with him. Based on personal observations, he was inclined to think that Alan's education challenges were due to dyslexia. I was surprised. No other educator had identified that Alan may have a learning disability, but it would certainly explain the struggles he faced in school. Bob suggested we contact School Selection Consulting, founded by Teckie Shackelford. (Bob knew from Teckie from her service on Wendy's Board.) After working with Alan, she confirmed he had dyslexia and suggested several distinguished boarding schools that successfully served dyslexic students.

Although I hated the idea of Alan living away from me, I was willing to make that sacrifice for his success. Bob, Alan, and I visited several schools in Ohio and New York. Returning from a school visit in the Wendy's jet, Alan was enthusiastic about the Gow program in Buffalo, New York, where students were involved in activities like skiing and horseback riding in the morning, and classroom time was pushed to the evening. We began the enrollment process in preparation of Alan beginning classes after Christmas break.

Bob and I had been casually discussing our wedding, but had not yet set a date. He wanted to keep the ceremony low-key so as not to upset his children or incite his former wife. On the Sunday after Thanksgiving, Bob suggested, "Why don't we go to the courthouse and get married this week?" It sounded like a good idea. I purchased an off-white suit and Bob mentioned to Dave that he needed to leave work early on Friday because we were getting married. And just like that, our wedding planning was complete.

On Friday afternoon, December 3, 1982, we drove downtown. After the judge declared us husband and wife, he snapped a picture. We stopped at Ollie's Grandview Inn on the way home to celebrate with a drink and shared a shrimp cocktail. We told Ollie we just married and would be returning for dinner that evening. In fact, later we did return with Dave and Lorraine Thomas.

The next morning Bob was scheduled to travel to a Wendy's function in Lexington, Kentucky, which involved attending a University of Kentucky basketball game. We enjoyed a quick trip down on the Wendy's jet with Bob's son Bryan, sportscaster Billy Packer, and Marquette University Coach Al McGuire. It was just Bob and me on the return trip, and I was glad for a little alone time with my new husband.

December was a busy time as Alan and I moved into Bob's home and we put the Stoney Bridge house in the hands of a Realtor. With Christmas right around the corner and Alan's impending departure for Gow, there was no time for a honeymoon, but Bob did surprise me with a Mercedes convertible as a combination wedding and Christmas gift.

I was delighted when our friends mentioned they wanted to celebrate this new chapter in our lives with a party, and infuriated when Bob adamantly refused their offer. I had agreed to a simple City Hall wedding, but mistakenly thought my husband would agree to a reception with friends and family. However, he was still smarting from his contentious divorce from Carol. He didn't want an elaborate party to exacerbate the situation, or possibly cause problems for his children, whom he adored. With Brad in college, Ann in high school, and Brian in junior high, Bob was desperate to maintain a relationship with them.

At the beginning, having a stepmother was uncomfortable for Bob's children. However, we all worked to make our new family function and, eventually, it did. I made things as welcoming and comfortable as possible, always ensuring Bob had alone time with his children when they came to visit. Because Brian and Alan were about the same age, they enjoyed many activities together on the weekends and their relationship played a big part in helping two families blend into one. Bob was an excellent stepfather and he and Alan got along extremely well. Alan responded positively to Bob's parenting, and Bob liked Alan's personality.

After the New Year we flew to Buffalo to settle Alan in his new school. He was excited. I desperately wanted Gow to be the answer for him, but I was nervous. My son had changed my life in so many amazing ways. He was a pregnancy the experts said could never happen. He was a beloved son who brought joy and fun into our lives. He was zany and energetic, loving and kind, and I nearly lost him. At thirteen, Alan was no longer a child and was relying on me less and less. With the effects of the crash behind us, I now worried about his happiness. My son had suffered more during the previous two years than most people encounter in a lifetime. We had traveled to death and back together, and I couldn't bear to think of him enduring any more sorrow.

I didn't need to worry. The young man I left in New York was the epitome of self-assured happiness. As Bob and I were preparing to leave, Alan gave us a quick hug before turning to join his new friends.

He was going to be just fine

12 | LIFE WITH BOB

1982—2005

> *"Dear Bob and Anita—*
>
> *Words simply cannot express how much Miriam and I enjoyed being with you and your friends at last night's Xmas party. As I told Bob before we left . . . I've attended many Xmas parties over the years, but never one as elegant as yours. Thanks, again, for your thoughtfulness and generosity. Best wishes for a joyous holiday season."*

Jimmy Crum
WCMH Sportscaster

Bob and I settled into a happy routine of married life and finally began planning our honeymoon. We decided on the Presidential Suite at Las Hadas in Manzanillo, Mexico, after learning a portion of the Bo Derek movie, *10*, was filmed on this beautiful property. Before we could head south, however, Bob had some Wendy's business to oversee in Japan and I was looking forward to my first visit to Asia.

Upon returning to the States, we headed to Pasadena, California, to attend the 1983 Super Bowl. With Mr. T and other members of the new television series *The A–Team* cheering in the row behind us, and Roger Staubach and friends seated next to Bob, we watched the Redskins defeat the Dolphins at the Rose

Bowl. It was my first professional football game and I had a lot of fun spotting celebrities and cheering on the Dolphins. Ten years later in 1993, I attended my second Super Bowl in Pasadena and had the honor of meeting former NFL player Marcus Gastineau on that trip.

After the game I was ready to head to Mexico, but it took some convincing for my travel-weary husband not to reschedule our honeymoon. He had plans of returning to Columbus and catching up on sleep while his body adjusted to traveling across multiple time zones. I had visions of romance on the beach while the Pacific waves crashed at our feet. I prevailed and we enjoyed a lovely week away from Ohio's winter weather.

At Las Hadas we had a private pool and deck, and our own butler. One evening, we decided to go skinny-dipping. As we exited the pool and attempted to re-enter our suite, we realized the door had locked when it closed behind us. We had not brought our keys, any clothing, or even a towel outside with us. "Well, Bo Bo, what do we do now?" Bob had taken to calling me Bo Bo in honor of Bo Derek. I responded, "Well, Dumbo, I don't know." Luckily we spied an employee delivering food to a nearby suite and, as we hid behind chairs on our deck, we called to him and explained our dilemma. The amused employee was able to grant us access to our room, and Bob handed over a sizeable tip for his trouble and discretion. Once we were alone, we laughed at the absurdity of it all. We were world travelers and he was the successful CEO and Chairman of the Board of an international company, and we couldn't keep track of our own keys.

***

Golf was a hobby we both enjoyed and we played as often as possible and wherever we traveled. Bob was quite competitive and it was a lot of fun as long as he was winning. But I was a fierce adversary and enjoyed making him earn every victory. We had the good fortune to play on prestigious courses like Pebble Beach and Spyglass Hill in California and were members at Jupiter Hills and Coral Ridge in Florida.

We also played golf while visiting locations in Japan, Hawaii, Africa, and Europe. Locally, we played at Tanglewood Club, Double Eagle, Worthington Hills, Jefferson Country Club (where Bob was an investor and lifetime member), and Muirfield, where we both were members. Our golfing companions included notables such as former OSU Football Coach John Cooper and football greats Archie Griffin, Jack Tatum, and John Hicks, as well as former OSU President Ed Jennings. We regularly attended The Memorial Tournament at Murifield and were in Augusta for the Masters in 1981 when Tom Watson beat Jack Nicklaus by two strokes.

In the early 1980s Bob became an investor, along with Dave Thomas, Arnold Palmer, Yankees Hall of Fame pitcher Whitey Ford, Boston Celtics Owner Harry Mangurian, and others of the exclusive Adios Golf Course in Coconut Creek, Florida. One day, shortly before Adios was scheduled to open, Bob and I stopped by to check on the progress and play nine holes. The manager called Bob over to the construction trailer that was still on property and reminded him that this was a male-only course and I was not permitted to play. Bob returned with the disappointing news. I was peeved! How unfair that my husband invested a large amount of money into this course and I was not allowed to play! Not one to be denied something I wanted, I made enough noise that they let me play that day. In honor (or perhaps, horror) of my being the only woman who managed to find a way to play on the "boys only course," Dave said he was going to have a sign erected proclaiming my stunning exploit.

Years later we were hosting three of Bob's childhood friends and their wives, including one friend whose long-standing nickname was "Brother." Bob decided to take the guys golfing at Adios while I took the ladies shopping. In the clubhouse Bob greeted Dan Marino, whom he knew casually because their lockers were adjacent to one another. Dan introduced Bob to O.J. Simpson, who was his guest for the day. Later from the fairway, both O.J. and "Brother" hit their balls into the same sand trap at the same time. They looked at each other, unaware of the protocol regarding who should proceed. Bob saw what was happening and after a few awkward moments he shouted to his friend, "Brother, hit the ball!" O.J. yelled back, "OK!" and took the swing as Bob stifled a laugh. Several weeks later Bob and I were in shock as we heard a news report that O.J.'s wife, Nicole Brown Simpson, had been murdered.

***

Bob's position with Wendy's afforded us many opportunities to interact with famous and powerful people who I discovered were generally entertaining and fun to be around. Shortly after we were married, we met Johnny Bench at a Christmas party at Dave Thomas' house. During a Wendy's event, Bob played tennis with Bobby Riggs, one of the top players in the world, and we both played tennis with John Sculley in Boca Raton when he was with Pepsico (before he joined Apple). In 1993, Bob and I were watching President Clinton's first State of the Union Address and there was John, sitting right beside Hillary. We pointed at the television in awe, delighted to know someone who rubbed shoulders with the President!

One week as the staff at Wendy's was preparing for a visit by former President Jimmy Carter and his wife Rosalynn, Bob invited me to attend the luncheon. In the next breath he mentioned that the Wendy's jet was available if I preferred to go to Florida for a few days. It only took an instant for me to decide on a weekend with the girls in the sun. Bob had been monopolizing most of my free time, so when I had the opportunity to hang out with friends and family I was going to take it, even if it meant missing out on meeting President Carter. I confirmed Alan's regular sitter, Mrs. Roebuck, was available to stay at the house for a few days, then I quickly made a number of calls and before dinner that evening had gathered a plane full of women including Angela and her best friend Martha Joseph. Utilizing every square inch of seating in the jet, we were cramped in the air but once the limo met us on the tarmac it was blue skies, warm sand, and wide-open spaces for the entire weekend.

***

The spring following our marriage, Bob was invited to attend a golf event in Pittsburgh sponsored by the Heinz Company, a Wendy's supplier. He was going to be gone for just a night or two and I decided to remain in Columbus. I had been traveling so much I had been missing time with friends and family, so I planned a small dinner party to reconnect with "the girls." Angela, my mom, aunts, cousins and a few friends ate and laughed and talked late into the evening. Everyone had so much fun that the girl's night out became an annual event. (We renamed the event "Hen Parties" because Bob said all the women clucking and laughing reminded him of a yard full of hens.) The guest list continued to grow over the years as the original crew invited friends of their own until we easily had 200 or more ladies.

I would purchase inexpensive watches and other small gifts from the Swap Shop in Fort Lauderdale to raffle off so everyone went home with a memento, and live entertainment became a highlight of the evening. At the beginning I invited Accordionist Esther Craw from German Village. Later it was famed Elvis impersonator Mike Albert, who put on quite a show for the guests. We would create a theater in the Great Room, complete with a stage on which Mike would perform before an audience of swooning women who might just toss lady garments his way.

One year I thought it would be fun to shake things up. I contacted Jack Hanna at the Columbus Zoo and asked if penguins could visit my upcoming Hen Party. We drained our pool and worked with zoo officials to ensure the replacement water was the proper pH and safe for the troupe of penguins that stopped by. I was thrilled to see how delighted my guests were to watch the animals waddle around the deck and dive into the water. It goes without saying those little guys were the best-dressed guests that evening.

In the beginning, Sisters Chicken & Biscuits, a restaurant Bob was instrumental in launching, catered the meal but eventually I pressed Bob and several of the husbands into manning the grills and cooking the steaks and chicken for our guests. Roy was our bartender and the only male guest was WCMH Sportscaster Jimmy Crum, who showed up one year uninvited with his wife Miriam, and returned year after year wearing one of his colorful sport coats. It was fun to watch as he circulated among the guests, always eliciting a laugh before moving on. Our relationship with Jimmy continued to grow until he had a standing invitation to all of our events including Hen and Christmas parties and Bob's birthday celebrations, where I would ask him to perform dramatic readings on Bob's behalf. With his distinctive vocal style and quick wit, Jimmy was one of the most popular guests. Bob became an enthusiastic financial supporter of Jimmy's philanthropic initiative, Recreation Unlimited Camps and Retreat Center for individuals with disabilities and health concerns.

***

When we weren't traveling for Wendy's, we would head to Florida when we needed some downtime. When we married, Bob owned a small condominium in Lauderdale-By-The-Sea and that became our escape. It was right on the beach and the sound of waves crashing on the beach was our constant companion. One week while we were vacationing at the condo Bob was feeling under the weather. He didn't feel like golfing or doing much of anything but suggested we go house hunting. We ended up driving through nearby Bay Colony, a premier community where a number of celebrities had homes including Shirley McClain, Lee Iacocca, Cal Ripken, Ray Kroc of McDonald's, and our friends Dave Thomas and Len Immke. We eventually purchased a lovely home and happily vacationed there, many times hosting family and Ohio friends, as well as many of Bob's childhood friends. We kept the Lauderdale-By-The-Sea condo so my parents and Bob's father could come and go as they pleased with their guests, whether or not we were in Florida at the time.

We had so much fun living in Bay Colony hosting and attending dinners and celebrations. Dave frequently had large parties on his ninety-foot yacht named the I. Lorraine, which he docked behind his home. It had a custom dining table to seat eight, complete kitchen, a master and two guest staterooms, and crew quarters for up to five staff. He even employed his own Captain. Dave's yacht was large and luxurious and because it could accommodate more than 50 guests, everybody, and I do mean everybody, attended his events.

***

Alan returned to Columbus from Gow for his first summer break and it was wonderful to have him home. He regaled us with stories of his new friends and experiences at boarding school. Bob and I had a Wendy's event in Las Vegas planned shortly after Alan's arrival. I wasn't crazy about leaving him so soon after his return, but the trip had been on the calendar for months. Mom and Dad happily agreed to stay at the house while we were gone. We were away for just a couple of days when I received an urgent call; Alan was experiencing extreme pain in his left leg, the one that had been severely damaged in the crash. I returned home immediately and took Alan to a specialist who, after a brief examination, diagnosed the discomfort as growing pains and sent us home. The next morning when Alan woke up his leg had tripled in size and was an ugly color. I called Dr. Johnston, the Orthopedic Surgeon who had operated on Alan after the crash, and he quickly arranged to come out to the house. After one look at Alan's leg he ordered us to get to the hospital right away.

E. coli bacteria that had lain dormant for three years following the crash had revealed itself with a vengeance and was now threatening to claim Alan's leg. The situation was quite serious. His doctor inserted a port which enabled Alan to receive intravenous antibiotic therapy, and he remained hospitalized for two weeks. He was back to using a wheelchair—no standing or walking on the affected leg. After he showed some progress overcoming the infection, Alan was discharged and we began daily visits to his pediatrician who continued administering antibiotics. It took several more weeks before Alan was out of danger of losing his leg.

Before long, summer came to a close and Alan returned to Gow to begin eighth grade. His enthusiasm for boarding school was waning and after the recent health scare I was reluctant to send him off, but we all agreed it was best for his education. Before long, however, we started receiving phone calls from Alan expressing his discontent. When I followed up with the headmaster to gather more details, he relayed Alan appeared to happily enjoy activities with his friends and was doing well in his classes, so I encouraged Alan to remain at Gow.

Bob and I continued traveling for Wendy's and spending time in Florida with Alan when he was on school break. One morning Bob planned to golf and asked Alan to join him. By the time they arrived at the golf course, they had picked up Dave Thomas, OSU President Ed Jennings, Len Immke, and Columbus Mayor Dana "Buck" Rinehart. I was proud to learn Alan didn't have any trouble keeping up with these "big boys."

**

When Bob and I were in Columbus, our evenings typically consisted of sharing about our day over cocktails, and then we would usually go out for dinner. He always wanted me to enjoy a drink with him at home, but I wasn't much of a drinker and often would discreetly pour myself ginger ale. When we went out, I limited myself to two drinks. Any more than that and things could get ugly. If we both drank to excess Bob could become a bully, I didn't know when to hold my tongue, and the evening could quickly spiral out of control. At home, he would demand and I would push back and before long crystal might be thrown against the wall or dishes smashed on the floor. As he said things just to hurt me, I hurled accusations in response, and we both behaved in ways we would later regret. We could be as passionate in our fighting as we were in our zest for life.

Reminiscent of my father's blackouts, the morning following one of these incidents Bob couldn't understand why I was angry with him, as his recollection of events was often hazy. A few drinks and Bob remained happy and easy-going, and could sing, dance, and talk the night away. Unfortunately, too much alcohol transformed him into a tyrant.

I remember one New Year's Eve in Florida in particular when things turned hostile between us. We were hosting our friends Ernie and Mariana Schwartzman, Stewart and Olive Brown, and Martin and Joy Blanco. After we watched the clock strike midnight, I retired to bed as we were hosting a rather large dinner party the next day for about twelve guests including Dave and Lorraine Thomas and Len and Charlotte Immke, and I needed to be up early. When I rolled over about 3:00 a.m. I discovered Bob was still sitting in the living room talking with Olive. I made a comment about him coming to bed that he took the wrong the way and he was immediately angry. I was upset about the scene he was making and things quickly deteriorated into a rather loud shouting match. I should have known better than to antagonize him when he got this way, but I was tired and had passed the point of no return.

Before I knew what was happening, Bob had opened our refrigerator and pulled out the four pork roasts I had purchased from Carmine's Gourmet Market for our party. (Carmine's was pricy, but they always had the best quality meats.) Unable to stop him, I watched as he stomped toward the canal behind our house and threw the roasts as hard as he could. I couldn't see where they landed, but they obviously missed hitting our boat because I heard all four splash in the water. I was panicked. I had guests coming in a few hours. What was I going to do? Without a well-formed plan, I grabbed a flashlight and a fruit picker and stood on the dock trying to spy the white butcher paper in the dark water so I could retrieve the roasts. I'm not sure what I would have done with the water-soaked packages even if I had located them. Certainly, I hope I wouldn't have served them to our guests, but at the time I was running on adrenaline and solely focused on those roasts.

Fortunately, I quickly came to my senses and devised a more logical and, most likely, safer plan. The local Publix would open in a few hours and hopefully I could replace the premium roasts with four less-expensive pork roasts. Later at dinner, everyone raved about the food and since it didn't seem anyone could recognize a difference in the quality, I never returned to Carmine's.

***

Alan's calls from Gow were becoming more frequent due to his increasing dissatisfaction. I was determined he would complete the school year before transferring out. My parents were horrified at my decision, continually insisting I bring him home. As their only grandson, Alan's happiness was paramount. Although his well-being was on my mind as well, I also knew the importance of teaching him about commitment and completing what one starts. Much to my parents' disappointment, I stood firm and told Alan once he completed eighth grade, he could return home and enroll in Dublin Coffman High School. With a clear ending in sight, Alan's phone calls became more positive and he transferred out of Gow the following June. He eventually graduated from Dublin Coffman and enrolled in The University of Southern Mississippi in Hattiesburg, where he had success as a member of the Men's Golf Team. It was during his time at USM that Alan became friends with Brett Favre and his brother Scott. Alan would often stay at their home and told many stories of their antics, including the three of them waking at 3:00 a.m. to hunt for armadillos. When Alan returned home from Mississippi he enrolled in Columbus State Community College and joined the Golf Team that won the state championship. He completed his education at Franklin University where he earned a degree in marketing.

***

The summer of 1984 was a sad one, as my father passed away. He was sixty-nine when he suffered a heart attack on the golf course. After an unhappy childhood, and living for years with the sorrows that alcoholism brings, he was sober and happy and doing something he loved when he left us. Wanting my mother closer to us, Bob and I convinced her to sell the little home in Lincoln Village. We purchased a lot and had a new home built for her on

Rings Road, adjacent to Steve and Angela and their sons, Scott and Sean.

***

Bob and I had met Danny Thomas at several Christmas parties at Dave and Lorraine's home, and then saw him again at The Athletic Club of Columbus during the 1985 wedding reception of Dave's daughter, Molly, and Charles Postlewaite. When Bob stepped away from the reception hall, Danny approached me and asked for a dance. As we returned to the table where Bob had reappeared, the music started again. Danny asked Bob if he could have a dance with me; Bob wouldn't allow it. Before we left, Danny discreetly slipped me a piece of paper with his phone number on it and said to give him a call. Well aware of Bob's jealousy, I wasn't willing to take the chance he might find the paper later and handed over the note with Danny's number. I never called him.

Some time later Bob and I were invited to attend a St. Jude fundraiser at the home of Danny Thomas, where I had the opportunity to meet many celebrities including Lucille Ball and Betty White. I encountered Betty in the powder room when I went to freshen up. I mentioned how much my mom loved her show, The Golden Girls. We chatted for a while and she asked my mom's name and where she lived. Shortly after we returned home, I received a package in the mail. Inside was a book from Betty with an inscription to my mother. I couldn't believe she would remember our conversation or care to follow up, and my mom was thrilled.

***

Bob and I saw Mike Tyson fight at the Las Vegas Hilton on four separate occasions as guests of the Hilton Hotel. For one fight, we had exceptional front row floor seats. Looking around I spied Wayne Newton and Eddie Murphy sitting behind us. After the event concluded and we were being escorted out, the usher said to a man a few seats down from us, "Right this way Colonel." I looked closer and recognized Elvis' former manager, Colonel Tom Parker, wearing his trademark hat and carrying a cane. Meanwhile, folks in the bleachers were pointing and calling out the names of celebrities they identified as the floor seats emptied. As we queued behind the Colonel I could hear, "There's Colonel Parker!" followed immediately by a reference to Bob and me, "Oh, they're nobody." And really, we were nobodies in an arena filled with household names. Oh, but it was so fun!

**

Bob and I had been married for a few years when he decided he wanted to build his dream house, something that would make a statement. I was quite content with our current house and didn't understand the need to make a change. The early stresses of a newly blended family had diminished and the concerns about remarrying that had plagued my mind were proven to be unfounded. I didn't want to rock the boat.

Nonetheless, Bob began looking for a lot on which to build and spied a promising location at 5600 Dublin Road, just up the road from our current address. It was a beautiful parcel with several waterfalls and a building site that overlooked the Scioto River. When he discovered the owners lived in England, we made plans to meet with them during our upcoming Wendy's trip to Europe. Unfortunately, despite Bob's best efforts he could not convince them to sell. We returned home disappointed and our search continued.

Eventually, we came across nearly thirteen acres at 7192 Dublin Road, on the north side of State Route 161. There was an old farmhouse, a barn, a little garage, and a chicken coop on the property. After some negotiation with the property owner Bill Guy, who also owned Air Force One HVAC Solutions, we became the proud owners. Bob possessed an uncanny ability to envision spaces and we immediately began planning what would become an architectural showpiece where we could entertain in style. In the evenings we would spread large pieces of newspaper on our garage floor and mark out different rooms and furniture placement as we ultimately designed a home that had seventeen rooms including five bedrooms, six full and two half-baths, and encompassed nearly 13,000 square feet.

At the very beginning of construction we had to make some dimension adjustments and the first one suggested was to reduce the size of my closet. I was indignant and questioned Bob, "What are you doing to my closet?" And then I caught myself. *What is wrong with you? Look at everything you have! Stop behaving this way!* At the newly reduced size of more than 500 square feet, there would still be plenty of room for all my clothes, accessories and nearly 300 pairs of shoes. I didn't necessarily buy a lot of new things all the time, I just rarely discarded anything I did purchase and my closet was filled with items I had accumulated over the course of more than twenty years.

It took nearly eighteen months to build our dream. As we began to decorate and furnish the interior, I worked with Christy at Lombard's Fine Furniture on Lane Avenue. Bob left the selection of all the furniture and lighting and flooring and cabinets—of everything—to me. He didn't give me a budget but asked that I keep track of what I was buying, along with the quantities and the pricing. As you might imagine when building out a house that was nearly 13,000 square feet, attempting to account for dozens of hinges and handles and outlet covers and reconciling invoices to orders and verifying pricing quickly became overwhelming. I confessed my inability to keep track of everything to Bob, explaining how unwieldy the task had become. He transferred the job to his secretary who was very detail-oriented, but it became too much for her to manage, as well. I can recall frequent lengthy meetings at Lombard's as we would try to make sense of all the purchases. I don't think we ever managed to untangle all the details.

With construction complete, but most of the furniture in transit, we moved into "The Big House" on our fifth wedding anniversary, December 1987. We invited our friends to celebrate our anniversary and new home with the stipulation that they bring a fifth of the drink of their choice as the price of admission.

Because Bob desired ample areas for entertaining, we built an open two-story great room on the main level measuring sixty feet by thirty nine feet to accommodate 100 guests and a dining area where we would regularly seat twenty guests. I paid special attention to creating cozy intimate conversation areas within the larger rooms Bob preferred so it felt like our home, not a convention center.

Our lower party level was designed for fun starting with "Barney's Bar," an entertainment room with dance floor measuring fifty-seven feet by twenty-nine feet, a sitting area for twelve around a fully stocked bar, a pool table, kitchen and fireplace. Other rooms on this floor included a professionally outfitted exercise room, billiard room, game room for a Ms. Pac-Man and other full-sized arcade games, and a climate-controlled area for the hot tub with the tanning bed and massage room nearby. A sitting area, overlooking the pool and Vermont stone patio, completed the space.

Our master bedroom suite included six rooms and was planned so Bob and I had separate baths, walk-in closets, and dressing areas—one at each end so we didn't crowd one another when we were getting ready. We also added a sitting room to our bedroom suite large enough to accommodate two sofas, two recliners and a refrigerator. This room opened up to a Vermont stone balcony overlooking the river. On warm Sunday nights we would sit on our deck and listen to live music spilling across the water from Scioto Park. I would often reminisce about my childhood and the pleasant times our family enjoyed at the park on the far shore, never imagining I would ever reach a point in life where I would be living in such a grand house on the river.

Once we had the space, Bob and I hosted all kinds of parties and I was always on the lookout for the next holiday or event where we could entertain. We were proud of Columbus and humbled when community leaders asked to make our home available for charity and civic events.

With the larger house and grounds, Lee, who had been with us for more than five years as a part-time house manager and groundskeeper, became a full-time employee with an annual salary of $60,000 and a nicely outfitted office in the barn. He took superb care of everything, including maintaining the grounds, and we never had to worry about a thing whether we were home or traveling. Lee would decorate for Christmas and help with all of our events, and would even go grocery shopping for us. Eventually I also hired a full-time and a part-time housekeeper, a laundress and several gardeners, the number depending on the season. With a regular staff of six, I had a lot of personnel to manage, but with all the charity events and parties we were hosting, it wouldn't have been possible without their enthusiastic assistance.

Our annual Christmas party—requiring male guests to wear a sports coat and tie and the women to dress up—was a formal and festive affair. Lee, his wife Teresa, our housekeeper Sabrina, cousin Carol Jean, and good friend Judy Nesbitt set out the holiday decorations. They trimmed four enormous trees, hung garland from the loft, and tucked holiday decorations on every available surface inside and out. Every November they dressed the house and grounds while we were in Florida, and when we returned home in December we walked into a Christmas wonderland. For the night of the big event, most of the furniture was placed in storage to accommodate the 100 or so guests who pulled right up to our front door and handed their keys to a valet.

On the main level guests were welcomed by a three-piece brass ensemble, and I customarily had three dining tables overflowing with appetizers, with a bartender nearby. We enjoyed cocktails for a few hours and then the party moved downstairs, and the real fun began. On the lower party level, guests were greeted by a DJ, two additional bartenders, and even more food. We converted the pool table into an enormous buffet, and separate tables were used to display boats filled with shrimp, holiday delicacies, and elaborate desserts for our guests to enjoy.

New Year's Eve celebrations were enjoyed in warmer weather with our Florida crew. The fun consisted of hats and noisemakers, food and decorations, and occasionally the guys dressing in wigs and performing a rehearsed dance number, with fireworks lighting up the sky at the stroke of midnight. Celebrating "out with the old and in with the new" was something we looked forward to all year.

***

Throughout the years Bob and I also enjoyed participating in or hosting a number of civic endeavors and charity events. The Bogie Busters golf tournament, which was a two-day event hosting 175 golfers—many of them celebrities or political powerhouses— was an event we always looked forward to attending. Held in Dayton at the NCR Country Club and founded to raise funds for the Multiple Sclerosis Society, it was always a great time. One year I recall meeting Notre Dame Basketball Coach Digger Phelps. In 1988 we met Vice President George H. W. Bush, who was in campaign mode. Bush said to Bob, "I'm going to be President!" Bob jokingly responded, "Well, I guess we'll have to see about that."

Several months later we attended the Republican National Convention in New Orleans, where George Bush received the Presidential nomination. We were guests of Roger Enrico, President and CEO of Pepsico, who was pushing hard to replace Coca-Cola as Wendy's soft-drink vendor. Bob and I were escorted to a large tent filled with lavishly decorated tables and dignitaries milling about. When we found our assigned table, I was delighted to discover I was seated beside Secretary of State George Schultz. Bob sat across the table with a member of the United Nations while other guests filled the seats between us. George was extremely easy to speak with and we kept up quite a lively discussion throughout the entire meal. After dessert plates had been cleared, Bob stepped around to my side of the table and George said, "I have certainly enjoyed talking with your wife. I think she could run the world!" I was beaming at his compliment.

***

One year we hosted a dinner for the Young Presidents' Organization for about 100 guests. We had all of the furniture removed from the great room and placed in storage. We created a French restaurant-themed space for the sit-down dinner where elite members of Columbus' business community dined on délicieuses spécialités françaises. The Columbus Boy's Choir performed that night, positioning themselves in three separate areas including the loft overlooking the Great Room. We were delighted to discover the acoustics in our home enhanced the performance as the voices blended to fill the space with captivating melodies and harmonies. It was an enchanting evening.

***

Bob and I had been invited to attend a United Way fundraiser with a performance by Kenny Rogers at the picturesque Darby Dan Farm, the estate of John W. Galbreath, in Galloway, Ohio. Galbreath was a well-known real estate developer and horse breeder. He had traveled the world, owned the Pittsburgh Pirates at one time, and remained a leading booster of the Ohio State Buckeyes. The event was billed as a formal gala and I wanted to look smashing. I immediately started shopping for the perfect outfit and when I found it, I gasped to learn the price for the little black dress that caught my eye was $1,000. Now, I had a credit card with a $100,000 monthly limit and Bob never asked how I spent my "allowance," he just sent the statements to his secretary to process for payment. But for a single clothing purchase of this amount, I wanted Bob's approval and I got it!

Before the evening program started, guests were directed to the big party room for appetizers and cocktails. I introduced myself to Galbreath who had been making his way around the room. We started chatting and before long he invited me to join him in a tour of his trophy room, which was lined with pristine display cases filled with impressive trophies, awards, and jockey silks. As we continued the private tour he began to explain the sport of horseracing. He enthusiastically talked about winning the Kentucky Derby, and Queen Elizabeth II visiting his farm in Lexington, Kentucky, where she was boarding a mare at his farm for breeding. For one magical evening, I truly felt like I belonged among those who played in the high stakes Sport of Kings. There is little doubt that dress was well worth the cost!

***

As 1989 drew to a close, things were changing at Wendy's and Bob made the decision to retire the following spring. He began his restaurant career in 1962 with the Bobcat Restaurant in Athens and joined Wendy's in 1968. Dave brought him on the board in 1971. It had been a good run, but Bob was ready to kick back, relax and enjoy life in a new way. He was 54 and I was 48. We were a fairly young couple to be retired, but we had our health, the world was waiting, and we had the resources available to do whatever we liked.

Bob always had a controlling nature, but it was fairly easy for me to tolerate his demanding ways when he was spending the majority of his time at the office. We weathered a few rough patches when he first retired as he struggled a bit in the transition from the highly structured routine and pressure cooker responsibilities of a CEO. He insisted I sit and have lunch with him every day, even though I rarely stop for a midday meal. He decided where we would have dinner and when we should go to bed. When Bob told me to do something, he wanted me to do it. There was little room for negotiation or consideration of other options. He was accustomed to giving orders and getting results, and it took some time before he was able to shed his corporate approach to our relationship. With years of uninterrupted time together stretching in front of us, I was determined to make it work for both of us, and Bob eventually settled down and embraced retirement.

We filled our days with family, golfing and traveling, fishing, tailgating, and vacationing with other couples, and spent most of the winters in Florida, where we developed quite a network of friends. In fact, our days in Florida were packed with so many activities we looked forward to returning to Columbus each spring to relax.

***

In 1991 after the story about William Kennedy Smith's alleged assault broke, I became curious to visit Au Bar in Palm Beach. The popular spot had become infamous due to it being the location where Senator Ted Kennedy, Ted's son Patrick, and Ted's nephew William Kennedy Smith visited the night of the alleged attack. Bob and I set out on a quest but we couldn't find it, so Bob stopped by Morton's to ask the manager if he knew anyone down at Au Bar. The manager at Morton's placed a call to Frances who managed Au Bar, obtained directions, and made arrangements for our visit. When we arrived we were ushered right into the VIP area. A few minutes later Donald Trump and Marla Maples arrived with several guests, and requested one of the vacant chairs from our table to accommodate their party.

I spied Roxanne Pulitzer sitting at a table across the dance floor with her French boyfriend Jean de la Moussaye, who was a Grand Prix driver. Upon returning from the ladies room, I stopped by their table and told Roxanne I admired her decision to follow her heart regardless of everyone's opinion of how she should live her life. (She had been in the headlines recently regarding her very public and messy divorce from Peter Pulitzer.) Roxanne was very nice and invited me to sit down as we continued chatting. Before I could excuse myself, Roxanne's dining companion returned to the table and sat next to me, greeting me as if I were a good friend. I turned to introduce myself and explain my presence and came face to face with Zsa Zsa Gabor.

As I returned to our table, Donald Trump called out to me, "Why don't you join us?" As I continued toward Bob I responded, "Oh, I would love to but I don't think my husband would want me to leave him." *Gosh! What was I thinking?* I should have accepted his invitation, grabbed Bob and returned to Mr. Trump's table. Bob was curious about the exchange. I told him about Mr. Trump's request and my response. After dinner, Donald and Marla got up to dance and then came to our table and asked us to join them. I danced with Donald and Bob danced with Marla. What a fun night and none of it would have occurred if I had not been curious enough to follow up on a news story.

A few days after meeting Mr. Trump, Bob and I were hosting friends in Florida. I had attended a number of parties at Trump's private Mar-a-Lago Club and wanted my friends to see the magnificent mansion. As we pulled up to the gate my friends were giggling and averting their faces and loudly whispering that we had better leave before we got in some kind of trouble. I quietly hushed them as a guard approached my Cadillac. I explained who I was and asked if Mr. Trump was available. The guard stepped away to make a call and when he returned stated, "Well, Mr. Trump said if you don't mind waiting, he'll be here in an hour." Without missing a beat I responded, "Well, tell him thank you very much but we really don't have time to wait that long." I turned my SUV around and departed as my friends sat in wide–eyed admiration at my chutzpah. In reality, I was in a hurry to leave as I feared if we waited for Mr. Trump's arrival, he would see me and ask, "How do I know you?"

***

Compared to our busy travel and event schedule when Bob worked at Wendy's, our retirement life became somewhat mundane. Looking for an adventure, I recalled that one of Bob's former coworkers had gone on several African safaris with A&K Tours and returned with unbelievable stories of animal sightings. I tracked down a brochure and after reading about the amenities and seeing the photos, I was convinced Bob this would be a wonderful trip for the two of us. He agreed, made arrangements, and in January 1992 we embarked on the trip of a lifetime.

We landed in Nairobi and stayed our first evening at a resort on a golf course. The next day the nine of us on safari boarded Land Rovers and headed out to the campsite. Our private tent, one of five, was well-equipped with a dressing space containing a simple closet separating the sleeping area from our private "shower" and primitive "bathroom" facilities. It was private but not secure, as the walls were simply thick canvas tarps. At night we could plainly hear the loud laughing of the hyenas and the lions' throaty growls and it was hard not to imagine they were standing mere inches away, just outside our tent. I would jump into Bob's cot and hide my head against his chest for protection. You can be sure there were no nighttime trips to the latrine.

The host team of about twenty locals prepared all the meals onsite and traveled to each campsite with portable ovens, china, and linen tablecloths and napkins. This wasn't your typical camping trip. If this was "roughing it," I couldn't have been happier. When we left camp to tour the area and search for animals, the staff remained busy refreshing our tents, doing laundry, and preparing meals. On the days we broke camp, they also dismantled all the tents and amenities and transferred them to our new campsite so when we arrived later in the evening, we didn't miss a beat.

Every day we encountered wildlife and particularly enjoyed watching the herds of elephants as they meandered across the plains or walked through the forests. The young male elephants were constantly play-fighting, and it was sweet to observe a calf run into the safety of his mother's shadow after he realized we were watching. We saw so many animals: giraffes, hippos, water buffalos, baboons and monkeys, hyenas, storks, and gazelles and numerous varieties of birds. One morning we came upon a lioness just lying at the side of the trail. Our drivers pulled impossibly close. She lay there, lazily watching us for a while, before slowly sauntering into the bush. Further up the trail we came upon a juvenile elephant that challenged us to continue. With a loud trumpet and agitated manner he blocked the way for quite some time. Staring us down, he begged us to take another step. *Bring it on!* It was quite tense and we wondered if he might charge us. Finally satisfied his position was secured, he abruptly turned and walked away. Later, we encountered a lioness that had just killed a good-sized waterbuck. She was standing over her prize and, as we were only yards away, we could clearly see her chest rapidly rising and falling from the exertion of the chase. After the large cat appeared to catch her breath, she proceeded to drag her prize into the tall grass and out of sight.

Witnessing the wild animals living on their own terms and finding a way to survive was astonishing. One afternoon as our

Range Rover came around a bend in the trail we discovered a lion and lioness resting in a shaded area guarding a leopard that appeared paralyzed in its hind legs and mortally wounded, yet still attempting to fight. Whenever the leopard would growl or attempt to move, the lioness would turn toward it and let out a heart-stopping roar. The scene was at the same time heartbreaking and marvelous. As we continued up the trail we spied another lioness resting with two cubs nearby. It was just another glorious day in Africa.

The land was exotic and hauntingly beautiful. I can't adequately describe the loud water falls, lush jungles, dry plains, muddy water holes, enormous trees with their branches outstretched like arms silhouetted by the setting African sun, or the majestic mountains in distant Tanzania. Nature shows can't begin to capture the sights and sounds and smells—the feelings you experience when you travel to Africa. My life was changed by the encounter with this mysterious land.

We were mesmerized by the routine and the extravagant costumes of the Kikuyu Warriors during their performance at the Mt. Kenya Safari Club. This area, sitting at an elevation of 7,000 feet in the shadow of Mount Kenya and on the equator, was magical. The dinner that night was formal and as we had not packed appropriate attire, Bob had to rent a coat and tie in order to enter the main dining room. For my part, I managed to put together a coordinated outfit accessorized with a neck scarf and newly purchased, locally made jewelry from the gift shop. I met the Club's standard for "formal" and no one seemed to mind I was wearing flip flops.

We took advantage of excursions including a hot air balloon ride across the savanna and a flight to Lake Victoria to go fishing for forty-pound Nile perch off Rusinga Island. Our flight was delayed until the airport staff were able to clear the runway of several hippos that were passing through.

After two weeks of living such an amazing adventure, we were homesick and ready to return to the States with hundreds of stories and hours of film.

***

By the end of 1992 Bob was itching for a change of scenery and decided he would like to build a home an hour north of Fort Lauderdale in the Jupiter Hills community in Tequesta, Florida. As an exclusive private gated community, we had to be accepted as members. The admission process included a personal interview with the President of the membership committee, which ironically took place in Toledo, Ohio. Once our application was accepted, we sold our fully furnished house in Bay Colony and began building a new 4,500-square-foot home. Others began building custom estates around us and before long our "small" home looked like it should be a carriage house for an adjoining property. Bobby Orr's home was down the street. Our neighbor on one side was Baltimore Ravens owner Stephen Bisciotti and on the other were Gordon and Jada Bailey, whose 8,870-square-foot French-inspired summer home was featured prominently in the prestigious Florida Design magazine. Gordon and Jada became two of our best friends.

Perry Como was another friendly neighbor of ours in Jupiter, and he regularly extended invitations for me to stop by and visit. One day, knowing Bob would be gone for a few hours on the golf course, I accepted Perry's invitation and walked over to his house. We spent an enjoyable afternoon chatting and even sang a few songs together. The next day a huge floral arrangement arrived with a lovely note from Perry.

***

In 1995 Bob started looking for a project and settled on developing a golf course. Bob and I, both of his sons, and Alan were golf enthusiasts, and he thought it would be a great business opportunity to involve the entire family. He purchased just over 180 acres in Marysville, north of Dublin, and everyone worked hard to make this dream a reality. The following year Rolling Meadows Golf Course opened. With our sons in place to oversee day-to-day operations, Bob and I worked at the course for eight years, opening up in the mornings and cooking for the guests. Many summer afternoons were spent on the course or hosting friends and family in the clubhouse. We had the good fortune to hire some terrific guys to help keep things running smoothly, including Lew Sanchez.

**

In October 1996 Alan was asked to assist his friend Tom Suddes with transporting two of Tom's Mastiffs, an adult and a juvenile, to New York City to appear on *The Late Show with David Letterman*, in support of a segment Jack Hanna was taping. Coincidentally, that same week I had planned to accompany Bob to New York for Wendy's business. At the airport I spotted Jack Hanna near our gate and we ended up sitting together in first class. Bob and Jack had become acquainted when Wendy's opened a location at the zoo, and a few commercials were shot on location.

When I mentioned that our son Alan was helping Tom transport the dogs, Jack was surprised to learn of the family connection. He then asked if I would be attending the show, which was taping later that day. When I lamented that I didn't have tickets, he apologized that he didn't have any extra to give me. "No worry," I told him. "I'll get tickets." This was long before smart phones and Jack knew there was no way I would be able to secure tickets until after we landed. Nonetheless, throughout the flight he periodically asked if I had found any tickets yet. "Don't worry. I'll get tickets," I retorted each time.

As we were disembarking in New York, Jack had a twinkle in his eye as he told me he would have tickets waiting for us at Will Call. We picked up our tickets and, not wanting to wait in the general admission line, I led Bob around the corner and down the street to a side door where celebrity guests entered. (My previous visits to *The Ed Sullivan Show* with General Lassiter decades ago were paying off.) At the entrance, of course we saw Jack, and we met Cindy Crawford and Lyle Lovett who also were waiting to appear. It was a kick being back in the Ed Sullivan Theater, this time with Bob and watching Alan assist Jack on national television. As I looked around the theater, I warmly recalled my last visit had been to see Elvis perform.

***

When we were in Florida, Bob and I had fallen into a daily routine of taking a brief afternoon nap so we would be refreshed for the evening's activities that generally continued until the wee hours of the morning. After we rested, we would shower and dress, meet in the living room for a cocktail, and watch an episode of our favorite program, *Coach*, before heading out for dinner. No matter where the evening started, it always ended by meeting up with friends at the local watering hole, Mulligan's Irish Restaurant and Pub, owned by our good friends Patrick and Lizzie Mulligan.

Back in Ohio, I learned of a fundraiser to be held at the Governor's Mansion benefitting the Ohio Alzheimer's Association. One of the top prizes being offered by the event's guest of honor, Shelley Fabares, were tickets for the final taping of her show *Coach*. I wanted those tickets. Bob didn't think I would be able to get them, but I didn't let his negativity dampen my enthusiasm. I called the individual organizing the event, mentioned my interest in the show and offered to make a $2,000 donation. I "won" the tickets and later was elated to learn Shelley wanted to come to my home and meet me. I called Angela and invited her to the meet and greet.

Shelley's visit was scheduled to last for only fifteen minutes as she needed to leave for a radio appearance. As soon as she arrived, I felt a connection with her; she was warm and sincere. She asked for a tour of our home. (This was at the "big house" so that took a little while.) At one point she mentioned she liked the fragrance I was wearing. "Oh, it's Wicked Wahine from the gift shop at The Kahiki." Both Shelley and Angela laughed because they were certain it would have been a designer fragrance like Chanel. Shelley stayed and visited for a couple of hours, missing the radio appearance entirely.

After we met, Shelley and I stayed in touch. When Bob and I were in Palm Beach, I would call her and see her speak or perform as often as possible. In fact, Shelley and I have remained friends through the years.

***

I was always a big fan of Regis Philbin and heard he was scheduled to appear with his friend Don Rickles at the Kravis Center for the Performing Arts in West Palm Beach. I desperately wanted tickets, but the show was sold out. Bob said I should call Allen Bernstein. I knew Allen and Regis were good friends, and often attended New York Knicks games together. I placed the call and when Allen picked up the phone, I explained my dilemma. Allen called Regis who said he had already distributed all of his extra tickets but suggested Allen call Don. A short while later Don's secretary called and told Bob that our tickets and backstage passes could be picked up at the Will Call window.

Regrettably, I had recently gained a little weight and couldn't decide what to wear that would be both flattering and comfortable. Looking through my closet I spied an inexpensive black velour tracksuit I had purchased recently at Walmart for fifteen dollars. I paired it with a white tee, high heels, and about $20,000 in jewelry. I felt great and no one could tell my outfit didn't come from a designer boutique.

We laughed all through the fast-paced show and afterward headed backstage. I spied Regis and struck up a conversation. It wasn't long before Regis called Don over. "Don, come and meet Allen Bernstein's friend, Anita." Don responded, "Any friend of Allen's is a friend of mine!" We laughed and chatted for several more minutes before the entertainers moved on to other guests.

***

In March 2000 Bob and I were in Florida preparing for bed when he picked up a call. I could tell from the tone of his voice that the nature of the conversation was serious and from his questions that someone had passed away. As he hung up the phone and turned to me, I knew it was my mother. He explained that she had not been feeling well and called 911, before calling Alan. Alan arrived first and kicked open the door and found his grandmother sitting on the sofa. He walked across the room and sat down beside her. He placed his arm around her. She put her head on his shoulder, and passed away. We made immediate plans to return to Columbus.

My mother was an outgoing and social person who hosted many parties and celebrations in her home, and always took time to make everyone feel special. Ruth was well-loved by family and friends alike, and it was an honor to plan a lovely service to remember the kindnesses and love she had shared. Although she never ran for office or held a public post, so many people came to show their respect, the parking lot at the funeral home was at capacity and the sixty-car processional seemed to stretch for miles. She would have been so pleased with the turnout on her behalf.

***

Around the end of 2001 Bob became restless and decided he wanted to sell "The Big House" in Dublin. "I'm tired of paying $50,000 in taxes every year," he said. Of course, unless Bob told me (which he rarely did) I didn't have any idea how much anything was costing us, but if he said we were paying too much in taxes, then I'm sure we were. It wasn't going to be easy to leave our dream home and, for heaven's sake, what would we do with all of the furnishings? It took more than two years to find a buyer, but eventually it sold for $2.2 million and we moved into our new home on Locherbie Court in Muirfield. At 3,666 square feet, it was nearly seventy-five percent smaller than the home we had just sold. Friends and family members became benefactors of all the furniture we couldn't take with us.

13 TURNING SIXTY

2002

"I would just like to say a special Happy Birthday to Anita tonight. I would like to say I love her very much and she has given me so much joy and that is all I'm going to say."	*Bob Barney*

As 2002 rolled around I was looking forward to my sixtieth birthday and decided a big celebration was in order. I mentioned my idea to Bob and before long the entire family was involved.

We decided the party should be a two-day affair. We would host a formal party on Friday evening at the Embassy Suites in Dublin with an open cocktail hour followed by a plated dinner for about 300 friends. For those friends who would be traveling from Florida—we expected about eighty—we would pick up the cost of their two-night hotel stay and would entertain our out-of-town guests with an informal lobster bake at our home on Saturday.

All the details were falling into place as I was driving along one day and thought it would be great idea to invite former President Bill Clinton to attend. *Wouldn't that be fun for everyone if Bill Clinton showed up?* I didn't have any connection to the former President, so I pressed the OnStar button and immediately I was talking with an operator. When I told her I needed to place a call to Bill Clinton's office in Harlem, New York, because I wanted to invite him to my sixtieth birthday party, she thought that was a cool idea and connected me. In no time I had Bill's secretary on the line. I explained who I was and the purpose of my call. She advised of the proper protocol to request President Clinton's attendance at an event, and provided the mailing address to send the paperwork. "Do you think he will come?" I asked. "Probably not," she responded. *Darn it!*

Since it was highly unlikely that I could convince President Clinton to attend my party, I thought the next best thing would be to hire an impersonator. Bob put the kibosh on that idea as soon as I mentioned it. Oh, well, back to the drawing board.

The formal party on Friday was a memorable evening I will never forget. Surrounded by friends and family and my loving husband, I truly felt I was the belle of the ball. More important, I felt validated for just being Anita, outside the shadow of being recognized as Bob's wife. I gained an unexpected confidence from all the accolades.

Bob's tribute to me was charming and witty:

> *I used to be married to a young broad. But Anita is sixty years old tonight. Anita has done one thing—she has stood by me in thick and thin. Anita, on December third you and I will have been married for twenty years. It's been so much fun it seems like thirty. It's only twenty. Now, I have a friend out here tonight and his name is Martin Blanco. Martin has a saying, "She has her faults, but then again, she has her ways." I could never figure out what that meant and I thought that no one else could figure it out either. So, I thought it would be safe to say in front of Anita. It must have been something Yogi Berra said or something. So, Anita has her faults, but then again, she has her ways. Do you want to hear her faults or her ways? Let me tell you one of her ways.*

Anita, she's probably like all you other ladies out there, but she loves to shop. About three months ago Anita was out doing some shopping. She came back home and like a week later she said, "I can't find my credit card. I've lost it." She said she was at this place and this other store. I said, "I'll take care of it."

Well, I forgot about it. Got tied up with some other things and forgot about it until the statement came in. And I looked at the statement and I thought, well, they must have made a mistake because the balance is too low; it's about half of the bill I normally pay for her credit card. So, I decided not to call anyone about replacing the card, so I could get away with a lot lower costs.

Anita and I have had a lot of good times. We've done a lot of traveling. We've been all over Europe. All over the East. We've been up in Canada. We've been down in Mexico. We've even been on safari. Let me tell you about our safari . . .

In all seriousness, we had a lot of great times together. In twenty years we've had a lot of great times together. And some bad times, too. She claims when she gets riled up she can walk through Harlem at midnight. And Cruz—her trainer—can attest to that. I would just like to say a special Happy Birthday to Anita tonight. I would like to say I love her very much and she has given me so much joy and that is all I'm going to say.

Bob wrapped his arms around me and planted a kiss on my cheek before handing me the microphone. I addressed my family and friends:

My turn. I'm going to be serious. I'm overwhelmed for all the people who have turned out for my party tonight. I'm just overwhelmed. No one can know what I feel inside. Thank you.

From the audience: Anita, we love you!

I really appreciate everyone being here—I really do . . .

From the audience: We can't wait until you're seventy!

Bob told me what to say tonight, so I wrote everything down. And then when I got here tonight, I pulled out my notes and it was my grocery list. So, I'm just winging it . . .

After dinner, we laughed at the comedy of our friend, Irish Comedic Grand Master Brendan Grace, and danced to the Phil Evans band. Turning sixty wasn't so bad after all.

For the Saturday night lobster bake, I planned many events for our guests to enjoy, including a fortune teller, magician, and animals from the Columbus Zoo. With so much food and entertainment we celebrated long past sundown.

It would be impossible to foretell that ten years in the future—the year I would turn seventy—nearly all of the friends who had toasted me on my sixtieth birthday would have abandoned me. Those who remained would be left questioning my integrity. I would be estranged from my family, file for bankruptcy, and plead guilty in court for the role I played in the Art Schlichter debacle.

In fact, I celebrated my seventieth birthday with Alan at a nondescript Chinese restaurant on Perimeter Parkway in the Giant Eagle plaza.

14 | END OF AN ERA

2004–2007

"I love you all. You are all wonderful, helpful, loving, and concerned. Thanks for looking out for Anita. I will keep fighting, and I hope to see all of you next fall."	Bob Barney

When it comes to the end, it's amazing how priorities shift and your mind focuses. Of course, we all know there will be a conclusion to our lives, but what takes your breath away is how it often shows up unexpectedly. There may be symptoms and medical appointments and diagnoses, but faith has a way of silencing the alarm and turning our attention to the details of today instead of the inevitability of tomorrow.

Hope is our security blanket and without it we would break down and collapse as the absurdity of death consumes our being. We would be in danger of abruptly discontinuing living the life that remains to be experienced before the final curtain call. We must stay engaged until it is impossible to keep death at bay. Otherwise, we will miss out on the intimate conversations, the memories, and the gratitude we've felt but perhaps never paused to say, as the daily grind of simply maintaining life pushes the non-essentials to a future to-do list. Love gives us the strength to attend to details, provide comfort, and communicate gratitude that might have been previously overlooked before a final farewell extinguishes the opportunity forever.

***

It was late summer of 2004 as we were preparing to travel to Maine for vacation when Bob received an unusual phone call in the evening. The woman on the other end of the line introduced herself as Linda and said, "I think you might be my dad."

After he disconnected the call, Bob explained that when he was attending high school in Ashland, Kentucky, he had a steady girlfriend who he left behind when he turned seventeen and joined the Air Force. A while later, a story reached him that his girlfriend had a baby she gave up for adoption. At the time he briefly wondered if the child might have been his. However, his former girlfriend had never contacted him about the child, and responsibilities of his Air Force assignment soon pushed the thought from his mind. Now, however, he had the opportunity to know for sure. We quickly made plans to meet Linda in Cincinnati and for Bob to provide a DNA sample. Shortly thereafter confirmation arrived that Linda was Bob's daughter.

Everyone—Bob and I, Bob's children, and even Carol—welcomed Linda and her husband into our lives with open arms. We learned she had been adopted by a couple who sent her to a Christian school, and she had enjoyed a wonderful life. When Linda became a mother she began wondering about her own heritage and a fervent search for her birth parents was launched. She found and reunited with her mother. When she asked about her father her mom said, "I think Bob Barney is your dad." So she looked him up and placed the call.

Linda and her husband joined us for Christmas that year and we visited back and forth several times. We enjoyed her company and relished the time we had together. I felt quite sad for Linda and the life and luxury she had missed by not knowing Bob was her father. Bob and I did what we could to make up for lost opportunities, but a lot of tears were shed about the separation and the time we would never be able to reclaim.

***

For our twenty-third wedding anniversary in 2005, I selected a flattering picture of Bob and me, wrote a nice tribute about us and had them both published in the *Columbus Dispatch*. Bob asked why I would do such a thing for an anniversary that wasn't marking a milestone. I showed him other postings for couples married twelve or thirteen years and assured him it was not unusual. The truth was rumors were spreading throughout the community that Bob and I were on the verge of divorce. I identified the source and wanted to silence her lies with a public notice that Bob and I were very much in love.

Even though my actions may have been motivated by less-than-honorable intentions, I don't regret what I did. Not even for a moment. You see, if I had waited until our twenty-fifth anniversary, when society deems these types of submissions appropriate, it would have been too late. Bob was already gone from me by then.

***

Late in 2006 Bob and I had decided to downsize, and the home we had built in Jupiter Hills was on the market. We were looking forward to remodeling a new home we had just purchased, planning for a year of travel and relaxation, and enjoying time with friends and family, but our lives took an unexpected detour.

As was our custom, we welcomed 2007 with friends in Florida. On Monday, January 15, I had an emergency hysterectomy. Over the weekend I had fallen going up the stairs at my friend's house and was in such pain that I went to the emergency room the following day. After conducting a pelvic exam, the doctor said he had not located any trauma from the fall, but had discovered several uterine tumors and had a strong suspicion they may be malignant. I was scheduled for surgery immediately.

The morning of my surgery, while Bob was waiting with me in the hospital, he mentioned an unusually painful backache that he dismissed as a result of sleeping in an awkward position overnight. At the hospital the day following my surgery he just couldn't get comfortable and no matter where he sat or stood, he was in a great deal of discomfort. I encouraged him to return home, get some rest, and not to worry about me. Although we talked on the phone, he didn't come to visit on Wednesday because he was still in so much pain. It wasn't like him to stay away, and I was becoming concerned about his health. By the time I was due to be discharged on Thursday, I had to call him to come and get me. After he dropped me off at home, he went to an Urgent Care that was just up the street from our home.

The physician assigned to him saw "Dublin, Ohio," on Bob's chart and, because she had played golf at Muirfield the previous summer, they made an easy connection. She conducted a brief examination and ordered X-rays, gave him a prescription for pain, and scheduled him for an MRI at the hospital the following day. The next morning Bob and I had planned to meet with a marble contractor at our new home. Bob was still in excruciating pain and drove himself to the hospital, but insisted I keep the appointment with the contractor.

Later as Bob and I were exchanging the details of our day, the Urgent Care physician called. She said, "I typically do not give the results, usually you would get this from your doctor in a few days, but I would like to speak with you privately. Can you come in?" Because I was still weak from surgery, Bob called our neighbor, Jada, to sit with me while he drove himself back to Urgent Care. When Bob returned about forty-five minutes later, he escorted Jada through the living room to the front door and I heard him thanking her for staying with me. Bob returned to the lanai and sat down next to me.

"Well," he said, "I have the big C." It was lung cancer. We both started crying. In that moment, with those words, regardless of the outcome, our lives were forever changed.

Our new home, which a minute ago was a fun new project for us to tackle, became an unnecessary distraction. I immediately called the builder and told him to put everything on hold indefinitely. The next day we made emotional calls to our family to let them know about the diagnosis and began planning to return to Columbus as quickly as possible. I called NetJets and other charter services for availability while Bob called Wendy's to determine if their plane was in the area. It was, and they generously offered it to us. On Monday friends drove us out to the tarmac at West Palm for the flight to Columbus. As we boarded the plane, we introduced ourselves to the two people already seated. We learned they were Wendy's employees. It had been seventeen years since Bob retired, and they didn't realize he had once been President of the organization.

On Tuesday Alan drove us to The James Cancer Hospital, as I was still unable to drive. Bob was scheduled for immediate surgery. My cousins Susie and Rock and my Aunt Lil waited with me during the operation. When the surgeon discovered that Bob was full of cancer, he concluded nothing could be done surgically, and terminated the procedure. The next day, we returned to The James to meet with Dr. Garrison, who explained treatment options; Bob began chemotherapy within a few days at the Martha Moorehead building. After a couple of weeks of chemo in Ohio, Bob was feeling better and asked about returning to Florida to continue treatment. He desperately wanted warm weather and sunshine. We both were pleased when his doctor granted the request.

I was convinced that the treatments would work and our life together would carry on. Probably not in the same way as before, but I *just knew* he would get through this. Bob was my hero—he could make *anything* happen, and I was determined to do whatever I could to ease his burden. As I accompanied Bob to his appointments I'm sure everyone could hear us coming down the hall. While most people only brought a book to pass the time, I pulled a rolling cooler behind us with Bob's favorite snacks and drinks, packed earphones and a radio so he could listen to news programs, a blanket, support pillow for his neck, special footies, and anything else I thought might make him comfortable.

After Bob finished three months of treatment in Florida it was time to return to The James for an update on his condition. By this point he had very little stamina and required a wheelchair at the airport. We booked seats in first class and during the flight home we reminisced and laughed and cried. Since Bob's retirement we had been together nearly every minute and had many memories to recall. We had enjoyed each other's companionship immensely as we explored the world together, golfed, vacationed with friends, and created memories with family. Any silly arguments were distant memories. It was a very intimate flight as we literally held onto each other for dear life.

At The James I remained hopeful and desperate to hear a positive report, but that was not to be. Despite the best efforts of modern medicine, the cancer had spread and Bob was given three weeks to live. I couldn't fathom how, before I would turn the page on the calendar, I would become a widow. *We had less than a month!* I was devastated.

Bob composed a letter to send to our friends in Florida, sharing his diagnosis and our bleak future:

May 2007

My Dear Friends:

I wanted to write a note to you all to thank you for all of the kindness that you have shown me. Words cannot express how much I appreciate all of the cards, letters of concern, food, and especially the love and prayers that came along with them. Thank you for the many, many phone calls asking how I'm doing. I'm sorry I was sometimes unable to talk. I have slept a lot because of my illness and the medication. We had so many offers to go to lunch, dinner, cocktails, take rides, drive us to the doctor, help with the house and the new condo, or just to come and sit with me. Even though I wasn't able (to) take you up on much of this, I felt the love and kindness that came with every offer.

Anita and I flew back to Ohio on April 25, and we'll meet with the doctors in the coming weeks to determine the next course of treatment. I'm sorry that I couldn't say goodbye in person, but Anita will (keep) you informed on how things are going.

I love you all. You are all wonderful, helpful, loving, and concerned. Thanks for looking out for Anita. I will keep fighting, and I hope to see all of you next fall.

Love,
Bob

I added this handwritten postscript dated May 15:

Bob is resting at home and chemo has been discontinued. We have about 3 (weeks) to live, talk & love each other.
Fondly,
Bob & Anita

I called Bob's daughter Ann, who lived in Texas, and we spoke frankly about the future. I knew Bob wanted to see her and I encouraged her to visit as soon as possible. Bob had designated Ann as the Executrix of his will and they engaged in several private conversations while she was in Columbus concerning, among other things, his will and estate.

Bob came into our lives when Alan was eleven, and regularly referred to him as his son. Over the years he had offered assurances that he would take care of Alan financially. We had also discussed his newly discovered daughter. Bob planned on including Linda in his will as he felt a responsibility for her even though they had been reunited for only a short while.

As is often the case when a terminally ill patient is making financial decisions, Bob made last-minute changes to how his wealth was to be distributed after talking with Ann. Both Alan and Linda were removed from the final version of Bob's will. I was disappointed about Alan, but knew that I would have sufficient funds to provide for my children. However, I personally resented Linda's exclusion and I told Bob that I thought his decision was wrong. Linda was his daughter, too, I reminded him. He told me his decision was final. There would be no more discussion concerning his will.

Bob began giving me a lot of advice. He rattled off practical and important wisdom: make sure to get the oil changed in the car, check the air pressure in the tires, change the furnace filters, don't buy a place that has a lot of taxes, don't let a man take your money, learn how to reconcile the checking account. I accumulated pages of notes as he went on and on with directives.

The cautions he provided about money were critical. Throughout my life I had rarely written a check and, in fact, managed my own money only during the short time I was a single mother before marrying Dick. Marcel refused to provide me with any money, and both Dick and Bob had secretaries to manage our accounts. Dick was generous with me, and Bob provided a credit card with a $100,000 limit, that was paid off each month. So, while I had conversed with heads of state, enjoyed meals with powerful politicians and famous entertainers, danced with Donald Trump, sang with Perry Como, dated General Lassiter, and have more items crossed off my bucket list than most, I was financially naïve.

Bob had his secretary continue to take care of our finances until two weeks before he died. Knowing the end was imminent Bob removed her from the accounts and added me. I was now in control of a sizeable fortune and, while I was resourceful and had management experience, to say I was ill-equipped regarding financial matters is an understatement.

Bob's health failed quickly. Even our morning routine of drinking coffee and reading the paper together took on special significance. He would look at me and ask, "I wonder if today is the day I'm going to die?" I would respond, "We don't know, so let's just enjoy the day we have been given." The sadness was overwhelming and often we would just hold each other and cry. He would say, "Do you know what I hate the most about dying? I will miss you."

We had nearly thirty amazing years together. But in the end, after the trips to exotic lands and the opportunities to meet famous people, entertaining friends and family and sharing the extravagances wealth brings, it all came down to "in sickness and in health." That was the vow we had made to each other, and I was committed to Bob even as my husband's robust approach to life dissipated into the indignities of death.

Bob became so weak he couldn't lift himself out of a chair and he was so frail I was fearful of breaking a bone when helping him; I purchased a lift chair to help him. When he could no longer use the bathroom facilities and needed to rely on disposable briefs, he was humiliated. I tried to lighten the mood with humor, "What's the matter? I've been kissing your ass for all these years, and you never minded before!" We both enjoyed a rare moment of laughter, which helped overcome an awkward situation. "Honestly," I told him. "I count it an honor and a privilege to be your wife and to be able to care for you in any way you need." I meant it wholeheartedly. Together we had enjoyed the riches of life, and together we would face the insults late-stage cancer was hurling at us.

Bob was insistent that I provide all of his care; he did not want me to hire in-home care for him. I never once was resentful of his request, but caring for him twenty-four hours a day was exhausting on every level. His pain became so severe that I couldn't even snuggle up to him in bed. We discovered that we could lie with our heads touching, and this brought us both comfort without causing him any pain. So we would go to sleep with our heads touching, but before long the pain would cause him to relocate from our bed to the hospital bed, and then to recliner. He was constantly on the move trying to find comfort and a few minutes of rest, calling for me to help him move from one location to another throughout the day and night. Rest, for both of us, was elusive.

During the final days of his life, travel and parties and entertainment a distant memory, we spent a lot of quiet time throughout the day together talking and reminiscing. During one chat, Bob said that when it came down to it, he wasn't sure I would have cared for him until the end. He was referring to his actions when he drank too much and became disrespectful, mean, and argumentative with me. The Bob I chose to remember was kind and generous. The Bob I chose to forget is the man who allowed alcohol to dictate behavior that horrified him.

A few days before we would say farewell to the man who generously shared of himself and his good fortune with so many and accepted my family as his own, he received a letter from my grandson, Sean; it was a fitting tribute and well-earned farewell.

Dear Bob,

I want to take this opportunity to let you know how much you have done for me. I also want to make sure that you are aware of how grateful I truly am for everything you have done for me. I'm so thankful to have someone like you in my life. Even though I grew up calling you "Uncle Bob," you've been so much more than that to me. I think of you as a grandfather.

You have taught me so many valuable lessons, not only about life, but also about the business world. I've always admired the accomplishments you've had with Wendy's, and even more than that, I admire the humble attitude you have always had along with all that success. I hope that I can take the lessons and values you've helped me to develop and become a success myself one day. The advice you've offered me with regard to being someone in a leadership position will be advice that I always carry with me, no matter where life takes me.

I also want you to know that I admire your generosity and caring nature. You have done so much for our family, and I cannot thank you enough. Your actions and the way you have lived your life have both inspired and taught me more than you could possibly know. I work as hard as I do at everything simply because of the example you have set for me. Saying thank you is not enough for all you have done.

Love,
Sean

When it became apparent I needed additional assistance, the nurses who came to the house persuaded Bob to enter Kobacker House, an inpatient hospice facility. At the time, I truly didn't understand what entering hospice signified. I knew Bob required care beyond my ability and his medication needed to be regulated as he had stopped taking the pain meds as they were prescribed. And, honestly, I needed a respite from the around the clock care I had been providing. I told Bob that we would stay at Kobacker for five days where he could receive treatment and I would obtain a much-needed break. I promised that soon enough we would return home. I simply did not have an understanding that this would be our final destination.

As the ambulance arrived to transport Bob to Kobacker he became hostile toward the medics. Fortunately, Ann and her husband John were there to assist with the transfer. Bob didn't want to leave the house, and he was angry and hurt by my decision. I felt terrible. We didn't talk during the short trip. When we arrived, Bob was assigned to a room where his nurse on duty attempted to give him medicine with applesauce. He refused. Her tone became stern in an attempt to communicate the seriousness of the situation. Bob was uncompromising in his refusal. I wasn't convinced I had made the right decision for my husband. At midnight, with Bob finally asleep, I left to go home and close up the house. We had left so quickly no one thought to check the locks.

When I returned the next morning, Bob was sleeping soundly. As his pain intensified he would awaken. The nurses would give him more medicine and he would slip back into sleep. The cycle repeated throughout the day and into the evening. During one of his conscious moments, I gently brushed my lips against his forehead and we said goodnight to one another before I left that evening.

I was greeted by several members of Bob's family when I arrived at 8:30 a.m. on Thursday. As I approached his room they stopped me saying Bob was in a coma. I was shocked at the change in his condition. Last night we had said our goodbyes and he was coherent.

Shortly after noon Bob was lying in bed still unconscious. I can't describe what happened, but as I was quietly talking to my cousin, Bob signaled for my attention. Even now, I can't say if it was a gesture or a sound, but I moved toward him, pulled a chair near his bed and sat down. I placed my head near his head, touching in the same way we had previously gone to sleep together, and placed my arm across his chest to let him know I was there. "Honey, I'm here. What can I do for you?" I asked. Without regaining consciousness, he took two breaths and was gone from me.

***

To sum up the life of a man, who was the light of my life for nearly thirty years, with a few fleeting sentences in a newspaper obituary seemed small and insignificant. Bob and I had worked on the wording together, but I added the closing paragraph after his death. It was a final message to the man I adored.

Robert L. Barney, age 70, of Dublin, OH, and Jupiter, FL, passed away peacefully after a courageous battle with cancer on May 31, 2007, at the Kobacker House in Columbus, OH. At his passing, he was surrounded by his loving wife Anita, his family and close friends.

He was born in Ashland, KY on October 28, 1936. He graduated from Ashland High School in 1954 and was a member of the United States Air Force. He attended The University of Kentucky. His highly successful restaurant career began in Athens, OH in 1962. His affiliations included Kentucky Fried Chicken, Arthur Treacher's and Wendy's. Bob retired from Wendy's International in 1989 where he served as Chairman and CEO.

After retirement, along with his 3 sons, he developed Rolling Meadows Golf Club, where he was active until his death. He served on many Boards of Directors, including COSI and Morton's Steakhouse. He was a member of the Elks Lodge and a 32nd Degree Scottish Rite Mason. Bob loved OSU football and Kentucky basketball. His hobbies included golf, fishing and tailgating at Ohio State football games with his close friends.

Bob never forgot where he came from or who he was. His contribution to family and friends will echo throughout the lives of present and future generations. Preceded in death by his parents Ernest and Wilma Barney. Survived by his wife of 25 years, Anita; proud father of Brad Barney, Gahanna, OH, Ann (John) Blateri, Irving, TX, Bryan (Cyndy) Barney, Worthington, OH, Linda (Matt) Bader, Cincinnati, OH, Angela Genereux, Delray Beach, FL, and Alan Valko, Dublin, OH; grandchildren, Reece and Ally Blateri, Scott and Sean Martin, Michael Barney, Dustin and Jacob Ubbing; sister, Marlene (David) Simmerman, Dublin, OH; many nieces, nephews, cousins, and friends whom he loved. Friends may call at the MORELAND FUNERAL HOME, 55 E. Schrock Road, Westerville, June 4 and June 5, 2007 2-4 and 6-8 p.m. Service will be held at Church of the Messiah United Methodist, 51 N. State Street, Westerville, June 6, 2007 at 1 p.m. Pastors Dale Dixon and Rev. Stan Fawley officiating. Interment Sunset Cemetery. In lieu of flowers, family requests memorial contributions to the Kobacker House, 3595 Olentangy River Rd., Columbus, Ohio 43214.

Bob, you had a fun-loving lust for life, strong convictions, and strength and quiet dignity when faced with the terminal illness that took you away from us. You are the man that I will always love. You said that you would wait for me in Heaven so I will see you then. Love, Anita.

After Bob died, I slept many nights in one of his shirts to feel close to him. His scent lingered on the fabric and memories of his leading me across a dance floor or of the two of us sitting together as we watched television comforted me as I would drift off to sleep, left to battle nightmares alone.

My life with Bob had been like living in a cyclone.

When the wind died down,

I felt like I couldn't catch my breath.

15 | ON MY OWN

2007—2009

"For years Bob had protected me from myself. I was a dreamer and he was the rock. I brought fun and adventure into his life. He brought stability and security into mine. I adored him. He believed in me."	*Anita Barney*

Loss has a way of emptying you in ways you can't even begin to understand until you have the opportunity look back at the event. We need time and distance to clearly evaluate what occurred and the price we paid to survive. Sometimes we become so caught up in the doing and managing and attending to details that we fail to see our life force swirling down the drain until it is far past too late.

***

After Bob's death, I was faced with a multitude of challenges from all fronts and was forced to step into roles and responsibilities that were new to me: writing checks, settling accounts, managing money, dealing with bankers and investment specialists, working with lawyers, distributing possessions, selling and buying real estate. These are big assignments to tackle even when you're part of a team, and details Bob had tended to in the past. I had never been responsible for managing money, paying bills, or participating in real estate transactions. Nor had I needed to account for my spending, work within a budget, or oversee any financial matters.

Bob's wealth and owning multiple properties in two states made for a complicated probate process. Bob's daughter Ann served as Executrix of his will, and I was charged to carry out many of the practical matters. Bob had been concerned about probate dragging out unnecessarily; I had assured him six months was enough time to dispose of our joint assets and secure a new home for myself. I was overwhelmed with details but my ability to manage projects and organize large events served me well as I navigated unfamiliar territory. Bob's family, including Linda, as well as my family and friends helped as I sorted through things, deciding what to keep, what to sell, and what to give away or donate to charity.

I also became aware of the responsibility of "my own" money. By October I had purchased and paid cash for a condominium in the Ballantrae neighborhood in Dublin, a little more than five miles from "The Big House" Bob and I had built twenty years before. I also paid cash for a small condominium in Florida as I intended to continue spending winters with my warm weather friends. Family members encouraged me to renovate my new vacation home as the finishes and appliances had not been upgraded recently. I refused. I was content with the way things were and didn't want to spend money unnecessarily. When I began looking for a convertible, I chose a brand new ruby red Saturn Sky instead of the much pricier Mercedes my friends expected. I just couldn't reasonably justify the additional expense. With major purchases out of the way, I placed the majority of my money—nearly $1 million—in an investment account for a financial expert to manage and continue earning money, which I planned to live off of for the remainder of my life.

While I was financially comfortable, Bob had left the majority of his estate to his children from his first marriage, and I no longer had the resources to pick up the tab for friends and family like I could when Bob was living. Nor did I possess the financial acumen to understand how much I could spend and still have sufficient money to provide for my expenses long term. So I erred on the side of caution. I was mindful and kept track. Gone were the big parties and the exotic travel. The extravagant gifts and the ability to purchase without regard to cost were distant memories.

Actually, a lot of things were gone, replaced by uncomfortable emotions. Alone in a new home Bob had never even seen, I was afraid of the sounds I heard at night. Without a financially savvy partner, I was uncertain my future was secure. Whereas before I had relied entirely on Bob to make decisions, now choices were mine alone.

I missed Bob terribly. I had no one to turn to for advice or to guide my decisions. In the past, Bob had been the one to veto my plans when they became too zany. He helped me see the other side of the story, stop to think before I took the next step, and not to believe everything I heard. For years he had protected me from myself. I was a dreamer and he was the rock. I brought fun and adventure into his life. He brought stability and security into mine. I adored him. He believed in me. I had trusted him with my life.

The months after Bob's death brought so much work that I didn't have time to grieve his absence. My friend Farley Daft from Columbus asked me out a few times. I always had a ready excuse for being unavailable. I didn't feel a connection with him and didn't want to misuse his time or lead him on, but also didn't want to hurt his feelings. In Florida, my friends tried to fix me up with a man they knew from New York. The entire group of us went out one evening. He was nice enough, but there wasn't a spark between us, mostly because I wasn't looking for anyone to fill the void Bob's passing had created. I preferred to be alone with memories of my wonderful husband.

By January 2008, I had endured the first Thanksgiving and Christmas and what would have been our twenty-fifth wedding anniversary without the love of my life. I was physically exhausted and emotionally drained. I needed a change of scenery. In February, I attended my first Buckeye Cruise for Cancer with Angela and Alan and we had a wonderful time. Surrounded by so many Columbus friends and Ohio State enthusiasts, it felt great to be among "Buckeye family" and enjoy myself while supporting cancer research. On the ship, I felt the pendulum of my life swinging from grief to release. Looking back, I probably laughed too loudly, drank too much, and flirted too conspicuously with the football players (most whom were just out of college), but I couldn't stop myself; I was having a lot of fun and made plans to attend the cruise the following year.

In Florida my friends kept me so busy during the day, I was too exhausted to go out again in the evening. I wanted to stay home, sit in Bob's recliner, and watch television. Nevertheless, nearly every night we would head back out, meeting around 5:00 p.m. to have dinner at a restaurant and then sit and talk for hours.

When I returned to Columbus that spring, I began to meet my new neighbors and it felt good to feel part of the community again. I forged a strong connection with Camilla Cox, a neighbor across the way, and we spent a lot of time together going to lunch, shopping, tailgating, and just generally enjoying ourselves. Most every Saturday in the fall I would give her one of my four tickets for the OSU football game. I also made sure my friends, the Lackos, had tickets for every Saturday home game they wanted. I met Keith and Gloria Beadell as they were moving in across the street. Keith was a professor at Fisher College of Business and Gloria was a nurse. Everyone was so nice and welcoming. I gladly took my turn hosting one of the monthly socials for the entire Ballantrae neighborhood. I called my event the *Anita Barney First Invitational 2008 at Rolling Meadows Golf Course.* I had caterers prepare steaks on the grill, awarded small trophies to the winners of competitions I created and, just like parties of old, had animals visit from the Columbus Zoo. Everyone had a great time and I couldn't wait until the following year to do it all again. I was finally beginning to feel at peace with the title of widow.

Although my life was going along swimmingly, I still felt lonely. I looked for activities to fill the quiet evenings, when Bob and I had always been together. I started going out three or four nights a week with different groups of friends: Giammarco's on Tuesdays, Arlington on Wednesdays, and The Knotty Pine on

Thursdays. The idea of sitting home made me sad but when I kept busy, I didn't have to face the fact that I was alone. When I was at home my mind never shut down. I would stay awake for hours and plan. I had notebooks scattered everywhere with lists of what events were taking place, what needed to be done, and how much I was spending.

When the 2009 Buckeye Cruise for Cancer rolled around, I took Alan and recruited several friends from Florida to join the fun including Lizzie Mulligan who shared a room with me. I also convinced Joy Blanco to attend and she brought her daughter and daughter-in-law. Everyone was having a great time until I bid $15,000 for the 2010 Rose Bowl trip and won it. Alan was furious with me for "spending" that kind of money. In no time our discussion became uncharacteristically heated and we were in the middle of a very public shouting match. I shut it down by saying, "Hey! This is for cancer research. It may save my life one day. I'm not just playing poker or gambling or wasting my money, like you are."

Perhaps Alan was anxious because my money had come from Bob and what I had, I had. There wouldn't be any more. Bob had been generous to Angela and Alan while he was living and I continued to be generous with my children and grandchildren after Bob's passing, never expecting repayment.

The money was secure.

I was being careful.

There was nothing to worry about.

Or so I thought.

Anita, age 4, with her parents, Ruth and Raymond

Anita with her parents c. 1946

Anita with her father, Mark, and her new bicycle, c. 1949

Anita at home, age 14

Anita, Andy Williams, Henry Mancini, and the band, c. 1968

Anita, Alan, Angela, 1971

Model Shot, 1972

Wreckage from plane crash, August 1980

Searching for Survivors

Preparing to remove Alan from the plane

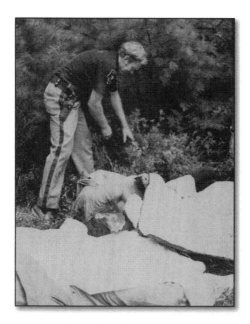

Removing other passengers

Inspecting the crash site

3 Ohioans die in air crash; boy survives

From staff and wire reports

EAST TAWAS, Mich. — A Columbus physican, an Air Columbus Inc. pilot and a Delaware, Ohio, contractor, all on a fishing trip in Michigan, were killed early Wednesday when their small airplane crashed into a thickly wooded area in northeastern lower Michigan.

Dead are Dr. Albert R. Valko, 50, of 3003 W. Broad St., a staff member at Doctors Hospital North since 1960; Robert L. Johnson, 45, of 151 W. Orange Road in Delaware, vice president of Arjay Construction Co.; and Paul Rinaldi, 22, of 522 Longhurst Drive, who apparently was piloting the plane, officials said.

A fourth man, William O. Walter, 38, of Algonac, Mich., a professional hunting and fishing guide, also was killed in the crash.

Valko's 10-year-old son, Allen, suffered a broken left leg, and cuts and bruises in the accident.

He was in guarded condition in St. Joseph Hospital in Tawas, a small city in Iosco County. He was undergoing surgery on his left leg late Wednesday, hospital officials said.

"It was a pleasure trip," Johnson's wife, Peggy, said Wednesday afternoon. "The four men and Valko's son were going salmon fishing near Oscoda, which is on Lake Huron."

Rinaldi and Valko owned Air Columbus Inc. and the twin-engine Piper Aztec aircraft that crashed a mile northwest of the Iosco County Airport during an attempted landing in dense fog.

Mrs. Johnson said she was told her husband would be flying the aircraft. She said the men left Bolton Field in Columbus about 3 a.m. Wednesday and flew to Bird-McCone Field near Detroit to pick up Walters before heading for Iosco County Airport.

Ironically, she said, Wednesday was Rinaldi's birthday. Her husband

Dr. Albert R. Valko

Robert L. Johnson

and Valko held a party for him Monday night, and Rinaldi's girlfriend brought a cake with an airplane on it.

Someone on the plane contacted Wurtsmith Air Force Base near Oscoda early Wednesday seeking instructions for landing at the Iosco County Airport, Michigan State Police said.

There was "very heavy" fog in the area at the time, police said.

"He was making an instrument approach. He was trying to find the airport in abnormal conditions," a police spokesman said. "He made one pass and then couldn't make it, so they gave him another."

A short time later, base officials lost voice contact with the plane, and the craft dropped off radar screens, police said.

The wreckage of the plane was located about noon about a mile west of the Iosco County Airport runway near East Tawas, police said.

The craft had slammed into several trees before hitting the ground, police said. The plane was demolished, but there was no fire, police said.

A rescue team pulled the boy from the wreckage shortly after the plane was discovered, but it took several hours for rescuers to right the plane and remove the bodies of the victims, police said.

Lone Crash Survivor Comes Home

By Wendy Langenderfer
Of The Dispatch Staff

Ten-year-old Alan Valko, the lone survivor of a plane crash in Michigan on Wednesday, was welcomed home Friday by tearful, smiling friends and relatives.

Alan and his mother Anita, 3150 Stoney Bridge Lane, arrived at Doctors West Hospital in an Army National Guard helicopter at 6:49 p.m. after a six-hour trip from St. Joseph's Hospital, Tawas City, Mich.

MEMBERS OF the helicopter crew, part of the 107th Attack Helicopter Troop based at Worthington, were finishing two weeks of summer training at Grayling, Mich. A family friend asked them to fly Alan home.

Dr. Peter Johnston, orthopedic surgeon, said Alan was sedated for most of the trip. The boy has a fractured left leg, multiple cuts and bruises and is in satisfactory condition.

Johnston said he expected Alan to be hospitalized for about three weeks.

SGT. MICHAEL Rokvans, Westerville, a paramedic on the flight, said the crew left Tawas City about 1:30 p.m. but had to stop several times to refuel. The helicopter was piloted by Warrant Officer Bill Miller and Capt. Bill Ashton, both of Columbus.

While Alan and Mrs. Valko were in transit, anxious relatives and friends expectantly scanned the sky from the hospital parking lot.

"I haven't been to bed since Tuesday," Alan's grandmother, Ruth Long, 258 Yarmouth Lane, explained with tears in her eyes. "I'm very happy for Alan I couldn't have taken it if something happened to him.

SHE SAID she had driven to Tawas City after the crash and was obviously surprised to find relatives using the crash

ANITA VALKO, Alan's mother, wipes away a tear after greeting waiting friends and relatives.

crashed in a wooded area near Tawas City early Wednesday. He spent several hours in the upside-down wreckage before the remote crash site was reached by Michigan State Police and Air National Guard helicopters, which were delayed by dense fog. Killed were Dr. Valko, a Columbus osteopath, of 522 Longhurst Dr., Lincoln Park West; pilot Paul Rinaldi, 22, who shared Valko's Lincoln Park apartment; co-pilot Robert Lee Johnson, 45, of Delaware, Ohio and William O Walters, 38, of Algonac, Mich.

Federal officials still are investigating the crash

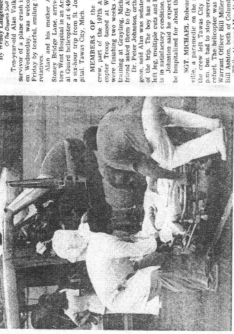

DOCTORS WEST Hospital personnel wheel Alan Valko from the Army helicopter Friday.

Columbus Dispatch   A-3

SAT., AUG. 30, 1980

Bombed-Out Hotel Opens For Holiday

STATELINE, Nev. (AP) — Slot machines whirred and blackjack dealers counted their chips as a bomb-scarred Harvey's Resort Hotel-Casino reopened part of its gaming floor for the lucrative Labor Day crowd.

Doors opened barely 48 hours after a powerful bomb planted by would-be extortionists ripped through the casino, causing damages estimated at more than $3 million. There were no injuries in the explosion.

Joseph Yablonsky, the FBI agent in charge of investigating the bombing, attended the reopening and held a news conference on a red-curtained stage behind the bar.

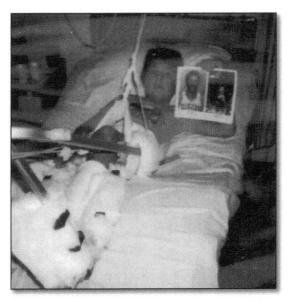

Alan in the hospital showing photos he received from Dr. J

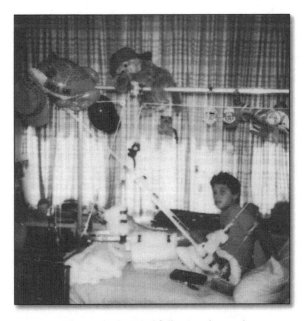

Alan in the hospital following the crash

Anita and Bob's Wedding Day, 1982

1983 Super Bowl, Pasadena, California

Florida, 1985

Wendy's Magazine

A publication for the Wendy's family

October, 1984
Volume 2 • Number 4

Bob receives the National MUFSO Operator of the Year Award, 1984

The "Big House" on Dublin Road

Rear elevation of the "Big House"

Ruth, Angela, Sean, and Scott, Bay Colony, Florida, c. 1985
Bob's boat is in the background

Golden Plate Award Ceremonies, Chicago, 1986

Anita's 60th Birthday Party, 2002

Angela, Anita, Alan, 2002

***

John Glenn, c. 1974

Rosey Grier, c. 1974

John McEnroe, c. 1981

Lorraine and Dave Thomas, c. 1982

Danny Thomas, Las Vegas, c. 1983

Johnny Bench, 1983

Clara "Where's the Beef?" Pellar, c. 1984

Eddie Fisher, c. 1994

Mike Farrell and Shelley Fabares, 1997

Perry Como, c. 1999

Regis Philbin, c. 2000

Jack Hanna, c. 2008

Alan, Anita, Angela, Monica, Sean, Scott, Landon, Yessie, 2013

VOLUME II

16 | DUBLIN POLICE TRANSCRIPT
FEBRUARY 7, 2011

02–07–2011

This date, Steve Schierholt and I conducted an interview with Arthur Schlichter at the Franklin County Sheriff's Office Annex. Franklin County Prosecutor Ron O'Brien advised Schlichter of his rights prior to the beginning of the interview. Schlichter was not represented by an attorney and waived his rights. The interview was audio and video recorded.

Reporting Officer: Detective Scott Davis
Dublin Division of Police

Art Schlichter: I asked (Anita) to help me almost right off the bat. I don't recall if it was borrowing money or buying tickets to make money. She didn't offer to help me—she asked how she could donate to the foundation. I pursued her. She didn't offer her money. **I pursued and pursued and pursued.** *She helped me a lot initially. I was asking her for a lot of money.*

Authorities: Do you have any idea how much money you asked her for?

On a regular basis for a year, year and a half, thousands and thousands, upon thousands.

More than a million?

> *I don't know. You lose track. I know she went into her investment account a lot. And got money, got money, over and over again. She was taking care of a lot of stuff. I promised that I would pay her back.*

> *I had her put money in accounts of people in Las Vegas, and then I would gamble. I just asked her to do it.*

People you knew from gambling?

> *The Las Vegas people, definitely. Howard Rickman. I've known him for twenty-five years . . . I sent a lot of money to this guy. In turn, he would bet for me through the windows or he said he bet on the Internet. I knew he was ripping me off. I can't imagine her doing this for anyone else. I assume most, if not all, of her Western Union or deposits she has ever made were for me.*

> *I would call Anita and tell her to send a certain amount of money. A couple of people she might have known. (Mostly), friends of mine. Some she did and some she didn't. If I told her I needed $20,000, $10,000 here, and $10,000 there, she would do that. Fax approval to the bank and I would tell someone to pick it up at the bank.*

> *I would tell her that we would make enough money to pay her back and get it figured out.*

> *She wrote a check deposited to John Amery's (Art's attorney) account to help me pay down my debt. To help me pay some people back.*

Did you intentionally not tell her you were gambling?

> *Sure.*

What did she think?

> *She thought she was helping me pay back debt. I never . . . she asked a few times if I was gambling. I said, "No!" I would*

try not to lie to her. If she did ask me I would say, "Don't ask. I just need the help and I will get it back to you."

Listen, she didn't know. Anita Barney is the nicest lady in the whole world. She didn't ask me a lot of questions. She is a smart girl but didn't ask a lot of questions. What I told her, it probably wasn't the truth.

Would she have loaned you any money to gamble?

I doubt it. Why would she? That wouldn't make any sense.

Was she ever going to get paid back?

When you're gambling, you always hope you'll get enough to pay people back. I did pay some back. But it was just a sprinkling. Pennies on the dollar. It was nothing. It couldn't stop one percent of the bleeding.

When you got money from her, was there a reality of her getting paid back?

When you're gambling you are always living in a false hope that . . . I won a couple hundred thousand dollars a couple months ago and gave her back $30,000 or $40,000. I always thought I could work my way out of it. But when I won that money and I gave it back, at that point I knew it was almost going to be impossible. I accelerated my gambling and borrowing. Made it ten times worse. Not with her, but with others.

17 | RECONNECTING WITH ART

2009

"Granted, I think an addiction, at some point, is a choice."	Art Schlichter 2009

In the fall of 2009, a little more than two years after Bob had passed, I was planning Alan's fortieth birthday party when I learned that Art Schlichter's book, *Busted*, was released. I hadn't thought much about Art in the thirty years since he visited our home on Stoney Bridge following the plane crash. However, I thought his book would be a novel gift for Alan and made a mental note to stop by Barnes & Noble on Sawmill Road.

Meanwhile, Ohio voters were being drafted into an intense battle over Issue 3, a constitutional amendment that would permit casinos to be built in our major cities. Opponents against and supporters for the issue were investigated and maligned. Smooth-talking lobbyists appeared on local talk shows, paid for prime time placement of their commercials, and scoured the state for any civic group or religious congregation that would give them a few precious minutes to address voters and, hopefully, influence their decision. Big money was at stake and you could feel it.

My friend Joy Blanco called me one day in October to let me know that Art was going to speak against Issue 3 the following

Sunday at Genoa Baptist Church in Westerville. I hadn't really followed Art's life or career—in fact, I hadn't even read his book I had purchased—but was aware he had been in prison for gambling, and thought it would be interesting to see him and hear what he had to say. Besides, it was the perfect opportunity to have him sign his book for Alan.

The invitation to see Art brought with it a flood of memories and emotions. The last time our paths had crossed, Alan was a broken little boy. After spending seven hours wounded, lying in the midst of plane crash debris, able to see his father and three other men hanging upside down strapped to their seats but not realizing they were dead, and questioning why they ignored his cries for help, he had been suffering from extreme depression. The son I had sent off for a day of fishing with his father—crazy fun, full of energy, always racing around—returned to me depressed, subdued, sad, and in pain. Even daily visits from a child psychologist had not produced the results we hoped.

When Alan's doctor recommended we put him on medication to help him cope, I resisted. I pleaded for more time to work with him. I had seen children who had been drugged and I couldn't bear to turn my son into a zombie, dependent on meds to function. The doctor agreed and I felt the clock ticking down without clear direction regarding the next steps I should take. Like an answer from heaven, it was during this time that Art had visited and dramatically changed the course of Alan's outlook and recovery. Alan enthusiastically shared the story of Art's visit with anyone and everyone who would listen. It was a game changer for all of us, and I was eager to thank Art for that gift. Thinking he would enjoy meeting Art again, I had asked Alan to attend the service with me, but he wasn't interested. My neighbor Camilla Cox accepted my invitation instead.

On Sunday, November 1, 2009, as I was driving to Genoa to hear Art speak at their second morning service, Joy called. Having just attended the early service, she offered to save me a front row seat and mentioned she was staying for the next service. "Anita, the service was so good. Art shared his story about his family and being in prison and how he has changed his ways. He has turned his life over to Christ! I want to hear him again. I just know you're going to be glad you came." Joy is generally very enthusiastic and outspoken about church and God, and this time her energy was contagious.

When I arrived, I connected with Joy, and she promptly introduced me to Senior Pastor Frank Carl. During our brief conversation, I mentioned the kindness Art had shown Alan three decades prior during a very dark time in our lives, and that I wanted to thank him and ask him to sign his book. He pointed to the other side of the sanctuary, where I saw a small group had congregated. Pastor Carl encouraged me to ask Art to sign my book before the service began, explaining that Art would be leaving immediately after his segment concluded.

I joined the short line of people waiting to speak with Art. He wasn't selling books, just talking with each person as they approached him. After several minutes it was my turn. I introduced myself and reminded him about our previous encounter, the plane crash, and Alan in a wheelchair. It felt great to finally extend my appreciation, albeit thirty years after his visit.

Whether he recalled the events of that day or not, Art was pleasant and said the right things. He graciously signed the book I had brought and asked how Alan was doing. I invited him to Alan's birthday party the following weekend, but he was unsure of his schedule. I gave him my phone number so he could RSVP. As I turned away, he was greeting the next person in line.

I sat with Joy in the front row and waited for the service to begin. This was my first visit to Genoa, and I was acutely aware of everything going on that day. When Pastor Carl introduced him, I watched Art walk across the front of the sanctuary and up to the stage. I noticed how put together he looked: dark suit, crisp white shirt, yellow striped tie, and brown shoes. As he turned I saw his profile and was surprised to see he was a bit out of shape. *I guess those years in prison really took their toll*, I thought.

Pastor Carl and Art took their seats at the edge of the stage in front of assorted gambling implements such as over-sized dice, a craps table, and roulette wheel. While I don't recall everything that was discussed that day, I do remember how I felt. Pastor Carl was enthusiastic, said he fell in love with Art as a person and a Believer after reading his book, called Art an "Ohio State Great," and said it was an honor to have him at Genoa. He showed a picture of Art working with children on behalf of his foundation, Gambling Prevention Awareness. I was pleasantly surprised when Pastor Carl shared the story of Art and Alan and the plane crash, using it as an example of Art's mission to help children. Pastor Carl also talked about the former football hero's important involvement as Co-Chairman of Families Against Issue 3.

> *Interestingly enough, Families Against Issue 3 may have been better served with the more accurate title of "Casinos Against Issue 3," as it was founded by TruthPAC, and was primarily funded by MTR Gaming. MTR Gaming operated gaming and racing properties in West Virginia, Pennsylvania, and Ohio, including Mountaineer Casino, Presique Isle Downs, and Scioto Downs. [2] Basically, you had a group that was funded by gaming interests and pretending it was against gambling.[3]*
>
> *Upon closer inspection, it was revealed $2 million of the $2.4 million Art Schlichter and Families Against Issue 3 amassed to fight the casinos was contributed by MTR Gaming,[4] where Art admitted in his book to being introduced to gambling—essentially where his gambling addiction began when he was a student at OSU—and where he continued to gamble throughout his adult life.*

Although Art briefly mentioned that his daughters went without a father for a period of time while he was incarcerated, he didn't talk about the destruction for which he was responsible. Instead, his remarks centered on himself and his losses: a million dollars, a profession, his dignity, self-respect, freedom, his life. What he neglected to mention was what he had taken from

---

[2] http://ballotpedia.org/Ohio_Casino_Initiative,_Issue_3_%282009%29
[3] http://www.nbc4i.com/story/20733948/anti-casino-ad-draws-criticism-from-issue-3-supporters-opponents
[4] http://www.followthemoney.org/entity-details?eid=10244090

unsuspecting and trusting people. The lives he had ruined. The relationships he had destroyed. The bank accounts he had drained. The lies and the pressure and the threats, and the people whose safety and well–being he had jeopardized.

Not once during the service did Art mention that overcoming his addiction was a work in progress, a fight he faced every day. Rather, he spoke about turning his life around, falling on his knees, turning everything over to God. Pastor Carl didn't ask Art about his recovery and Art allowed the congregation to believe that gambling was a thing in his past: he had served his time, paid his debts, and was a *free* man in every sense of the word.

Another missed opportunity for Art to be truthful and forthcoming about his addiction that day came when Pastor Carl stated that Art *was just getting his land legs on during the past three years* (since his most recent release from prison in 2006), indicating he was becoming accustomed to a healthy life without gambling. But that wasn't true. It would be more than two years later, in February 2011, when Art would admit to authorities that he began gambling shortly after his release and was betting heavily again by 2007. While he stood on the stage in front of a sanctuary sharing the evils of gambling with unsuspecting congregants, Art was in the throes of his own addiction, and losing.

Art had not won the war over his addiction, but no one had the courage to ask hard questions and demand truthful answers. The bright lights of long-ago accomplishments were still valuable to the community, and looking too closely felt disrespectful of this hometown hero. So, Art was placed in a position of prominence by the gambling industry and endorsed wholeheartedly by churches in the community without proper forewarning to their congregations. In fact, pastors provided credibility by mentioning Art's association with 610 WTVN where he rubbed shoulders with on-air radio personalities. Art was a scheduled host on The Bucks Line at Buffalo Wild Wings on Bethel Road on Thursday nights, talking sports and spreads and giving his opinion on OSU football players and opponents. He was interviewed for sports blogs, written about in newspapers, and featured in periodicals.

Art was back, baby!

After I reconnected with Art at Genoa that day, I really didn't have any intention to see him again, unless he was able to make a surprise appearance at Alan's party the following week. He did call me to say he couldn't make it to the party but would like to get together soon to catch up on Alan's life and hear about what I had been up to for the past thirty years. He also mentioned that he would be wishing Alan a happy birthday during his weekly appearance on the John Corby radio program on 610 WTVN at 3:00 p.m. that Wednesday, and encouraged me to listen.

True to this word, during the program Art said he wanted to wish Alan Valko a happy fortieth birthday. He shared a brief summary of the plane crash and how he came to meet Alan thirty years ago. He and Corby discussed the story for few minutes and the segment concluded with Corby stating he would like to meet Alan one day. Interestingly, I did have the opportunity to eventually meet Corby when Art invited me to the station during one of his Wednesday appearances. Art and Alan never met up again as adults, although several heated telephone conversations eventually took place between them.

Looking back, I realize Art had likely set his sights on me immediately after I had him sign the book for Alan. I wouldn't be surprised if he was working on a plan to separate me from my cash before he left the church parking lot. I was unfamiliar with the signs of a compulsive gambler and he would use that to his advantage. It would be just a matter of days before Art took the first step in engaging me as his next victim.

Shortly after I heard Art speak at Genoa, I read his book, *Busted*. I was so impressed with his life story. The way he had suffered at the hands of an abusive father, battled a gambling addiction, survived prison and after calling on God, was able to turn himself around and find a way to help others in need, spoke to me. I purchased several copies of his book to give to my friends. Art gladly signed them for me.

At the time, I thought his inscription to my friend Mary was sweet. When I read it now, I understand the chilling implication of his message.

How thrilled he must have been when he understood my position in the community and the balance in my bank account. That he was able to so easily manipulate my goodwill and feelings of gratitude were icing on the cake.

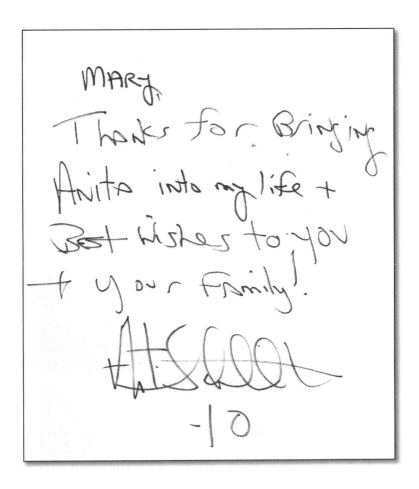

18 | THE CON WAS ON

2009

"Bob and Anita were constantly giving. It wasn't about what they owned, but what they were able to give."	*Vincent J. Margello Jr.* *Margello Development Co.*

On Friday, five days after we spoke at Genoa Baptist Church, Art called me at home. He said he was in the area and wanted to know if he could bring lunch over. He suggested Wendy's, which I found endearing, and when I told him my housekeeper Sabrina was working that day, he also purchased a meal for her.

Before long, he was knocking at my door, Wendy's bags in hand. The three of us sat at the table eating our sandwiches and talking about what had transpired since we had originally met all those years ago. He recounted how his days were now filled with book signing events and public speaking and talked about the foundation he established to help people struggling with the torment of gambling addiction.

Sabrina returned to her cleaning while Art and I continued our pleasant conversation until he unexplainably became interested in my television. "I wonder what's on TV?" he asked. He walked across the room, turned on the television, and increased the volume. At the time his actions seemed nonsensical; he wasn't interested in the programming. *What on earth did he want with the television?* Looking back, I see that he wanted to mask our conversation from Sabrina. He was about to ask me for a loan.

Without any preamble, he jumped right in. "I would love to be able to buy a better car so I can drive back and forth to Indianapolis to see my kids. I'm trying to build a relationship with my daughters." With the television blaring behind him, he returned to the dining table, took out a piece of paper and began writing out how much money he needed.

Art explained he didn't have a dependable car. The dark blue Dodge Durango he drove had been stored in a garage for years and had more than 200,000 miles on the odometer. Without a dependable car it was difficult to travel from Washington Court House, where he lived with his mother, to Indianapolis where his children, Taylor and Madison, lived with their mother. His voice dropped as he told me his older daughter had been in grade school when he went to prison and he had missed a significant portion of her life. His girls were everything in the world to him, and he was desperate to re-establish a relationship with them.

Would I be willing to loan him $10,000 to purchase a vehicle?

At this point I must pause to tell you that Art is a compelling storyteller. He is able to target his audience, convincingly weaving details and emotions into compelling arguments. He can pull on heartstrings, appeal to one's willingness to assist, and explain ideas that make sense to even the most tenacious realist.

Have you ever encountered a skillful salesperson? You may not even be in the market for the item or service being offered and have no intention to purchase anything, but from the start you are aware of the sales pitch. The poking and prodding, looking for a weakness, before pulling back, assessing, and beginning the sales assault anew. Successful salespeople know how to lead you across the dance floor. At first, it might feel a bit unnatural but before long they are speaking your language and their argument makes sense.

Even while you are fully aware that you can end the engagement at any time, have you ever returned home with a new car or a timeshare that you hadn't planned on purchasing? When you think about the encounter later, it's often difficult to explain why. It's nearly impossible to detail how you went from barely interested to a new owner. *"It made sense at the time,"* you tell your friends. *"If you only could have heard the salesperson's spiel, you would have purchased one, too."* And while they may snicker behind your back, most everyone has been there—a victim of a master salesperson.

That's how it was with Art and his ability to turn a scheme into a gleaming new opportunity, or a favor or a desperate crisis that only I could solve. However, there was one critical exception when it came to his targeting me: I didn't know I was being sold, until it was too late to spot the con or recoup the enormous cost.

When Art first broached the subject of a $10,000 loan, he said his publisher was going to release money to him in January and he would pay me back at that time. He only needed the money for ninety days max.

How could I deny his request?

Sitting across from me was the man who had dramatically helped my son achieve a breakthrough in his recovery, asking me to help him with his children. I was glad to be able to return the favor in some way by providing him with the money. He wrote me a post-dated check for $10,000 from his mother's account to cover the request. He assured me the funds would be good on that future date. Before the date on the check arrived, Art asked me to hold on to it. I didn't mind; I certainly didn't expect his mother to cover his debts.

While Bob was alive, we were delighted to help our friends and family members with personal loans, gifts, and opportunities. Among numerous loans (of which more than $1 million was never paid back), Bob loaned $35,000 to one good friend when his restaurant was struggling. He made sure others had opportunities to acquire Wendy's franchises and loaned money to purchase them. He pledged $1 million in Wendy's stock to help launch The James Cancer Center on the OSU Campus. He gave every year to our local United Way. He was a generous contributor to Church of the Messiah United Methodist in Westerville when they were building a new gym, which they named "Barney Gym," and was instrumental in assisting Beacon of Hope Church in Lincoln Village to purchase a building they desperately needed. He spent time consulting with business owners personally and by serving on their boards.

We purchased or built homes for family members, provided the start-up capital for new ventures, invited friends and loved ones on all-expense-paid vacations, took them along on private jets, hosted them at extravagant parties, gave them our first row Ohio State football tickets, purchased cars, and covered college expenses. We didn't keep track; we kept giving—sharing the blessings we enjoyed.

After Bob's death, I was able to continue the generosity for friends and family, albeit on a smaller scale befitting the now-limited finances I had available. I donated generously to the Buckeye Cruise for Cancer fundraisers and invited friends and family to accompany me, covering many of the costs. I offered my home to friends who were down on their luck, and continued hosting parties and trips. If my loved ones had a need and I had the resources to help, I would. Time and time again.

What I couldn't know when Art made that initial loan request was that the con was on. He was prodding to see how willing I would be to "help" him. I misread his ask as a friendly request, and I engaged him as I had all of my friends for decades. I have no doubt now that he specifically targeted me after we reconnected at church. He was a gambling addict—a wolf in sheep's clothing—focusing his leer on a wealthy widow who felt a debt of gratitude for a decades-old kindness. I saw a man once broken by his illness who had paid his debt to society, struggling to reconnect with his family, welcomed by the community, celebrated by the OSU fans, endorsed by local pastors, broadcasting weekly on the radio, vowing he hadn't gambled in five years.

I could easily obtain money from one of my investment accounts and write a check to meet his request. His promise to repay the loan seemed sincere, the purpose was legitimate, and the amount was small enough that I could afford it. Honestly, it was the least I could do for this man. I needed to move some money, but I was able to write out two checks, made payable to Cash, for $5,000 each.

Early the next week, Art called and invited me to lunch at Applebee's on Ackerman Road. He talked about his problems, which mostly centered on several old gambling debts. *Would you be willing to loan me $100,000?* He said he would use the money to pay off the debts and would help other gamblers who had contacted his foundation. He promised to pay back the loan—with ten percent interest—by the end of January, when he was expecting a $125,000 check from his publisher. To be sure, the amount he was requesting was a lot of money, but it wasn't an inconvenience for me to provide him a short-term loan for that amount. After considering it for a couple of minutes, I agreed and told Art that it would take me a few days to have the money transferred to my checking account. Meanwhile, Art said he would have his attorney prepare paperwork to outline the terms of the loan.

Before he left, Art asked for my help with something else. He explained he was in a desperate cash flow situation and asked if I could help him out until things picked up. I gave him one check for $5,000 and post-dated three additional checks for the last week of the month: two to him totaling $10,500 and $8,000 to his friend Chester Meeks. I felt really good about being in a position to help him obtain a new lease on life. I had recently heard both Dr. Phil and Oprah discuss the importance of giving people a second chance. Here was my opportunity to do just that.

Shortly after that meeting with Art, I received a call from an unknown number. The man identified himself as Art's attorney, and wanted to review and confirm the details of the $100,000 loan so the promissory note could be prepared correctly. We discussed the details, and I appreciated his thoroughness. Art began calling on a regular basis, inquiring when the funds would be transferred to my checking account and be available. As soon as the money hit my account, his requests started in earnest. Between December 1 and December 4, Art had me prepare five checks to his creditors for a total of more than $61,580. Additionally, I wired $25,000 to an account he specified.

My attention turned from Art and his troubles to the holidays. It had been more than two years since Bob's passing and I finally felt like hosting a Christmas party again. My days became filled finalizing details for the upcoming festivities.

The Christmas party I was planning at La Scala in Dublin that year wasn't close to the scale of previous events Bob and I had hosted, but I did have a large guest list including long-time friends Dom & Terri Tiberi, Jack Hanna, Dimetrius Stanley, Justin Zwick, and members of both my family and Bob's family. My friend Phil Evans and his band provided the entertainment. My cousin Rock dressed up as Santa to dance and flirt with the girls. My life was feeling hopeful, as I looked forward to the new year and traveling to the Rose Bowl in January with Alan.

At the end of the party, after stepping away from my remaining guests and settling the bill—which came to around $10,000—I received a call from an unknown number. The individual on the other end again identified himself as Art's attorney and indicated he didn't have a lot of time to talk as he was at the airport heading out of town. He simply wanted to touch base regarding the $100,000 I had agreed to loan Art. I confirmed everything was on track. Before I could explain that I had already made several disbursements to Art, the caller disconnected.

A few days later, on December 7, Art asked me to meet him at the office of his attorney, John Amery. As I pulled into a parking spot, Art was exiting the building holding the promissory note for the $100,000 loan we had discussed. He gave me what looked to be a legitimate legal document specifying the details of the loan and payment terms. We talked for a few minutes before he requested a check for $5,000 made out to Birch, Amery & Golson, LLC, for John Amery, which I wrote out and handed to Art. And with that exchange, I had now written checks to or on behalf of Art for more than $115,000, satisfying his initial loan request.

19 | MY RELATIONSHIP WITH ART

> "I was fond of Art, but I wasn't in love with him. I realize my feelings toward Art weren't always obvious to others, and my actions muddled the perception of our relationship."
>
> Anita Barney

It had now been more than two years since I said a final farewell to Bob, the love of my life. He had retired early and we spent nearly every minute together, even holding hands when we sat side by side in our matching recliners watching television at night. Bob took care of everything for us. While he had left me financially comfortable, I missed having a partner to ask advice, talk over the day, and plan for the future. My life wasn't difficult, per se. But it was different. It was more complicated and less fun than before. The brightness was gone. The comfort and laughter had faded.

My friends continued to ensure there were plenty of fun things planned, but it wasn't the same. I didn't want my loss to be a source of my friends' sadness, so there was a lot of pretending. Pretending to like watching movies in the middle of the afternoon. Pretending I was interested in the men they suggested I meet for dinner. Pretending I looked forward to the same routine every single day and then returning home alone to an empty house.

When Art and I reconnected we became fast friends. I was flattered by the attention of a much younger guy. He would call and sing to me, casually referred to me as *honey,* expressed interest in what I was doing. Of course there was a bit of excitement when he showed up unexpectedly at my regular Wednesday night haunt to meet my friends. My pals warmly welcomed the former OSU and NFL quarterback—even if his body was out of shape and his reputation a bit tarnished.

Art was witty and engaging. The men wanted to talk football and reminisce. The women were enamored by his charisma. And I was enjoying the company of a companion who was accepted so easily and enjoyable to be around. He came across as humble, the glory days of past accomplishments rarely acknowledged.

When I showed him the photos lining my staircase of the many celebrities I had encountered during my life and shared the backstories of how I came to meet them, he acknowledged, "Well, I guess I'm the low man on your social totem pole." He was right; my association with famous and influential people far exceeded the fading glitter of this long-ago college athlete.

I had purchased a conversion van specifically for tailgating at OSU home games and invited Art to join me and my friends. He stopped by one Saturday and, while my family was hanging out in the van watching the game on TV, Art and I sat outside in lawn chairs. I had given my four season tickets to friends so they could watch the game inside Ohio Stadium. No one ever turned down the chance to sit in the first row at the 35-yard line, behind the visiting team.

While I remember an enjoyable, if predictable, day chatting and joking with my new friend, others present recall there was a bit of flirting and a kiss passed between us. I tend to be a very physical person, kissing and hugging friends a greeting of welcome or farewell. Patting an arm or squeezing a shoulder during conversation is customary. And I assume this is the behavior that was observed because while I was fond of Art, I didn't have any romantic feelings toward him.

Sometime in December 2009, I called my friend Suzi Rapp, Director of Columbus Zoo Promotions, and scheduled a behind the scenes tour for Art and me. As she had many times in the past for my friends, Suzi graciously organized the visit for the following week and I was delighted to learn that Brian Green, Promotions Assistant, would be our guide. After the tour, Art and I turned our attention to the Wildlights display and the twinkling wonder of millions of lights celebrating the season. With a chill in the air, Christmas around the corner, and enchanted children snuggling close to their parents, it was a happy evening.

Art spotted an empty bench and I agreed it was time for a quick break. As we were sitting talking about the tour and the animals, the conversation turned personal when Art made an awkward romantic overture. I quickly rebuffed him by replying, "Art, I don't need you for anything and I don't want you for anything. I just want to help you." That appeared to put an end to his intentions for the moment. However, he was relentless and later he would repeatedly tell me that he wanted to make me fall in love with him. Obviously, it was clear to him that I wasn't in love. But my feelings toward Art weren't always obvious to others, and I now realize that my actions muddled the perception of our relationship.

Now, let me set the record straight about one more thing. There has been a lot of speculation and rampant rumors about Art and me having sex. The unvarnished truth is that Art and I never had sex. There was one time when he got a little frisky and I wasn't opposed to indulging him. I had never connected sexually with any man and had no preconceived idea that Art would be the one to break the streak. However, when it quickly became apparent that he would be unable to perform, I came to my senses and wondered what in the world I was doing with this man who was much younger, a convicted felon, and someone to whom I wasn't even attracted. I put an immediate stop to the charade.

20 | NOVEMBER & DECEMBER 2009

"Eventually it appeared Art had one huge hot mess on his hands, but he was making sporadic repayments to me, and I believed in him."	*Anita Barney*

I had agreed to loan Art $100,000 and he provided a signed promissory note specifying repayment terms. However, because he didn't request the money in a lump sum and, instead, frequently requested smaller amounts arbitrarily, and I was confident his word was good, I ended up giving him a more than twice that amount in less than seven weeks.

Art said the money was being used to repay old loans he had incurred years ago, before he was incarcerated. He explained the creditors were men prone to violence and retaliation, and they were threatening him, indicating that if the outstanding balances were not satisfied quickly, he could end up back in jail, or worse. Repeatedly, he vehemently denied he was gambling. I believed him.

By the time November 30, 2009, rolled around, just thirty days since I reconnected with Art at Genoa Church, I had written six separate checks totaling $33,500.

Between December 1 and 24, Art requested sixteen checks and one wire transfer which drained my accounts of nearly $185,000.

With the exception of one payment to Art's attorney, John Amery, the remainder of the money went to people I did not know.

The amount I loaned to Art during November and December 2009 totaled just over $218,000. In the process of money exchanging hands, I became acquainted with his circle of "friends."

John Amery was Art's attorney and agent. Early on Art took me to John's office so we could meet. As I was writing a check to one of Art's creditors in his presence, John said, "Are you ever going to run out of money?" As I recall, we all shared a laugh. *Run out of money? Nonsense!* The idea of not having enough money had never even crossed my mind during the past thirty years.

John would eventually tell authorities that at one time he had provided Art with a blank promissory template to use, but had never prepared one on Art's behalf. Months later John would share with me that Art would use his offices to shower and change clothes when he was in Columbus. One morning, John arrived to find that Art had been in his office overnight and, inexplicably, a check was missing from John's desk.

Charles Grubb was a friend and gambling companion of Art's. Art wrote in his book *Busted*, that Charles covered for him, gambled with him and on his behalf, and let him sleep on the sofa at his home when he was on the run from the Columbus Police. Although I never met him, I talked to Charles on the phone a few times, and he told me he wasn't going to loan Art any more money. In fact, Charles had instructed Art not to contact him anymore but Art kept calling and harassing him for money. Art told me Charles "Chuckie" worked at The Red Mile racetrack in Lexington, Kentucky.

Herschel DeLarge and his brother, Douglas, owned a construction company in Columbus. They supported Art financially before I reconnected with him, and I'm not sure they were ever paid back. Herschel refused to give Art any money this time around. Nonetheless, Douglas folded to Art's demands without telling his brother. I spoke to Douglas on the phone multiple times and recall meeting him in the parking lot at Thurn's Specialty Meats on Greenlawn Avenue. I gave him a personal check as collateral and he gave me cash for Art. At the time, his business was experiencing financial difficulty and Douglas was quite angry Art wasn't paying the loan on time, which resulted in penalties to which Art had agreed; I would be surprised if the principal, interest, or penalties were ever collected.

Sue Paveleski and her husband Boris were hired by Art to transport money. They met me several times in Columbus and when I was in Florida to deliver or pick up money. Often they said they were going to Indiana to meet Art. Although it was never proven, the authorities speculated they were taking a percentage of the money they were transporting or placing wagers on behalf of Art or both. They were never charged.

***

Art would occasionally stop by my home to pick up the checks he demanded. He was constantly promising the checks would never be cashed, adamantly pledging, "I'll have the money before this check ever becomes due. You don't have anything to worry about." Other times (and especially if I was going to be out) he would instruct me to leave checks under the cushions of my porch furniture with promises of repayment. Frequently, he would have me meet people to hand off a personal check. With my check in their possession as collateral, they would release funds to Art via cash or an account transfer to whomever he designated. It wasn't unusual for Art to have me write several checks to the same person with different dates and give them to his long–time friend Bill Hanners to deliver. Bill was also a money runner for Art.

Later, when Art would send me into the bank to retrieve funds, he would instruct me to initiate transactions of less than $10,000 so they wouldn't be flagged. I didn't know what that meant, not understanding that transactions of $10,000 or more are reported to the government so they can be reviewed for illegal activity. Art was always worried about people knowing what he was doing and was very secretive. When I was in Florida and authorized Bill Hanners to make a cash withdrawal at my Columbus bank, Art insisted I tell the banker it was for a home remodeling project I was having done. At some point and for reasons I still don't understand, he no longer wanted checks from my UBS bank account. "Don't you have a PNC account? Write the check from that account," he instructed. His demands were spontaneous, fast, and furious. Immediate action was required or destruction was imminent: go to the bank, approve a withdrawal, write a check, meet someone right away!

Eventually, Art's promises of repayment on my loan to him became vague, undependable, and often came with last minute delays. *The money will be released after 1:00 p.m. tomorrow but I won't get it until the following day. I'm still waiting for the money but I'll let you know when it arrives. Hopefully, the guy will be able to get it to me before Friday. I know I said I it would be $10,000, but all I was able to get was $2,000.* No doubt he was playing people on the other end of those promises, like he was working me to get money to pass on to creditors or to gamble.

It appeared Art had one huge hot mess on his hands, but he was making sporadic repayments to me, and I believed in him.

21 | SPOTTING THE SCAMS

"There is no one in the world Anita is not interested in helping. Unfortunately, some people aren't worthy of the help."	*Bill Loveland* *Attorney*

Even now, after everything that has transpired, I'm not sure I could spot a scam. I know that probably sounds insincere to those who can identify a whiff of fraud a mile away. But I'm not like that. My life experiences didn't train me to be alert for those who plan to inflict loss. And I still question why God would create people with a mind bent on destruction of others. The idea that I need to inspect the motives of others before offering assistance is foreign to me. If someone needs help, and I have the means to offer it, I want to make life easier.

Several weeks ago I received an email from a business acquaintance reporting he was in a foreign country, robbed of money and identification, and requesting a cash transfer. My desire to help anyone in need kicked in immediately. I was concerned for this man's safety and well-being and placed a call to the mutual friend who had introduced us. My friend said this individual should not be asking me for money; he explained it was probably a scam. I was incredulous. "Why would he contact me if he didn't need help?" I asked, not understanding. "Are you certain he is OK?"

I now know it's quite common for hackers to commandeer someone's online account and email contacts with a crisis message requesting immediate action. I hear about it on the news. I just never expected that I would be the target. Evidently, there are a good number of folks who think like this; otherwise scammers would search for a different line of work.

A few months back Art, through his attorney, tried to bargain to be moved to a different prison by claiming he would be willing to reveal where he had stashed his ill-gotten gains. As I related the story to a friend, I said, "If I could, I would want to make the deal if it would mean I could repay my friends the money they had given me." And I meant it. Surely, if there was a way to reclaim funds and attempt to restore relationships, I was in.

My friend interrupted my musings by asking if I thought there was any money left to find. I was shocked by her response. "Well, why on earth would Art say there was money if there wasn't any left?" I questioned.

Her blunt reply left me speechless. "Because Art is a liar. He scams. That's what he does."

I was stunned. I couldn't wrap my mind around the fact that Art would lie to me, to his attorney, and to the authorities while sitting in jail. The question crossed my lips before I could think, "Do you really think he would lie about this?" My initial response toward anyone is to give him or her the benefit of the doubt, to hope that I can somehow make the situation better. But I understand not everyone feels that way. Some people mistakenly assume there is a hidden motive of love or greed.

Before you rush to judge my gullibility, consider the scams and cons that have taken down business owners, politicians, religious leaders, sports heroes, and ordinary folks just trying to make a living. Hackers slip links into emails, online services advertise unbelievable opportunities, job applicants misrepresent their experience, on-line dating profiles are filled with half-truths. Accidents on purpose. Fake illnesses for gain. Illegal use of performance drugs. Reports engineered to disguise the facts.

Evening news programs lead with the stories. Movies glamorize the con. Television programs expose the criminals. Senate hearings are convened. And yet wolves roam Wall Street devouring bank accounts and reputations with regularity. Too often we hear, "On counsel's advice, I invoke my right under the Fifth Amendment not to answer, on the grounds I may incriminate myself" instead of "Let me come clean and tell you what happened." The truth remains elusive.

Perhaps you've heard of cons perpetuated by Charles Ponzi (creator of the Ponzi Scheme); Frank Abagnale Jr. (Catch Me If You Can); James Frey (A Million Little Pieces); Bernie Madoff, or Enron. More recently, you could have read about the IRS, Veteran's Administration, General Motors, NFL players and coaches, elite athletes and, closer to home, The Ohio State University football team's tattoo "scandal."

No one is immune to being conned. Everyone has been victimized in one way or another because those perpetuating the scam often don't look dangerous and their stories contain enough truth to hook the target. We buy the lie. Hope for the best. Want to help. We either can't see the truth or deliberately look the other way out of solidarity, pride, greed, misjudgment, love or, sometimes, even abuse. Sure, some scams create more embarrassment than financial loss or criminal charges, but there is a reason these schemes continue to exist: they are overwhelmingly successful.

Now that I've had a chance to sit back and reflect on everything and read through the police file, I have been able to identify five different scams Art had going in the sixteen months I knew him.

On Monday, February 7, 2011, a little more than a year after we connected, one day after Super Bowl XLV, and a week before he went to jail, Art detailed his actions during an interview session with then Franklin County Assistant Prosecutor Steve Schierholt and Dublin Police Detective Scott Davis.

***

Scam #1: Personal Loans

At the beginning, Art would simply ask that I personally loan him money, which he would instruct me to give directly to him or to one of his associates. He would provide fraudulent promissory notes and have people contact me posing as his attorney to convince me the transactions were legitimate. Although he did make irregular payments to keep me hooked, it's embarrassing to admit that, on average, he was costing me $6,200 per day between November 6, 2009, and February 7, 2011. His requests were sporadic, frenzied, and demanding. While I attempted to keep records at the beginning, he destroyed them in May 2010 before federal investigators interviewed me. The transactions were coming so fast and furious that I woefully misjudged my remaining available cash. One minute I was confident I had a comfortable amount of money, the next I realized I was broke.

Eventually, trying to save the little money I had left, but feeling the pressure from Art to put out fires and keep him out of jail, I would write checks that couldn't be presented to the bank because they were indecipherable. He would call enraged, "WHAT ARE YOU DOING? I can't read the son of a b**ch!" I would beg and plead that I didn't want to write a check. He would coerce and threaten until I eventually felt compelled to acquiesce. Then I came up with a new plan to circumvent Art's scheme and started using a felt pen so that I could smear the ink. Same result. Art would call screaming and threatening and swearing. When I couldn't take the pressure any longer, I would break down and write a replacement check. I was trying to drag out the process as long as possible, hoping he would give up on me and search for money elsewhere, while still appearing compliant so he wouldn't make good on his threat to leave town with everyone's money.

***

Authorities: When all this started with borrowing the money from Anita, realistically, did you ever have any intention of paying her back?

Art Schlichter: Absolutely. Always. I have given her money back. When it first started, $20,000, $30,000, $50,000, $100,000, that's not "worrying about winning it" money. It was later when I was trying to survive for me and for her. I promised, promised, promised that it would be OK.

Is it safe to say you got over $1 million from Anita Barney?

Probably. Maybe more. I mean you can go to Chip Greene (Best Seat Tickets), $150,000 on her credit card was from him right off the bat. And then any money that she gave me is probably $1 million right there.

Did Greene know (Anita) was getting tickets for you?

Let me tell you what Greene did. Absolutely. Anita wrote him a check. I don't know why she did this. He knew I didn't have any money. When it started out, I owed him $50,000 to $60,000, maybe more. He would front me the tickets. Help me get them . . . let me have them. Same thing. She went in there swiped the card, swiped the card (for) $150,000. Then I had debt to him. I wrote him checks for that debt. I don't even remember the circumstance. She never got a ticket from him. No receipt or anything. He sued or threatened to sue her for $22,000 for my debt. It's not her debt. She wrote a check to cover my debt that wasn't any good. Now she's getting sued for it. I don't know how you can sue anyone for that. She didn't get a thing from him. He's still grinding her for the last $22,000 that I owed him. Literally, threatening her on a daily basis. That's the stuff I don't understand. How he could do that?

Scam 2: Ohio State University Football Tickets

Another scam Art pushed was selling season tickets for OSU football games. Bob and I had been season ticket holders to the same four seats in the first row of The Shoe for years. I expected that the season tickets Art was selling would be like the ones we purchased: same seats every game, with the entire season of tickets and parking passes arriving prior to the first home game. Not even close.

Art would ask, "Do any of your friends want to buy tickets? I have an opportunity to get tickets they can't." Art really knew how to use the enthusiasm of Ohio State football to sell his scheme. In fact, my neighbor Keith, who is a professor at OSU, wasn't even able to get tickets, and was excited for the opportunity. Art didn't want me to tell anyone that he was the one supplying the tickets. He crafted a back-story that involved a friend of Bob's who could buy extra tickets and had offered me the chance to obtain some for my friends.

Art was very specific on the location of the seats. When I questioned how he was able to get them, Art explained there was a guy at OSU who got the tickets for him and they would meet at the Applebee's restaurant across from the Union Cemetery on Olentangy River Road to make the transfer. Months later, as the investigation was winding down, but before everything came out in the press, I called OSU Athletic Director Gene Smith. I had previously gone to dinner with him and his wife, and we had golfed together at OSU. I explained what had happened to me because of Art's scams. Gene responded, "Anita! How could you do this? Art has nothing to do with OSU." But Art was so believable when he explained how it would work. He had answers for all my questions and confidently addressed every detail. It sounded authentic.

I was thrilled to be able to offer my friends season tickets, because I knew how much fun Bob and I had with our friends tailgating and attending games. But things went bad from the beginning. Most weeks I would meet Art behind the Buffalo Wild Wings on Bethel Road on Thursday nights after he finished broadcasting The Bucks Line with Coach Earle Bruce. He would have a box of tickets in his back seat and dole out random tickets— even for my friends who had purchased season tickets. Other times, he wouldn't deliver tickets until late on Friday night or early Saturday morning. I was a nervous wreck waiting for the tickets each week and so embarrassed by the fiasco; I couldn't understand why season tickets were random every week: different seats, different sections, and often the seats weren't together. I was initially excited to help my friends, but it turned into a disaster. The good thing—if you could call it that—was everyone who had purchased tickets did receive them, or a refund if they requested their money be returned.

***

Authorities: Did (Anita) know you were gambling with the money?

Art Schlichter: No. Never. Never. Listen, I wasn't always gambling with the money. If you look at all the tickets she helped me buy, in a roundabout way the people got the tickets.

If someone paid you $2,200 for tickets, did you gamble that money?

I never sold tickets for more than face value. Some of the money Anita gave me to buy tickets—when you are in a gambling cycle it's a constant hurricane—I would gamble. Some I would need to pay back a debt or whatever.

So you wouldn't take the money Anita gave you to buy tickets? You would use it to gamble, pay down debts, etc.? But when it came down to the wire, you would need to buy tickets?

Let's say a ticket at face value was seventy dollars. I would presell (collect the money for a future ticket delivery date). So, 200 tickets equals $14,000. My hope was really to just return the money to the people and tell them I couldn't get the tickets this year. (Short-term, no interest loan.) But I was always worse off when September came around and I had to go to a ticket broker who knew I was screwed up and I would have to pay $250 or $300 or whatever (per ticket). I would use their money free for several months. But except for the three or four or five people who didn't get their tickets. I would wait until right before the game and buy the tickets (with someone else's money I had "borrowed") at the broker price of $250-$300 a ticket. I was losing money.

Best Seat Tickets?

Chip Greene is who I dealt with. Last year I dealt with Chip. And then more recently I had someone go in and get the tickets. I didn't want to go in. I was under federal investigation, (but) he had to know it was me. He was charging me outrageous prices for tickets. Brokers can name their price. And especially if they know you're desperate . . . and he knew I was desperate. He cut me at the jugular. I did give OSU tickets to Anita. It was fifty to sixty tickets a week to her friends.

How many seasons did you sell tickets?

Three, maybe.

Is it fair to say that some people did not get all of their tickets?

Very few. Fletcher said he didn't want his tickets. He just wanted his money back.

Are you sure?

I'm positive, in fact.

Weren't there a number of people from Washington Court House?

That's where the majority of the people were from. Two to three last year. None from this year. That I can think of. If you give me some names, I could tell you.

Was one a chiropractor?

Yes. I think we paid him in full. Morgan Miller.

A printer?

He got tickets. Dennis Foster. I still owe him a lot of money. I borrowed it from him. Some was attached to tickets. Most of it was just going in and telling him I needed to borrow. He has checks from Mom and maybe from people in Indy that bounced. I'm going to tell you something. There are very few people who say they bought tickets from me and didn't get them. And if they didn't get them, there was a story behind why. Either they didn't want them. They wouldn't accept the money back. They wanted to throw me in jail.

Walter Fletcher was paid back in full. In November he came to a broadcast at BW3 at Bethel. Came up. Hugged me. Told me, "I love you, brother." Introduced me to all of his friends. He got paid back. I saw him right before the Michigan game. Maybe he was playing along.

How did you get OSU tickets?

I get tickets from the University. I'm entitled to them. If I need extras, I call up Justin Brooks' secretary, mostly, and say I need extras. I have to pay money to the University. That's been a few years ago. I didn't get any from the players. I always told people I had a source at OSU or elsewhere. But I didn't have a source. People that got tickets from (me) the first time, all of them came back, for the most part, to get more. They would call me. I pursued a lot of people initially. When I did this I was real careful most of the time. I told them I need money. Not paying it to OSU. I was on the fence bragging about it, "I've got this source." Most everyone, except for a handful of people would get the OSU tickets. I might send Bill (Hanners) or Boris (Paveleski) to drop off tickets. That was part of them helping me out. I didn't pay them. Every once in a while I would give them gas money, but they considered it a favor. They knew I was struggling and needed some help. They cared for me.

OSU Tickets. At Player Will Call . . . ?

None of that. Never been involved with that. I never got tickets from OSU except for the ones they send me for being a varsity player. Two or four. That's it. Not one person from OSU did I get tickets from.

So, (Anita) really doesn't know?

No. She's got enough faith. She thought the fifty to sixty tickets that I got for her friends each week, she thought we had bought and paid for them.

Scam 3: Loans from My Friends

Art asked about obtaining loans from my friends. These would be short-term loans that he would pay back with high interest. I had seen Art come through with OSU tickets (even though the process was a mess) and was making an effort of (slowly) repaying the loans I had made to him, so I was confident he would make good on these promises and my friends would benefit by making a little money for their trouble.

But there was one big problem. I was really uncomfortable contacting friends—some with whom I had not spoken for years— and asking for money. I hesitated and he became angry. He would write out a script for me to read, but then criticized me when it sounded like I was reading it. "Sound natural!" he commanded. He would meet me in a parking lot, jump in my car, go through my address book, dial the number and hand me the phone. Then, while I was on the phone, he would coach me because I "wasn't doing it right." It was humiliating.

***

Authorities: How did they pay her?

Art Schlichter: No checks. I didn't know these people. I knew of them.

Did you ever talk to any of these people?

I can't think of one time I talked to them. I doubt her friends knew about me (then). They know now. Read it in the paper.

Did people know you were getting the money? That you were involved?

I know they all thought, at some point, after the fact. Rumors. That she and I were dating. That wasn't true. She really was just trying to help me get my life back together. She had no idea.

Ben Roberts?

I don't know him. Just know the name. Anita went to him to borrow money. Told him some investment. If he would help for a month or two she would make him some money. Probably paid him back $10,000. Maybe.

Her going to him would have been at your suggestion?

Yes. Not because it was Ben Roberts. Just because he had money. Any time she ever called anyone up, she did it with the purpose and faith of knowing I was going to pay her back. And get tickets for these people. I think he gave her $20,000 but is suing her for $30,000 for missed profit.

So, if she got $20,000 from Roberts, she would give it to you?

Yes.

Would you gamble it?

Or I would buy tickets or whatever I needed to buy or do at that point. Did I gamble some of it? Probably. Did I buy some tickets? Probably. Did I use some of it to pay someone back? Probably. Whatever I needed to do. When she was in Florida she sent a lot of money back (to Ohio) to pay people back for gambling purposes.

Scam 4: Using My Reputation and (Alleged) Wealth as Collateral

When I was out of disposable income, Art would ask me to write checks he could use as collateral for loans he wanted to obtain from his friends and acquaintances. We both knew my bank accounts were empty, but Art guaranteed the checks would never be cashed; he would get the money before the check would be presented. Generally, these checks were made out to people I did not know.

***

Authorities: How did that work? Did she know them or did you?

Art Schlichter: I knew them. She didn't know any of these people. All she did was write a check to these people either to guarantee it or for me to use.

If she didn't have any money, how could she guarantee?

Well, they didn't know that. And I told her the checks would never be cashed. I would get it handled before that.

Did you give (people) Anita's checks as part of getting (their) money?

Yes. She post-dated the checks and I told these people to not cash the checks until I told them they could. I told Anita they would never be cashed. All these checks she wrote for these people, we did not represent that the money was there. We told them we would let them know when the checks were good. My whole plan was to make the checks good. When you're gambling, your hope is to take the $20,000 or whatever, and turn it into a lot more.

Was it always you instructing (Anita) who to write it to and for how much?

She might have included that in how she borrowed the money. Saying the check should be good in a couple of weeks.

If she said that, was it because you told her it would be good in a couple of weeks?

Yes.

Did you tell these guys who she was? How did they know her?

They asked me who she was and I said Bob Barney's widow. You want to look it up, you look it up. That what I would tell them. She didn't know these guys from Adam. They came after her like it was blood money. I owed The Tree Surgeon $4,000 for four tickets. And he texted me that said, "Say hi to your dad in hell." You would have thought that I assaulted his family. And Tim Baker is the same way. "Hope you get butt-f**ked in prison. That's what we're doing to Anita Barney."

What did you have her tell people that were looking to collect their money?

I wasn't there on the back end. Only on the front end to get the money. I would tell her to tell them, here's what we are going to do for them. Tickets. A little extra money. And then she wrote checks to them as a guarantor. All those checks came back to haunt her.

Did you often tell her that a check would never be presented?

If Anita wrote me a check and I presented it to someone, I would tell her it would never be presented. Because my plan was always to go back and pick up the check, so it would never be presented.

But that was contingent on your winning a sport bet or at the track or casino?

Absolutely.

Scam 5: Super Bowl Tickets

The final scheme, and the one that caused everything to implode, involved Art collecting money to purchase Super Bowl tickets that he supposedly had access to through the Indianapolis Colts organization. His plan was to buy the tickets, at face value with investor's cash, and sell the tickets for a profit. He would then split the proceeds with the person who fronted the money. He would tell these investors that I, a wealthy widow, wanted to purchase the tickets from them, while telling me there was a "guy in Chicago" who wanted to buy them from me. After he was arrested I found out there never were any tickets. Art was simply using me to collect money that he would then squander.

I repeatedly asked Art what he was doing with the money I was giving him. His response was that he was just retiring old debts and trying to stay out of prison so he could turn things around and reestablish a life with his daughters. He would play heavily on my sympathies and mentioned his children often. That was our connection, the children: my son thirty years ago and his daughters today.

Art assured me he was not gambling and hadn't gambled in five years. (After he was arrested, Detective Davis told me Art had been captured on recent security camera video footage in area casinos. *Was anything Art said true?*) When I asked if he was using drugs, he said he didn't do drugs. He never sounded like he was on drugs, nor did he appear to be under the influence the times I saw him. He was so believable, and what choice did I have? I felt I had to roll the dice. By the end I was in so deep I didn't know what to do. When a compulsive gambler is calling the shots, it is like being swept away by a powerful avalanche. I was frantic—in the middle of a tumultuous situation—and I couldn't see any way to escape it.

22 | GAMBLING

| "Every day I'm reminded of the debts I owe. I keep lists nearby that contain the names of my friends to whom I owe money." | Anita Barney |

It's no secret that my notoriety is tied to gambling. Not my own act of risking money, at least not in the way you might think. But in the risking (and eventual loss) of something with greater importance—things that are too valuable to be appraised in monetary terms: the caring and meaningful relationships of friends and family—for that I plead guilty. I don't blame any of my friends, family, or acquaintances who hold a grudge, refuse to take or return my phone calls, or publicly shun me. I understand that my choices and actions caused financial strain, unnecessary hardship, and guilt by association. I severely damaged and in some cases permanently destroyed relationships with people who are dear to me.

How did it happen? Where did it begin? Why didn't I see it? Why couldn't I stop it? These are questions that keep me awake at night. I've cried out to God repeatedly for answers. I've talked about it with therapists, discussed it with friends and family, and confessed it to authorities. How did I manage to allow such a disaster to occur? When did my actions transform from good intentions, to taking advantage, to a frenetic quest for survival?

How could I not see that my attempts to save a man drowning in a sea of gambling addiction was pulling me under and threatening my very survival?

There are so many questions. I'm sure when you look at the surface, it appears smooth, and a direct line from the question to an answer is easy to follow. But if you're willing to take a look beneath what's easily visible, perhaps you'll understand there are legitimate explanations—not excuses—that reveal predispositions, suppositions, and actions that resulted in the destruction of what was and what could have been. Even an eventual court judgment against me failed to adequately atone for the trail of destruction I permitted to occur. Every day I'm reminded of the debts I owe. I keep lists nearby that contain the names of my friends to whom I owe money.

I am not a gambler. Yes, I've occasionally visited a casino for pleasure, and risked a small amount. (When I was married to Bob I would put fifty dollars in a Ziploc bag and this was my limit for the evening.) But I viewed the money I put in the slot or placed on the table as entertainment. No different than the cost and fun of attending a show or spending an evening with friends at a nice restaurant. I know people who would regularly spend thousands more on a shopping spree for new clothing than I would shell out for a few hours of fun with some casino chips.

Waging money to score big wasn't even in my consciousness. Bob liked to gamble occasionally and would play what I considered large amounts of money, but this was of no consequence to me. He had worked hard and been successful in business. He generously shared his wealth with family members (both his and mine), friends, and strangers. With a good deal of discretionary income available and without placing anything but the money in his pocket at risk, I considered Bob's gambling to be a pleasurable, yet innocent diversion from the demands of his work life. Not something that would increase our wealth. I was never holding out for a "big win" in the future. Gambling is not the same as investing in reputable income streams. I understood financial wealth was the result of hard work, not a happenstance of gambling.

In fact, having seen the devastating effects of gambling, I was predisposed not to support it. Many Saturdays my father would go out gambling and drinking, which resulted in terrible fights between my parents upon his return. Then his gambling escalated to weeknights and after playing golf, he would go out gambling and drinking. My uncle, who had five children, would gamble so much at Beulah Park Racetrack my aunt had no choice but to garnish the wages he earned at General Motors so the family would have enough money for groceries and rent.

Too many people refer to a gambling addiction as if the person is suffering with a cold. It's very nonchalant. They don't realize what that means to the people who become victims. In part, this is because victims often feel too ashamed to share their stories, or are too belligerent to cooperate with authorities.

People would never be so casual with the term sex offender. That term implies evil darkness and contains within itself the warning to stay away, be cautious, and protect those who may not be aware. We place faces on offender websites and legislate where convicts can and cannot live. The person must be watched. The community must be warned.

But a gambling addict? Come on! Gambling is fun and enjoyable, harmless, in fact. Voters pass legislation to legalize betting. Tour companies schedule trips to casinos and offer special incentives to reserve a seat. Casinos are bright, happy, busy places. We plan vacations to the Kentucky Derby to see and be seen while we wager on the ponies. Houses of worship depend on games of chance to fund social programs. So what if you lose a couple hundred—or couple thousand—betting on actual or fantasy games over the weekend? It's a victimless crime. No need to warn. In fact, offering caution about the evils of gambling can land one on the receiving side of scorn and mockery.

The truth is, if we want fewer victims of compulsive gambling, our opinion of gambling must change!

At one point, Art told me he was *sick of this sh***. But the truth is that Art created his own life. And as I talked with Art, many times pleading for money simply to keep my electricity on, he rarely expressed remorse about my situation. He was always the one who felt inconvenienced. He was annoyed because someone had called *him* about *their* money, or *I* didn't get a check to him fast enough, or *I* didn't answer the phone every single time he called. But it wasn't just his treatment of me that was bewildering; he had a sense of entitlement about everything. I was incredulous when he was adamant that a victim of his should enthusiastically express appreciation to *him* for *his* efforts to repay the $60,000 she had loaned him.

My reputation of generously loaning money to people that was never repaid, paying for college, buying homes, and hosting vacations, was destroyed by helping a gambling addict who was able to turn his craziness into my destruction. Toward the end, Art told me that no one has ever helped him as much as I had.

But had I really *helped* him? Or had I simply helped him feed his addiction?

23 | THE FEDS SHOW UP

JANUARY—MAY 2010

"It's rare we are able to get to a potential victim in advance of a crime taking place, which is what happened with Anita. The story with her son, she told us that. In her mind, Art saved her son's life. It blinded her."	*Terrence Brown* *Special Agent* *U.S. Treasury*

With Christmas behind us, Alan and I traveled on a charter plane filled with OSU fans who had purchased event packages to Pasadena, California to attend the Rose Bowl. On New Year's Eve, the night before game day, we were enjoying the company of fellow Buckeye fans when someone asked Alan what he recalled about the airplane crash from his childhood. While Alan doesn't remember many specific details, he said, "I remember my mom always being there for me." No doubt the guys sitting at the table that evening were anticipating hearing about being stranded in the midst of debris or airlifted out of the forest, but Alan chose to honor me. I wiped away tears as his unexpected answer caught me by surprise.

The following day we cheered as the Buckeyes defeated the Oregon Ducks 26 to 17. Alan and I enjoyed a wonderful couple of days in the California sun and we brought happy memories back with us to Ohio. As I dropped Alan off at his house, he gave me a big hug and kiss and said, "Mom, this trip was one of the best times of my life. Thank you." His previous disapproval and our subsequent argument over my "extravagant" bid to win the trip (and support cancer research) were forgotten.

As soon as I returned to Columbus, Art requested additional money for his associates. Because he was making small payments to me on the original $10,000 loan I had given him, I agreed to help him. He had provided me a cell phone to use exclusively for us to communicate. He was worried about people—primarily thugs to whom he owed money—being able to record his conversations or track his movements with a regular cell phone, so he used prepaid cell phones and frequently switched them out. Not wanting to reveal his whereabouts or place him in jeopardy, and because I knew Sue Paveleski and Bill Hanners carried disposable phones for Art, I agreed to carry a TracFone.

Between January 4 and January 11, I wrote checks and initiated wire transfers to Chip Green of Best Seat Tickets and other associates of Art's totaling $81,000.

By the middle of the month I was weary of the cold weather in Central Ohio and I packed my bags, loaded up the Escalade, and headed to my condo in Florida. I caught up with my friends and in no time we were back in our routine of shopping and movies and dinners out.

Of course, I told my friends about Art. They were curious and wanted to know if he was my boyfriend. For goodness sake—he was younger than my daughter by a few months. But the fact that my friends thought a younger man might be interested in me gave me all the motivation I needed to play up my new "boy toy." We laughed and joked and made silly comparisons like we were schoolgirls at a slumber party. I fueled their speculation with half-truths and eye rolls and allowed them to think I was keeping secrets. From my perspective (and knowing the truth), it was all in good fun until Angela received a call asking about her *mom's new boyfriend*. And when she learned this new man in her mom's life was Art Schlichter, she contacted Alan right away.

On Thursday, January 21, I received a frantic call from Art. He told me a woman from Washington Court House was going to the police to file charges against him if he didn't pay her $8,000 by the end of the day. "Anita, you need to help me or I'm going to jail. And if I'm in jail, I won't be able to repay the money you've loaned me." I was panicked. I couldn't let him go to jail, but I explained that I didn't have any cash on hand. What could I do? There was only a second of hesitation before he offered, "You have jewelry with you, right? You could pawn it." And before the absurdity of his plan could even register with me, he said, "You'll get the money back in a few days. I promise. If you get me the money today, I'll repay it before the end of the month."

Bob had enjoyed giving me fine jewelry and most all of the pieces I had with me were from him. In fact, he had given me six pieces that were insured in total for more than $92,000. I loved his gifts because they were an expression of his love, but I enjoyed wearing costume jewelry as much as the real stuff, and would often purchase knock-offs at the Swap Shop for less than $100. Bob was annoyed that I preferred to wear the fun stuff and only permitted it if I promised not to tell anyone I was wearing cubic zirconia.

I had never stepped inside a pawnshop, but I knew there was one we drove by frequently in Jupiter. With a heavy heart I stuffed multiple jewelry pouches into my purse and drove to Prestige Pawn on West Indian Town Road. The man who greeted me as I entered was nice enough but I'm sure he could sense my nervousness. I explained how I had never pawned anything before, but I had a friend who was desperate and needed $8,000 immediately. I placed the jewelry on the counter and he got to work inspecting and placing a value on each piece. In the end, he selected sixteen different items including necklaces, bracelets, rings, and a watch to hold as collateral against an $8,000 loan at an annual interest rate of 243.33%. I would need $9,600 to redeem my jewelry by February 20 or $11,200 to redeem it by March 22. Instead, I began making monthly payments of $1,600. Toward the end of that year with no money in my accounts and the fear of losing my jewelry a constant threat, I would begin begging Art for the money to make the monthly payment. My final payment of $1,600 on December 27, 2010 wasn't enough to cover the debt and in the end, I lost it all.

With an $8,000 check in hand I called Art. Because he needed the money immediately, he instructed me to send the funds via Western Union. I had seen one of their kiosks at the local Publix, so I drove there and initiated the transfer. With the crisis averted, I returned home satisfied that I had been able to help Art but unsettled by the day's events. Art began calling on a daily basis, often multiple times a day. Sometimes just to chat and see what I was doing, other times to ask me to transfer money to someone's account or authorize my bank to release funds for Bill Hanners to retrieve at a Columbus location.

***

One day while I was driving down the street, I noticed a car behind me. I saw it stay with me as I made several turns and felt uneasy as I continued to watch it follow me. I made my way back to my condo and the driver pulled the car right behind mine. My heart was beating fast before I recognized Alan through the windshield. I was shocked and couldn't imagine why he was in Florida. "Alan! What on earth are you doing?" I nearly shouted. He explained he had become suspicious of my association with Art when Angela, friends, and family members heard I was loaning him money. As we entered the condo, Alan said he had gone to my home in Dublin, found and looked through my financial statements searching for answers. Desperate for information, he had even called my banks and financial planner. But because Alan was not listed as an account holder, no one would divulge details regarding my account activity. With his anxiety rising and every door closed to him, he had flown to Florida to confront me in person.

I was displeased at Alan's meddling into my affairs but attempted to calm his fears by explaining that I had indeed made a short-term loan to Art that would be repaid when the proceeds from his book were released at the end of the month. Even with the loan, I still had plenty of money, and I was in control of my finances. I appreciated his concern, but there was no need to worry. Satisfied things were OK, but still apprehensive, he reluctantly returned to Ohio.

By the end of January, Art had not said anything about his publisher releasing the book funds or the $100,000 he owed me. I mentioned it in passing and he said the payment had been delayed. I wasn't to worry; he was good for the money.

By early February, I was tired of Florida and ready to return to Ohio. When I heard the Endeavor Space Shuttle was making its final "evening launch" on February 8 at 4:14 a.m., I closed up my condo, packed my car, and drove up the coast to witness history. On my way out of the parking lot after the launch, I became disoriented at the unfamiliar route and stopped at a rest area to check a map. Fortunately, I met a young couple heading toward Reynoldsburg, Ohio, and they invited me to follow them for a while. Once I got my bearings, it was a straight shot north to Columbus.

I returned to Florida a few weeks later with Joy Blanco and Camilla Cox to attend the Buckeye Cruise for Cancer. Art, in a useless attempt to court me, sent a dozen red roses to the condo. Fearing the flowers would be dead before we returned from the cruise, I gave them to a neighbor. Joy, Camilla, and I enjoyed ourselves on the ship hobnobbing with OSU elite and celebrating in Key West and Mexico. Mindful of recent cash outlays for Art, I was conservative with my purchases but did go home with a cedar chest handmade by a cancer victim for $400. On March 1 we docked in Tampa.

There were two separate occasions while I was in Florida when Art had me meet with Sue and Boris Paveleski. One time they were traveling to Florida on vacation and Art instructed me to pick them up at the airport and transport them to a hotel. Oh, and while I was at it, I was to give them $30,000. Another time, I was supposed to meet Boris and Sue at a certain location to give them money but I was having difficulty finding the meeting place. I phoned Art and let him know I was on the Interstate but I was lost. He asked for the mile marker and when I relayed it, he hung up. A few minutes later the phone rang and Art told me to pull over to the side of the road. I didn't understand what was going on, but did as he said and turned on my hazard lights. Before long, a vehicle slowly pulled up behind me. Sue and Boris got out of the car and, after some small talk, we exchanged money right there on the side of the road.

During February, Art had me write checks or process wire transfers to his associates—including a realty company in Indiana, a moving company in Florida, and Best Seat Tickets—totaling $112,604. He assured me he would be able to repay my loans within a few weeks.

In March Jeff Snook, who co-wrote Art's book, *Busted*, was celebrating his fiftieth birthday. Art had received an invitation to the party and invited me to attend with him. Because the celebration was taking place at Jeff's home in nearby West Palm, I agreed. However, Art never spoke of the invitation again and if he ever traveled to Florida, he didn't tell me. Although Art was calling me multiple times a day with stories and threats and directives, I never saw him while I was in Florida.

At one point, and almost casually during one of his calls, Art asked what I would be willing to do for a million dollars. I was taken aback with his tone and what the question implied. Of course, I didn't have an answer. In the ensuing silence, he said in a serious tone, "Well, I would s**k a dog's d**k for a million dollars." His answer was so vulgar I was deeply offended. He didn't laugh; it wasn't a joke. I had no idea the depths Art would travel to obtain cash, but he had previously gambled away his family, his friends, his freedom, and his future. There is little doubt he would sell his soul for whatever he wanted.

Meanwhile, my Florida friends were becoming suspicious of Art and worried about my relationship with him. Several of them contacted Angela again to discuss the situation. I could tell Angela was upset with me as soon as I picked up the phone. She wanted answers and explanations. I gave her promises and reassurances. She wouldn't be silenced. Believing I was a victim of an ongoing financial scam, she placed a call to the Ohio Attorney General's office to ask for assistance. Because she was not listed as an account holder on any my accounts, she learned the only course of action would be to have me declared legally incompetent—which is a rather lengthy process—before she could be named as my administrator and oversee all of my decisions. Angela didn't believe I was incompetent, but she felt that Art was involved in suspicious behavior and swindling me. Without any proof of financial impropriety, frustrated by not finding a meaningful solution to thwart Art's schemes, and without my cooperation, she was forced to let the matter drop.

During March, Art instructed me to write five checks or wire transfers, which totaled $81,100. One single transaction for $50,600 was to Best Seat Tickets. I lent him this money reluctantly. I was feeling unsettled by Angela's inquiries and Art's behavior.

One of the last times I was in Florida with my friends, we were sitting in Classico's Italian Restaurant in Juno Beach discussing our plans for the summer. I mentioned that Lizzie Mulligan and I were going to Mexico on vacation. I also had a trip planned to Dubai, and had joined a mission group traveling to Thailand to help women enslaved by prostitution. My friends roared in laughter at the thought of me doing missionary work in a developing country. I was annoyed by their skepticism. I was sincerely committed to helping others—and not just Art—with my time and resources. After all, wasn't that what life was really about?

My cousins Carol Jean, Susie, and Sharon, and my Aunt Lil came down to Florida for a few days and then accompanied me to Ohio. Before we left, Art had demanded I withdraw cash as he was going to have me make a delivery on my way home. We were driving two cars and Sharon volunteered to ride with me. On the return trip Art kept calling and asking where I was. *Give me your mile marker. OK, I'll call you back.* Evidently he was coordinating with a third party because as we approached an exit in Ohio with a sign indicating a McDonald's, he told me to pull in. I did and made an excuse for the stop, encouraging my family in the other vehicle to continue without me. While Sharon went into the restaurant, Henry Garcia approached me and I handed over the cash as Art had instructed. There was simply no escaping Art; he was stalking me. He was constantly contacting me and keeping tabs on my whereabouts at all times.

In April, Art convinced me to write sixteen checks or initiate wire transfers, totaling $235,000. The disbursements included $42,000 to Charles Grubb, $25,000 to the moving company in Florida, and $49,000 to Cash. When I attempted to deny his requests for money, Art explained he would be unable to pay back any of my previous loans unless I funded these new requests. He had backed me into a corner.

By April, Art had begun threatening to disappear with all my money if I was reluctant to accommodate his requests. He initially threw out the idea as a joke accompanied by a little chuckle. *Hey, honey, if you don't write this check for me, I could just disappear and then you'll never get your money back.* I felt uncomfortable when he said that, but I didn't believe him. Besides, he was repaying the money he had borrowed from me, albeit very slowly. I had faith everything would work out as long as I did as I was told. I just had to be patient.

When Art's fiftieth birthday arrived on April 25, I was worried about him spending the day alone, so I called and left a message for him in the morning. When I didn't hear back, I called again. And again. And again. All throughout the day I called and left messages for him. *Had he been serious about leaving town? Would the money ever be returned to me?* By evening, I was calling and leaving messages non-stop. I was irrational and desperate. Finally, Art left a nasty voicemail calling me all sorts of names. He said he was celebrating with his mom and daughters and I had ruined his day. I didn't believe his story. When I finally got in touch with him the next day I apologized and said I was just worried about him spending the day alone. I never mentioned the money or my fear of his leaving town.

A few hours after my apology for ruining his birthday, Art called me. I could hear voices and loudspeaker announcements in the background, and he sounded panicked. He explained he and his ex-wife were at the airport taking their daughter to a drug treatment facility. They had just been informed that insurance was not going to cover the cost of treatment and the facility would not admit her without advance payment. *Can you help? We're desperate! My daughter's future depends on this program.*

Of course I would help. I was willing to do whatever he needed for his daughter! He quickly gave me his account information before we disconnected. I immediately drove to the Chase bank branch on Perimeter Drive and wired $24,000 from my checking account to his bank in Indiana. A week or so later when I inquired about his daughter, he brushed off my question like he didn't know what I was talking about.

At the end of April, Art mentioned he was going to work at the Kentucky Derby the following Saturday, and anticipated making a lot of money. He didn't specifically say what he would be doing, but assured me he wasn't betting. Confident of a paycheck, Art instructed me to meet him at 9:00 a.m. the Monday after the derby in Washington Court House; he said he would be able to pay back a significant portion of the money he had borrowed. I was overjoyed at this turn of events! Finally, I would be able to replenish some of my accounts. During the sixty-minute drive to Washington Court House on Monday morning I could barely contain my excitement. However, when I pulled in the driveway at his mom's house, he walked out to my car and told me that at the last minute the money hadn't come in. "Oh, Art!" I couldn't hide my disappointment. He quickly assured me he was working on something else and he would have some money for me very soon. I was so angry I couldn't stop crying as I returned to Columbus empty-handed.

***

Sometime in the spring Art told me that "The Feds" had talked to Chip Greene of Best Seat Tickets as part of an ongoing investigation into Art's activities. During the meeting, Chip had provided my name as someone who was helping Art.

With the Feds poking around, Art became even more suspicious of everyone and everything. He told me to expect my own visit from the authorities. "Why?" I asked. "I've not done anything wrong. Why do they need to talk with me?" He was convinced the authorities had a chip on their shoulder and were trying to find something—anything—that would violate his probation and send him back to prison in Indiana to finish out his sentence. "Why," I wondered, "would the Feds care what you are doing, or what I am doing with my money? We're not doing anything wrong."

"They have it in for me! They want to see me back in jail!" he would say time and again. The idea that federal agents wanted to speak with me did raise some red flags, and I wondered what in the world I had gotten myself into. I suddenly felt cautious. Because Art had most of my bank account numbers, I thought it would be a good idea, although I didn't know why, to update all my accounts with new numbers.

In May, I received a call from Special Agent Terrence Brown with the U.S. Treasury Department in Cincinnati asking to schedule a time to come to my home and talk with me. He was very cordial on the phone, and we set a date and time for the following week. Still not understanding why the authorities thought they needed to meet with me, and confident neither Art nor I were doing anything wrong, I told Art about the appointment. He was immediately concerned. I told him not to worry. I was gathering together and organizing all my receipts and records and planned to present the documents as proof that everything we were doing was legitimate.

Art became agitated and asked if we could meet within the next few days. I agreed and before leaving the house to meet him, I grabbed the tote with all the information I had assembled and placed it in my car. There were check registers, copies of checks and payments, receipts, Art's signed promissory note from January, and a record of every transaction involving Art and his associates. I certainly didn't want that information sitting around in the event Alan came by looking for "evidence" of something, and I thought by showing these items to Art it would put his mind at ease. When I pulled up to the meeting location, Art jumped in my car. We started talking and before long he was coaching me on how to deal with the authorities.

What are you going to say if they ask about you and me? What are you going to say about all the cash transfers? His quizzing went on for a while before he spied the tote in the back seat. "What's that?" he asked as he reached for the container, pulled it to the front seat, and began looking through it. "You *can't* show the Feds this stuff," he exclaimed. "They will misinterpret it and twist it around and use it to prove I'm guilty of something, and probably that you're guilty, too! I'd better take it and hold onto it until after your appointment."

"Are you sure?" I asked. How could proof of innocence be used by authorities as proof of a crime? Everything was all turned around and nothing was making sense. However, certain that Art knew what was in my best interest, I let him take the tote. How would I know what I should do? I'd never had to deal with the Feds, and I could tell Art was nervous about their visit. When I pressed him about it, he explained it was because he still owed people for ticket money from his past and things were coming back to haunt him.

Regrettably, I didn't know what was going on, but Art knew exactly what he was doing. He realized the records I had collected would incriminate him and probably be enough to revoke his probation and send him back to prison where he belonged. Instead, he never returned that tote or the information it contained. Months later, Detective Davis said he wouldn't be surprised if Art had destroyed everything.

As scheduled, Terrence Brown, accompanied by Robert Murchland, Law Enforcement Liaison with the United States Attorney's Office, interviewed me at my condo in Dublin. I wasn't nervous to meet with them; why should I be? I hadn't done anything wrong. They shared that they thought I was being victimized by Art or, at the very least, was on the verge of being exploited. I shared Alan's story and how Art had literally saved his life.

Some of their questions seemed odd to me, but I had never been interrogated before so I wasn't sure what to expect. *Is Art taking money from you? Is he stealing from you? Is he threatening you?*

I answered truthfully and assured them I was acting reasonably and on my own. Art was not coercing me. In fact, he was working with his attorney, John Amery, to repay me. I still had money. I wasn't worried about my utilities. I was paying my own bills. My life was normal with the exception that I was financially supporting Art. I mentioned that Sue and Boris Paveleski had also helped Art recently with a $4,000 loan. Special Agent Brown asked how they could afford to do that. I didn't have any idea.

The agents provided information regarding their investigation and what they knew about other victims. Nothing they said could persuade me that my situation was serious or something other than the way I had interpreted it. Before they left, Special Agent Brown handed me his business card. The meeting lasted about an hour. The men were friendly enough, but all business.

Later, Special Agent Brown would say I was too naïve to understand what Art was doing. "It's rare we are able to get to a potential victim in advance of a crime taking place, which is what happened with Anita. The story with her son, she told us that. In her mind, Art saved her son's life. It blinded her."

Art was extremely anxious the day of my interview with the Federal Agents and, depending on the outcome, was prepared to flee. He was especially concerned that I might be arrested, which he interpreted as a signal that he would be next. I was supposed to call Art immediately after the agents left and tell him what happened. Unbeknownst to me, Art had instructed Sue and Boris to watch my condo and report any activity—including when the agents arrived and departed. Each time Art called them for an update, there was no information to report. Nothing was going on. No one had arrived or departed. With his imagination getting the best of him, Art was already in the car heading out of town when I reached him. He was panicked at first but calmed down once I filled him in on the details. We subsequently learned that Art's "crackerjack" surveillance team had been watching the wrong condo.

At one point, Art told me Sue and Boris were summoned to an interview at the Federal Courthouse in Columbus regarding their dealings with him. After their appointment, we all met up in the parking lot of what appeared to be an empty hotel in Mount Sterling. Art pulled up in the same blue Dodge Durango he was driving when we first met. *Hey, what had he done with the first loan I gave him to purchase a new vehicle so he could re-establish a relationship with his children?* (I never asked him.) Sue said that during the course of their meeting she told the authorities that there weren't many people like Anita Barney who were willing to help others. I was flattered by her comment.

Shortly after my meeting with the Feds, Art said he could purchase extra 2010-2011 OSU football tickets and wondered if any of my friends might be interested. *We're talking season tickets at face value, with parking if they want it. It's all legit. I'm working with my friend Mark in the OSU ticket office.* I was a bit skeptical at getting my friends involved. Art told me that he regularly sold "a lot" of tickets to a guy in Chicago. To prove it, he had the man call me and confirm that he had been doing business with Art for a while and was quite satisfied. Art also mentioned there was a company in Cleveland who sold tickets on his behalf. To further bolster his claim, he called them one day and let me listen in as he inquired about the balance in his account, which was substantial.

With my concern alleviated, and recalling the wonderful times I had enjoyed with Bob tailgating and attending home football games, and knowing the difficulty of obtaining season tickets, I enthusiastically began calling my friends. Art cautioned me not to mention he was my source, as people may be reluctant to take advantage of the deal. Most everyone I contacted was eager to pay the $2,240 per package of four season tickets (seventy dollars each for eight home games), and some even paid an additional $500 for a parking pass. Within a few weeks twenty-three of my friends and neighbors purchased a combined twenty-nine packages and I collected just over $65,000, which I transferred to Art for delivery of tickets in the fall. Over time several people changed their mind and requested a refund instead of tickets, and Art returned their money.

The fifteen checks and wire transfers Art had me prepare in May totaled $166,700 including multiple checks to individuals not known to me: $34,000 to the Indiana Realtor, $10,000 to a trucking company, and $10,000 to his attorney's office. Now that my encounter with the Feds had ended without incident, Art began intimidating me if I showed any hesitation in complying with his demands. He threatened that if I didn't continue loaning him money, he would leave town and I would never see him or my money again. Out of options and filled with fear, I did whatever he requested.

Looking back over the lists of checks that the police reconstructed during their investigation of Art, I find it interesting how many names reappear month after month, as well as how many different people Art became involved with in one way or another. Even after knowing his past history, people were willing to "go into business" with a convicted criminal and give him one more chance to make them money on their investment.

As I continued to hear about federal authorities systematically contacting Art's associates without any charges forthcoming, his claim that they "had it in for him" appeared justified and I felt I had been caught up in a witch hunt. We couldn't know it at the time, but the investigation continued to grind away behind the scenes. Witnesses were interviewed and information was gathered as authorities followed the money . . . and it eventually lead them right back to Art.

24 | FROM BAD TO WORSE

JUNE—DECEMBER 2010

"Art trained Anita to be his tool of deception. She couldn't act, didn't know what to say without him."	*Detective associated with the Art Schlichter investigation*

In June Art mentioned that he knew a person in the Colts Ticket Department, and he would be able to purchase 2011 Super Bowl Tickets. *Do you know anyone who might be interested?* Initially he told me the cost would be $1,400 per ticket, but quickly dropped the price to $1,100 per ticket for seats in the lower level, outside of the end zones. This was the opportunity I had been waiting for—a chance to earn back all the money I had loaned to Art.

In no time, I was on the phone calling friends to give them a chance to purchase tickets to the biggest football game of the year. I collected $19,800 for eighteen tickets. My neighbor Perry Shasteen purchased six tickets for his family to go to the game. Floyd Rogers, son-in-law of my friends Lew and Annabelle Sanchez, purchased ten tickets for $11,000. As I was recording these transactions in my notebook, thoughts about the federal investigation flooded my mind and I realized Art was my only contact—the trail ended with him. As I handed him the money I asked what I should do if something happened to him. "I mean, I don't have any details on who I would contact to get the tickets if you were unable to follow through for some reason." He brushed off my concern. "Just call Bill Hanners. He will take care of things on this end and be able to get you the tickets or whatever you need." I called Bill later that day and relayed the message that he was my "go-to guy" in the event Art wasn't around. Bill seemed a little surprised by my announcement but assured me he would be able to figure things out, if it came to that. Within the hour, Art called me, asked why I was calling Bill, and told me to knock it off. "Don't call Bill!" he snarled through the phone.

Occasionally, Art would ask to use my Escalade for a few days. I always said no. I didn't know what he was going to do or whom he was going to meet. Art had told me that some of his past associates were involved in criminal activity. Was he going to commit a crime? I just didn't trust him with my car. Other times he would say, "Why don't we go out and get you a new Cadillac? Then I can take your old one off your hands." *Did he think I was stupid?* "That's a dumb idea," I would retort. "Then I would have a car payment. No, thank you. I'll keep my car."

In June Art made me write checks totaling $46,000. Douglas DeLarge received $25,000 and Buster Jurik the remaining $21,000. Art explained these loans would be repaid with money we earned from the sale of Super Bowl tickets.

During the summer things with Art went downhill quickly. The nice guy I wanted to help earlier in the year transformed into an unpredictable monster. He was becoming angry and unstable and I became tense and afraid from his constant pressure. When I would inquire about repaying my friends or giving me funds to pay my bills, he would threaten to leave town with all the money: *Ask me about the money one more time and I'll disappear and you'll never get the money!* On especially stressful days when I would make demands for cash and answers, he would scream at me and call me every vulgar name you can imagine, telling me I was so stupid and I didn't understand. That I was going to ruin EVERYTHING! With so much at stake I would retreat and become a submissive mouse again. I had nothing—literally nothing—but

Art's promise to make things right and I couldn't risk everything by driving him away.

At the end of my rope, I placed a call to Father Lavelle, the priest who had led me to a Catholic conversion and conducted my Marriage Mass to Marcel so many years ago. By this time, Father Lavelle had retired but had access to an office at St. Paul's in Westerville, and this is where we met. As I drove to meet him that day, I was an empty, broken woman. How would I even begin to describe what had happened since the beginning of the year? It was unbelievable, even to me.

When I entered the office, I was overcome with emotion at seeing my dear friend. His kind greeting and warm embrace overwhelmed me; it had been ages since I had felt any measure of safety from the raging storms Art had conjured, and for which I felt powerless to escape. Father Lavelle's office offered a respite from the prying eyes and the threats and interrogations and before we were situated comfortably in our chairs, I was pouring out my heart to him.

I explained everything: my desire to help, the mess I had made, and how I had disappointed my friends and family. Between sobs, he heard about my shame and regret, my fear and humiliation. How I had lost my way and in the process, lost everything. *Everything!*

Before our session concluded, Father Lavelle offered to be my prayer warrior. I met with him a few times after our initial session, but mostly we would talk on the phone in the evening when the growing shadows of nightfall ushered in fear and apprehension like a heavy blanket. We discussed many things during those chats and he always encouraged me to "Hold on! Easter is coming."

I started attending Mass most every morning at St. Brendan on Dublin Road near my home and, between calls from Art, spent time in prayer. I was desperately seeking God and His direction for my situation. Quiet time in the church and conversations with the pastor, Father Rod, became my lifeline, a reprieve from my assailant. And even though Art knew about my new routine, when I returned to the car from the church and turned on my phone, I would find he had left three or four urgent messages and I could feel myself withering under the intensity of his torment.

Where are you? Where have you been? Who are you with? Why aren't you answering the phone? We have fires to put out today! CALL ME! IMMEDIATELY!

And just like that, the insanity that had become my life was off and running for another day.

Art called one day and told me if he could gather some money, he could invest in a short-term loan that would yield high interest in a matter of days. *Do you think any of your friends would like to make some quick money? The more we invest at one time, the higher the yield. I doubt most of your friends would be able to meet the minimum threshold to invest at this level on their own; this would be a great opportunity for them!*

At first I was excited at the prospect of helping my friends earn a little money for their trouble. But when Art said to meet him at Lee Garden restaurant off Sawmill Road and things quickly became complicated, I wanted to back out. *Here's what we really need to do, you'll ask your friends for a short-term loan, because we'll need to invest it in your name. And then you will pay them back with interest. But don't let them know that I'm involved or it will spook them and they'll miss out.* When I asked why on earth I would "need" to borrow money from my friends, Art said I should say my money was tied up, maybe in an off-shore account, and by the time funds would be released the window of opportunity will have closed.

"That's ridiculous!" I exclaimed. "I don't have any offshore accounts." With a gleam in his eye he said, "Sure you do. You've already invested with me and I've tied up your money in foreign accounts." An alternate story he concocted for me to tell was I had an immediate opportunity to purchase a large number of OSU tickets that I could sell for profit. I was supposed to say, *I had ordered money from my UBS account and it typically takes three to five days to transfer, but I needed money before that.* Art was able to take a bit of one story and add in a portion of another and by the end there were so many stories running around I couldn't keep track of what he told me.

"No! I don't want to do this!" I pleaded. Art began flipping through my address book, came upon a name, grabbed my personal phone, and dialed the number. I heard the ringing from the speaker as he handed it back to me in time for me to hear a female voice on the other end of the line say, "Hello?" I couldn't just hang up. As I looked bewildered at Art, he grinned and pointed to the name in my book, Tina Lewis, the wife of one of Bob's associates from Wendy's. How embarrassing! I hadn't spoken to Tina in quite some time and for me to be calling her under these circumstances and asking for a loan was ridiculous. After brief small talk I started in on the spiel Art had cooked up. Tina interrupted me. "The answer is no. What do you think I am, a bank?" I was shaking in humiliation as the call disconnected. I turned to Art, "I'm not making any more calls."

"Well, you were terrible!" he yelled. "You need to practice a little and you'll get the hang of it." I protested and he became angry. The more I resisted, the louder and more vulgar he became. In no time he was throwing papers and I was rattled as he embarrassed me in a public place. "OK, calm down," I said keeping my eyes on the table in front of me. "I'll try again."

As he wrote out a script for me to read, he kept saying reassuring things and convincing me this was a really good deal for my friends. I wanted nothing more than for my friends to earn some "easy money." Most of them were good people, really hard workers who had earnestly saved for what they wanted. I would be thrilled if I could relieve a little of their financial burden. I read over the paper he had written and before I looked up he had dialed another number and handed me the phone. Not sure who was on the other end of the line I stumbled over my words, but eventually got back on track and read the script. The caller said no. Art was furious. "It sounded like you were reading. D**n it! You CAN'T just read the f**king thing. You have to act like you really mean it!"

I was near tears. I was never the one to ask for money. Bob and I had always been the ones to *give* money when others needed it. I was uncomfortable being on this end of things. I didn't like it, not one bit! "No, I'm not going to do it."

"It's up to you, but your friends are the ones who will be losing out. What kind of a friend are you anyway, keeping something like this to yourself? Are you selfish?"

I remembered Bob had shared investment opportunities with his associates and from what I heard, everyone had profited. And I really did want to help my friends. How had things become so complicated? I didn't know what to do. Art pointed to the paper in my hands. "Let's practice once or twice so you feel better about it," he suggested gently. Even after our impromptu rehearsal, I was steadfast. I wouldn't call my friends. Art simply dialed numbers and handed me the phone. Too embarrassed to hang up when people were already on the line and would have recognized my name from their Caller ID, I worked through the script and tried my best to sound believable.

After Art was satisfied that I was performing to his expectation, he began making lists of people we would call. Eager to ensure I was following his direction, working from the script and sounding believable, he would instruct me to meet him in a restaurant or a quiet corner of a parking lot and dial numbers repeatedly, handing me the phone as soon as he heard a voice on the other end of the line. Occasionally, he wasn't in town and harassed me to make calls when I was alone. I hated asking people for loans. Along with the short-term high-return loan story, he would terrorize me with other reasons to make the calls: *If I don't get money, people will kill me and you won't get any money. Thugs in Toledo beat me up and broke my ribs; I need money to pay them what I owe. If you don't make these calls, I'll disappear and you'll never get your money. If you ever turn me in, know that I can't make money from jail and it will be all over.*

In the end, the following individuals had loaned me money with the expectation of a return of their investment with varying amounts of interest.

My good friends Roland and Judy Nesbitt jumped at the chance to make some healthy returns in exchange for a short-term loan. In June, Roland withdrew $90,000. I provided him with three personal checks in the amounts of $6,000, $12,000, and

$50,000, and a promissory note for the remaining balance of $22,000.

Cruz Hill, our beloved personal trainer who worked with Bob and me at "The Big House," provided me with two loans of $15,000 each in July.

Farley Daft, my old friend who had asked me out, loaned me $20,000 in August to buy tickets with a promise of $10,000 interest.

Betty Gabor, the mother of my long-time housekeeper Sabrina, loaned me $10,000.

Friends Lew and Annabelle Sanchez, who had vacationed with us and stayed in our condo in Florida, loaned me $50,000 with an expectation of $10,000 interest.

Friend and business owner Rod Cheetham gave me $30,000.

Long-time friend and entrepreneur Hugh Buttke loaned me $28,000 to buy tickets.

Jessie Muse, a singer who had entertained at so many of my parties, gave me $10,000 in exchange for a promise of $2,000 in interest.

One of my dearest friends, Joy Blanco, invested $31,000 and in return was to earn $5,000 interest. (Bob had once provided financial support when Martin and Joy's restaurant was struggling.) My good friend Lizzie Mulligan loaned me $25,000. Both Joy and Lizzie attended the Buckeye Cruise for Cancer with me. We had shared many happy memories over the years.

A former schoolteacher, Eric Turner, loaned me $10,000 and was promised he would earn $5,000 interest.

Harris Jackson, one of my favorite guys who was always working in the maintenance garage at Rolling Meadows Golf Course on one project or another, gave me $14,000 to purchase tickets and Art promised I would be able to pay him $4,000 interest.

Lew Sanchez started working for us when we opened Rolling Meadows. Lew and his wife Annabelle, and Bob and I had become friends and they would often join us in Florida and stay in our home. They were invited to all of our parties. Lew loaned me $39,000 when I presented an opportunity to purchase OSU tickets and earn $10,000 interest. Later, his wife Annabelle also loaned me some money, but she didn't tell her husband right away. Annabelle and I went together to the Chase bank at Kingsdale Shopping Center. I knew Art was watching from the adjoining Macy's parking lot. Annabelle was taking forever in the bank and I became a nervous wreck. I was seconds away from going in to see if there was a problem when she exited with $10,000.

In total there were more than twenty-five people who gave me money for tickets—either for themselves or as an investment—and as personal loans. Everyone I contacted was identified and mandated by Art, and my requests of them were a result of coercion or threats. All the money I collected was transferred immediately to Art. Although my accounts were dwindling, I never kept a dime of anything I collected for myself.

Art didn't make me write any checks in July, but in August he had me write four checks totaling $55,000. Art's attorney received $10,000 and the additional funds went to an individual I did not know. When I resisted his demands, Art posed a frightening scenario. If I didn't loan him money this time, he would never be able to repay my previous loans. Without any money, he wondered aloud how I would be able to take care of my family. "You will become an embarrassment to them and they will disown you."

Art's icy tone reached through the phone and I could feel my blood turn cold. In a heartbeat, my childhood fear of being abandoned consumed me and my will to fight was destroyed. Driven by a deep-rooted anxiety I could not control, I was unable to resist Art's commands.

By the time Art called another friend, Richard Head, and handed me the phone, I was exhausted by the process of asking for loans. Art, sensing blood in the water, amped up his demands as if it were even possible to take *more* advantage of me. As I was talking with Richard on the phone, Art was sitting right beside me feeding me the script about buying OSU tickets and selling them for a profit that Richard and I would share. I knew Richard when he worked at Wendy's. Richard and his wife Mara would visit us in Florida, and we would visit them in Bonita Springs. Even after

Richard's departure from Wendy's, he and Bob had remained friends.

Art convinced me he needed the money immediately or he was headed to jail. "Then, you won't get any of your money, will you? Besides, I told you when the money will be coming in. You're not going to lose anything." In late August, Richard agreed to loan me $20,000, however, he required collateral before he would release the funds.

Art rode with me to the LeVeque Tower downtown where Richard's attorney, Jude Gallipoli, had an office. Art planned to wait in the lobby while I went up to sign the papers. As I turned toward the elevators, he threatened, "If you don't come back with the paperwork, I'm gone!" In the few minutes it took to arrive at the 25th floor, fear overtook me and I began crying and couldn't stop. In the office, I emptied the tissue box waiting for Jude and he grabbed another one for me as he entered the conference room. As the process dragged on, I became anxious thinking of Art impatiently waiting for me downstairs. I signed over my two cars— the Saturn Sky and the Cadillac Escalade—as collateral, while my tears fell on the paperwork. Jude gave me copies of the contract. When I met up with Art downstairs, he was furious. *What had taken so long? Let me see the documents!*

Later I met Richard, as we agreed, at the McDonald's on Bridge Street in Dublin. "Why don't we go in and get a cup of coffee?" he asked. Knowing Art was sitting across the parking lot watching me, I said, "I'd love to, but I can't." Richard wrote me a check for $20,000 and as I watched him drive away, I could see Art heading my way to confiscate the money.

As the summer was drawing to a close, friends and family members were becoming more suspicious of my actions and increasingly demanded answers. Angela's calls from Florida were filled with angry accusations as I continually reneged on promises of financial assistance. Alan was regularly cornered by friends asking about my situation and my unusual requests for cash. My cousin Carol Jean was fielding calls from family and acquaintances desperate for information.

Feeling anxious about the situation I found myself in with Art and his schemes, and bewildered by the cash hemorrhaging from my bank accounts, I felt isolated. When I stopped calling friends, began refusing offers for lunch, and rarely answered my phone, it was obvious something was very wrong. With few answers, speculation abounded.

Is everything OK with your mom? How's Anita? Bob left her a lot of money. She was more than comfortable. A millionaire! How could she lose all of her money? DID she lose ALL of her money? Is she on drugs? Drinking? Gambling?

And then there it was, a quiet little question creeping around the edges, *Is she involved with Art?*

***

What does it mean to be *involved* with a compulsive gambler? What would that look like? It's not obvious like witnessing someone become drunk at a party or shooting up in a parking lot. There are not signs you can point to like erratic driving, vacant stares, or the faint odor of drugs. Because no one in my circle of friends was familiar with the way a compulsive gambler operates, it was nearly impossible for anyone to imagine how Art could be responsible for my losing hundreds of thousands of dollars. As ridiculous as it seems now, it was much easier for my friends to believe I had become a drug addict.

Art? Really? She wouldn't just hand over all her money to him. Would she? No way! She's smart. She wouldn't allow that to happen. She must be doing drugs.

Alan finally caught up with me one day and demanded answers. I didn't have anything to offer. I can't even imagine how difficult it was for my son to be so forceful with me. He was worried, and he had a right to be. I'm sure it felt like he was boxing a shadow: expending so much energy chasing the unknown, only to come up empty-handed. And it only added to his confusion that I side-stepped his questions, dried my tears before I answered his calls, and put on a brave face when he visited.

"No, nothing's wrong. Everything's just fine." I repeated again and again in response to his inquisitions.

When all of Alan's efforts to obtain an explanation failed, he pleaded with me to see someone. If I wouldn't talk to him, perhaps I should talk to a therapist. Hoping to distract Alan from looking too closely into my predicament, I mentioned that I had been meeting with Father Lavelle. Knowing Father Lavelle was conducting Mass the following morning, I invited Alan to attend with me and promised to make an introduction. Alan did accompany me the next day, but remained unconvinced I was receiving the help I needed. Both he and Angela continued to insist I seek more formal counseling.

I asked Father Lavelle if he could suggest a therapist and he provided me with a list of people. He highly recommended Dr. Ezra Jayson, a psychologist whose office was convenient for me. When I contacted Dr. Jayson he agreed to meet with me right away and we scheduled an appointment for Labor Day, September 6. When I relayed the information to Alan, he said he would join me.

Alan and I drove separately and I arrived first. We barely even spoke to each other during a brief wait in the small second floor waiting area. Once we were seated in the office, Alan let loose with a barrage of questions and observations and conclusions. I sat silently in an adjoining chair, wiping tears from my eyes. It was the first time I could understand what the situation looked like from my son's perspective. I knew things looked desperate from my side of it, but listening to him speak I witnessed how terrified he was, how much he cared for me, and how helpless he felt.

Dr. Jayson listened intently, made some notes, and asked a few questions. I couldn't offer any response to Alan except, "I'm sorry you feel that way." If I revealed what was really happening, I feared Alan would seek revenge and drive Art—and any hope of restitution—far away. Honestly, at that point I couldn't imagine receiving help from anyone that would result in a favorable outcome. I was convinced I could still manage Art to the point where he would repay the debts we incurred. That was the hope I clung to; there was nothing else.

When our hour was up, I scheduled a time to meet with Dr. Jayson alone. During my next session I revealed what truly was the source of my bizarre behavior. I didn't hold anything back. Nothing was off limits. During subsequent sessions I shared, for the first time ever, that I had been raped as a child. We talked about my marriages and divorces and the crash that killed my second husband and nearly claimed the life of my son. How I had been coping since the loss of my loving husband Bob. The ways I had become enslaved to Art while he pilfered my life.

I looked for Dr. Jayson to provide answers to extricate me from the mess I was in. He preferred to accompany me on a journey to discover the solutions I needed. I talked a lot. He said little. I asked questions. He asked questions. I wanted him to give me direction so I could take action. He encouraged me to pause and consider the way in which past experiences had influenced current decisions. And although at times I didn't feel like I was making any progress, along the way I was learning about myself. Where I was strong. Where weaknesses were hidden. What I needed to do to survive.

And while my circumstances related to Art continued to deteriorate, I felt the tiniest flicker of strength begin to glow. It was just a whisper of confidence and I wasn't even sure what it meant, but something was changing. I discussed the possibility of inviting Art to attend a session with me. Dr. Jayson agreed there might be value for the two of them to meet. I was pleased when Art accepted my invitation, thinking maybe a little therapy would help him, too.

When the day of our joint session arrived, Art and I met in a parking lot near Dr. Jayson's office so he could follow me to the address. Before we had reached our destination, Art flashed his lights to get my attention. He put on his turn signal. I pulled onto the next side street and he followed. He jumped out of his car and quickly came up to mine as I rolled the window down. "What's wrong?" I asked. Things were blowing up! Art needed me to write a check to Buster Jurik so he could deliver it immediately. Art was frantic. *I promise Buster will never cash this check. I just need it for a while to secure a loan he is going to give me.* I handed over a check before watching him turn around and drive away.

Like most things Art promised, his word was worthless. Was he afraid of what Dr. Jayson might see or was he just playing another game? I doubt he had any intention of attending a therapy session with me. It was so easy for him to make another promise, tell another lie, or say anything in the moment just to keep me engaged in his schemes.

***

Meanwhile, OSU football season had started and I was facing another disaster. All the people who had purchased season tickets began calling. Nothing made sense about the way Art distributed the tickets. Instead of a single packet for each person containing all the tickets and parking passes at the beginning of the season, I had to meet with him each week to pick up the tickets, which he had stored in boxes in the backseat of his car. It was very haphazard and unorganized. Sometimes we would meet on Thursday nights after his appearance on Bucks Line. One time I met Sue and Boris on a Saturday morning to pick up the last of the tickets. Sue explained they just received the money that morning and were instructed to immediately go to Best Seat Tickets to purchase the tickets I needed for the game later in the day. I rushed to meet my friends in front of the stadium and hand over the tickets literally minutes before kick-off. Every week I was nervous about getting the tickets in time and then when Art finally gave them to me, I was driving all over Central Ohio to deliver them to my friends.

In September Art demanded I write checks totaling $114,500. Buster Jurik received $39,500. Brad Johnson received three checks for $25,000 each. By this point, Art had broken my will to the point that he could easily bat away my reluctance to help him. When I told him I was out of money, he laughed. "Write these checks," he snarled. "Or everyone will find out how stupid you are. Your so-called friends will be laughing behind your back!"

When I met Art at Genoa Church in November I had $1 million in an IRA and $500,000 in a separate investment account. With no debt, I was able to live quite comfortably on the $70,000 per year I was earning from my investments. Now, however, my money was rapidly disappearing. I wasn't quite desperate, as Art was making an effort to repay me and I thought I still had a sizeable amount of money in an account I hadn't yet touched. I had promised myself that I wouldn't give him a dime of my reserve. If or when it came to it, the answer would be a resounding, "No!"

One afternoon my nerves were getting the best of me and I peeked at the balance in my reserve account to prove to myself everything was OK. I was shocked to see such a small balance. I was panicked! What had happened to my security blanket? Certainly, there had been a mistake! I calmed down and reviewed the transaction history only to see I had inadvertently been dipping into this account all along. There was no reserve. I was nearly out of cash and at the end of my rope. I felt stupid and afraid. This had been my last chance to save myself, and I had blown it because I didn't have a handle on my finances.

Various times in the past I had told Art I was out of money in an attempt to get him off my back, but this time when I summoned the courage to say it, there wasn't a hint of deception. "Art, I don't have any more money. I thought I had some in reserve, but I was mistaken." He didn't believe me. "Come on, Anita! I know you still have money. I really need you to come through for me on this. It's serious. If we don't put out these fires, I'm going to jail and no one is getting paid back—especially not you." Trying hard to choke back tears of shame I'm sure he could detect the despair in my voice. I was a failure, unable to help Art any longer or even, at this point, help myself. I confessed, "This is it. I don't have anything left to help you, or to help anyone. I'm broke."

From the other end of the line I thought I heard him ask, "What about your house?" I asked him to repeat the question. He wanted to know how much I owed on my house. "Nothing. I paid cash for my condo. I'm not selling it." His suggestion was offensive. I had given him everything. EVERYTHING. How dare he ask for my home. "No, I wouldn't ask you to sell your home," he explained. "I was thinking you could get a reverse mortgage." He described how a reverse mortgage worked and that I could continue to live in my house, I would just take out a loan against its value. I had purchased my condo for a little more than $336,000 in October 2007, five months after Bob died. It was probably worth about the same now.

I wasn't convinced this was a good idea, but he wouldn't let it drop. He called repeatedly: non-stop ringing on my house phone, personal cell, and the disposable phone he had given me. Reminding me of our dire circumstances. Prison was our fate. *What was I waiting for?* He was diligently chipping away at my resolve little by little until I was willing to make a call to a mortgage lender. And in the time it takes to process a reverse mortgage for more than $186,000, Art had claimed everything I owned and I was his complete prisoner.

Soon after Art told me he was expecting a large amount of money, around $600,000, coming the Monday after the upcoming weekend. He sounded relieved with such a large windfall and I was excited because I would be able to pay everyone back. I was walking on clouds. When Monday arrived, I drove to an exit off I-71 south of Grove City to meet Art and pick up the money. Well, he met me all right, but he didn't have any money for me. He said he had used all the money to invest in a thoroughbred racehorse. I was so angry I couldn't be contained. "THAT'S MY MONEY!" I screamed. "I COULD HAVE GIVEN IT TO MY INVESTOR AND HAD HER MAKE US MONEY AND I WOULD HAVE SPLIT IT WITH YOU." I was devastated. There was no calming down that day.

Later, I asked about the horse and when we could expect to receive a return on it. He was ready with a quick answer explaining that I didn't understand the process of buying and selling thoroughbreds. "We can't do anything until the horse is drug tested and passes all sorts of other tests. It takes time."

In October, Art made me write twenty-one checks or initiate wire transfers totaling $384,500. Tim Baker received two payments totaling $105,000. Brad Johnson received $25,000, and

$12,000 went to Yanni Rivera, a local businessman. The remainder was distributed to Art's associates who were unknown to me. I cried and pleaded with Art; I didn't want to write any checks. Couldn't he see how desperate my situation had become?

Art had become tired of my complaining and crying, and was unwilling to tolerate my defiance. His threats increased but his story remained the same: if I didn't do exactly what he said, I would never see any of my money again.

By the end of October, with my account balances nearing zero, I was writing checks only on the promise that Art would deposit the money to cover them before they were due to be cashed. To my knowledge most of the checks were used as collateral against personal loans he needed. He would tell the payees that the money wasn't in my account just yet, and they couldn't cash them until he told them it was OK to do so.

By November Art had depleted my resolve, just like he had drained my bank accounts. When Art demanded nine checks or wire transfers during the month totaling $126,000, there was nothing I could do to stop him. Calder Fenwick received $32,000; Brad Johnson received $25,000 and $8,000 went to Yanni Rivera. The remaining amount went to Art's associates, including Bill Hanners.

I had to ask repeatedly, but Art was continuing to provide me with just enough money to buy groceries, pay my utilities, and make the monthly payment to the pawn shop for my jewelry. Any money he gave me to repay my friends went directly to them. I didn't keep a penny of the money that wasn't mine.

With the holiday season approaching, I began reminiscing. Just a year ago I was celebrating Alan's fortieth birthday with a lavish party among dear friends and family. This year I could barely afford to purchase a card. Thanksgiving was a bust. Memories of previous holidays with a house filled with loved ones and family and friends talking happily as they passed the turkey, now mocked the meager dinner Alan and I planned to share alone. With little hope that a turnaround would happen before Christmas, I was flooded with despair. I couldn't keep living like this.

Although I had been attending Mass everyday and often visited the church several times throughout the day, talking to Father Rod, praying, crying, lighting candles and begging for God's help, I couldn't find any answers. It felt like all the oxygen had been sucked out of my life. Art called insistently with urgent demands. *We have fires to put out. You need to call this person. You need to go here or there. Pick up money, Go! Go! Go! NOW!* He was the coach calling all the plays and I was at his mercy.

***

At the end of my rope, I placed Bob's pistol in my purse and drove to his gravesite. I missed my husband so much and needed to be near him. I wanted to find comfort in the bench we had engraved with our favorite quote, "Can I have this dance for the rest of my life?" But I had made such a mess of everything I couldn't find any relief. As I sat in my car in the cemetery, I began praying for forgiveness: first from God, then from Alan and Angela, and finally from my friends. I was sobbing and could barely see through my tears. I removed the gun from my purse and switched off the safety, intent on taking my life and putting an end to the madness.

Suddenly, my phone rang. It was Alan. I cleared my throat in an attempt to sound calm. He wanted to know where I was. I wouldn't tell him; he persisted. As I returned the gun to my purse and drove out of the cemetery, I told him I was visiting Bob's grave. Sensing things were desperate, he immediately set out to find me. By the time he arrived at the cemetery, I was gone. I had driven to an undeveloped cul-de-sac behind the Wendy's on Rome-Hilliard Road. I couldn't let my son see me in such a bad state, and I certainly didn't want him to find out I had the gun with me. But Alan sensed what was going on and begged me not to kill myself. "We've been through a lot together. Please don't leave me," he pleaded. His desperate tone cut through my self-absorbed sorrow. I promised I wouldn't harm myself and, in that moment, I meant it. He was right; we only had each other. How selfish of me to solve my problems by causing him permanent pain. Alan wanted to find me and confirm I was OK. I was such a mess I wouldn't let him see me, but assured him I was fine.

Although Alan didn't know exactly what was going on, all signs pointed to Art's involvement. Immediately after Alan was convinced I was out of danger, he placed a call to Art. "What are you doing to my mother? Leave her alone! You are killing her!" he screamed. Art told Alan he would call me and find out what was going on. My next call was from Art, the predator I was trying to escape.

Barely waiting for a response between questions, he was talking ninety miles a minute. "Anita, are you trying to kill yourself? What are you doing? Stop it! They will put *me* in prison for murder or something. Your son is all upset. You are hurting Alan. Are you going to kill yourself? Stop it!" He continued to lecture me about the ridiculousness of my plan and concluded with, "Don't do this now. Just wait. We can commit double suicide together." I was so angry at his selfish tirade. "You go first," I said before throwing down the phone.

I returned home and went to bed and cried for the rest of the day. My mind was frantic with regrets and broken relationships and the destruction of a future that was once bright with joy. With no money and little hope of anything changing, I wondered what would become of me. Since I could no longer afford to live in my condo, where would I go? What could I find that I could afford? What about my utilities? And taxes? Questions circled round and round and round until my thoughts turned to panic and then to despair.

On December 3, after days of enduring Art's torments, I relented to his demands and wrote a check to Steven Grundy for $60,000. Unbeknownst to either of us, this would be the final check I would ever write for Art.

Things were about to change.

25 | TURNING POINT
EARLY DECEMBER 2010

"Would I survive the evening? Was this the night Art would kill me?"	Anita Barney

One night in early December Art showed up at my front door unexpectedly. He rarely visited my home and I did not welcome his arrival. He looked more disheveled than I had seen in the past and his eyes were wild. I was immediately on guard. "What's wrong?" I demanded.

He pushed his way through the front door as he grumbled, "We have BIG fires to put out!"

Something was different; the air was electric. Art's manner was eerily calm, but beneath the surface I could sense hysteria lurking. He began pacing around my coffee table. I was afraid to speak, certain that uttering one syllable would push him over an unseen precipice and the result would be disastrous—for both of us.

I took a seat at the kitchen table while he continued nonstop pacing. His incoherent mumbling took on a threatening tone. I was aghast at Art's deranged behavior mere inches from where I was perched. As I tried to remain inconspicuous, I began perspiring heavily and trembling from fear.

Was this the calm before the storm? Would I survive the evening? Was this the night Art would kill me? I could feel my heart racing as I willed myself to remain silent.

I sat quietly, reluctant to make eye contact with him as the minutes slowly ticked by.

I spied my cell phone on the breakfast bar, too far away to reach discreetly. It didn't matter; whom would I call? It had felt for months that there was no way out of this nightmare. Who could help me? Who would *want* to? I had destroyed my life and made a mess for most everyone who knew me.

If tonight was going to be the end, then so be it. I deserved whatever happened.

In the past, when Art screamed and called me awful names I was intimidated and afraid. But tonight was different. I was terrified and the fear surrounded me like a cloak.

I stole a glance at the clock and calculated that nearly thirty minutes had passed since Art arrived when I noticed something out of the corner of my eye. Art had abruptly changed direction and was heading toward the entry. "I'll call you later!" he growled as he walked out and slammed the door behind him.

I quickly raced across the room and engaged the deadbolt. A flood of emotions overtook me as I began sobbing uncontrollably. Relief, fear, grief, and shame ripped through me like a howling tornado. I was reduced to a pile of human rubble.

As I fell to the floor in the living room, I cried out. "God! I need Your help! I turn my life over to you. I thought I could get through this on my own. But I was wrong! I don't know what to do or where to turn for help. Please show me what to do."

There. I had said it aloud and acknowledged it to myself. I was in way over my head and the safety of solid ground was a long distant memory. Whether Art's visit had been a legitimate mental breakdown or a charade intended to manipulate me into obedience, it had the unintended consequence of causing me to see how misguided it had been to put my hope in him and his promises of future payoffs.

The threats Art manufactured of lawsuits and charges and jail time for both of us if the authorities found about *his* schemes slipped away. Gone was the fear that had dictated my compliance with his crimes, and with it the certainty that betraying him or disobeying his directives would cause him to leave town with all the money. I was no longer convinced he could fix any of this.

Suddenly, I knew exactly what needed to be done.

26 | CALLING FOR BACKUP
DECEMBER 2010

| *"I was trying to save you. And now I need to be* | *Anita Barney to* |
| *saved. How have you done this to me?"* | *Art Schlichter* |

I opened a drawer in the kitchen and there it was. Special Agent Terrence Brown's business card was right where I left it after he had visited six months before. It was too late to call Terrence tonight, but I was determined to talk to him first thing in the morning. If there was no hope of repaying my friends and family, I didn't care what happened to me. I wanted Art taken off the street and it was time to get the Feds involved.

My conversation the next day with Terrence was brief. I introduced myself, reminding him of our meeting earlier in the year and told him Art was taking advantage of me and I was in desperate need of help. He instructed me to call Steve Schierholt with the Franklin County Prosecutor's Office. "He's a nice guy and will be able to help you. Call him right away," he said after he read off Steve's number. As soon as I disconnected my call with Terrence I contacted Steve. Steve listened as I briefly recounted what Art had been doing and explained I needed help to make him stop. We set up a time to meet the following day.

When Steve arrived at my home he was accompanied by Jane McKenzie, Franklin County Prosecutor Victim Witness Advocate. I began telling my story, my history with Art, and how he had used my generosity to blind me to the fact that he had taken everything. Here I was, spilling everything to the Prosecutor. The guy who could—and whose office would—eventually charge me for my involvement in Art's schemes. Not only did I not have an attorney present to advise me of my rights, I didn't even have an attorney to consult. At this point my only concern was doing whatever was necessary to stop Art. I couldn't continue to live under his constant threats any longer.

Our meeting lasted quite a while and throughout most of it my phones were continually ringing as Art tried to reach me. Steve asked clarifying questions in an attempt to understand exactly what had been going on and the level of my involvement. He also wanted to know if Art and I were having a sexual relationship. We weren't. Jane explained she was available to serve as a resource and support for me. She would be my liaison with the Prosecutor's office, provide information about the court system and social service agencies, or answer any other questions that might arise regarding my involvement as a victim within the legal system.

When I told Steve that neither Angela nor Alan knew what was going on, he agreed to meet with Alan and place a call to Angela, who was living in Florida. Alan came to the house and I could see a torrent of emotion wash over him as Steve relayed what he knew. Alan cycled through disbelief, anger, fear, disappointment, and concern over the disaster Art had caused. Angela's response mirrored her brother's. They were infuriated with Art and angry with me. Because both the investigation and my safety would be in jeopardy if Art discovered I had met with authorities, my children were literally sworn to secrecy.

On December 13, 2010, Steve returned with Detective Scott Davis of the Dublin Division of Police. Because the Franklin County Prosecutor does not have jurisdiction to conduct investigations, Detective Davis would be leading the investigation into Art's activities and would serve as my primary contact. Detective Davis took my statement. I told him how Art had depleted all of my money and that I had borrowed or collected money on his behalf for Ohio State tickets and Super Bowl tickets totaling around $450,000.

Detective Davis provided me with a digital recorder and a telephone microphone to immediately begin recording telephone calls with Art and anyone else who was or might have been involved in ticket or money scams. It was a very simple device for me to operate. Detective Davis stopped by every couple of days to retrieve the tapes and bring extra batteries; Art was calling twenty to thirty times a day and I was recording a lot.

Detective Davis also requested that I keep notes regarding all the calls with or involving Art and to write a detailed statement about what had taken place prior to my calling the authorities. I was instructed not to meet with Art and to advise Detective Davis if Art requested funds or gave me money, or if anyone else were to give me money.

I turned over several TracFones Art had previously given me and were now depleted of minutes. The only data that could be retrieved were three phone numbers I had used to reach Art. I also informed Detective Davis that Yanni Rivera of True Blue Truck Rentals had two checks I had written totaling $15,000 that Art had used to obtain money for Super Bowl tickets. Yanni had been calling me repeatedly to find out what was going on and why the checks were no good. Throughout my meetings with Detective Davis, Art called me incessantly.

For some reason I cannot explain, I felt that John Amery, Art's attorney and agent, had a right to know what Art was up to. After Detective Davis left I placed a call to John and explained that Art had been selling tickets and had conned me out of all my money, along with convincing me to write worthless checks that he could use as collateral to obtain money from his friends. John became outraged and in a turn of events I had not expected, asked to meet at my house. Not knowing what I had stirred up, I asked Alan to come and be with me. When John arrived, I explained the situation in detail and he became adamant that I call the police. Not being able to tell him I was already cooperating with authorities, I put him off, explaining that if Art got even a whiff that I had called the police, he would skip town with all the evidence and all my money. I was able to convince John to wait. In addition to John being Art's legal representative, the other reason I could not reveal I was working with the Dublin Police was because no one knew if John was involved in Art's schemes. Detective Davis instructed me to record my conversations with everyone, even John, until he could be cleared—or implicated—in Art's madness.

John shared that he had recently received a text from a man in Baltimore stating if Art did not pay the $200,000 he owed the man and his daughter, the caller was going to call the police. John had been working out deals for past victims to be repaid but had threatened to call the authorities if he learned Art was gambling again. He called Art a thief and a liar and said Art was sick. Meanwhile, John offered to begin working on finding me an attorney. "You're going to need one," he warned. He quickly made an appointment for me to meet with Attorney Hamilton in German Village within the next few days. After I learned the attorney required a $5,000 retainer to take my case, I was devastated. I didn't have that kind of money.

***

The authorities were seeking specific information to use in their case against Art, and when I placed the following call, Detective Davis was sitting at the table coaching me. During the conversation, Art chastises me for only dwelling on the problem and not working on a solution to help alleviate our money problems. He says I need to learn to figure out things for myself. When I ask about the horse he had purchased with money that belonged to me and the profit we were supposed to realize, he assures me it's on the way.

Anita Barney: You know I've been sitting here calculating all this money that has gone out. I started out just helping you, if you remember, a year ago. And loaning this money and everything, it has just snowballed. I just really don't know what's going to happen. Do you remember how much you owe me?

Art Schlichter: Yeah.

Barney: It's a lot, isn't it?

Schlichter: Yeah. It is.

Barney: Two million? Something like that?

Schlichter: No!

Barney: All right. What is it? What you've borrowed from me, plus with the credit cards and plus what I've borrowed from all these people. 'Cause that's what you said one day, "It's about two million dollars, I owe you. I'm indebted to you." OK. There's no way you can pay me back. I know this. So, that's why I'm going to be losing what I have. Because people are going to take my homes. And that's why it's important for me to go down and get this jewelry, because at least, I have some memories there. That meant a lot to me.

Schlichter: There's no need to lose your homes. It's just paying your debt off. OK? Then you work on the other stuff.

Barney: Which debt are you talking about?

Schlichter: All of it!

Barney: How are we going to do it? How in the world . . . I really thought that horse was going to get us out of this. Remember you telling me that?

Schlichter: It is!

Barney: But when? Where is it?

Schlichter: Very, very soon.

Barney: It's just causing me problems and you problems and everyone else.

Schlichter: I know it is, but, you know what? On a situation like that, you just gotta maintain until you get it done. And if you fall apart, like you're doing, you're no good to anybody.

It'll *never* get worked out. So, you gotta, you can't sit there and just dwell on it and dwell on it. You know, you could get a little creative yourself.

Barney: And do what?

Schlichter: I don't know. But just sitting there thinking about it and dwelling on it. I don't know.

Barney: Oh, you mean go out and make myself active, you mean?

Schlichter: No, you might be able to figure out a way to help get it taken care of. You know what I mean?

Barney: No, I don't even know how I could do it, though.

Schlichter: Well, that's because all you are doing is thinking about it instead of thinking about a solution.

Barney: Well, see, you told me you had a solution and it was all going to work out—

Schlichter: I do! But, you know what? It's always good to be able to maybe, maybe get yourself a good night's sleep by trying to figure out, that's how I've always handled it. And as you try to figure out maybe what the next step is, if this goes wrong then you do this. If that goes wrong, then you do this. If this goes right, then it will give you a chance to do this. OK? It's like a process. Trying to get it taken care of. And the problem is that you're just dwelling on the problem so bad that you can't even breathe.

Barney: I know.

Schlichter: You've got to get to the point where you can breathe. And answer your phone. And take care of being able to communicate with people. It works.

Barney: But see, I'd have to lie to them.

Schlichter: You know what your problem is? You don't have to.

Barney: Why not?

Schlichter: You don't have to lie to them. You can just say it's going to work out. You don't have to give them numbers. Go ahead and do that. But, it's going to work out. And I'm going to get it taken care of. OK?

Barney: All right.

Schlichter: And you can do that. But your problem is that you fold about one-third of the way through and then you sit there and . . . when you do that, it will never work. OK?

Barney: I know you're right.

Schlichter: All right. My battery is beeping . . . I'll call you back . . . take some deep breaths and . . . try to figure it out how to make it better. And, just maybe, something might come up where you'll figure it out.

Barney: I'm not smart like you are. I don't know how to do things like that. I can't—

Schlichter: You know what? You're one of the smartest people I've ever met.

Barney: No, I'm not.

Schlichter: How old are you now?

Barney: You know how old I am. I'm sixty-eight years old.

Schlichter: Well, you sell yourself short. You've been doing that all your life. You don't need to do that anymore.

Barney: Yeah, but you're the one that knows how to figure out things. I can't. I've never really had to figure things out for myself that much.

Schlichter: Well, I'll help you do that. OK? You've got to stop having someone do this stuff. OK?

Barney: Oh, gosh. I really thought we'd have that money from the horse by now and take the pressure off—

Schlichter: We're going to. Let me call you back in a little bit.

***

A few days later John Amery told me someone had contacted Art's employer, 610 WTVN, and possibly other radio stations about the Super Bowl ticket scheme. John hadn't heard anything definitively, but was fairly certain this was going to result in Art being fired. John was preparing a letter to withdraw as Art's attorney.

John Amery: Hey, Anita, It's John . . . so, what do you know?

Anita Barney: I talked to him last night, and talked with him briefly this morning. I'm waiting for him to call me back. He told me I was supposed to meet Boris (Paveleski) or Bill (Hanners) today for some money. This morning I asked him about the situation, that I was supposed to help him when he was having problems and now it is me having problems because Fenwick Calder called and left a message that they went to an attorney. And they don't think I ever intended for these checks to be good and they are going to go to the police. This is this morning, already. I had been trying to keep Art out of jail and now I'm probably going to end up in jail. It's unbelievable.

Amery: Listen, you're not going to end up in jail, Anita. Don't worry about that.

Barney: Well, I hope not, I've never been inside of one.

Amery: Well, you're not going to be.

Barney: I'm waiting for him to tell me whether I am to meet them or not for some money. Art said I have to pay my bills, which I do, but I was supposed to pay Rod Cheetham $1,000 starting today. That's what Art told me to make the arrangements and I did it with the attorney. Signed the papers and everything and I have no money. I have no money.

Amery: Unless Art shows up today.

Barney: Yeah.

Amery: A back alley meeting. Anita, I have to be really careful. I want to help you. I don't know that I can continue to represent him. Here's what I wanted to run by you this morning, is to tell him that you and I, just to give you additional cover, because if I withdraw I don't want him to think we are talking. So, what I want to do is write him a letter that says, I've drafted part of it. Listen and tell me if you are OK with this: *Art, per my numerous letters to you I directly and clearly advised you that my representation would only continue if I believed you were not engaged in any form of illegal activity. I cannot accept your recent explanations regarding the monies you borrowed from Tim Baker. Anita Barney will not return my phone calls and I have no explanation for the checks she has written without funds in her account. I cannot express my disappointment given all I have done for you but I am afraid you've relapsed into conduct which requires me to withdraw as your counsel.* I want to kinda do that thing but I want to do it so, Anita, it protects you. I don't want him to think that I'm doing this, that's why I'm asking you if I can put your name in there in that vein so that—

Barney: Yes. Yes. It sounds good.

Amery: I just do not want to, at all, ever, ever cause you any problems. And, listen, I'm going to help you through this whole thing. I mean, whether it is with Attorney Hamilton or helping him, I'm going to help you through the whole thing. So, I don't want you to panic, but I ethically, because I do think he is engaged in illegal activity, I can't continue to represent him. So, if you're OK with that, I want to get that to him.

Barney: Yes.

Amery: I think if I clearly say that you're not even returning my phone calls, that he won't suspect anything there. I think, I've got enough with Tim Baker and the crazy call I got yesterday from Chester Meeks.

Barney: No, I'm fine with what you're saying. It's absolutely fine. Because one of his complaints about me, Art is always saying that I never answer my phone. I never call people back. And I don't like to call them back because I know what I'm going to hear on the other end. And I'm going to have to lie to them. And I can't lie. I just can't handle it. It's not me. It's just not me. I can't lie. I've lied enough, not intentionally. I was lying and I was telling them what I thought was the truth at the time. It turned out to be lies and everybody is calling me a liar and a thief, now. That's what tears me apart because I'm really not. Oh, god! I just wanted to ask him this morning and I want to talk to him more about it if he will talk to me. I want to understand how everything turned around like this? *I was trying to save you. And now I need to be saved. How have you done this to me? Why can't you give me this money from this horse and that way I won't lose my homes or anything! I'm losing everything.* He said, "Oh, you're not going to lose anything. I'm not going to let that happen." And stuff like that. I told him I was going to. People putting liens on everything. I'm going to lose everything. I was just trying to help him get a life with his mother and his children again. He was going to go out and give all these speeches to save families. And that was supposed to be our goal.

Amery: You need to absolutely pin him down on that. I mean, just keep asking him that, Anita. Because I, I don't know. Maybe he will admit to you what he has done. Obviously this money is gone. I got to thinking about it. I'm not sure that he hasn't used it pay back some people that have threatened him. He had that issue in Indianapolis a long time ago. But he may have messed with the mob and is trying to pay back mob money.

Barney: Oh, gosh! Well, last year when I was coming back from the Michigan game, around that time, he said he had to go up to Toledo or around that area. He didn't say up into Michigan. I wasn't paying that much attention. I couldn't care less where he was going or anything. He said I'm not going to be able to talk for a while. He finally called me after so long and said these goons beat him up. He thought he had broken ribs and all that but I thought he might have gone up there to gamble.

Amery: I'm sure he did. Sure he went to Detroit and gambled. Oh, Anita. Oh, my god! I just put two and two together. He said, I didn't even realize this. But three or four months ago, which is probably the time you were borrowing some of this money, he was going up and seeing some girl in Detroit. I'll bet he was up there gambling. I didn't even make the casino connection. But I bet you that's what he was doing.

Barney: I never believed him when he said that, and he had his brother drive him because his ribs were so bad. He's dramatic anyway.

Amery: Well, I never heard anything about the rib story. So, that must have been a total lie.

Barney: Well, one day he took his daughters to an Indianapolis football game and said he fell down the steps and sprained his ankle. *I can't hardly walk. I'm on crutches and all that.* Well, two days later he wasn't on crutches. You know, he forgets his stories, maybe.

Amery: Yeah, I just think he makes that sh*t up.

Barney: Yeah, I think so, too. And this one time his car was so bad he wanted to buy a car. He asked to borrow some money from me to buy a car, like $11,000. He was sitting in the car dealership and I sent it to him and all that. He needed a car so bad he couldn't get back and forth. He told me I was going to love this car. Well, I've never seen that car and I keep wanting to ask him.

Amery: Art lied to you. He got that money and he gambled it. That's what he did. That son of a b**ch!

Barney: I could write a book on the lies he's told me. I'm so stupid for believing it. That's what's embarrassing.

Amery: Oh, my god! Oh, my god!

Barney: But that's me! I'm such a believer in everybody. That's my problem. I just always believe everybody. It's unbelievable. I'm a wreck . . . Dr. Jayson called me yesterday or last evening, I believe. Wanted to know how I was doing. He asked about the meeting with Attorney Hamilton. I told him not too well. I can't afford him. He was going to try and find somebody that would not charge me and if someday down the road if I had any money I would be able to pay him.

Amery: Well, I'm still working on this. This guy is really, really good. And believe it or not, $5,000 sounds like a lot of money—it is a lot of money—but not for the work he is going to have to do. So, I think it is a reasonable request. Especially when Kim Gamble is talking about $50,000 or $60,000. So, let me keep working on this.

Barney: But that was just a retainer.

Amery: I know. But I think the goal, which I talked about before, is that we got to get these people to understand that you didn't do anything wrong so they are not going to chase you for this money. We've got to stop the liens so you have equity in your condo. What did you pay for your condo?

Barney: Well, it was maybe $340,000 or something.

Amery: Well, it's probably lost value . . .

Barney: But that's what I paid, cash. And then I paid $300,000 cash for the one in Florida. In fact, Ben Roberts and Phil Evans have all that paperwork at their attorney's office. Because I took the paperwork over there and they were going to put a lien on here and have me pay it off in a year and I was going to take them the paperwork and they were going to make me a copy of what they needed but they won't give it back to me now. It's at their attorney's office because we still owe them like $18,000. Phil called me last night and left a message, asking me to call him. I haven't called him yet. I just can't call him. I don't know what to say to him. I have nothing—

Amery: You can't. There isn't anything to say to him because you can't keep calling people and telling them, dependent on Art, when there is no money coming in, right?

Barney: He told me, I think it was last night, Linda Scott called, she lives in Dayton, to tell her that I ordered the money and the money will be in there next week.

Amery: No! Do not lie for him anymore.

Barney: I'm not. I haven't called her. I'm not going to. That's when he got mad at me about Calder, because I wouldn't call him. I kept putting it off. He said, "You're going to f**k this up if you don't call him. Oh, god.

Amery: Art is a bad, bad person. Let's keep working through it. OK?

***

Dr. Jayson referred me to his friend, Attorney Bill Loveland, as it was clear I needed legal advice and representation. Bill called me and said, "It sounds to me that you're a person that could use a hand at this point in time." His gentle and caring demeanor spoke volumes.

He offered to meet with me on Monday, December 20, 2010, a few days away. I shared that things were starting to fall apart around me, but since I've waited this long, Monday would be fine. After he provided his address and we decided on a time, Bill continued, "My understanding is that there is an investigation around an individual. Ezra (Jayson) did not identify that person for me. Could you give me the names of a couple of the most important people involved in this to ensure I don't have a conflict?"

I told him it involved Art Schlichter, who had extorted all my money and Hugh Buttke and Rod Cheetham, both well-known business owners and very good friends of mine who trusted me and I trusted them, as well as several others. I said, "I thought I was doing something right. It turns out I was wrong."

***

The weekend before Christmas John texted Art to notify him he would no longer represent him and confirmed the radio station had, indeed, fired him. And then things became complicated. Art told me not to talk to John until he had a chance to talk with me. John told me he was leaving on a cruise and to just tell Art we didn't talk; he would contact Art via text. While I continued to keep in regular communication with John, I denied doing so to Art.

In the following conversation when Art questioned me about where I've been and I tell him I've been at home, he responds with, "I know." I didn't realize it at the time, but he had people watching me and reporting back to him about what I was doing. He told me Sue and Boris had been watching, and I have no doubt there were others. He was becoming more and more paranoid. Frankly, he had a right to be nervous, as the walls were closing in on him, he just didn't have proof . . . yet.

Art Schlichter: Did you talk to John?

Anita Barney: No. But I'm going to try to call him.

Schlichter: Why?

Barney: You told me to try and I haven't tried.

Schlichter: Don't lie to me! Come on, Anita. You're starting to go rude on me. Tell me the truth.

Barney: I have not talked to John. He left a message, I told ya. I think he is probably out of town for the holiday. I don't know where his family lives.

Schlichter: Have you been trying to get a hold of him?

Barney: I've only tried two times.

Schlichter: Where have you been last night and today? What's going on?

Barney: I've been home! I haven't left my house. I have been in bed all night. I'm just getting up to do my hair and I have to be at Dr. Jayson's at one o'clock.

Schlichter: Anita.

Barney: What?

Schlichter: We've been through the mill here. You've got to tell me the truth on stuff. OK?

Barney: Art, I have been home!

Schlichter: I know. But who have you talked to?

Barney: Hadley Higgins called. I didn't answer. Harris Jackson has called. I don't know who else has called.

Schlichter: I want you to swear on your grandson's life that you have not spoken or left a message of any negativity for John Amery.

Barney: I have not.

Schlichter: Swear!

Barney: Swear.

Schlichter: Swear on my grandson's life.

Barney: Yes, I swear.

Schlichter: I want to hear it. I swear on my grandson's life.

Barney: I have not left anything negative on John's voice mail.

Schlichter: All right. OK, what have you said?

Barney: That I'm trying to return his call. I don't know where he is. He has tried to call me. He's told you that and left messages.

Schlichter: When was the last time he tried to call you?

Barney: Oh, gosh. I don't know. Why? Have you heard from him?

Schlichter: He's wrote me negative things.

Barney: Today?

Schlichter: Yes.

Barney: Well, here's something blocked, that's yesterday some time. That's why I don't know who it is. I don't know anybody else it would be. His calls are blocked sometimes, that's it. Probably. It doesn't have any time. Yesterday. No message.

Schlichter: All right.

Barney: Then Hadley Higgins. Then 866, that's American Express calling me. That's today. Might have been today. The other two are yesterday. And it was so full, I erased all the others. It was too full. I didn't hear from you; where were you last night? Where did you spend the night?

Schlichter: Washington Court House.

Barney: Spend it at your mom's?

Schlichter: Yeah . . . put my truck in the . . . just a minute. All right, I've got to deal with John. I'll talk to you later.

Barney: Have you talked to him yourself?

Schlichter: No, he won't take my call.

Barney: Oh. Maybe he's out of town for the holiday. I don't know anything about his family life or anything. Where his parents live. Or even if they are alive. I don't know. I thought maybe you might know that. I don't know where he is.

Schlichter: All right. I'll call you back. 'Bye.

***

I met with Attorney Bill Loveland on Monday, December 20, 2010, and we discussed my situation. I explained I had no money to pay his fees. Nonetheless, Bill agreed to take my case and contacted Detective Davis to advise that he was now representing me. He assured the detective I would continue to fully cooperate with the investigation.

27 | PLEASE LEAVE ME A MESSAGE
DECEMBER 2010—JANUARY 2011

"Hi, this is Anita Barney. I can't come to the phone right now, please leave me a message."

***

. . . taking my money. My family needs that money. I'm going to lose my house. I'm losing—my kids will have to change schools. I'm going to get divorced over this. All of this because of you! You are ruining my life. This needs to end.

***

Anita, it's me, Cameron Vaughn! You never send the money. You never send documentation. This has gotta stop. I'm going crazy here. I need money. Christmas is coming up and I'm broke. I mean, shame on you! Shame on you, Anita Barney! Bob Barney would be saying shame on you, too. Now, you've got to do something about this. I can't figure out how you do it, but you've got to do something. You can't owe $45,000 that you're promising to pay it back and not do anything about it. You own a couple pieces of property and you can borrow money on them. You better do something, 'cause we're already talking to a criminal lawyer and you could lose everything. Call me.

***

Anita? Lew Sanchez. I don't know what's going down. I don't know what you have yourself into but it's to the point now where I need that money and I told you that this week. You told me you would get it to me. And nothing has happened. You told my sister-in-law and my wife that they would have $2,000 each day. You're going to have to take out a secondary mortgage or something because I want paid before I leave here. And I told you I needed $2,000, but to pay this off, I'm borrowing $2,000 to pay this event off. And I need money. And I expect to hear from you somehow in some way. Otherwise, things will have—I don't want to do what I want to do—but I'm trying to be nice about it and . . . you're not explaining anything to me and until you tell me the $300,000 was deposited, there is no money coming in. Something's wrong, Anita. And you're not fooling me. I'm just going along with this and my patience is waning. My daughter, she is very upset, too. So, I'd love to hear from you. It sure would be nice. Thank you.

***

Hello, Anita, it's Buster Jurik. It's 2:30. I've just gotten back. I had a meeting with Ben and his staff. Totally unrelated thing, so, that was the reason nobody was available. And I already told you yesterday, I think it was. That yesterday I had met with "The Great" Schlichter's people and not to expect anything for a few days. Now, if you get anything, just give me a call. 'Bye.

***

Hello, Anita, it's Chuck Taylor. It's about 3:20 on Monday afternoon and I've just got to get my finances in order. I have to put a new kitchen in German Village. I have to put a new kitchen in a condominium in Naples, Florida. I've got a vacancy in the condominium in Upper Arlington. So, I need to figure out when I'm going to get my money here this week. I look forward to hearing from you . . . Thanks, Anita, very much. 'Bye. And Merry Christmas.

***

Anita, it's Cruz Hill again. I just want you to keep praying. I've been praying for you everyday. And that money's gonna come. We'll keep praying that money's coming in. It will be here. And everything's going to be OK. So, I'll keep praying that the money is coming in. I know there's a lot of pressure on you. There's a ton of pressure on me. I'm just broke. I don't know what I'm going to do from day to day. And it's not your fault. I want you to know that. But I wish you'd pick the phone up. But if you come across any money, just give me a call because I am in dire straits. I'm stone broke. All right, Anita. You take care of yourself. And God bless. I love ya. 'Bye.

***

Anita, this is Joy Blanco and it's 10:44 on Thursday, December 16. I don't know why you haven't called me back. Because you know I love you. And you know I'm your friend. And you know, friends don't walk out. They stay with the person they like and love. So, I don't know why you're not calling me, because I care for you. We both know our Lord. I believe you made a commitment to Him, and I did, too. So, we're sisters in the Lord. He loves you. I just want you to know that. He loves you so much and He wants you to be with your friends. And we love you, Anita. And, please let us talk to you. Let us be your friend. It's very important. We're not throwing any stones. We're only throwing our love to you, because Jesus died on the cross for each one of us. *Oh, Lord Jesus, please be with all of us. Help us to love one another and care for one another. Lord, I love You. And I know Anita loves You. Lord, be with all of us.* Anita, please call me. I love you.

***

Anita, this is Ida Croft, and I don't blame you for not answering the phone. I wouldn't either. But if I don't have this money by the first of the week, I'm going to turn this in.

***

Hi, Anita, it's Lew and Annabelle Sanchez. I think it's about ten after nine o'clock. Didn't know if you were able to get any money this week. Yeah, we leave January 1. So, we're hoping and praying, OK? Hope things are going well for ya. We think about ya. OK? Take care. I'll wait to hear from you. OK? Happy Holidays. Talk to you later. 'Bye.

***

Anita, Lew Sanchez. I'm leaving for Florida January 1. I'm to the point where I just have to do something and you said do whatever you think I should do, go ahead and do it. What I intend to do is go to the Dublin Police Department if I don't hear from you within the next hour, to file criminal charges, as well as sending you a letter, certified letter from the post office. My intentions are that in ten days you respond. So, if you have something to say to me before I leave in an hour, then call me. If not, then let it be as it is. Thank you.

***

Anita, it's Chuck Taylor. It's January 27. Anita, we've got to clear this up. You created major difficulties for me and I know that's not what you intended to do. But that is what is happening. I need our dollars, please. January, February, March are negative cash flows in my business, not positive cash flows. And I need some help. Thank you.

***

This is Janette Niles. What's going on? Two missed payments. I really need that money. And Nathan always said don't lend money to friends; it ruins the friendship. Oh, *please*, Anita. *Please contact me.* What's going on? I gave that to you in good faith, Anita. You said in six months you would pay the whole thing off and now you've even missed two payments. Please contact me. I'll have no other choice but to contact my lawyer and this could destroy your credit rating. Please, Anita! Please let me know what is going on!

***

My friends waited and waited for their payments. They called, stopped by, mailed cards, sent collection letters, and eventually threatened to call the police. By the time Lew Sanchez made good on his promise to contact authorities, I was already cooperating with the local investigation and recording phone conversations and doing whatever was necessary to bring Art to justice.

28 | THE PREDATOR BECOMES THE PREY
DECEMBER 2010

"Oh, yeah. He's relentless."	*John Amery about Art Schlichter*

Shortly after I started working with authorities, I received a phone message from Calder Fenwick, a local businessman who had ordered Super Bowl tickets from Art with the intention that I would purchase them at a mark-up, and Calder would make a profit. I had written checks to Calder as collateral. Art knew I didn't have the funds to cover the checks, but had promised they would never be cashed; however, at some point Calder had presented them at his bank and discovered they were worthless. Infuriated, Calder left me a voicemail message threatening to go to the police and the local newspaper if I didn't rectify the situation immediately.

Good morning, Anita. This is Calder Fenwick one more time. I won't be bothering you with any more phone calls after this one, but I wanted to let you know that I need a phone call back from you today. You told me that the funds would be in the bank and you would meet with me on Monday. It's Thursday. I had to cancel my meetings

242

*for the rest of this week because I need to take care of this.
My arrangement was with **you**. I bought those tickets—
ordered those tickets—for **you** and I have two checks. At
this point in time, they are bad. So, if I don't hear from
you today—and I don't care to hear from Art, I want to
hear from you, **we** have the arrangement—if I don't hear
from you today I will be going to the police tomorrow and
also contacting my attorney and the press. So, I'm up to
my eyeballs with this. You broke a promise to me and you
wrote bad checks. You need to resolve this today. Thank
you. 'Bye.*

With no resources to make the checks good, I contacted Art in
a panic. Art became frantic and demanded that I write additional
checks to other people who would then loan Art money he could
give to Calder and extinguish this fire.

Calder's call and Art's response created a tense situation for
me as I was no longer permitted to meet Art or write any checks
for him. I called Detective Davis for instructions and left a message
when his voice mail answered. He called a few minutes later and I
filled him in on the details. He made plans to stop by later in the
afternoon.

Meanwhile, Art called back to explain the plan he had worked
out to keep Calder quiet.

Art Schlichter: I may have to borrow this money off of Douglas
DeLarge. You may have to—

Anita Barney: I can't understand what you said.

Schlichter: Borrow the money off of Douglas DeLarge.

Barney: Yeah. And you want me to do what?

Schlichter: You may have to s**k him for it. He thinks you're
wonderful. All right?

Barney: I want to ask you a very personal question. Do you have a
lot of girlfriends around that you are taking care of that you

spend all of this money on? Don't you hang up on me! I asked you a question.

Schlichter: That's the question you have for me?

Barney: Yeah! What are you doing with all this money? Where has all this money gone?

Schlichter: Ha. Ha. Ha.

Barney: Only a female would spend this kind of money. Right?

Schlichter: Well, that ain't true. Well, maybe there's ten or twenty of them.

Barney: Well, I hope they are living better than me now but I sure don't have a d**n penny now.

Schlichter: I can't believe you'd say that.

Barney: Just curious about where all the money went.

Schlichter: I've gotta get Bill (Hanners) on a call. 'Bye.

***

Douglas DeLarge called me but I refused to answer. I simply couldn't talk to him. I had nothing to say. He left a message indicating Art sounded desperate and to give him a call.

My phones began ringing repeatedly as Art, no doubt enraged at my refusal to speak with Douglas and agree to write checks to back the loan Art needs to satisfy Calder's demands, attempted to reach me. At the end of my rope, feeling pressure to act from Art, Douglas, and Calder but knowing that I wasn't permitted to write any checks, I broke down and began sobbing at my predicament. Not knowing what to do, I cried until there were no more tears. Then I took a deep breath, regained my composure, and called the Prosecutor's Office.

***

Anita Barney: Hi, Steve, it's Anita. Can you talk a minute?

Steve Schierholt: I can for a minute. Not very long, though. I'm getting ready to go into a meeting, but go ahead.

Barney: OK. All right. I just talked to Detective Davis a little while ago and he was going into a meeting also and that's why I can't get ahold of him and I need a quick answer of what to do.

Schierholt: OK.

Barney: OK. This Calder is going to press charges and go to the press if he doesn't have $5,000 by four o'clock tonight. I already told all of this to Detective Davis. Art knows it. Art's talked to Calder. Art just called me and said that he's going to call Douglas DeLarge and borrow $5,000 from him and he needs me as a back-up to say I will cover it. Now, what am I supposed to do here?

Schierholt: Who is Douglas DeLarge?

Barney: He owns a construction company. I'm not sure where it is. He's been a supporter of Art for a long time.

Schierholt: I am not comfortable with you saying you'll cover that debt.

Barney: So, what do I do?

Schierholt: What if you tell Art you won't do it? Or you can't do it? Or . . . you just can't.

Barney: He'll get angry. That's always been my predicament. If I don't do what he tells me he gets angry. And, oh god!

Schierholt: Now, this Calder . . . where this debt arises from, I know it's a Super Bowl ticket thing, right?

Barney: Yes, he went into partnership with Art to buy these Super Bowl tickets and then Art told him I would buy the tickets from them. And I already supposedly paid for my tickets. And I gave Calder two checks and he pulled the money out and gave it to Art already. And Art was supposed to put the money in there to cover the checks (I wrote) and he didn't.

So, my checks to Calder have bounced. Calder is taking them to the police, because of me.

Schierholt: OK. Now, who gave Calder the two checks? Did you give him the checks or did Art?

Barney: Art did.

Schierholt: Do you have Calder on tape?

Barney: Yes. Yes.

Schierholt: Do you have Calder on tape saying, or acknowledging that Art is the one who gave him the checks?

Barney: Oh, I don't think I have that. He just says *I have two checks here with your name on it.* I think is all he said.

Schierholt: Does he acknowledge on tape that this is Art's deal, not your deal?

Barney: Well, I was supposed to be buying tickets from the two of them. Yes, that's all I can say. That's how it was set up. I am buying Super Bowl tickets. I've given them two checks now. And Calder took the money from those checks and gave it to Art. And Art was supposed to go buy the tickets with that money. They had to have an advance is my understanding. What I've been told before. I don't have that on tape now. That was before.

Schierholt: How did you leave it with Art about this DeLarge fella?

Barney: I didn't say anything. I changed the subject and said I had a personal question to ask him, if he had any girlfriends . . . I'm trying to work my way into that.

Schierholt: Sure. And to get him to acknowledge that it is $2 million?

Barney: Well, I think he kinda did last night. You have to listen to the tapes. Because I asked him if he realized how much money. First of all he said *no.* But I said by the time you add everything up . . . I think it is on tape.

Schierholt: OK. All right.

Barney: I don't know what to do now.

Schierholt: How did you leave it with him? Is Art going to call you? Are you to call him, or what is the next step?

Barney: All he said was "Be prepared." That either means . . . I don't know if Douglas is going to call me and ask if it is OK to give Art this money, or if I will cover the money. I don't know what is going to happen.

Schierholt: What if you . . . let me throw this out and you just evaluate it. I'm thinking out loud, OK? You tell me what you think. You said that when you cry (Art) gets angry and hangs up and won't talk to you. What if you say something to him like—and maybe start crying if you can turn it on and off.

Barney: Oh, my god! I'm crying all the time. That's easy!

Schierholt: OK. What if you say that you just can't? Because then it's going to be one other person calling you and cussing you out because you're not going to be able to pay him. You can't. And just kinda keep repeating that. And kinda talk like you can't talk, you're crying. And try that first.

Barney: OK. I can just hear him now. Excuse my language, but he will say *You're just going to f**k this up. That's all you're going to do. It's going to be your fault. You're going to f**k it up because you won't do this!* That's how he talks all the time.

Schierholt: But if you stick to your guns and just keep saying, you know, "He's just going to keep hounding me and he's going to call me and cuss me out and on and on and on." Try that first. See what happens. And if it gets to the point, just pretend you're crying and can't even talk and he's not going to sit and listen to that forever, is he?

Barney: He hasn't before. But under this circumstance he is so desperate he may just tell me to *Shut the f**k up! Stop the f**k crying!* and talk that way to me. *Buck up! We're in this* *together!* I don't know. I don't know how he is going to react. I can try it.

Schierholt: If he says we're in this together, what if you say, "We're not in this together. I tried to help you and now look what you've done to me?" or something like that? What would his reaction be?

Barney: When I say I'm going to lose everything he says *Well, that's not going to happen. I won't let that happen.*

Schierholt: Try that first and then call me and update me.

Barney: OK, I'll try it.

***

Art Schlichter: Hello?

Anita Barney: Alan was here, I couldn't answer the phones.

Schlichter: OK, I'm going to get us some money today, but it's going to take a couple of checks from you. OK? One to Douglas. And one to another guy that I know. He's just going to hold them until I pay him back. OK? He thinks you're helping me. And I'm going to give you part of the money and give the other part to Calder. You'll get a little cash, too.

Barney: So, I'm supposed to write a check to Douglas DeLarge?

Schlichter: You need to get on the freeway and meet Bill in Polaris.

Barney: Let me write this down. Just a minute. *Bill at Polaris.* What's he going to do? What am I meeting him for?

Schlichter: You're giving him a check and he's taking it to Stuart DuPont. You've talked to him on the phone before. A nice guy.

Barney: Where's he? I can't remember.

Schlichter: He's in Cleveland. A very nice guy. Old school.

Barney: So, about Douglas DeLarge. What am I supposed to do here? I'm supposed to meet Bill at Polaris? I'm writing this down.

Schlichter: Write a check to Stuart DuPont for $14,000. And I don't know about Douglas. It's going to be about $10,000. All right? I told him you were going to back me up and you would have money by next week. He said his brother may lend it to him and have him write a cognovit note.

Barney: His brother may do it?

Schlichter: Write a check and a cognovit note. Yeah. So, we've got to go with that. OK? But we've got to hurry now because Douglas DeLarge is expecting you to call him. Just say, "Douglas, I'll have the money in that account no later than next Thursday or Friday." OK? That's all you got to say.

Barney: Well, wait a minute I'm writing this down. *Next Thursday or Friday the money will be there.* OK.

Schlichter: Yeah. You ordered it from your investment.

Barney: Where's my investment? I don't have any, do I?

Schlichter: Don't worry about it. I'm getting a little cash for us today! We got fires to put out! I'm going to get cash starting on Monday again.

Barney: But you know what? I'm really afraid. Do you know how many people are saying they are going to the police against me?

Schlichter: Right.

Barney: I've never been in a police station in my life.

Schlichter: Don't worry about it. Who sued you the other day?

Barney: I don't know. I'm afraid of all this. I'm scared to death.

Schlichter: Well, don't be scared now.

Barney: Why not?

Schlichter: If you're scared now, you're going to be in trouble. You've got to move forward.

Barney: Why, if I'm scared now, how am I going to be in trouble?

Schlichter: I said if you're scared now you're going to be in trouble. You just won't make it. You can't be scared now.

Barney: I'm probably going to end up in jail.

Schlichter: We're just starting to get it worked out. You're not going to end up in jail.

Barney: How are we working it out? I haven't got any money from you. How are you working it out?

Schlichter: What do you mean you haven't got any money from me? I gave you about $40,000 in the last three weeks.

Barney: Where did it go, though?

Schlichter: You just pay people.

Barney: For myself, though? I have my condo fees and my taxes. Personally, I'm not getting the money. I don't know what I'm going to do.

Schlichter: You will, eventually.

Barney: I don't even have any gasoline money.

Schlichter: I'm going to pay you back.

Barney: I don't know how you're going to do it.

Schlichter: OK, I'll call you back, OK? If Douglas calls you and says, "Come on down," say OK.

Barney: I'm supposed to wait for him to call me?

Schlichter: Yeah, but you gotta go see Bill first.

Barney: Well, wait a minute.

Schlichter: Get on the road! I've got somebody on the other line.

Barney: But I don't know what to tell Linda Scott. What did you tell me to tell her?

Schlichter: She call?

Barney: I think it's her number. I'm not sure. I've got to look it up. But if it's her—

Schlichter: Get in the car and I'll tell you what to say. I've got to talk to this guy. OK?

***

My attempts to slow down this process were ineffective and Art was expecting me to write a $10,000 check to Douglas DeLarge, and a check for $14,000 to give to Bill Hanners. Art would use them as collateral to collect cash from a man named Stuart DuPont in Cleveland. I was in quite the dilemma and could feel the pressure building. I couldn't write any checks, not even as a ruse, but I didn't want Art to become suspicious because I didn't have a plausible reason for refusing him at this point. It would be odd for me to drive to Polaris and meet Bill without a check. What would I say? I was out of excuses with no visible means of escape when John Amery called, and we began working together on a solution.

***

Anita Barney: I just thought I could do that, though. Just tell him my car is not starting. He'll probably say, "Bill will come to your house."

John Amery: Well, that's right.

Barney: I've got to think about what to say because—

Amery: Well, don't let him intimidate you.

My phone begins ringing.

Barney: He's calling again. One right after another.

Amery: Oh, yeah. He's relentless.

Barney: All right, well, this has been my life. I've been on the scale today and I've lost twenty-five pounds or more. I can't eat. I can't sleep.

Amery: Well, that's not the way you are supposed to be losing it.

Barney: I know it. But I just feel terrible about everybody. But we'll get it done. We'll get it resolved. I'm doing better.

Amery: Good! I'm glad to hear that. That's for sure.

Barney: I still feel devastated, but I will get through this. Because I don't want him doing this to anyone else. I really don't!

Amery: That's right. That's the key. Do the best you can. Just say you can't do it.

My phones continue ringing in the background.

Barney: There he goes again.

Amery: You can't write another bad check. Don't believe that crap of "one more time," one more time! OK?

***

Before I dialed Art's number, I cried out a prayer, "Oh, Lord, show me what to do!"

Art Schlichter: Yeah.

Anita Barney: OK, I guess my car is going to be all right. I left an interior light on. The dome light on. It's going now, but I didn't think it was going to start.

Schlichter: Who have you been talking to?

Barney: I wasn't talking; I was out in the garage.

Schlichter: Hey, listen.

Barney: What?

Schlichter: You've got to get to Polaris right now. At the, where did you meet Bill last time?

Barney: Uh, Max & Erma's, I think. Yeah, Max & Erma's.

Schlichter: I thought you said it was the BP Station?

Barney: No. Max & Erma's. But, Art, I hate to do this. I'm scared to do this. People are calling right and left for these bounced checks.

Schlichter: Yeah, these won't bounce. These are my friends. OK?

Barney: Art! Please don't—

Schlichter: I'll have them paid by Wednesday. I'm going to put the money in your account myself.

Barney: Please don't make me do this! I can't do this any more.

Schlichter: You know WHAT? We HAVE to do this today. We've got to pay Calder!

Barney: I CAN'T! He's not going to do anything.

Schlichter: OH, MY GOD! You should have heard what this guy told me and all the names he was throwing out at me. OK? Write the f**king checks! They will never be cashed. OK?

Barney: Oh, Art! I'm in trouble for all of these bounced checks.

Schlichter: I will not let you get in trouble for bounced checks!

Barney: Well, what about—

Schlichter: Have you got in trouble yet?

Barney: No.

Schlichter: OK. You've not been in trouble yet; you're not going to be in trouble.

Barney: Oh, god!

Schlichter: All you've got do to is pay 'em. Get over there to Bill!

Barney: I've had so many threats now. I just hate this.

Schlichter: No, these people won't threaten you.

Barney: Oh, Art!

Schlichter: All right?

Barney: I'm just devastated. I've lost twenty-five pounds now. I'm so sick over this. I'm going to lose my condos with all these liens. I was supposed to pay Rod Cheetham money today, even.

Schlichter: Go give him $1,000; you're going to get it. OK?

Barney: Oh, Art! Please? Please! I'm just—I really—I don't have any way to do it. I've done so many I'm scared to death. I'm really scared.

Schlichter: If you don't do this, we will be buried. Today!

Barney: Oh, Art! It's not going to happen. Calder's not going to do anything, I don't think.

Schlichter: Let me tell you something. He's got checks. OK? He's got checks . . . and you're not burying yourself. You just need to get him paid off or paid today and work on the rest.

Barney: I haven't got paid anything. I'm going to lose everything. This is what's bothering me!

Schlichter: We will get the money today to pay Rod Cheetham.

Barney: OK. How are you ever going to pay this $2 million back to me that you owe? How are you ever going to do this?

Schlichter: All right. Do we want to talk anymore?

Barney: I just want to know how are you going to pay—I'm writing all these bounced checks to these people and I'm not getting any money in return.

Schlichter: Have I asked you to write a check? I haven't asked you to write a check in months. OK?

Barney: That's true.

Schlichter: And, this is an emergency. Please. It's not going to hurt you.

***

I didn't write any checks. I didn't leave my house. I sat at my kitchen table feeding Art story after story to keep him occupied and myself out of trouble, waiting for Detective Davis to arrive and help me resolve the situation.

***

Art Schlichter: Where are you located?

Anita Barney: (long pause) Are you talking to me?

Schlichter: Hello?

Barney: Are you talking to Anita?

Schlichter: YES! Where are you located?

Barney: Uh, I'm just getting on the freeway.

Schlichter: Sh*t! All right. I'll talk to you later.

Barney: 'Bye.

Schlichter: Do you know (where) to meet him at?

Barney: Did you say at the BP?

Schlichter: Is that where you met him before?

Barney: No. Max & Erma's.

Schlichter: All right.

Barney: So, where am I supposed to go?

Schlichter: BP.

Barney: OK.

***

Art Schlichter: You're not even out of the house yet.

Anita Barney: I wanted to tell you I'm sick.

Schlichter: You know, Bill is sitting there waiting for ya. He's been there for fifty minutes.

Barney: He's not been there that long. I am so sick to my stomach. I'm going back in the house. I don't know—I'm crying I'm so sick. I don't know what I'm going to do.

Schlichter: What do you mean?

Barney: You've had those feelings you've been sick before. Haven't you been sick the last few days?

Schlichter: Yeah. OK. You need to meet me. I'll have to have someone else go besides Bill. He can't go. F**k it!

Barney: Where are you?

Schlichter: I'm coming up to Grove City and I'm sick. I haven't taken a shower. I look like sh*t. I got sick as a dog this morning. I vomited so many f**king times. I had to stick my hand down my throat and ripped the skin off my knuckle.

Barney: Well, me, too. I've been going through hell today . . . and I haven't showered or anything. And I'm a mess, too. And now I'm sick. Why did you say I hadn't even left the house?

Schlichter: I can tell.

Barney: How can you tell?

Schlichter: When you're in the car you can tell.

Barney: Oh, I see. Because I just walked in the house and went to the powder room here. I'm still at home.

Schlichter: I've got to call Bill and I've got to call Boris and, please, get this done.

Barney: Well, I'm trying.

Schlichter: Can't you go and meet Bill?

Barney: I'll try my best. I can't—

Schlichter: You've got to go down to see Douglas right now.

Barney: I can't do everything! I can't do everything here!

Schlichter: All right. I'll have Bill not go. I'll have Boris go.

Barney: Well, wait until I feel good. I'll have to call you back. I don't know—

Schlichter: Hey, we're going to GO TO JAIL TODAY! OK? This time's for real! A lot of these other guys wouldn't, but this guy (Calder) is for real. I've got a guy that is helping us today. OK?

Barney: Yes.

Schlichter: This guy is giving us a loan for four, five, six days. F**k! That's all I can ask. OK?

Barney: Yes.

Schlichter: TWO guys are willing to help us a little bit. And all you've got to do is write a check and post date 'em. You can always stop payment on 'em. But you have to go. Or we are running out of time. Calder is going to bury us today.

Barney: Oh, god! Well, I guess we should have paid him this week some time and calmed him down.

Schlichter: I didn't know that we owed HIM! I didn't know he was going to give us all the money. You weren't listening.

Barney: You told me to call and calm him down and I did.

Schlichter: That was two weeks ago.

Barney: No, I called him Monday and you told me to tell him at the end of this week we would have money for him. Either yesterday or today! $5,000 is what you told me to tell him, and I did. I told you that. And that hasn't happened, so . . . I'm just sick. I'm trying to get out of here the best I can, as quickly as I can.

Schlichter: Bill (Hanners) has to see his mom. He has to pick up his wife, and he's driving to Cleveland. He's doing that for *us!* Trying to help.

Barney: I know. I appreciate that. Well, I'll try my best. I don't know what to tell you. You know I've always done my best for you.

Schlichter: Well, we're in trouble right now.

Barney: I'm trying. I'm trying. I'm trying. I will leave as quick as I can. I've got to change my clothes and everything. I've got vomit all over me.

***

Art Schlichter: Where you at?

Anita Barney: I'm in my car.

Schlichter: All right. Bill is meeting me at the BP. All right? And then you need to drive down to Douglas DeLarge's office. I will meet you there. I'll call you back.

Barney: OK. I think that's off of 317 or something. I don't know what it is.

Schlichter: Well, it's on Groveport Road.

Barney: OK, I kinda remember.

Schlichter: All right. 'Bye

***

By the end of that call Detective Davis had arrived at my condo and created a story for me to tell Art that I had been stopped and questioned by police. This cover served two purposes: It was a legitimate reason I was unable to meet Bill (or Art or Douglas or Bill or Boris) to hand over checks, and with the police involved, the pressure on Art would dramatically increase.

***

Art Schlichter: What's going on?

Anita Barney: (Whispering loudly) OK, I'm in a police—the police are taking me to the Powell Police Station. I don't know where it is. They want to talk to me about a bad check. Another cop had pulled up. I don't know where I'm going. I

258

have no idea where it is I'm going. But I'm scared. I'm scared to death. I'm scared to death!

Schlichter: They are taking you for a *bad check*?

Barney: Yes. What am I to do? What do I tell them?

Schlichter: They're gonna arrest you!

Barney: What do I say to them, then? What do I do? Tell me what to do.

Schlichter: Oh, my god! Why would they arrest you? If they had a warrant out for you they woulda come and got ya.

Barney: I have no idea. I have no idea.

Schlichter: They've got you in the back of the car?

Barney: Yes . . . Yes.

Schlichter: Can Bill (Hanners) see you when he drives by?

Barney: I'm probably past there. I don't know where I'm going. I'm in the back. I'm whispering. I don't think they can hear me; there's a window between us. They can't hear me. I don't know what to say.

Schlichter: Did they arrest you?

Barney: They just said they would have to take me and they have some questions about a check is all they told me. What do I do? What do I tell them? *What do I tell them? I don't know what to do!*

Schlichter: Tell them you didn't know about it. You didn't know it was a problem.

Barney: OK.

Schlichter: If they ask you about it, you say, "I owe it and I'll get it handled. Nobody ever told me about it."

***

I disconnected from Art. Detective Davis prepared answers to questions he expected Art to ask me about my "encounter" with the police:

1. I will get a summons in the mail within 30 days.
2. I have 30 days to get checks paid back.
3. I didn't say why, only that I was having financial problems.
4. Detective Davis was cutting me a break because he knew Bob.
5. I had to write four to five pages for handwriting comparison purposes.
6. I didn't mention Art's name and he didn't ask about him.
7. Detective Davis did not act like he knew anything other than the checks. He said Lew Sanchez called him about a check.
8. I told Detective Davis that I was selling the condo and will have the money to pay everything back within a month.
9. I told Detective Davis just what Art told me to say. I cried a lot!

He also had a list of questions I needed to ask Art:

1. How are we going to pay everyone?
2. What do I do?
3. Please tell me what is going on.
4. Should I have an attorney go with me to court?

And suddenly I wasn't just passively recording phone calls for the police, I had become an integral member of the investigation team, creating scenarios, and soliciting information that could be used as authorities built their case against Art.

***

When Art called me later, I continued fabricating details to conceal my involvement with authorities, while providing plausible answers to his questions.

Art Schlichter: What's going on?

Anita Barney: I'm at home now. They told me they were talking to me about a check and they gave me ten days to make it good. So, I'm at home and I'm crying and I'm devastated. There's my phone—I don't know what to do. They didn't give me much information. That's all I know. I'm back home now.

Schlichter: Anita. Anita! Where you at right now?

Barney: I'm sitting in my kitchen.

Schlichter: Well, what's the printer going off? Are you at a police station or where you at?

Barney: A printer?

Schlichter: Yeah. I can hear the—

Barney: That was my phone that was just ringing. I'll go back over. It was just my phone ringing. I told you. My house phone is ringing.

Schlichter: Anita. Anita. They left your car to be towed?

Barney: No. I got my tire and they fixed it. They put a spare on it.

Schlichter: I thought they took you away.

Barney: They did. I went to the police station.

Schlichter: What police station?

Barney: Powell. And they told me and I said, "Why are you talking to me?" They said something about a bad check and they allowed me ten days to get the money to cover it before they would do anything. So, they let me go and I'm home now. You can come by if you want. I'm home. I cannot write any more checks!

Schlichter: I knew you—I knew that you weren't where you said you were. That's how good I am. OK? You weren't f**king hauled off by them.

Barney: I wasn't hauled off.

Schlichter: Yeah, you did. You said you were in the back of car.

Barney: While they were talking to me. Yes!

Schlichter: No! You said they were driving with ya.

Barney: Well, that's true. Yes, that's true.

Schlichter: OK. And you went to the Powell Police station. I called the Powell Police station and they said, "No Anita Barney has even been brought in for questioning today."

Barney: That's not true. Why would they tell you I was, then? Why would they tell you that? I don't know.

Schlichter: Because it's record. Let me tell you something. You were standing inside someplace when you were talking to me. You said you were standing outside with the police. I just hate when you lie to me. You know, you didn't have to lie to me. Just say you didn't want to (write checks). I understand. But, you just sent everybody into a f**king frenzy.

Barney: Well, if you want, call the police department. Do you want to do that? They gave me a card.

Schlichter: What's with the paperwork?

Barney: Well, I had it but I also have a number here to call, too, if you want to do that.

Schlichter: Well, what's the f**king check? Who's the check?

Barney: *Who's the check?*

Schlichter: Who is the check from?

Barney: Oh, they didn't tell me that. They just said it was a bad check.

Schlichter: Well, you can't bring somebody in and say you've got a bad check and not tell them where it's from.

Barney: Well, it's for $30,000. That's all I know. That's all he told me. "You wrote a bad check for $30,000 and there is no money there to cover it." They didn't tell me who, what name, or anything.

Schlichter: You know what?

Barney: I don't know. I've never been in a police department in my life so I wasn't going to argue with him. I didn't know what to do.

Schlichter: Did they put you in the holding tank?

Barney: No. No, I just sat at some desk and talked to some police officer. That is all.

Schlichter: Was it a detective that came to see ya?

Barney: Yes.

Schlichter: Who was it?

Barney: A Scott Davis.

Schlichter: Oh, you're right there with him, right now.

Barney: No, I'm not! I have his card. I'm reading his card to you. You asked me who it was. It's right here. Right here. (I wrinkled the card so Art could hear it.) Hear it? Scott Davis. I'll give you his number if you want to call him.

Schlichter: When you gonna find out what the check's about?

Barney: I'm afraid to find out. I don't even know, I've got to go to the bank, I guess. PNC. I don't even know who turned me in or what it's for. I don't know! I don't know anything. They said, "If you can make it good within ten days, we'll let you go." I'm supposed to go to PNC and find out who it is from. I don't know who we wrote a check to for $30,000. We've written so many. I have to find out.

Schlichter: Never heard that before. Well, everything got blown up today.

Barney: Well, it certainly wasn't because of me.

Schlichter: Well, I mean, it *was* because you wouldn't tell me the truth.

Barney: I am telling you right now. Here is this guy's number. Call him. Hear the card? I'm beating the phone with it.

Schlichter: Well, what did they say besides, "Here's a check."? Did they talk about anything else?

Barney: No, no, not really. No. So, I don't know what I'm supposed to do now. I don't know what I'm supposed to do. It's already late, so I'm not going to do anything.

Schlichter: Call them.

Barney: PNC? You think I should go? I probably should go there then, shouldn't I? I've got to go through my checkbooks, I just got home, and see who I've written a check to.

Schlichter: You just told me you *were* home.

Barney: I said *I am* home! I have to go through my checkbooks. I said I just got home a short while ago. I've got to go through my checkbooks. They are on the table. Hear them? I've got to go through these checkbooks. Do you know how many checkbooks? What do I have six, seven checkbooks? Hear the phone ringing?

Schlichter: If Douglas DeLarge calls you, answer it! *Answer it!*

Barney: It's maybe Ben Roberts. I don't want to hear it. He'll leave a message. He's been calling and cussing me out. And Chuck Taylor, Ida Croft, they are all calling me. I can't talk to them, Art. Don't you understand? I don't want to lie to them. I don't know what to say to them. Listen, it never stops. The recorder should come on soon. You'll hear it in just a minute. I really need money. I don't know what I'm going to do for my utilities or anything. I don't know what I'm going to do.

Schlichter: I told ya I had one way . . .

Barney: Well, it sure wasn't fun. I'm embarrassed. I hope my son doesn't find out about it. Or my daughter. I've never been in a position like this in my life. I mean, this is terrible. I'm mortified. I don't have any tears left I've cried so much. I'm just shaking now. I'm just shaking. I can't get over it, Art.

Schlichter: I've got to go talk to Calder. Go, try to make amends . . .

Barney: I'm sorry.

Schlichter: Why didn't you CALL ME BACK?

Barney: I wasn't able to call. They made me turn my phones off for a while. And then I started driving home and Alan called and I was talking to Alan and it didn't take me that long to get home, but now I'm home and I've just got to go through the checkbooks now. I don't know where to turn right now. But I need money and I don't know what I'm going to do. I need money as bad as you do. Probably worse. Because I have condos to take care of, taxes. I have a gas bill to pay. Electric. So, I need money more than you do.

Schlichter: What are you going to do if I give you $2,000 today?

Barney: I don't know! I don't know. I've got to pay bills. I've got my electric bill. Gas bill came in. I don't know. Bills. That's all I can do. I let Sabrina go because that will save me sixty dollars a week. I cut back.

***

Art Schlichter: Well.

Anita Barney: Trying to relax here and unwind. Have a cry.

Schlichter: Bill drove two-thirds of the way to Cleveland and the guy wouldn't give him the check because he didn't have your check to hold for safe keeping.

Barney: Hold? For safe keeping? Is that what you said?

Schlichter: He was going to hold it to make sure I got his money back to him. I just needed you to cosign for me. I was going to give you about $3,000 or $2,000 and I was going to take $2,000 or $3,000.

Barney: I know.

Schlichter: If you want, he will start driving right now and I'll have Bill turn around and meet, oh, no. I'll have Boris meet him.

Barney: But the Detective told me that I'm not allowed to write any more checks until I have cash in my hands to cover the checks and, in ten days, I have it written down here. He said ten days to make good for that $30,000.

***

Art had a right to be suspicious. He had built a complicated web of lies and deceit and, no doubt, could feel it beginning to unravel. Trying to get to the bottom of what had happened, he placed a call to the Dublin Police Department, posing as my husband. The two-minute call creates more questions than answers and showed the lengths that Art would go as he tried to control my every action.

Dublin Police Dispatch: Dublin Police, can I help you?

Art Schlichter: Yes, where's your impound lot that takes your cars?

Dispatch: Well, it depends on who impounded it.

Schlichter: I guess it would be Dublin Police.

Dispatch: OK. Right. But I mean we have several different places that take vehicles. Was your car towed?

Schlichter: Yeah, on the Sawmill Parkway.

Dispatch: Well, that's not our jurisdiction. You're sure Dublin Police did it?

Schlichter: Whose jurisdiction would that be? Sawmill Parkway?

Dispatch: That would probably be Delaware County Sheriff. Do you know what your license plate is?

Schlichter: Uh, no. It's my wife's. We're just trying to figure it out. She's not here right now.

Dispatch: Why was it towed?

Schlichter: I don't know. I think they hauled her in.

Dispatch: OK. Was your wife driving the vehicle, or who was in the vehicle?

Schlichter: Wife was.

Dispatch: What's the last name?

Schlichter: Barney. B–A–R–N–E–Y.

Dispatch: First name?

Schlichter: Anita.

Dispatch: I'm not seeing—when was it towed?

Schlichter: About three hours ago. Two hours ago.

Dispatch: OK. Yeah. That wouldn't be us. It's probably Delaware County, let me give you their phone number.

Schlichter: OK. She hasn't been, uh, they haven't—

Dispatch: I'm sorry. What?

Schlichter: She hasn't been arrested, has she?

Dispatch: Not by our agency. No. I have had no contact with her today.

Schlichter: So, would it be Delaware County or Powell? Which one would it be?

Dispatch: Do you know where she was on Sawmill Parkway?

Schlichter: About Vittoria's, the restaurant.

Dispatch: You said, "Vittoria's"?

Schlichter: And the fire station.

Dispatch: Let me give you both phone numbers because I'm not sure which one it would be and you'll just have to check with both of them.

***

I felt a flash of empowerment surge through me as the tables turned, and the predator became the prey.

29 | WE WON'T MAKE IT TODAY
DECEMBER 23, 2010

| *"You get your panties on, girl. I'm trying to save our lives. I'm not going to let us down."* | *Art Schlichter* |

Art used to call it, "Putting out fires." There was always a looming deadline, or threat of prosecution, or jail time, or other urgent need that he presented to keep my adrenalin high. Frenzy was his secret weapon. Early on when he would call me in a state of panic, I was immediately motivated to respond in a reckless and reactionary manner and would take whatever action (write checks, wire money, pawn jewelry, etc.) he demanded to keep the wolves at bay. Because he kept the accelerator pressed to the floor, there was little time to actually process what was happening until it was too late.

By the time the following call took place a couple of days before Christmas, I had been cooperating with the authorities and recording calls for several weeks. I was instructed not to meet with Art or to write any checks on his behalf, but it was difficult to put him off without tipping my hand.

This conversation reveals how Art would introduce an emergency situation and, depending on my level of compliance, cycle through his approach from calm to conspiratorial to angry to accusatory to protector to persuasive, until he heard the response he needed.

Interestingly enough, the reason he told me *his* funds were delayed and he wanted me to write a check to Pastor Hartwell as collateral was because his money was being wired from an offshore account. This is the same story he had me tell my friends: I needed a short-term loan because *my* money was tied up in an overseas account.

Regarding Pastor Hartwell: I never met him or gave him checks. I knew about him only through conversations with Art and later, seeing his name on a police report where he was listed as a victim. Meanwhile, Calder Fenwick, the local business owner who wanted to purchase Super Bowl tickets from Art and sell them for a profit, continued to create problems for us.

Not knowing how to handle this situation—which threatened to explode at any moment—I called Detective Davis for guidance and he quickly devised a plan; it was time for him to intervene. I called Calder and arranged to meet him at his office. As Calder pulled into the parking lot and exited his Hummer, Detective Davis arrived in his unmarked car. From my vantage point sitting across the street, I watched them shake hands and exchange a few words before they entered the building together.

***

Art Schlichter: OK, I want you to listen to me now, OK? I can't tell you how important this is.

Anita Barney: OK.

Schlichter: You hear me?

Barney: Yeah.

Schlichter: I've got money that's coming in to an account today . . . it usually hits around one to three o'clock. I have to be at Calder's office by noon. The money is not in the account yet. I have a guy, a preacher, Seamus Hartwell, who goes to Marble Heights Church. He's the preacher there, and a nice guy. He is going to help me. OK? To put cash up. I need a check from you. All right? Given to me made out to this guy (Hartwell). If I don't go get this money right now, before noon, this f**king Calder is going to bury me and you. So, I promise you, cross my heart and hope to die, that this check will never be cashed. OK? EVER! It won't be run through. This man is a minister. He is a fine gentleman. I spoke for him. Remember when I went to Marble Heights and spoke?

Barney: OK.

Schlichter: Listen, nobody'll know that this happened. All this is going to be is a form of hold for me. To get the money, I got him involved in something. It will be fine. But you need to help me here. I am driving right now. I'm going to be, I need you to meet me behind Kroger's right now! OK? I just got on 270. Don't tell me your car broke down. Don't tell me the police took you and put you in a car. Don't tell me we're in trouble. Don't tell me any of that. Honey, I need to get Calder paid off.

Barney: I don't have any checks.

Schlichter: Yes, you do.

Barney: I do not have any checks. I wrote the last one. I promised.

Schlichter: U.S. Bank account. You have checks. Anita! ANITA! We won't make it today if you don't write me this check now. I've worked this out. It will never be cashed. OK? I promise you.

Barney: I hear you, but I don't want to go to jail. I'm afraid that they are watching me.

Schlichter: Let me tell you something! Calder has got two checks that he wants to throw you in jail on. This guy (Pastor Hartwell) is a friend. He will NEVER, he will NEVER DO ANYTHING. I'M GOING TO PAY HIM BACK! OK? You cannot—this is a friend. Calder is gonna throw us both in jail today. I want to get him taken care of today! All right? PLEASE! . . . you don't know what I'm saying, g*d*** it!

My ass and your ass will be dead as of today. This morning. At noon! That was my time. All right? Unless you haven't told me something. You haven't told me the truth on something, then you need to tell it to me right now! What the f**k is really going on?

Barney: I'm just scared to death. I'm scared to death!

Schlichter: Calder has got checks that he is ready to prosecute you on today! OK? I can get those checks today, no problem. And transfer it over to a friend. All right?

Barney: The detective said, "Do not write another check!" or I will go to jail.

Schlichter: This guy is not . . . HE'S A PREACHER! HE'S THE NICEST GUY IN THE WORLD. HE'S MY FRIEND! I ask him to do me one favor. And he said, "I will." OK?

Barney: Yes. OK. I'm scared to death though, I'm telling you. I'm scared.

Schlichter: He just has to have something to show his wife. All right? That's it! That's all he has to do.

Barney: Will you write him a promissory note or something?

Schlichter: NO! HE DOES NOT WANT THAT! Get in your f**king car and get to behind Kroger's right now! OK? You know, let me tell you something. If f**king Calder is an a**hole, his wife is a b***h! Calder is a good guy. His wife wants him to hurt you and me. We've got enough . . . that if Calder comes down on us, then they'll all come out on you. OK? They'll kill us.

Barney: Oh, god!

Schlichter: We're all right. Pastor Hartwell is going to help me. He just needs something to show his wife. You are a rich woman . . . all right? All he has to say is, "This lady is a member of the foundation, donated money to Art's foundation to help him. Here is the money she has written, uh, I'm gonna help Art until his money becomes clear." That's all he is going to say. It's as simple as that. You need to stay out of it. He is fine with it. And it will work out very well. I've got to get Calder taken care of. And let me tell you something, not only do I have to get this taken care of, I've got to get it taken care of by noon. And I'm driving up to Route 33 and 161 right now. OK? I thought I was going to need Bill (Hanners) to get this done. But he just called and the money will not be in the account until probably two or three o'clock. So . . .

Barney: He can't get the money any sooner?

Schlichter: Who?

Barney: Bill.

Schlichter: It's wired into the account from an offshore account, OK? Offshore account.

Barney: I hope they are not watching me to see if I write checks. That is what is scaring me.

Schlichter: WHO IS GOING TO WATCH YA? NOBODY IS EVER GOING TO SEE YOUR F**KING CHECK!

Barney: OK.

Schlichter: Come on, let's go! I'm sitting here waiting. Just getting off the exit.

Barney: Well, I'm not even dressed.

Schlichter: You get your panties on, girl. I'm going to save our lives. I'm not going to let us go down. All right?

Barney: OK.

My house phone begins ringing.

Schlichter: No one is going to see you writing the check. Who is calling you?

Barney: I don't know. It's 267.

Schlichter: Area code 267?

Barney: Yeah.

Schlichter: You've got to get in the car and come on!

Barney: OK. All right.

Schlichter: Listen, Anita. I love you. You have been a godsend to me. I have been a nightmare for you. All right? I have to get us through this. You are incapable of doing it. If I don't get us through, nobody will. I have . . . a little bit to keep us going. OK?

Barney: I know. OK.

Schlichter: You've got to be a little stronger than this. Don't act like, *OK*.

Barney: I've been falling apart. I'm very emotional.

Schlichter: Let me tell you something. Wouldn't you like to get Calder out of the way?

Barney: Yes.

Schlichter: OK. Who would you rather have a check into? A friend of mine that is a preacher who would NEVER do anything? Or Calder? That wants to F**K us? All right? He wants to bury us. Because his wife thinks we f**ked him.

Barney: She was angry that day I met her in the parking lot.

Schlichter: Do you understand that I can get rid of this c**ks****r right now!

Barney: I understand.

Schlichter: OK! Come on!

Barney: I have to get ready here, so, I'll get moving.

Schlichter: I'm past, down by the Marathon Station on the other end.

Barney: But, I've got to get ready.

Schlichter: You don't have to get ready. I look like sh**! I haven't taken a shower. I jumped in the car. I got a pair of old beat-up jeans on. A stained shirt and my long coat. And bad breath. All right?

Barney: I've got to get organized here. I don't even know where the checks are. So—

Schlichter: Oh, F**K! You've got a million of them.

Barney: I threw some away, I'm telling you. Because I don't want to be—

Schlichter: U.S. Bank. Just U.S. Bank, that's fine. It doesn't make any difference what bank! Any account, he's not even going to cash it. I want to give him a current account. Come on! Let's go!

Barney: All right. OK.

My tactic was to agree with Art verbally to keep him engaged and stall him, but never follow through. With Detective Davis' warning that if I wrote another check for Art he would surely arrest me, I didn't meet Art that day and I had hell to pay later. Meanwhile, Calder Fenwick shared his version of what took place during the unexpected meeting with Detective Davis, which was outlined in a Dublin Police Report:

12–23–2010

This date, I met with Calder Fenwick at his place of business. Fenwick advised he was contacted by Schlichter in October 2010 by telephone. Schlichter told Fenwick that he had heard from a friend that Fenwick may be interested in Super Bowl tickets. Fenwick stated that he was not interested.

Several weeks later Schlichter called again and met with Fenwick at his office. Schlichter told Fenwick that he had an investor (Anita Barney) who wanted to buy twenty Super Bowl tickets. If Fenwick gave him the $32,000 to buy the tickets he could keep four of the tickets and go to the Super Bowl. The rest of the tickets would go to a rich woman (Anita Barney) who was willing to write Fenwick a check for the remainder of the tickets and that any proceeds from the tickets would be split with Fenwick for fronting the money.

The "deal" was he could buy tickets for $1,100 apiece and sell them for $4,000 apiece. Schlichter told Fenwick that he had a connection with the Indianapolis Colts who could get the tickets at cost. He gave Fenwick the two checks from Barney for a total of $32,000. As a guarantee that he was getting the tickets as promised.

Fenwick withdrew $22,000 from his company account and gave the cash to Schlichter to buy tickets. Fenwick became suspicious when he attempted to cash the checks and found out they were not good. He called Schlichter and eventually received $11,000 in repayment. As of this date he is still out the additional $11,000 including $3,000, that he gave Schlichter (copy of check provided) for Bowl Party tickets.

Fenwick agreed to make a recorded call to Schlichter concerning his refund or Super Bowl tickets. Fenwick stated he will provide a written statement and does wish to pursue charges. During the call Schlichter promised to repay Fenwick the money for the tickets within two days. Schlichter stated repeatedly that he was getting the tickets from his connection as soon as they were available.

Reporting Officer: Detective Scott Davis
Dublin Division of Police

30 | CHRISTMAS 2010

"After the first of the year things will be a lot better for everyone."	*Art Schlichter*

Two days before Christmas Art instructed me to meet Bill Hanners in the Borders parking lot off Sawmill Road. Bill gave me $2,000 as a loan repayment from Art who said I was to buy Christmas gifts with it. However, there were no gifts to buy or decorations to hang or elaborate parties to lavish on my friends this year; I desperately needed the money for basic necessities like groceries and utilities.

I didn't receive any Christmas cards, but I could have covered the mantle with the paperwork from lawsuits filed in November and December by Hugh Buttke (seeking repayment of $14,140), Tim Baker (seeking repayment of $219,500 plus interest), and Rod Cheetham (seeking repayment of $30,000 plus interest) as they began proceedings in an attempt to collect the money I borrowed at Art's direction. On Christmas Eve, my postman delivered certified letters from former friends Cruz Hill, Farley Daft, and Lew Sanchez. Too ashamed to read their condemnation and see their signatures affixed to promises of lawsuits, I couldn't bear to open the envelopes until after Christmas Day, so I set them aside.

Looking for solace in tradition, Alan and I suffered through a quiet Christmas Eve meal at La Scala. The previous year I had reserved a private room and hosted a holiday extravaganza at the restaurant, toasting friends and family. This year I didn't even have a tree.

Alan and I visited Aunt Lil on Christmas afternoon. Later he called, expressing his frustration at my situation and sorrow over broken dreams. He didn't understand how my life had become such a wreck. Nothing I said made any sense, even to me, and I could feel myself falling down an emotional black hole. As soon as Alan ended the call, I began weeping uncontrollably.

Art called several times on Christmas. During his final call of the day, he assured me that on January 2 or 3 we would have at least $100,000. "It won't be all of it—it's not a million dollars—but it will be a substantial amount." He promised we would sit down and look at all the bills and everything and take it from there. I felt a tiny bit of hope at his declaration. I asked if he was serious.

"You can take it to the bank or I'll be dead by then. That's the way it is," he said confidently. He asked me to hold the fort down five more working days, until Monday, January 3, 2011. He instructed me to find out about the bounced checks. "Call the bank. Call the detective on Monday (December 27) and find out what you're supposed to do so you don't get thrown in jail. Talk to people. Answer the phone. Keep everyone at bay until after the first of the year." To all the people who called and made me feel bad, I was supposed to say, "After the first of the year things will be a lot better for everyone."

"I'll call you tomorrow," he said before he hung up.

Of course you will, I thought wearily.

***

A few days after Christmas I finally summoned the courage to open the certified letters that had arrived. I was aware my friends had met recently at the home of Joy Blanco to discuss what was happening with me. Joy had invited me to attend the meeting. I declined. Since I was working with the police and couldn't talk about Art, there wasn't anything I could say to explain my inability to repay the money they had loaned me. Long ago people had grown tired of hearing my apologies and excuses; they wanted their money, and rightly so. They deserved answers I couldn't give them.

As I feared, the envelopes did not carry wishes for a Merry Christmas or Happy New Year, only promises of legal action:

From Cruz Hill, a close friend and our former personal trainer:
> *On or around July 11, 2010 I loaned you $15,000 on two different occasions . . . I have received nothing. It is now December 23, 2010. If I don't have my money within ten days I will be forced to take legal actions against you Monday, January 3rd, 2011. Sorry it had to come to this.*

Lew Sanchez and his wife had stayed in our home and regularly took advantage of our OSU football tickets:
> *I am writing to you today as a final request for remuneration relative to the loan you requested of Annabelle Sanchez and myself . . . the remaining balance due is $29,400. This of course does not take into account the additional $11,100 that was promised as interest for our alleviation of your short term cash requirements . . . you have 10 days to provide the funds as stipulated in our agreement and make restitution or I will make a formal complaint with the Dublin, Ohio police department . . .*

Farley Daft, the school friend who asked me out after Bob's passing:
> *This letter is in reference to your personal check #1135 in the amount of $30,000 . . . for the payback of personal loan, loaned to you by me. Anita, please respond within 10 days . . . if you fail I will have no other option but to take legal action.*

Roland Nesbitt and his wife, Judy, who were our good friends for years:

> *I am writing this letter as a final request for repayment of a cash loan in the amount of $90,000. Your personal checks could not be cashed because the account was closed. Additional promises by you to pay your debt have come and gone. You are in default of your agreement. The balance must be paid in full, including accrued finance charges and interest . . . if you do not return my money in full in 10 days as promised, I will file civil or criminal charges against you.*

31 | LINDA FROM DAYTON
December 2010—January 2011

"In my ten plus years of doing this job, I have never come across anyone who had the ability to persuade others to do whatever they asked, like Art could. And that's saying something."	Official assigned to the Art Schlichter investigation

I knew Linda Scott only through Art. As you will read in the following transcripts of the recorded conversations that took place from late December 2010 through January 2011, Linda had been involved with Art for quite a while (even supporting him while he was in prison), and they had discussed marriage at one point. She appeared to still have feelings for him and, at the beginning of our interaction, was either unaware of or unwilling to grasp the gravity of the situation he had created and his potential for destruction. When federal investigators contacted her earlier in 2010, she was insulted by their questions and responded belligerently.

By January 2011, however, when it's clear Art isn't going to deliver on his promises of payment and she is struggling under the massive debt incurred on his behalf, she revealed new details about Art's activities and threatened to send him to prison. In a last, desperate attempt to keep Linda at bay, Art told her he has signed loan papers with me, and that I will give her money on his behalf. This is a blatant lie, as Art is well aware at that point I didn't have any money, nor had I had any for months.

Art was a master storyteller and could string together details on the fly that were quite believable. These recorded conversations reveal Art's ability to devise a plan in intricate detail that was completely false. There was no check that had been mailed to Florida. Nor were there elderly neighbors sent to retrieve it and return it to me in Columbus. Art was spinning a story to delay a payment to Linda that may or may not be forthcoming, depending on whether he could beg, borrow, or gamble the money from someone else. He was constantly in a frenzied state, borrowing from Peter to pay Paul.

Also interesting to note in these exchanges is that Linda was able to hurt Art's feelings with a seemingly harmless comment. *"I hope those panties your mom gave you fit your fat ass when you're back in the slammer,"* bothered Art so much he mentioned it to me over the course of several phone calls.

I couldn't understand how a convicted felon, who literally stole millions of dollars from people and withstood threats of physical harm, public humiliation, and incarceration without batting an eye, could cry foul over a seemingly innocuous insult from one of his victims. I recall learning in school that everyone has an Achilles heel—a weakness that can be exploited—and the taunts from Linda that seemed juvenile and humorous to me revealed Art's bruised ego. No doubt there are countless therapists who would be willing to discuss a compelling theory regarding Art's levels of insecurity.

I was continuing to work with Franklin County Assistant Prosecutor Steve Schierholt and Detective Scott Davis of the Dublin Division of Police, and checked in with them when I wasn't sure how to proceed with regards to interacting with Art and his associates. I used my conversations with Linda to mine details to provide information to support the investigation. I generally didn't have Davis nearby to coach me during phone conversations and often had to invent my own stories as I went along. It was nerve-wracking. I didn't want to inadvertently say the wrong thing and sabotage the investigation. I also couldn't afford to alienate Art and send him packing. Every call was a performance. It was a real-life game of cat and mouse, with my future hanging in the balance.

***

One afternoon in late December Art called and said he needed me to call a woman named Linda Scott. "Let me think about what I want you to say and I'll call you right back. OK?" A dial tone was humming in my ear before I had a chance to respond.

He called a few minutes later to give me Linda Scott's number, and I realized she had a Dayton area code. Then Art began filling me in on the story I was to tell Linda. I was supposed to say I had ordered $9,000 (at some point this number grew to $9,900) from my bank and it was inadvertently sent to my condo in Florida. My elderly neighbors agreed to retrieve the check and forward it to me in Dublin, where I would deposit it and then transfer a portion of it to Linda. I was not going to order any additional money until after January 1, 2011, because I didn't want to incur any more tax debt in 2010.

"Tell her you're gonna wait and then you're going to order a big gob of money after the first of next week. And you'll get back with her and figure out how we can get her some money, OK?"

He was adamant that Linda realize I had made this decision of my own accord, and that it had nothing to do with Art or anyone else. He stressed this point several times. "Make sure she knows!"

As I began to ask Art questions, clarifying the message I had been ordered to deliver, he quickly developed a story in astonishing detail. "OK, let's say, your neighbors sent the check to you last week, but you have not yet received it. There was a delay because your neighbors, who are quite elderly, did not have a key to your mailbox and you had to mail it to them so they could access your mail." He continued, "Your mail is typically delivered around 4 p.m. and it should arrive today, tomorrow, or the next day. You don't know. They don't know the first thing about trying to overnight anything, so they sent it to you regular mail."

Art went around and around with the details for more than an hour: the check was supposed to arrive in Florida last week, elderly neighbors waiting for a mailbox key to arrive, they sent the check via regular mail, I've been waiting, ordered $9,000 and won't get any more until after the first of the year due to taxes. Once it arrives, I'll have enough money to help Linda out next week.

He made me repeat the details back to him as I read the story from the notepad where I had scribbled his directives.

"That's all you gotta say. It was *your* decision. You made the decision on your own. For your own benefit. That's it. All right? Call me back," he barked. "Just be real upbeat with her! All right?"

I felt sick about this charade. "I need to work up the courage to do this. I hate lying to her like this."

"You're *not lying!* Your *are* ordering money after January second. You're ordering it from me."

I didn't understand. "I'm ordering it *from* you?" I questioned. "I don't have any money to order."

I could hear the anger seeping into his tone as he clipped his words. "We're getting money. You're ordering it from me and I'm giving it to you!"

***

Unsure of how to proceed, I tried unsuccessfully to reach Detective Davis for guidance and then, in desperation, placed a call to Steve Schierholt in the Prosecutor's Office.

Steve picked up and I jumped right in. "Art wants me to call this Linda Scott and tell her I will have money for her. I told him I didn't want to. Starting about 2:15 p.m., Art has called me about twenty times. He is calling relentlessly now. Linda is calling and texting me, too. But my attorney said not to make the call until I spoke to you or someone who could tell me what to do. I didn't want to get in trouble for lying again."

Steve asked about the woman Art wanted me to call.

"It's Linda Scott. She lives in Dayton. He had me write some checks to her that she was going to cash or deposit, but he hasn't put the money in my account yet to cover them. He wants me to tell her that the money will be there next week."

Steve said he would call me back with instructions regarding what to tell Linda, which he did a bit later. Meanwhile, Art had been calling for more than an hour and I needed to create a story to explain why I had not answered. The phone rang seconds after I disconnected with Steve. It was Art. I quickly answered and told him that Alan and his sister from Philadelphia had stopped by to visit and had just left.

"You know I can't have your phone around when Alan is here. It will create questions." Before I can even finish my explanation, Art cut me off with a string of expletives.

"Jesus Christ! You scared me to f**king death! F**king, all you had to do is call this g*d***n f**king Linda Scott and you didn't. She has blown my phone off. She called me a fat ass. It really hurt my feelings."

I can't stop myself from chuckling at someone calling Art a fat ass. He becomes indignant.

"Let me tell you what she wrote me. *I hope those panties your mom gave you fit your fat ass when you're back in the slammer.* That's what she said to me!

I'm laughing now and can't contain myself. Art's on a roll and there's no stopping his tirade.

"F**king b**ch! F**king whore! See that sh**? It hurts my feelings. No one calls my ass fat."

I ask a few questions about Linda and he finally composes himself. Then he reviews all of the details of the story of the $9,000 check sent to Florida and the elderly neighbors, and the mailbox key and the proverbial check in the mail. "Tell Linda that she will be taken care of. That's all you got to say! Understand?"

I tell him I understand and I'll make the call, but there's no stopping him. He makes it clear it's *my* fault Linda has been harassing him over the past hour.

"Listen! I'm ready to f**king blow up again today! OK? I've had to deal with 9,000 texts from this woman and all I wanted you to do was just call her about an hour and a half ago. And that would have taken care of it. But I had to deal with it the whole time. Then I had to worry about what happened to you. Because you didn't call me back. Call Linda and tell her you'll put some money in the bank when the check arrives."

***

I look over the notes Art had me write down, recall the guidance Steve had given me, say a quick prayer, take a deep breath, and dial Linda's number.

Anita Barney: Linda? This is Anita, I couldn't answer my phone. I had a relative stop by.

Linda Scott: Oh, OK. Art was really worried about you because he said it was unlike you not to answer your phone.

Barney: Well, I'm a little shook up right now because Art has been calling repeatedly. OK, what has he said to you and what are we supposed to be doing and how much money does he owe you, or I owe you? What is going on? The whole situation exactly? Can you explain it to me or not?

Scott: Well, I can explain it to you. I know that Art had said that you were going to try to get money out after the first of the year to help with the bulk of what we were trying to do in the past few months. But there was a tax reason you wanted to wait until after the first of the year. But I have the problem that I have credit card bills that I have to pay at the end of this month and I'm at an absolute panic because I don't have the money to pay those credit card bills. And Art's been telling me all this time that you were going to be able to help and I've been making plans based on that and now I'm in a disaster, personal financial disaster because of what I, because of listening to Art. And I need $3,000 to pay credit cards this month or I am just, I'm not going to be able to make the payments, is the problem.

Barney: What about next Monday? Is that too late? Because there should be some money coming in today or tomorrow. My check was sent was to Florida and the neighbors are sending it back here.

Scott: Oh, OK. Yeah, he did mention that to me. Um, I can. Monday is not a bank holiday, is it?

Barney: No, I don't think so; it's the third, I think.

Scott: Yeah, I have some bills due on the fifth, but I can probably arrange, if the money can be cleared in my account I can probably arrange to do a bank transfer to them and make those on time. I have two that are due on the fifth. And those are the ones that I am really freaking out about right now. I have one due on the thirty-first. I don't know if that is a holiday, but that is what the statement says. But I can cover that one myself. It's these others that are coming up and I'm just an absolute basket case over. I have just maxed out everything to help Art when he needed it. Everything was betting on it to come and nothing has come and that's the problem. Now, I've exhausted every resource I have to keep myself afloat. I'm just going completely berserk here. But if you're pretty sure Monday can happen, then I can wait until Monday, but I can't wait any further than Monday.

My TracFone is ringing continually in the background.

Barney: Well, maybe this week, even, it will happen. So, we'll see. That's Art calling. Have you known Art a long time?

Scott: Oh, yeah. Oh, gosh. Seven or eight years? He was in prison when I first got hooked up with him. But I've been with him every day since he has been out of prison. He and I talk on the phone every single day. I've been with him through all of his family issues and issues with his kids and issues with everything. Art aged me ten years.

My phone continues to ring.

Scott: He's aged me more than ten years, at least.

Barney: How did you get in touch with him when he was in prison? That's a personal question, maybe I shouldn't ask you. You don't have to answer that.

Scott: Well, I actually met his mom and then I ended up writing to him. I visited him a lot when he was in prison. Yeah. It's a long emotional tale. (Laughing). I've visited him in four separate prisons. He got moved around all the time. When he had nobody else visiting him, I would go and visit him.

Barney: My goodness. How nice of you to do that.

Scott: Yeah. I would take his mom out for dinner and stuff when he was still in prison and I would come visit his mom. I sent Christmas gifts to his kids when he was in so that he felt like he was still a dad to them. He was always worried about not being seen as a dad to his kids. So, I helped him by sending cards to them. I also helped pay for the calling from prison; it is very expensive. So, I helped fund the account to put minutes on his phone so that he could call his kids when he was in prison.

Barney: Oh, Linda! My goodness.

Scott: Yeah. Oh, my gosh. It's crazy. Art and I, we've been through a lot.

Barney: I guess so. Well, there aren't many people like you to support someone like that. That is really wonderful of you.

Scott: I know a lot of Art's family drama since he has been out of prison, you know relationship with his kids and his sister and his nephews. It's been so up and down for him. He just doesn't have a whole lot of people who have remained constant there with him that he can call and unload on. And that's kinda been my job.

Barney: Wow. I guess so. My goodness. That's incredible.

Scott: He's worth it. But I tell you what, he can sure test your nerves some times, that's for sure.

Barney: It sounds like it. It sounds like he's done that to you. My goodness. When you visit his mom, did you come to Ohio? Or she was over there?

Scott: No, my parents live here in Dayton. I was living in Texas for part of that time. When I would come home and visit my parents, I would also go see him in prison. And I would go over and see his mom. And then I moved back to Dayton about four years ago. Not too long after he got out of prison was when I moved back to Dayton. That was very strange timing. I got a job. I work at Dayton Industrial Supply now. I just have a normal job and a normal life, and then I have Art.

Barney: Oh, my goodness. Well, you guys should have gotten married.

Scott: Well, we thought we were at one time, but then Art needs— his life needs to settle down a little bit before I can invite that chaos into my life. Yeah, we talked about it. We did. We thought we were going to at one time. I just realized in the cookies of life I'm kinda a vanilla wafer and Art is more something like a double-stuffed Oreo and all. He's more hyper than I am. Maybe one of these days, the moon and stars will line up and it will work out for us.

Barney: I've only met his mother once or twice. Not many times. I've never met his children.

My phone is ringing non-stop in the background.

Scott: Yeah, very nice lady. I haven't met his children but I've talked to them on the phone. He's very private about his kids. He's also trying to repair the relationship with them. You know, after all the years when he was in prison.

Barney: That would be difficult to do in anybody's situation like that. I mean, I could put myself in the children's place. How embarrassing it would have been.

Scott: Oh, yeah. There was one time, there used to be a show on TV called *Prison Break* and they mentioned his name on the show, and then the kids were talking about it in school and his older daughter was hearing about it the next day. It was really hard for her. I think there have probably been a lot of little things over the years that have damaged his relationship with the kids. Just aside from him not being there. But all these other little embarrassing things that come up.

Barney: Oh, absolutely. Because at that age you're kinda shy about things anyway. And then to have that happen.

Scott: I hear your phone going crazy. Is that Art all that time?

Barney: Yeah, he wanted me to be sure to call you, so I did. I even have it covered up because it was driving me crazy here. I better answer it and see what he has to say. And let him know I called you.

Scott: OK, and then you just want to call me the next time that you have, when you can help me? Is that how you want to work this? I don't want to be a pest.

Barney: Don't you worry about that. I may just tell Art, depends on who I have around and what is going on, I may just have him call you or something. We'll work it out somehow. All right?

Scott: OK. Thank you so much. I feel so much better.

***

As I answer the phone I can hear Art, "What happened?"

"Girl talk," I respond. "She just needed to vent." I explain Linda's financial situation and how she has credit cards due on the fifth. "She'll probably tell you what she's going to do to."

"I don't want to hear it. I'm the fat ass that has to fit into my mom's panties that she bought me," he sulks.

I scold him. "She sounds like she has been a good friend to you. Don't do that! Don't feel that way toward her."

He can't see beyond Linda's childish comment. "How about if I said that to you? Would that hurt your feelings a little bit?"

I'm incredulous at the path this conversation has taken. I can't make sense how *his* feelings are hurt because of a silly comment yet he can't understand the dire financial situation he has caused for me and many others?

Anita Barney: "*That* wouldn't hurt my feelings. My feelings are hurt that I'm losing my condos and my jewelry. That is what my feelings are hurt about."

Art Schlichter: You're *not* losing your jewelry and your condo!

Barney: Really, my condos are gone, to be honest with you. I have liens on them. You know that. And that Wells Fargo reverse mortgage I got for you. All that stuff is gone.

Schlichter: No, it isn't. You've got a couple of liens for $25,000 on a condo worth $300,000 to $400,000. How's that gone? The liens here don't mean anything. The liens in Florida, that's like $25,000. What's going on with your cars? I don't get it. These people, it's not like they got a $500,000 lien on you. It's $10,000 here, $20,000 there, $10,000 here, $20,000 there. You know? Those things are correctable. G*d***!

Barney: Well, that hurts my feelings. I don't care if anyone calls me a fat ass, because I am. I am fat. I do have a fat ass. It's reality. I don't care. Financially, I could kick myself for putting myself in this position, that's all. At my age. I shouldn't be doing it. I was sitting on top of the world. Trying to get us both up there on top of the world. So, I'm hoping to do that again. Hope we can do it. Think you're going to do it?

Schlichter: I know I'm going to do it.

Barney: OK.

Schlichter: This f**king craziness over the course of the day.

Barney: Well, how much, does she call you a lot?

Schlichter: Crazy. A LOT?! Well let me just say how many times she texted me. I erased about ten of them. About twenty-one times, and I erased ten of them. And that started at 2:26 p.m. It's now 4:20 p.m. Thirty-one times in two hours.

Barney: Well, she texted me, I don't know how many times she called me. She's in panic mode right now.

Schlichter: Called me eighteen times. Texted me thirty-one times in two hours. So, I mean, I can't even talk to anybody about anything or try to do anything. I'll call you back.

***

In an attempt to elicit additional information for the authorities on how Art is behaving toward other victims, I placed another call to Linda.

Anita Barney: I'm a little confused. I wrote you some checks, right?

Linda Scott: Yes, I still have those.

Barney: Did Art give you money in exchange for those checks? Or how does this work? I don't know.

Scott: Well, I will give them back to you. I mean, he didn't tell me what to do with them. So, I've just held on to them. I can give them back to you at any time. That's no problem.

Barney: Sometimes I get confused on what I'm doing or what we're doing. So I wanted to clarify that with you.

Scott: Art had said that, my impression was that you had changed your mind about checks and that you would rather just withdraw cash. It never really fully came to anything. So, I've just been holding on to the checks until someone tells me what to do with them. Or who to give them to. Or what. It doesn't matter to me.

Barney: Well, have you given him money, and has he given you any money back?

Scott: Yes to the first. And no to the second. I've helped him. He had somebody that he owed money to from a long time ago. And he needed to pay that person back and that's where I've helped him recently. And that's why I'm in the mess that I'm in right now.

Barney: Was that a lot of money you had to pay him? For that guy? Was it a lot of money?

Scott: Well, it was a lot for me. It was $11,000.

Barney: OK, because, you know, I'm trying to help him get out of debt, as well. Or help his organization. So, that's where I come from, as well.

Scott: Well, I don't know what all debt he has other than to me. It seems like he has been accumulating it over a long period of time. I'm just to the point now where I'm just breaking under all this credit card debt that I have taken on for all the times that he's needed money. I don't know how much he has told you, but when he got out of prison, it wasn't like he came out to a clean slate. He got out of prison and he still owed people money who didn't forget that.

Barney: Really?

Scott: And, they were threatening to expose him, and I think he spent a lot of time borrowing from people to pay this person to get them to be quiet. He just kept, it was just a cycle that he kept going on and on, and finally got to the point where he couldn't take it any more. And I said, "Art, you've got to pay these people back so they won't go to the newspapers or whatever and threaten your radio job or all your other jobs that you've been managing to get. You've got to get your life straightened out." So, that's why I helped him out. But it was always under the condition that he was going to pay me back when he got some of his book money. Well, then the Feds stepped in and now they are tying up the book money and so I didn't get that. There's just all these things where I was supposed to get paid back all along and it never happened.

Barney: Oh, I see. Did the Feds ever talk to you?

Scott: Yeah. They came and talked to me.

Barney: Oh, me, too.

Scott: Yeah. I told them to basically shut up and leave me alone. I'm handling my own finances, and thank you very much but please leave me alone.

Barney: Oh. And they have?

Scott: They have, yeah. They haven't called me back. I said, "This is my money I can do whatever I want with my money. I would appreciate if you would just stop wasting my time." So, they did. 'Cause I haven't done anything wrong.

Barney: No, I haven't either.

Scott: They just don't like that I helped Art. But frankly, it is none of their business.

Barney: It's true. He's always talking about the Feds. He's always worried about them. Always looking over his shoulder about them, I think.

Scott: He's always paranoid. Because I think he is still on probation in Indiana. I think if they do anything his probation can be revoked quite easily.

Barney: And he would go back to prison? Is that what you mean?

Scott: I don't know if he could go back to prison. But they could make him start having to report regularly again. And make his life more difficult. And, he worked with his attorney to get the Indiana Probation relaxed enough to where he can travel when he needs to travel and work when he needs to work. And not have to keep reporting back every time they snap their fingers. It was just really becoming a huge hassle in his life. He doesn't want to have to go back to that. Because they could call him one night and say, "We need you to report here at 8:00 a.m. tomorrow morning." He would go there and be there at 8:00 a.m. and at 1:30 p.m. they had not even called his name yet. He's just sitting there, waiting in the hall. Waiting for them to call. They were just screwing with him.

Barney: Oh, my gosh. See, I'm afraid to ask him any questions. I'm glad I'm talking with you. I've had a lot of questions but I didn't want to ask him. You understand?

Scott: Yeah, because he gets so paranoid. Because every time he hears a police siren I think it's ingrained in his psyche now that every time he hears that it triggers a response in him that he can't even shake. They are just messing with him. I don't understand why. They would have him report the next morning and not even talk to him until three or four in the afternoon. And then say, "OK, well, seems like everything is all right here, you can go." And in the meantime, how is he supposed to work? How is he supposed to work with that hanging over his head all the time? He doesn't want to go back to that life because he's scared. He's just scared that something else might happen and he might not get to come home one of these times.

Barney: Well, that would be terrible. To have to live that way.

Scott: Oh, yeah, yeah! And it's really taken its toll on him. His health has suffered and he is under so much stress all the time. He just needs to be able to relax. I don't know how to get him to do that. I don't even know if that's in his personality. I don't know if he is ever relaxed. I think he's always been a hyper guy. According to what his mom has told me. Always been jumpy. You've known him since his college days, haven't you?

Barney: Yes, but I lost contact. Off and on. Just off and on. Not steady. Hasn't been steady. I don't know if he was a junior or senior. I can't remember now, what it was. When I first met him. But it hasn't been constant, like with you.

Scott: It's been every day. He used to coach. A couple of seasons ago he coached a high school football team down in Southern Indiana. He was up for that job, to get the head coaching position this year, and the Feds went down and talked to the school and to people that he knows and recommended they not hire him. They spooked the school so bad that they didn't hire him.

Barney: The Feds went down and talked to them?

Scott: Yeah or they called somebody. It was just, nothing was coming of this. The Feds talked to me it was probably a year ago that they talked to me. Absolutely nothing has come of it.

Barney: I wonder why they are talking to . . . see, the Feds, I don't know what the Feds are.

Scott: It was someone from the U.S. District Attorney's Office that came and talked to me. Because they thought I had been defrauded because I gave Art money. I said, "No, I haven't been defrauded." They thought he either took it from me without my knowing it—like I would be too dumb to know that I was missing my own money—or that he lied to me or somehow defrauded or tricked me into giving him money. Which never ever happened. I said, "No. I totally know where every cent I've ever had has gone. Now you just need to leave me alone so I can get back to work." It was really an insulting kind of interview. They said, "We think Art Schlichter is up to no good and we think you've been giving him money." I said, "Well, I have been giving him money, but it's been my choice and I'm aware of every cent that I have given him. So, do you have any other questions?" (Giggling) So, they've left me alone ever since then.

Barney: You're a strong woman.

Scott: Well, they irritated me. It's like they are calling me stupid for not knowing where my money was. Which, I knew where it was. It's been an interesting ride.

Barney: I guess so. Ten years, though? My goodness. I've never been inside a prison in my life. I would be scared to even go into one.

Scott: You have to go through metal detectors and there are certain things you can wear and certain things you can't wear. You can't wear things that are in layers. If you go in wearing a sweatshirt you can't have on a shirt under the sweatshirt. I guess they figure it's easier to hide things in there. They make you take off your shoes and look inside your shoes to make sure you're not trying to get anything in your shoes. It's probably one of the safest places I've ever been, believe it or not.

Barney: I guess so.

Scott: The security is phenomenal. I've never felt bad one time. I'll tell you what, it was interesting. I'm glad in a strange way— I'm not glad Art was in prison—but I was glad I had the opportunity to do that. Because I never would have known what a prison visit would be like, of course, without Art there. The only time I've ever been to prison was just to see Art. It was really interesting . . . I know it's a lot of money Art owes me. But the problem was when he got out of prison he was behind the eight ball in a big way. Because right before he went to prison, he went crazy and he borrowed a lot of money thinking he could gamble and get himself out of his jam. And he didn't. So, six years later when he came out of prison he had all these problems haunting him. And no money to help dig himself out and really, no job at that time either. Anyway, I think he's back on the level now. But the problem is that I'm in the hole. (Laughing)

Barney: Well, I don't know what he can do now. I don't know how he can even, what kind of a job he can get or anything.

Scott: Well, you know, the radio thing is doing well. And he's doing a lot of the interventions (with gambling addicts). I'm not sure what all he has in the fire, but Art's never had trouble making money.

Barney: Really?

Scott: He never has had trouble making money. He just has trouble managing his money. So, I'm hoping to help him out there.

We said our goodbyes, and I ended the call. I couldn't believe what I was hearing. How could Linda not understand the truth about Art? She sounded brainwashed. I wondered if she really was so brazen with the Feds or had she embellished the story with the retelling?

And if she thought Art was on the level now, she was badly mistaken. He had taken everything from me and a lot from my friends and family. He wasn't close to level. However, one thing she said was true. Art was really good at *getting* money, and he was terrible at managing it.

Before long, Art was calling and he was fit to be tied!

Art Schlichter: I'm a little bit pissed off at you.

Anita Barney: Why?

Schlichter: You made it sound like she was f**king trying to ask the questions and she said you asked her all the questions. *"Where did you meet him? How long have you known him? What's going on? How did you get the checks? Did he give you any money?"*

Barney: I was seeing if you were boyfriend-girlfriend.

Schlichter: We're not boyfriend-girlfriend!

Barney: That's what I wanted to find out. I asked her.

Schlichter: All you had to do was ask me!

Barney: Well, she said you talked about getting married one time. That's what I wanted to know.

Schlichter: Let me explain it to you. When I was in prison, she used to come and see me all the time. When I got out of prison, there wasn't anything at all. That was it. It was just nice that she came to see me. When I was in prison, hell, anything could have happened to me. But, hold on a second. But for you to do that, you shouldn't be doing that behind my back.

Barney: Now, just a minute. Let me tell you what. She told me that she came to four different prisons. I didn't have any questions to ask her. I just said something like *you've known Art a long time*, because I wanted to find out if you were boyfriend-girlfriend.

Schlichter: I've known her since she was eighteen years old.

Barney: I didn't know that. I didn't know anything.

Schlichter: I TOLD YOU WHAT THE TRUTH WAS! I'll see ya.

Many times Art would get himself worked up until he was yelling and then abruptly disconnect the call. Even though I had become accustomed to his rudeness, it was still jarring to be treated that way.

A few minutes passed before he was calling back. I knew from past experiences that if I ignored him, he could call repeatedly for hours, his anger transforming into outrage. I answered the phone. I was surprised to hear his anger wasn't directed at me. He was still consumed with Linda's comment about his "panties."

Art Schlichter: You called Linda back twice.

Anita Barney: I called her when you wanted me to. And the phone kept ringing and ringing and she kept saying, "Is that Art calling?" I said, "Yes, it is." So, I hung up with her to answer your call. We had been in the middle of talking and I called her back. That's what happened. You kept calling and calling. That's all.

Schlichter: Anybody that would say that about me. It's ridiculous.

Barney: Say what?

Schlichter: You can't say *that* about people, it hurts their feelings.

Barney: Oh, about the panties?

Schlichter: Yes!

Barney: I never heard that before.

Schlichter: You never heard about it because it was the first time someone ever said it to me. It wasn't very nice. All right. Well, I'll talk to you in a little bit.

Linda must have been holding his feet to the fire with her demands for money, because a few days later he was scheming again.

Art Schlichter: You need to do this for me, OK?

Anita Barney: Just a minute, let me get my pencil and paper. OK.

Schlichter: Now, you know, everything that I ask you to do, you never do. So, if you're not going to do it you need to tell me you're not going to do it so I don't have to call back and then you don't answer for three or four hours and then tell me you can't do it. You know, you're not writing anybody any checks. All you're doing is calling Linda Scott and telling her that you'll be putting money in her account Monday morning, OK?

Barney: Art, listen to me—

Schlichter: Which I will do myself.

Barney: Art, I have had detectives at my door and call me and talk to me. I'm scared to death. Don't you understand that? I've never had that before.

Schlichter: I understand that part. OK?

Barney: I'm being afraid of everything. I'm very paranoid now.

Schlichter: You are?

Barney: Yes.

Schlichter: Linda Scott is not going to bother you. She just wants to hear that you're going to be putting money into her account on Monday. And I'm going to do it myself. OK? All right?

Barney: Yes?

Schlichter: So, all you got to do is say, *"Linda, I'm going to put $9,900 in your account Monday morning. I ordered money and I'm going to put money in your account Monday morning. I just cannot do it today because I'm not in town. The money will be available in there Monday morning. I'll go to the bank. Give me your account number."* Don't tell her I'm going to do it. Tell her *you're* going to do.

Barney: OK.

Schlichter: And I will go deal with her on Sunday if I need to. Tell her you've already done it all. You've already ordered some money. You owe her money. The first thing you're going to do is put $9,900 in her account on Monday. OK?

Barney: OK.

Schlichter: And you'll call her Monday afternoon. You need her account number. Call her Monday afternoon to make sure she got it and then make arrangements for the next step. That's all you got to say.

Barney: OK. All right.

Schlichter: You'll put $9,900 in her account Monday morning. Get her account number. OK? And you will call her Monday afternoon to make arrangements for the rest of it, or the next step. That's all you got to do. Put $9,900 in her account Monday before noon. Get her account number right now. Cash. You're going to put cash in there.

Barney: OK, what's her number?

Schlichter: 937-###-####. Say, *"Linda, this is Anita. Sorry I haven't gotten back to you this week. I've made arrangements. I'm going to put $9,900 in cash in your account on Monday morning."*

Barney: Is that your phone ringing?

Schlichter: Yeah. Eighteen times in a row. OK? It never stops. Listen to me. Linda has called me fifteen times today. All she needs to do is hear from you. I can't concentrate if she is f**king driving me crazy. Don't get into any other conversations with her. Say you're in a hurry. Tell her you're doing some business stuff today, *"I just want to* *touch base with you today because Art keeps calling me and asking me what is going on. OK? Art is bothering me. I'm going to put $9,900 in your account in cash Monday morning. Give me your account number."* Right now. All right? *"I'll call you Monday afternoon or Tuesday morning to make sure you got it in there and to make arrangements for the rest."* OK? That's ALL you gotta say! NOTHING ELSE!

Barney: OK!

Schlichter: Call her RIGHT NOW and call me right back.

With Art's commands ringing in my ear, I called Linda immediately. She didn't answer. I didn't dare mention Art's name, but I wanted to convey the information I was providing—and the money—were coming from him.

Hi, Linda, this is Anita calling. I was going to get your account number because I'm told that Monday morning, the money would be in your account. And I would check with you Monday afternoon to make sure it was there and everything. So, I was just calling to tell you I was told there would be money there Monday morning. If I don't answer my phone and I can't, just leave your account number, if you want to. I don't know what else, nobody sees this number anyway but me. So, you can just go ahead and leave it on voice mail and then I will erase it immediately. OK? OK. 'Bye.

As soon as I disconnected from Linda's line, I called Art as he had instructed.

Art Schlichter: Hello.

Anita Barney: Hi, her voicemail came on and I left a message and told her she could call me back and leave her account number on my phone. Nobody sees it but me. And then I would erase it; it wouldn't stay on my phone. I don't know why she didn't answer.

300

Schlichter: Call her back. She'll answer. She was probably f**king ringing my number 100 times.

Barney: Oh, OK. I'll try it again, then.

Schlichter: Call her back right now.

***

On January 26, 2011, Art called in a panic. From the sound of it, he had failed to come up with the money Linda desperately needed when I had spoken with her a month ago. She was now threatening to go to the Prosecutor.

Art Schlichter: Oh, my god! If I read you everything she said to me. This is what kind of person she is. *Your life is over. Go . . . and have some fun because you're never gonna see daylight again except for the rec yard. You may as well leave the attorney's office and go gamble somewhere. One last hurrah for #10. Um, I'm going to be fine. You're going to get f**ked in the ass in prison, literally. You're going to prison. Enjoy the Ramen Noodles! Steve Haller is a Prosecutor. Appointment tomorrow morning. You're toast! You are a lying motherf**ker! You will see your daddy in hell.* Uh, let's see. What else? *You may as well crash your car into a tree tonight because today is the last good day you'll have left.* All right?

Anita Barney: Wow.

Schlichter: *I'm going to prosecute your mother, too. She is going down, too. And I'm going to make sure your kids know exactly what a piece of sh** their father is. And I'm going to bury you. You will be hearing from the Greene County Prosecutor tomorrow. You're dead. Your mother is going to die in that house alone.*

Barney: Oh, my gosh.

Schlichter: *You will never see your kids again. You're a rotten motherf**ker. I'm going to do everything I can to put your ass back in prison!*

Barney: She texted all that to you?

Schlichter: *(Taylor) will probably go back to being a crack whore. Good job, dad!* That's the sh** I got in the last hour.

Barney: Wow.

Schlichter: Anyway, I'll call you back. Get some rest. I don't know. I'm late. I'm sick. 'Bye

Art called later, convinced Linda was going to the authorities.

"They are going to make you look like the victim and make me look like the bad guy," he said. "I don't want to talk about it on this phone. We are going to meet in person and talk about it because I'm going to give you three thousand bucks. I explained some stuff to my lawyer, about what you and I had going."

I acted shocked when he said the Prosecutor had painted him out to be the worst guy in the world.

"They are gonna put me in jail for my life. Life in prison!"

I asked about the validity of Linda claiming she had an appointment with the Prosecutor in Dayton.

"She said that I could buy her silence by giving her money today. I told her to go f**king do whatever she wants to do . . . I'm working on some stuff. So, I'm just, uh, been banging the phone (to find money). I hate to do that but . . . just hang tight and we'll talk in a little bit. All right?"

I mentioned my neighbor had been asking about the Super Bowl tickets we owed him. Art said to tell him the tickets would be available within the next three or four days.

***

Art told me to call Linda and tell her money was on the way. He was grasping at straws to keep her from going to the authorities. As soon as she answered the phone I clearly heard her exasperated tone, which was in stark contrast to her easygoing attitude during our previous conversation when she spoke fondly of Art and talked of possible marriage. She sounded desperate as she told me she couldn't afford to continue paying Art's debt.

Linda Scott: I can't afford to do it. I don't have the money! I've withdrawn from my 401(k). I've liquidated everything I have because he kept telling me that I was going to get paid back. And I haven't been paid back and I don't know what to do about it anymore.

Anita Barney: How long has it been since he has paid you?

Scott: Oh, he gave me $1,300 yesterday, but that doesn't even cover the minimum on the credit cards.

Barney: I thought he was covering it. I thought he was going to take over.

Scott: NO! HE'S NOT! He hasn't paid me in months! I've been, I've taken out of every retirement account that I have. I'm going to have a tax bill from hell and here he is telling me I just have to wait. I CAN'T WAIT for Art's problems to go away.

Barney: So, that's what he told you, you're going to have to wait?

Scott: Well, that's . . . always the excuse. We just need to wait for things to settle down. With Art, it's NEVER going to settle down.

Barney: Well, I'm finding that out as well. It's a terrible situation.

Scott: And I'm sorry I'm upset with you because you shouldn't even be involved in this, but he brought you into it because, I mean, the last time I loaned him money it was because he exchanged the cash that I gave him for a check from you.

Barney: Oh, is that what he did?

Scott: Yes! That's exactly what he did. So, that's why I'm like, OK, how about the check? Let's cash the check from Anita! I can't cash the check because the account is closed. And you know how I got that cash? I got the money from a cash advance on my credit card. So, I'm paying like nineteen percent interest on that. I just can't do this anymore. I am NOT a wealthy person. He has drained me of everything I have. And he just keeps telling me to wait; it'll be OK.

Barney: Oh, god! Well, he told me I didn't have to do anything. He was going to take care of it. So, that's why I didn't do anything.

Scott: He always says that. *He always says that!* And then he doesn't return my calls. I've been taking care of him for four years now. All I have to show for it is debt! He keeps telling me, it will be OK. It will be OK! And every time I turn around he has another issue. I am just sick of being his fricking private—I'm sick of being his friend. I can't be his friend anymore. I'm his creditor and he has to start treating me like that.

Barney: Oh, I didn't know it had been four years you had been doing this with him.

Scott: I have been helping him since he's been out of prison! And he does things like say, *"Well, don't worry I'm coming through, we'll stop for dinner. We'll talk. We'll get things straightened out."* He doesn't stop. He calls me when he gets home and says, *"Gosh, I'm just too tired."* Or, *"I don't feel good."* He's been using me for four years! And all I have to show for it are credit card bills from hell. And all I want him to do is do what he said he would do.

Barney: Yes, I know that feeling. I know exactly what you are saying. Are you going to go to the Prosecutor?

Scott: I haven't decided yet. I haven't decided yet because I'll tell you what, if I have to take anything else out of my retirement account, he's not just going to walk away scot-free. I will absolutely go to the Prosecutor and file a complaint. I'll call the police. I'll do whatever I have to do. Because he is not just going to walk away from this.

Barney: I agree with you. It's the way it should be. He shouldn't do that to you. I totally agree with you. It's sad. I can't believe you were being such a friend to him and look how he is treating you.

Scott: That's exactly right. And every time I say, "Art, I thought Anita was going to help you, you keep telling me she's going to help you." This has been going on since, September 1 was the first day that he told me about your involvement. And here we are, January 26, and all I've done is go deeper in debt because he kept promising that *"No, Linda, there's a sunny horizon! It's all going to get taken care of. I've got a deal with Anita. I signed the papers. You're going to get paid back.*" And all he does is just, it's just one fricking delay after another.

Barney: It's lies. He's just lying, to both of us, I guess. And that's what . . .

Scott: Well, that's what it seems like to me because he's not communicating with me.

Barney: Well, he's always saying it's going to get greater, later. Where's the later? And how great is it?

Scott: When is the later? Later is now! Later is now as far as I'm concerned.

Barney: Well, I don't want to lie for him anymore. I'm tired of doing that. I just was going to read to you what he wanted me to say to you.

Scott: Well, it doesn't fix anything is the problem.

Barney: No, it doesn't. I know that. He's going to call me back and I'm going to tell him I didn't want to lie to you about anything. And I'm not going to lie and cover for him. He's supposed to be taking care of this and he should be taking care of it. And stop using me. Because he's the one who should do it.

Scott: He's been using you to buy time with me. And I don't know exactly how much of that you've been a part of or how much of it is even true! I don't know what to believe any more.

Barney: I don't think, I don't know what he's told, he's told a lot of stories about me. So, I don't know what he's saying. He's saying things that are not true in many cases. So, I don't know what all he is telling you, but he doesn't want us talking, I know that. So we can't compare notes.

Scott: Well, he never wants me talking to anybody. He had somebody helping him last year work through all this and he never even let me have that guy's phone number. When that guy called me he would block his phone number. It's crazy. *It's crazy!* All I want is out! I just want my bills paid and I want away. I want Art to handle his own debt. I can't be Art's MasterCard any more.

Barney: I don't think you're the only one. How much does he owe you now?

Scott: Credit card bills? About sixty grand.

Barney: Sixty?

Scott: Yeah, yeah! Sixty grand. On my credit cards. All because of him. ALL! One hundred percent because of him! That's almost as much as I make in a year. Gross. It's going to take me the rest of my life to dig out from under that! And if I have to do that on my own, then by god he's going to prison! He's going to prison for it and everybody else who is involved is going to prison for it if I can help it.

Barney: I think you should do that! You should just go ahead, he's abusing you and taking advantage of you. That's what he's doing.

Scott: Yep.

Barney: You make your choice; do what you want to do. And I think you're doing the right thing, though, by thinking that way.

Scott: I've just waited long enough. I can't be a friend any more, because he's not mine. He's been accusing me of not being a good friend. But, he hasn't been a good friend to me for a long, long time! And I've been way better to him than he deserves and I'm sorry it's turned out this way. But he's in a world of sh** right now, and I can't help him get out of it this time.

Barney: So, you don't know who helped him last year, then? You never did find out who helped him?

Scott: No. It was one of his coaches. Braxton Bell.

Barney: Is that someone from Indianapolis? I don't know any—

Scott: Someone from Washington Court House.

Barney: Oh, I see, he helped him out?

Scott: Yeah. And I got all of these promises then. That, "*Oh, no, Braxton is going to help. He has agreed to help me get my life straightened out. All these problems of mine sorted out. Just sit still.*" And nothing has gone any better for me. All I've done, ALL I'VE DONE to Art is help him when he needed it.

Barney: And this is the thanks he gives you?

Scott: This is all I get. Now, I'm fricking buried in debt. How in the hell is anybody supposed to pay $60,000 worth of credit cards back?

Barney: What does he do with the money?

Scott: He pays people that he owes.

Barney: Do you think he's gambling again?

Scott: Right now? I don't think he is right now. I think he, I don't know. I don't think he is right now.

Barney: I don't know either. But there is so much money going out there, that I just can't see him, he's been paying off people for so long, I just feel that he is gambling again, myself.

Scott: I don't know where all the money is going. I don't know how else you can lose this much money if he stopped gambling.

Barney: That's my point. There is no way. There is nothing to show for it.

Scott: Absolutely nothing to show for it.

Barney: He lives out of his car and lives with friends and I don't know what all he does. Don't care what he does. He's not in my category. That's for sure. I can't imagine somebody living like that.

Scott: That's why he's stressed out all the time.

Barney: He should be! He's bringing it on himself.

Scott: He's brought it on himself. And I was stupid enough to believe everything he told me when he said, *"No, Linda, if you give me this money I'm going to pay you back."* I've got . . you know, I have a stack of checks from you, Anita! That you were supposed to, and I thought well, this makes me feel really good because now I'm finally, Art's going to take responsibility for his debts. And I won't have to be the one carrying this load anymore. I have a mortgage that I would love to refinance. How? No one is going to even look at me with $60,000 worth of credit card debt. So, I don't know how many hundreds of dollars every month I'm pissing away on extra mortgage payments that I could have refinanced by now. And now I'm screwed. I'm screwed!

Barney: See, he was supposed to cover those checks that I wrote to you. He was going to cover them.

Scott: HOW?

Barney: Well, I didn't know. I thought he was getting it from somebody, I didn't know what he was doing. I didn't know where his money was coming from. But he said, *"I've got money to cover those."* I assumed he was doing it.

Scott: Oh, no! I still have every single one of them!

Barney: See, he was supposed to cover those. So, that's where he is lying to me.

Scott: Oh, my god!

Barney: When I said to you that I was told the money was going to be there for you, he was telling me it was going to be there.

Scott: He was telling me, you were going to put it there.

Barney: He said he was going to put the money there. He was. When I was telling you *I was told that*, he was supposed to cover them. So he lied to me and he lied to you. We've both been lied to. You do what you have to do. And don't feel bad about it.

Scott: I won't. I mean, I will. But I'm still going to do it. Because he is not just going to do this to me and get away. It just doesn't happen in my life.

Barney: I don't blame you at all. That's terrible. He just told me to touch base with you and tell you that this is what he wanted me to say.

Scott: OK, well, thanks for calling.

Barney: I hope things turn out better for both of us.

***

One of the final times I heard from Linda was when she left a distressing voice mail message for me. Art was still stringing her along with a bogus story about my loaning him money to give to her. Her message reflected my situation. Without money to pay my own bills, I was also desperate. I couldn't help her. I couldn't even help myself.

Hi, Anita, it's Linda Scott and um, I've been talking to Art here lately. And he told me that he signed some papers to make it all legit so that when you loan him money it will all be on the up and up. And I was kinda hoping that you were ready to do that because I've given everything I can to Art and I am absolutely desperate for your help. And Art promised me that you would help me. Or that you would help him. And that was sorta my understanding when I loaned him all this money and now I'm kinda really desperate. I have no money I can't pay my bills and I am in the deepest sh** you can imagine. I really need your help. Could you please call me back and let me know where you stand on this? I would really appreciate it. Thank you. 'Bye.

32 | OUT WITH THE OLD
NEW YEAR'S EVE 2010

"There are just too many problems. I don't know how we're going to make all this money fit with all the problems."	*Art Schlichter*

Thursday, December 30, 2010

Art called me after 11:00 p.m. and said he was sitting alone somewhere between Kentucky and Indiana looking out over the Ohio River. His voice sounded flat, unusual. When I asked what was going on, he said he was just thinking about what to do next. Wondering how he was going to survive everything. He had a long talk with John Amery earlier in the evening but nothing had been resolved.

"Everything has gone wrong," he said. "It's a tough situation. Sh*t's been going on I didn't know about. You've not made one call when I've asked you to make a call to keep people afloat for a day or two. Not one time. We might have gotten arrested today from Calder Fenwick for all I know. He may have turned us in. Can't do anything about the money until Monday or Tuesday. I owe Calder and Douglas . . . I can't get the money."

Things *were* getting desperate with our creditors, and I asked Art if any money would be available tomorrow.

"No. I don't think I can get it by tomorrow. These people just can't wait. They're going crazy. There are just too many problems. I don't know how we're going to make all this money fit with all the problems. They are talking out there. All the people that are mad at us. You. Me. Starting to call the Prosecutors and the f**king detectives. We've got to nip that in the bud. I don't know if it will be enough money to do it. I don't know. F**king got to give $30,000 just to Lew Sanchez, you know. That's a big chunk of it right there."

"How much are you going to get on Monday?" I asked.

"Supposed to be $80,000, but I need some of it. $50,000 or $60,000, whatever. I don't, honey, I don't know what's going to happen. I know you haven't told me the whole truth, which kind of hurts me. You didn't tell me you went and got a lawyer. You didn't tell me about anything else. He probably told you not to talk to me, or whatever."

Then, once again, Art asks for my assistance.

"I'm going to need your help in the morning with two people, just to calm them down. You seem to be able to do that sometimes when I can't, and if we want to survive the weekend and get to the hope of the money, then maybe you can make a couple of calls for me. If you don't want to make them or you're not going to make them, don't tell me you're going to make them but then don't make them. Because when you don't make them, it just makes it worse. Makes it bad."

I explain I'm afraid to lie to anyone about anything, especially with the detective on my case. In typical fashion, Art has an answer for everything.

"You don't have to promise them anything! Just tell them we'll get it handled on Monday. That's all you have to say. You don't have to say you'll have the money on Monday. Just say, 'Listen, I need until Monday. I'll get your money to you.' Please . . . don't make it any worse. *Please.* That's not lying to anybody or doing anything wrong . . . It will be all over with Monday. Tuesday.

If I don't have it, it will be all over with. A lot of pressure to get it done. All right. Call me at eight o'clock in the morning."

Friday, December 31, 2010

The following morning I called Art at 8:00 a.m. as he instructed.

He asked me to make a phone call and made me promise to be "real positive." Then he said he would take care of the money on Monday or Tuesday. I asked if there really would be money on Monday. I personally wanted to know because I needed some to help with my bills.

"There will be money. There's gotta be! If there's no money on Monday, I've cooked our goose. And I'm not going to cook our goose."

He tells me that Tim Baker sued me and before I can react he says, "I think your lawyer will be able to stop all that. You'll probably get a letter in the next couple, three days. By the time they get done, we'll negotiate and get away from this piece of sh*t. OK?"

I told him I probably had six or seven suits filed against me. He corrects me. "Five. They are all your friends. Except for Tim Baker." Art then instructed me to call Douglas DeLarge and Calder Fenwick and put out fires.

I called Douglas on his office line. As I explained the convoluted reason Art could not pay him until Monday (or Tuesday), Douglas reminded me of his conversation with Special Agent Terrence Brown that had occurred months ago, when the Feds were making the rounds and interviewing Art's associates.

"It's (Art's) d**n fault. Terrence Brown said it was a scheme, about Art and banking. Remember when they were investigating Art, and Terrence was questioning you and me?" I was surprised to learn Douglas had been questioned and silently wondered how many others were notified about Art's schemes, but failed to heed the warning.

When I asked Douglas what he thought Art was doing with the money, he had a ready answer. "He told me some guy was going to get him in trouble that he owed from years ago. That he had to have the money within an hour, and on and on, and I went and begged it out of my brother. Art promised me I would have it returned the following Tuesday and now another Tuesday is already going by and my brother is ready to blow. It's a mess. Art's got to deal with whatever happens. It's not my fault. It's his own d**n fault."

Whether a housewife from Dublin, Ohio, like myself, or a business owner like Douglas DeLarge, when Art got involved everyone was going down.

***

This was the worst New Year's Eve ever.

Last year I had been in Pasadena with Alan, preparing to watch the Buckeyes defeat the Oregon Ducks in the Rose Bowl.

Recent years were spent celebrating in grand style with beloved friends in Jupiter, Florida. Before that, Bob and I hosted parties brimming with shenanigans that caused all of us to laugh until we cried.

It had been years since I had been in Columbus on December 31. I had a small glass of champagne alone in my kitchen before heading toward my car. I left the TracFone Art had given me on the counter and heard it begin to ring as I closed the door to the garage. Under the circumstances, it was the biggest act of courage I could muster. I didn't have a destination in mind; I just wanted to get out of the house and away from the mocking silence and tormenting memories.

I found myself driving through the Short North, interested to see what was happening in the city. A Blue Jackets game had just ended and people were partying in the streets. Further downtown families were enjoying First Night Columbus activities. It seemed everywhere I looked groups were celebrating and couples were drawing close. I could feel the energy as the community eagerly anticipated the fresh start of a new year, which only magnified my misery.

As I turned toward home, tears blurred my vision.

33 | HAPPY NEW YEAR
JANUARY 2011

"Faster, Mom! You've got to move faster than that!"	Alan to Anita while rehearsing survival drills

I don't know what I thought would happen when I contacted the authorities in December. I guess I was hopeful that they would quickly get Art off the street and behind bars . . . that I would be protected from the madman who had become my tormentor . . . that the constant phone calls and orders and threats would end. But three weeks had passed and I was still at Art's mercy. And now I had the added pressure of recording calls, playing a part, obtaining information, and helping build a case against him. The stakes were high and I couldn't escape the burden of my role. If I didn't gather enough evidence to prove Art's level of involvement, all the blame would be mine to bear alone.

Personally, things were bad and deteriorating by the day. I was receiving regular demands for payment from former friends, multiple calls from credit card companies, and notices of lawsuits that had been filed against me. I didn't have money for basic necessities like food or utilities, and when I was able to scrounge a little money for groceries, I avoided my local grocery store so I wouldn't accidently run into any acquaintances. Art was calling repeatedly—it wasn't unusual to receive more than thirty calls from him in a day—with directives and requests, many of which I had to creatively avoid so as not to violate the boundaries placed on me by Detective Davis.

There was also a great deal of concern for my safety; I had been warned to be careful by my son, my attorney, and the authorities. Detective Davis requested the Dublin Police conduct additional patrols in my neighborhood. There was a lot at stake. If Art and his accomplices were to learn of my involvement with the investigation, I could become a target. If I were unable to testify, there would be precious little to tie Art to the crimes.

Alan was worried about me and developed a plan in the event anyone tried to break into my condo. First, he had me practice shooting Bob's guns until I felt comfortable handling them. Then he had me place the pistol in my bedside table and the rifle and a cell phone in my closet. At the first sound of someone entering the front door, I was to jump out of bed and run to the closet, pulling the door shut behind me. I was then supposed to call 911 immediately, report the intruder, and prepare to shoot at the person who opened the closet door. Alan said if someone was so determined to harm me that they would bust through three doors, I would be justified to shoot. We practiced the sequence repeatedly, with Alan timing me. "Faster, Mom! You've got to move faster than that!" he barked.

I was 68 years old and rehearsing how to save myself from an attack in my own home. I was under so much stress I began suffering from double vision and wicked headaches. When I couldn't stop my nose from bleeding for a couple of days, I went to the doctor who had to cauterize it. For the first time in my life I began taking pills to help me sleep. I had lost so much weight; I was a mess. When I ran into an old friend, he took one look at me and demanded, "Tell me who is doing this to you! I will take care of it." I brushed him off by implying I would deal with the situation when the time was right. I didn't dare breathe a word of Art's abuse or the investigation.

Art was pushing me to meet him in person. He was desperate to talk face-to-face. At first I dismissed his requests. Eventually,

Detective Davis approved of our meeting in a controlled location and suggested a local Panera. He mobilized a team to scout the site, determine where I should sit, and where the undercover agents would position themselves should a rapid response be required to maintain my safety or that of others in the restaurant. I received specific instructions on what to say and how to behave, and how to record our conversation covertly. It was a high-risk operation that could offer a big payoff if Art divulged valuable incriminating information.

On the day we were to meet, I was breathless as I started my car and backed out of the garage. I settled myself down on the drive to the restaurant. Several minutes before I arrived, Art called. He wanted to know where I was, before he told me he wasn't able to make it. After we concluded our call, I contacted Detective Davis who called off the operation. Art would try repeatedly to get me to meet him at his mother's house in Washington Court House or some other remote location. Detective Davis said it was out of the question; he wouldn't take the chance that Art or one of his associates would try to harm me.

On one especially dark day, I took inventory of the pills in my medicine cabinet and envisioned how easy it would be to escape this hell of a life I had created by slipping away peacefully. My thoughts were interrupted by a routine call from Steve Schierholt. He was just checking in to see how things were going, but I believe his call was divinely timed. I blurted out how difficult everything had become and my desire to end it all. "Oh, Anita," he said calmly. "You don't want to do that." He reminded me how hard I had been working, and that I was still needed to collect evidence. Steve explained that if I threw everything away now, Art would most likely just move on to another victim. I couldn't imagine another person suffering the abuse I had been forced to endure. Steve's words were exactly what I needed to hear to refocus my efforts.

Meanwhile, Alan was willing to do whatever was needed to be done to fix my situation, and would plan various scenarios that could be enacted to make everything right again. One day he said, "Mom, everything is going to be OK. If we have to, I have stuff I can sell to get some cash. I've even got my boat up for sale. We'll start paying these people back. If we have to, we'll move away and live in a trailer. It doesn't matter what it takes, as long as we're together. Don't do anything to harm yourself. You're all that I have."

I was still visiting my psychiatrist Dr. Jayson regularly, and finding solace in the safe haven of his office. Concerned about my mental health and constant isolation, he and his wife invited me to their house for movies and popcorn one evening. It was such a gracious gesture, but one I couldn't accept. I wasn't their problem, at least not in that way. I didn't want to drag my misery into their home.

Bill Loveland, my attorney, checked in with me every day not only to keep me updated on what was happening with my case, but because he could tell I was emotionally fragile. He was thoughtful with the information he provide; enough so I would be aware of what was going on, but not so much I would sink deeper in depression. He was my anchor and I was so thankful that Dr. Jayson had connected us.

Whether out of guilt, compassion, or something else entirely, John Amery (Art's former attorney) called frequently. He would offer advice and try to lift my spirits. He encouraged me to call him whenever I was feeling down and needed a lift. He said, "I feel so bad about the whole thing I just want to shoot myself here thinking that I could have stopped this if I had been more persistent and just kept after you to find out what was going on."

Art had repeatedly said he had people watching me, and I got in the habit of keeping the blinds in the condo closed all the time. My home became a dark dungeon; I was on constant alert. Looking around for anything or anyone out of place, I even became conscious of cars driving around me on the road. One day I spied an unknown sedan sitting out on the street across from my drive. A short while later I caught my breath when the doorbell rang a few times. Then there was pounding at the door. Even after all was quiet, I was too afraid to move from my hiding place in my bedroom. After several long minutes of silence, I crept to the front window and parted the blinds. The car was still outside. I panicked and called Detective Davis. In no time he showed up and approached the driver. It turned out to be a process server, delivering notice of another lawsuit that had been filed against me. He had wrongly assumed I was away, and was just waiting for my return. With Detective Davis standing just a few feet away ensuring my safety, the young man nervously handed over the envelope and promised to never come to my home again.

A few weeks later another unusual car sitting at the end of the street for several hours turned out to be associated with a workers' compensation investigation surveilling my neighbor's house. Days upon days of hyper-vigilance took their toll until it felt like everything was coming apart at the seams.

34 | LETTERS FROM FRIENDS

| *"Every day the postman delivered heartbreak."* | *Anita Barney* |

Even after Bob's passing, I would have Sabrina come and clean my condo every Friday. In fact, she was working the day Art had brought Wendy's over for lunch in November 2009. In the middle of December 2010, when I was no longer able to pay her fee of $60 a week, I had to let her go. I knew it was bad timing for her, being right before Christmas, and I agonized over that decision. But the truth was I had no choice. I was broke.

What complicated our parting was that I had approached her earlier in the year, at Art's insistence, to request a short-term loan. At the time, Sabrina's situation didn't permit her to invest, but she did speak with her mom, Betty Gabor, who gave me $10,000 which I had been unable to repay. Toward the beginning of January 2011, I received a letter from Van Mitchell, Sabrina's husband. Sabrina sent me a separate note toward the end of January inquiring about the money I owed her mother. These letters are just an example of the type of correspondence I was receiving on a regular basis. Every day the postman delivered heartbreak.

January 8, 2011

Dear Anita,

 I hope this note finds you in good health. The reason I am writing is on behalf of Sabrina's mom and the money you owe her. Things are getting kind of uneasy around my house, between my wife and her mom. We need to know something. That was her life savings. Now she wants us to pay her back. We don't have that kind of money. You just can't drop out of the human race and not contact anyone. Note the date of this letter. If we don't hear from you by 1-20-2011 I am contacting the Attorney General's office. My wife does not know about this letter. I would prefer that you call me at 614-###-####.
 Also, I don't appreciate the way you let my wife go. 15+ years means nothing to you. You just brushed her aside like a bag of trash. She is very worried about you and also very hurt.

Hope to hear from you
God bless

Van

***

January 24, 2011

Anita,

 I hope this letter finds you in good health and that things in your life are getting better. I have been thinking of you.
 I gave my mom your numbers because she is worried about you also, but doesn't want you to think she is only calling about the money. She keeps asking me questions and I have no answers for her.
 I hope that you will call her and let her know something. If I had known things would turn out like this, I never would have asked Mom for you, for this is her savings and she already lost all

her money before, and this was what she had left when Daddy died. She has a new phone #, it is 1-614-###-####. Please call her.

> *I wish you well*
> *May God bless and keep you safe,*
> *Fondly,*
>
> *Sabrina*

***

When Art's friends would call and make threatening demands, they could strike fear in my heart. But when my friends contacted me out of care and concern for me and also to inquire about our financial agreement, I was devastated. I had nothing to offer them by way of answers or finances to alleviate the hardship I had allowed Art to create.

The trail of destruction Art left in his wake was horrifying: financial stress, distrust, broken relationships, legal fees, threats, and uncomfortable encounters. These are the situations created by a compulsive gambler.

35 | JANUARY 2011

"You have been a godsend to me, and I have been a nightmare for you."	Art Schlichter to Anita Barney

To keep my mind occupied so I wouldn't have time to wallow in despair, and to assist their case, Detective Davis asked me to keep a chronological timeline of calls and activities involving Art. My "diaries," were not a comprehensive report of the day's activities, but became part of the official police file.

During January Detective Davis kept increasing the pressure on Art with different strategies in the hope that Art would either commit an offense that would result in arrest, or turn himself in. One scenario was that I had been summoned to the Dublin Police Station for a meeting. The second was that I had been subpoenaed to testify before the Grand Jury in early February.

Art was flying out of control, calling nonstop with desperate ideas, suggesting outlandish schemes, and exhibiting the insanity that comes when one reaches the end of the proverbial rope.

Monday, January 3, 2011

11:07 a.m.   Calder texted me that he was meeting his attorney at 9:00 a.m. on Tuesday. He told Art he had not heard from me. Art asks me what is going on.

12:35 p.m.	Art told me to call the detective to see what to do. He's dealing with WTVN now.
1:30 p.m.	Art calls to see what the detective said. He said money is in the process. Keep the faith in him.
10:30 p.m.	Art has called many times today wanting to know if I had heard anything. He said he wants to do some cashier's checks. $100,000 worth. He told me to make a list of people to pay. I told him that when I did it before, I didn't get any money. Is it going to happen this time? Yes! Within the next few days. Cannot get it all at once. Red flags to Feds, banks, etc. He was saying prayers. Told me to call the detective again. I told him I'll believe it when I receive it. Told me he loves me and I'm a helluva woman. I know he is trying to keep me calm. I don't want to hear that talk from him. I just want the money back that I loaned him.

Tuesday, January 4, 2011

8:00 a.m.	Art wants me to meet Calder and ask for twenty-four more hours. I told him I didn't want to do it, but he said we'll end up in jail if I don't meet Calder face-to-face. Detective Davis took over.
11:00 a.m.	Art and Calder are both calling at once. I'm not answering. Art called thirteen times and at 12:20 p.m. I finally answered and he wanted to know where I had been. He called me a liar. I said Calder didn't show up. I said I was looking for his Hummer and didn't go into the office. Art was angry and yelled, "He has other f**king cars!" He wanted me to write Calder a post-dated check or give him my car title. I did not!
5:00 p.m.	Art thinks I may need to drive to Cincinnati to get the first part of the money. I can't. Suffering from a bad headache and double vision.

8:30 p.m.   I have not heard from Art. He said he would call early in the a.m. Doesn't know how much money he'll have for me.

** Tim Baker received a judgment lien against me today for $194,600.

Wednesday, January 5, 2011

10:55 a.m.   Art is driving to Evansville to collect some of the money. He says it's in different accounts. I told him I couldn't meet him in Cincinnati. Bad headache. He will have Bill Hanners bring me the money.

1:00 p.m.   Art has Bill Hanners meeting him in Cincinnati to bring me money later tonight. He says it will be $30,000 to $40,000.

3:00 p.m.   Art called to say he was waiting to get money so I can pay my friends.

10:15 p.m.   Have not heard from Art since earlier. If I do get any money, I'll tell him I've used all of it to pay debts. I don't want to be robbed. You never know.

Thursday, January 6, 2011

8:15 a.m.   I called Art. He was sleeping in a hotel in Evansville. Told me to go to the doctor (for my vision problems).

12:15 p.m.   John Amery talked about Art going to rehab instead of to jail. *The Columbus Dispatch* reporter (Mike Wagner) had called John saying he had heard stories around town about Art. John will ask him to be easy on me. They are friends and I will be part of the story. John doesn't know the situation with Art but is waiting until after the Super Bowl to do anything.

12:30 p.m.   Called Art. He is "rocking and rolling" and has Boris Paveleski coming to meet him to give some money. Art will be busy for three hours. Use regular phone if I have an emergency. I told him not to lie to me and he said he wasn't lying. I tell him I need money! He tells me, "Don't worry, we'll pay these motherf**kers." I know he is trying to keep me quiet. He is still lying to John, telling him I have a lot of money. Art has been using me for a long time. I know this, but I didn't know how to end it. I was still hoping to get back the money for my friends and myself, so I've been playing games with him.

5:00 p.m.	Art is with Coach Devlin. Will call me back.
6:00 p.m.	Art called to say he can't talk now—walked outside to call me and will call me at 10:00 p.m. my time. Things will be OK. Said he loves me. He probably is telling many other women the same thing, in order to take their money.

Friday, January 7, 2011

9:45 a.m.	Called to ask what is going on. I asked where all my paperwork is located. (I'm referring to the tote of papers he removed from my car back in May when the federal agents were coming to interview me.) He has it somewhere. He is in Southern Indiana. Wondered why I didn't call him to check on him when he didn't call last night. Next Monday he will get big money. Will have no trace for us.
11:15 a.m.	Art says we'll have big money on Monday or Tuesday. Wants me to call Linda Scott. Said we'll get a lot of money. I ask, "REALLY?" He hangs up on me and refuses to answer my calls. He finally calls back and said he is under a lot of stress. Had me call Linda Scott. Tell her money will be in her account on Monday morning: $9,900, and the rest later. He will put cash in her account on Monday morning. He said I haven't been doing the things he as asked. He was very accusatory and suspicious.

1:30 p.m.	Art has been with Hagan Temple (a Realtor). Asked me if I had given anyone his cell phone number.
4:30 p.m.	I called Art to see how he was doing and how his meeting with Hagan went. All was fine. He said, "I know you need money for bills."

Saturday, January 8, 2011

12:40 p.m.	Art finally answers his phone. Had not heard from him since yesterday afternoon. He's working at a basketball game. Wondered why I had not called and checked on him. Asked if I had talked to John. He's upset. Nobody thinks he can put this together. I told him I still have faith and trust him. He promised to always answer his phone and I will do the same. We worry when we don't answer.
4:00 p.m.	I called Art to tell him I was jealous about him being with all these girls. It's a ruse to misdirect his suspicions.
5:15 p.m.	He had been helping his friend, who is a coach. Will call back. Boris was calling him. He is at a bar watching a Colts game.
8:15 p.m.	He has been asking me to do a lot lately. I told him I was scared. The detective came to my door. I'm paranoid. He was calm and said he understood.

Sunday, January 9, 2011

Detective Davis had developed another ruse about my being called into the Dublin Police Station for questioning. This news worried Art a great deal and he wanted to be sure I was prepared for what awaited me. He called me repeatedly, explaining exactly what I was to say and how I was to respond to questions.

11:00 a.m.	Art called and said he is trying to work things out.
4:45 p.m.	Art called. I told him about my upcoming meeting with the detective. Art will be meeting Tim Baker

and Calder Fenwick on Monday to keep them at bay. We need to talk at 9:00 p.m. He said he hasn't asked me to do much recently.

8:30 p.m.   Told me what to say to the detective. Call early AM.

I still think God had wanted me to help Art and other families. Sometimes I don't understand—maybe this is all to be, to get Art to stop all of this. I just wish all my friends could be paid back. It is so sad. I never dreamed my life would be like this. I must stay strong!

***

Art Schlichter: What I would do when I go in (to talk to the detective), they are going to want to ask you a lot of questions about me and you. That's what the guy's going to ask. They are going to try and scare you to tell them the whole thing and (they want you to) say, "I gave all this money to Art." You probably should take a lawyer in there 'cause it's going to be a disaster.

Anita Barney: Maybe I should see if I can wait a couple of days or so then.

Schlichter: No, just ask them, "Do I need a lawyer?" Say you're getting it all resolved. Don't say, "*we* are," say, "*you* are." You have just been writing these checks as collateral. You didn't know they were actually going to come back and throw them at you. You were going to pay the money back and then they could use the checks to cash them. It wasn't like giving me money and here's a check or anything like that. They are going to ask you a thousand questions. Did you give Art—they probably got a full-blown investigation going with the Feds and the State and—what this is all about and why have you done this? It's probably going to get really ugly tomorrow if you don't, if you don't say, "Listen, I didn't know but I have the wherewithal and will go ahead and take care of this. I haven't known what to do. You told me I needed to pay the bank. The banks closed my

328

account. Tell me what I need to do and I'll get it done. I'm trying." But they are going to pull a full-court press. Maybe you want the guy to come to your house. You don't want to go there because there might be four, five, six, seven, or ten people there. You know?

Barney: I will call him in the morning and see what I can work out.

Schlichter: Say, "I just want this to all go away. I have the wherewithal to make it all go away. I've just been waiting to hear what you wanted, how you wanted me to handle it. You scared me."

Barney: What do I say if they ask me to show them the money?

Schlichter: Tell them you need a few days and you'll have it all. And they'll tell you who to pay, and you'll get a cashier's check and make sure everyone gets paid. The bank accounts got kinda screwed up and you've got to figure out how to do it a different way. Say you'll get a cashier's check and that will be it, if that's OK. That might be it, but I think it's going to be much deeper than that. If they ask you about football tickets, say, "I had access to tickets and I helped people out and got people their tickets."

Barney: What about Super Bowl tickets? Because my neighbors—

Schlichter: You don't have no Super Bowl tickets. You don't have anybody but one or two people involved with that. There's a question you've got to answer, "Where did all this money go?" They will want to know where did all the money go that you borrowed.

Barney: They're going to ask me that, you think?

Schlichter: Hell, yes, they are going to ask you that.

Barney: Do you have money to give me tomorrow? Or Boris or somebody?

Schlichter: We don't have money to give you tomorrow. But I want to know what's going on before we go any farther with this. I've got to know.

Barney: All right. I'll find out. I've got bills to pay, too.

Schlichter: You better think about what you're going to say when they ask you where all the money went.

Barney: Well, what I'll do is ask if I can have a couple more days.

Schlichter: If the detective asked to talk to you, they want to find out what you know. They don't care about a couple more days. They want—

Barney: Maybe he'll be on vacation. I hope! We'll see what happens.

Schlichter: He told you to be there Monday at ten o'clock! HE'S NOT ON VACATION!

Barney: Oh, that's true. I guess I'm daydreaming here.

Schlichter: Don't do none of that going in there. When they say you won't be under arrest, that means that they are considering hammering you and me and whoever. Your friends . . . ask if you can work out a payment plan with some of these people and you'll get the rest of them taken care of. They will want to know where the money went. That's a touchy subject right now. Because you can't answer, you can't say you gave it all to me. That's not going to be good. At all. That would be a disaster. That would be an IRS nightmare. All right? Think about it . . . Call me back at seven-thirty in the morning. We'll talk. You can call the detective at eight. We'll see what he's actually about to say. You're almost better to have him come out to your house and do the meeting there. You hear me?

Barney: I can't believe my life.

Schlichter: I know. This is ridiculous.

Barney: We're going to be OK, right? You've got the money coming?

Schlichter: Without the State of Ohio and the Feds we'd be fine. But they still f**ked with you . . . I'll try to get it all worked out. Call me early.

Monday, January 10, 2011

Art Schlichter: You've got to listen to me very closely. OK? What they're going to do is, he's going to want to know where all the money went. OK? And what they're going to do, they are going to have you, turn you against me today. Then they will say either you go or he goes. He goes or you go. Yep. That's what I think is going to happen. I think (the detective is) going to ask you if I got all this money from you and all this kind of stuff.

Anita Barney: Maybe it's not. It's just about that check.

Schlichter: This Detective Davis has called around to people that you have written checks to and brought my name up and tried to get people to talk about tickets and all kinds of bad things.

Barney: Who did he call?

Schlichter: He's called some people from, well, your normal Whit Beatty, your buddies, my guy from Wilmington, a friend of mine who lent me some money and we wrote a check to. Lance Sellars. Tim Baker. They are going to talk about him today. They are probably going to talk about, I wouldn't be surprised if Calder has been in there. Wouldn't be surprised if Buster Jurik has been in there. Wouldn't be surprised if any of them has been in there and saying that I got a connection to all this through tickets. OK? And let me just give you some words of advice, OK? Hold on a second. John's texting me. He said that I have hurt you and that they are going to prosecute me for hurting you. I've been talking to him back and forth—texting. He said, "If you've hurt that lady, Art, you deserve to go to prison."

Barney: Oh, Art! Oh, no.

Schlichter: Have you heard anything? Has anybody approached you or is any of this news to you? Or have you already been approached by all these people?

Barney: You say "all these people," I haven't been approached by anybody. That detective came to the door and I didn't answer it. The phone didn't ring at all yesterday. Chuck Taylor this morning. But I haven't heard from anybody, just Chuck wanting money. He's going to Naples and wanted money before he left.

Schlichter: Listen to me now, OK? I don't even know how to get through this. What you need to do is say, "Listen, I've made arrangements to clean this all up." OK? "Sorry it's gotten this far. I wrote some checks because I just thought that would be good collateral for them. I didn't know they were going to prosecute me. I'll pay them back." If they ask you about tickets, well, you got tickets for everybody.

Barney: Where did I get them from, though? What do I tell them? They will ask where they came from.

Schlichter: Well, you can say some of them were yours, some of them you bought.

Barney: OK. That's true. I did.

Schlichter: You didn't get things you thought you would, so you went ahead and just purchased them yourself. OK? They are going to ask you if you have given me money and what I am doing with it. And you're going to say, "I've helped Art out." Say, "I borrowed the money in good faith from people because yes, he needed some stuff." He will ask you that and just say, "I can't tell you because it's private. I've got a confidentiality agreement."

Barney: I can say that to them?

Schlichter: Yes, if you have a confidentiality agreement. I don't know what to say to them on that. They are going to ask if you gave me all the money and you're going to say *yes*. Once you do that it will be all over with. So, you really can't say that. And they are going to ask if you talked to me before you came in here and you can say *no*, because they don't know that you and I have talked. Let me just tell you what's happening. They are going to bring you in and say

332

it's either you or him. OK? I think they are going to say that because you have the checks out and they want to know where the money went. If they want to, they could prosecute you for the checks. But if you agree to testify against me, I'm sure they will let it go if you pay it back or whatever. But we're not going to be able to pay it back if . . . and they can't know anything about anything about the money coming in. Just say, "I've made some arrangements and I'm going to get this stuff handed out."

Barney: Do I ask for a little time? A few more days?

Schlichter: Yeah, you want time. Just say, "I'm going to get all these lawsuits straightened out. I've got a condo. I've got property. I'm not very good with money. My husband handled it most of the time." But that's how I would do it. I would not let them—I would say, "I've helped Art some, but it's not all about Art. This money will be replaced. This money will be paid back by the end of the month. I've got a condo worth about $400,000 and I've got money owed to me that I'm going to be collecting." Don't tell him who. Just that you have money from individuals owed to you.

Barney: What if they keep asking me? Do I have to tell them? What do I say? That is what scares me.

Schlichter: You do have a condo. OK? You do own your own condo. It's worth half a million dollars. You can say, "I've got that up for sale. I plan on selling it to pay debt." Just don't tell them that you lent me the money.

Barney: But I can tell them a little bit you said?

Schlichter: Yeah. Say, "I've helped Art, I've donated money to his foundation. I've helped him through his lawyer. And I have backed him up on a couple of things when he needed help. Write checks to let people know that they would be getting paid. I didn't know what they were. I didn't know I could be prosecuted for that. I just wrote them a check so when the money was available they could go ahead and cash the check. I didn't know they were going to use it against me. I didn't write the check for them to give me money. I mostly signed agreements with them. And it has taken a little bit of time to pay them back." Which you have paid back some people and you will be paying back others. You'll have this all sorted out by the end of the month. God forbid I would go to jail because I still owe you money and I'm capable of working. "Why would you put him in jail? I did everything of my own free will." That's what I would tell them. Which you did! Really! The other thing is, "Should I have a lawyer here with me today? I don't want to get arrested. I just want to get the people taken care of. I'm not very good at communicating because I was embarrassed that I had not got them paid back yet. I didn't know everybody was going to start suing me." If they ask you about Tim Baker, just tell him that Tim Baker is—well, that's going to be one problem because what they are going to say is that your checks made the deal and Tim Baker took the deal and you were going to buy tickets from him. That was how Tim got involved. You just wrote those checks to co-sign until the deal went through. No big deal. Say, "I didn't think it was illegal, I was just trying to help him and co-sign them until we actually got the tickets."

Barney: The problem is, when they went to put the checks in, the money was not there. So, they will ask, "Where is the money?"

Schlichter: Just say you told them not to put the checks in yet. There's not one person you haven't told not to put the checks in yet, because the money wasn't available and everybody you wrote a check to, you told them that you would call them and let them know when those checks would be good. You didn't give them a specific date. And Tim Baker the same way. You really weren't getting anything for it. I think it's too late.

Barney: What do you mean by that?

Schlichter: John just talks so negatively about me that what I think has happened is that these people have been complaining,

334

and you've got these checks out and I'm involved with those people. And as a result, then, they think that it's a con . . . listen, if it gets bad, just say, "Sir, I don't feel comfortable with this. Would you allow me to go home and come back tomorrow or the next day and bring my lawyer with me? I don't want anybody to go to jail. I don't want to go to jail. I don't want Art to go to jail. I want to pay everybody back and that's what we're going to do." Don't sign anything. You need a lawyer there if you're going to do anything like that. OK? Don't sign a statement against me. If you do that, it will be all over with.

Barney: Oh, dear. OK. Well, send Bill Hanners with some money for me. I'm nervous about my bills. I'm afraid they are going to turn the electricity off or something.

Schlichter: Listen, they are going to say so many bad things about me today and make you think that I'm a piece of sh*t. OK? . . . Don't talk about Bill or Boris or anybody else. OK? . . . Call me immediately after you get out of there, no matter what. Please!

Barney: I'll call you when I get out of the parking lot.

Schlichter: They are going to try to turn you against me and say I stole all this money from you, which is bullsh*t! That's not true. Say, "Any money I've given to Art or anybody else I gave of my own free will." And then they can't do anything about that. If they prosecute me, I'm not paying anyone . . . All right, I love you. Be very careful. Call me immediately.

***

As I drove to the police station for my 10:00 a.m. appointment, Art called. I could hear the anxiety in his voice as he warned me not to be surprised if the Feds or someone from Prosecutor Ron O'Brien's office was there with the detective. He cautioned if I find myself outnumbered, I was to stick with my story. He made me rehearse my answers by asking again, "How are you going to answer their questions about where all the money went? What are you going to say if they ask what you told the people you took the money from?" He was insistent I present a reasonable and believable explanation for the big question, "Where did all the money go?" Before disconnecting the call he told me his whole life was riding on a thread and wished me luck.

At the Dublin Police Station, Detective Davis met me and the two of us sat together in a conference room, drinking coffee, and discussing the case. He downloaded recorded calls, and I provided him with an American Express statement that showed Art had used his cell phone to make telephone charges to my account.

He provided me with responses I was to give Art when he asked about my "interrogation." When an appropriate amount of time had passed, he encouraged me to keep up the good work and escorted me to the exit.

Art called on my way home, desperate to know what happened. I told him the meeting wasn't as bad as we had anticipated. I had thirty days to cover the PNC check written to Lew Sanchez. When I said Detective Davis had not mentioned his name, Art became suspicious and replied, "I can't believe that." Art was happy when I told him I cried a lot and quiet when I said I got a break because the detective knew Bob.

Art began probing, looking for an inconsistency, a tell that I was lying. Before long he dispensed with the subtly and asked directly, "Sure he didn't bring up anyone else? So, tell me the real story. What really happened?" Once I convinced him we were OK, he said he had to get to work. "Thank God it wasn't worse than that," he said before hanging up.

Later Art calls and said it was a shame my friend Lew Sanchez would do this to me. *How can Art not see that HE did this to ME? He's the one to blame—not my friends!*

***

5:00 p.m.   Art wants me to open a PayPal account. I've never heard of it. Told me the guy who is hiding the money for him has almost all of it in PayPal.

6:00 p.m.   Told me to call people back! He said he has a lot of money to put in my PayPal account. No way; it will be traced. Says he can transfer money into a PayPal account confidentially. Explains even if you have a billion dollars in a PayPal account, the authorities can't find it. Will have a lot of money for me in thirty-six hours.

Tuesday, January 11, 2011

7:15 a.m.   Art called and wanted me to call Douglas DeLarge and plead with him not go to Prosecutor O'Brien's office. Gave me Douglas' cell number. Art wanted me to say: *I will handle this, this week. I've invested a lot in Art and he has done a lot of good things. Had a long talk with Art and we have a good game plan. I've always helped with issues. Art's having heart and many other health problems. He could have a breakdown. Why go to the police on me when I'm just trying to help people? Do I need to sign a note? Please don't do anything.*

Art asks if I'm writing down what he's telling me to say. He wanted to listen in when I made the call to Douglas. I didn't know what I was going to say with Art listening. He mentions PayPal again. I ask why, if he has access to the money, he needs me to open a PayPal account. He just needs PayPal. Art says he is in Lexington. *Thank God* the minutes ran out on the phone before I could call Douglas.

12:00 p.m.   Art's voice changes. I told him about Chip Greene calling and his letter. He thinks I could sue Chip and get my money back because I didn't receive anything. I'm just paying Art's debt. Art told me Steven Grundy wasn't going to deposit the checks until I have (Super Bowl) tickets in my hands. Art had told Steven before that I couldn't order money until first of year for tax purposes.

6:30 p.m.   Bill Hanners put $300 in my U.S. Bank account.

11:30 p.m.   Art called to say good night.

** American Express has been calling at all hours.

** Art tells me I'm making a lot of mistakes and creating a lot of problems for him with Douglas DeLarge.

Wednesday, January 12, 2011

10:15 a.m.   Art sounds sleepy. Says his buddy gave him a sleeping pill. Told him again that I didn't want to do PayPal. Can't lose my small credit card and last bank account. OK. Art said he took care of Douglas DeLarge, Calder, and Tim Baker *for me.* "I gave them money," he said. All three men have checks of mine and Art said after Super Bowl they'll get their money and I'll get all checks returned. I said, "I want money for my jewelry." He said I would have money next week and could go to Florida Monday or Tuesday (to pickup the jewelry I pawned for him a year ago). Monday was a relief for him. He thinks things are going to be OK now.

I went to the doctor for prescription and we were talking about Art. My doctor has known Art since before he played football. He said Art is trouble. Bipolar. Doesn't care about anyone but himself. Shows no remorse to anyone. He's a thief and will steal from anyone. Bad news!

12:30 p.m.   Art called my doctor's office to see if I really was there.

2:20 p.m.   He still sounds sleepy.

4:00 p.m.   He wants me to open a PayPal account and he will put $150,000 in it. Doesn't cost anything. Isn't illegal. There will be money going into that account.

338

Maybe $150,000. Says next week I can go to Florida and get my jewelry, get bills paid, pay people.

4:45 p.m.   Bill Hanners' mom in Grove City called Bill and asked if Art was in trouble. Art said Bill is freaking out and is a pu**y. Art asked me if I mentioned his name on Monday (when I interviewed by the Detective). I told him NO! He wanted me to swear on my daughter's life. I told him that was childish and we had a deal. He wants me to call Linda Scott and calm her down. He put no money in her account. He does not want me to call Douglas DeLarge. He said he gave him $5,000 of the $9,500. Bill is to put money in Calder's PayPal account. Tim Baker is getting Super Bowl tickets and money.

6:30 p.m.   His voice sounds normal now. I've heard him change his voice on many occasions. I think he's doing it with me and forgot who he was talking to. He's talking to Ron? Says Charles Grubb works at Red Mile Racetrack. Art tells me not to tell people I don't have the money.

8:30 p.m.   I was going to ask Art questions, but he said he'd call me back in ten minutes. Someone was going to help him to the bathroom because of his dizziness. He called Douglas DeLarge. Thinks this was a few days ago.

11:30 p.m.   He just now is calling me back. I didn't answer the phone.

** When I wrote checks for Art, sometimes he wanted me to remove a check from the middle of the checkbook. Why?

Thursday, January 13, 2011

8:10 a.m.   Art is calling all three phones. I'm not answering. Many calls and voice mail messages like this one: *G*DD**N IT! Where you at? . . . I've been calling and calling and calling you. Called your home phone. Called on your cell phone. Called ya!*

9:15 a.m.   I was going to call him now, but he's calling me instead. He's checking to see if I'm OK. Worried about police and people threatening me. He has to sell Super Bowl tickets. If all goes as planned, after Super Bowl I'll get some money and all checks back. He talked to Buster Jurik yesterday. Tim Baker expects to get $100,000 plus more from Super Bowl tickets.

10:30 a.m.   Wants me to call my people about paying them back. I won't call anyone. Don't want to lie to them anymore.

1:45 p.m.   He's going to put money in my account. Needs number. Called back to say someone called his regular cell phone and asked for me (Anita.). The caller wouldn't give the number but Art said he'd take their number to give to me and they said they had another number for me.

5:00 p.m.   He said he was sick. Going to have someone drive him home tonight. Wants me to look at PayPal. He could put $10,000 in my account if I opened it. He's got to spread the money out. His voice changed. I told him my cousin wants me to go to Wheeling Downs with him. Art said he will give me some money to go and have fun. He hasn't been there in a while. Art was told it was nice. I said I couldn't spend money that way when my friends need repaid. Told me to check out PayPal Again. He says that only I can use it. Not him.

| 10:25 p.m. | I called him to see how he was feeling, and he is still in Lexington. Says he has to work tomorrow. Big payday. |

Friday, January 14, 2011

| 9:00 a.m. | Art said he was putting money in my account today or Tuesday. He told Steven Grundy money would be in bank Tuesday AM. Plan on getting my jewelry. |

Art said there would be $155,000 deposited to my account on Tuesday. Some to Steven and Sam. I'm supposed to call my attorney and try to settle some lawsuits. He'll take care of Tim Baker.

He doesn't want to come to Columbus since John no longer represents him. He's afraid of the police and the Feds.

I think if he puts money in my account, it's to keep me quiet and to tell the Feds that he is paying me back.

| 10:00 a.m. | Had me call Brad Johnson and tell him there will be money in his account Tuesday AM. Check or wire into account. (Art gave me Brad & Lisa Johnson's account # and routing # at 5/3 Bank.) |

| 1:40 p.m. | Art calls. Wheels are in motion. Money will be there Tuesday AM. Boris is delivering basketball tickets. Says we have a long way to go. |

| 5:30 p.m. | Art called to say his mom has to go to the Grand Jury. She was crying and ready to kill herself. John Amery thinks all the attorneys who have sued me have gotten together and are trying to build a case against Art and me. Art said if I had talked to these people this would not have happened. *Really? He's blaming me? If he had not conned these people, this would not have happened!* |

** Art has ruined many lives, but he also ruined his own life. So sad!

***

Art Schlichter: Honestly, tell me the truth, will you, please? Please, honey! I've gotta have the truth here, OK? You've got my mom involved now. I'm asking you: Did Ron O'Brien call you?

Anita Barney: No.

Schlichter: Did the Prosecutor for Franklin County call you?

Barney: No.

Schlichter: Have you been in to the Prosecutor's office?

Barney: No.

Schlichter: Swear to God?

Barney: Swear to God.

Schlichter: What happened then? I'm going to ask you something. Somebody who sued you has now taken this case to the Grand Jury. Trying to get an indictment against me for dealing with the stuff that I dealt with you.

***

8:30 p.m.   Art said he wants to straighten his life out and get people paid to get the stress out of his life. I reminded him that was my goal when I met him and he only needed $100,000.

** He gave me a check from his mom in February 2010. I think the check is in the tote bag Art took when the Feds were coming to talk to me in May 2010. I had all the receipts from banks, etc. He says they just want him.

342

Saturday, January 15, 2011

10:00 a.m.   He thinks police are looking into checks from about three years ago. He is sad about his mom. He had Stan Jackson speak in his place this morning at a church in Sunbury. He says Stan's one of the good guys. They did radio shows together. Art said the money is taken care of for Tuesday. I tell him I trust his decision. I trust him. That he is a very smart man.

12:15 p.m.   He doesn't want to talk on the phone. Easy to tap. He's going home to Washington Court House and I can come down and we'll talk then.

3:15 p.m.   He's still out of town. Afraid he'll be arrested if he goes to Washington Court House. Bill Hanners was calling to tell him which tickets he had available for the OSU Basketball game at 5:30 p.m.

I reminded him of when we were supposed to go to Chicago to get that money. Someone in Chicago was to buy many OSU tickets. We were to drive the Escalade to Chicago after I met him in Indy. It did not happen. I told many people I was in Chicago getting the money. I lied to keep them calm. Art told me many times to get packed that we were going to go and get the money.

He asked about my friend Joy Blanco. Joy and I don't talk now. She is owed $18,000.

6:00 p.m.   Buster Jurik called to say he talked to Art. He and Art are going to Indy one week from Tuesday. Going to a ticket outlet to have Buster go in and buy tickets. Buster gave Art money already. Buster bought forty tickets and will make $30,000. Art will make $40,000. I told him I bought twenty-five tickets. He heard that Art was kiting. He told me what that meant. I'd never heard the word.

** Art said the car his mom is driving is the one I gave him money for. It's a Buick. *That's a lie. They were driving that car a year ago in December when we met at Applebee's for lunch before Christmas. The money came to him in January 2010.*

** Art used to sit with me most of the time when I tried to sell his OSU tickets. He would go through my address book over and over.

** Art told me his mom is a board member of his foundation. She doesn't do anything. It's being reconstructed. Gave the money to Maryhaven. (A treatment center for individuals with addictive and mental illnesses.)

** A woman named Maci Paskell created his website and he owes her $200,000? She is checking into rehabs for him.

Sunday, January 16, 2011

10:00 a.m.   Art called sixteen times.

1:30 p.m.   I finally answered the phone. Just chit chat. He doesn't want to answer any questions on these phones.

8:30 p.m.   Chit Chat.

10:30 p.m.   Called to say good night.

** I just remembered meeting Boris' (Paveleski) daughter at Walmart on East Main Street and at Bob Evans at Crosswoods and behind Applebees. I'll get her name.

Monday, January 17, 2011

8:30 am.   Just checking in. Is sad about his mom.

1:00 p.m.   John called, told me about Art's mom being called to testify at the Grand Jury.

1:30 p.m.   Just checking in. Chit chat. Weather is forty degrees where he is. He'll call later.

9:30 p.m.   Art said he was being arrested by the Feds. Would call me back. He said he saw a man outside who was wearing FBI shirt and needed to go.

Tuesday, January 18, 2011

12:45 a.m.   Art has left his friend's house. I don't know where he is. He asked if they (FBI) came to my door. Said he'd call in the morning.

1:00 a.m.   I called his cell. He answered his phone said he'd call in the AM.

1:30 p.m.   Art is acting paranoid. John told Art he has to go to Ron O'Brien's office this week. Art wants to talk to me in person, not on phones. I need to go to my Aunt Donna's funeral Wednesday. Cannot see him. He said he'd meet at Lee Garden restaurant on Thursday to talk about plans.

Detective Davis and others are concerned about my safety so I cannot meet Art unless we control the meeting.

9:30 p.m.   Buster Jurik called to say he talked to Art today. Art told Buster he was still in Indy and would be in Columbus on Thursday, and they will have lunch. He told Buster they are still going after the Super Bowl tickets next Tuesday.

Art told me he would give me money within twenty-four hours. I need to pay bills, jewelry, etc.

** Rod Cheetham filed a complaint for foreclosure against me today.

Wednesday, January 19, 2011

1:00 a.m.   Art called to talk about meeting today.

8:30 a.m.   Art wanted me to meet and talk. I told him I had to go to the funeral.

Afternoon | In the afternoon I attended the funeral for my Aunt Donna at First Community Church in Columbus. I ran into Calvin Renwick, a friend of the family and local business owner. He had given me money, plus he bought tickets from me. Our cars were parked beside each other at the church. He said he thought I owed him some money. It was about $19,000. I was caught off-guard being confronted in person by a creditor and quickly searched for an explanation. I told him I did owe him money, but that I had a problem. I opened my purse and showed him the recorder. I mentioned Art Schlichter was involved and I was recording for authorities. I wasn't supposed to tell anyone. I swore him to secrecy. At the funeral, Alan and my grandson Sean sat near me, but none of my other family members spoke to me or acknowledged my presence. Due to my involvement with Art, and now the authorities, I had pushed them away and they were unsure of what to do or how to respond. My heart broke at our estrangement.

7:00 p.m. | Art is insisting that I meet him tomorrow. Told me that he knows I lied to him about the police. He said if I don't meet him he'll know that I talked and told everything. I told him I'm pissed at him for ruining my life when all I wanted to do was help him. Liens on my cars, condos, jewelry gone, family not talking to me and broken promises about money. I'M PISSED! I told him I think Linda Scott is behind all this and he disagrees. He says I met Prosecutors and they told me not to meet him. Told me to ask them if I can meet him.

8:30 p.m. | I'm going to tell him, when he puts money in my account, I will meet him. He was talking with anger in his voice. He said he's pissed at me.

** My son Alan and grandson Sean each sleep with a gun by their beds for protection.

** I asked Bill (my attorney) if Linda could charge Art even though she lives in Dayton. Yes.

Thursday, January 20, 2011

8:15 a.m.   Brad Johnson calls about checks.

10:45 a.m.   Art asks if I was hiding from him. He won't give or take information over the phone. Will get it in person. Hung up on me. Said I called the police.

11:45 a.m.   I talked to Art and told him I didn't want to argue with him and he said the same. Wants to use the money as a bargaining tool. Told me to put checks in the mail.

3:00 p.m.   He'll put $5,000 cash in my account within forty-eight hours. Says all my friends are going to the Grand Jury on Monday and that's why they are not calling me. Art said Buster Jurik is working at the Franklin Depot, and that I should work there and pay off the debt owed to Ben Roberts.

5:30 p.m.   Called to see if anyone had called me to tell me to call a judge. Thinks Douglas DeLarge turned him in. He's in Indy to see his kids. Bad storm. He says all my friends turned him in to Grand Jury, not me.

8:30 p.m.   He said I must have told all my friends that it was him not paying them back. Told him I would not do that. His mom must give a handwriting sample to authorities.

The authorities requesting a handwriting sample from Art's mother, Mila, was simply a tactic Detective Davis and Steve Schierholt used to put pressure on Art. At the time, she was not the target of any investigation.

9:00 p.m.   I asked what I will do if he goes to jail and he said that is what he wanted to talk to me about. He's going to talk to his attorney on how to pay back the money. I reminded him I have nothing now! He said we'll meet Sunday PM. He sounds very sad. He said it is his fault. I reminded him how I kept telling him my friends were very upset. Douglas DeLarge has a friend who is a judge.

** Basil Philpott, my girlfriend from grade school who was invited to my birthday celebration and accompanied me to the Ohio Theater to see Snow White, filed a complaint on promissory notes against me today: two for $25,000 and one for $60,000.

Friday, January 21, 2011

8:00 a.m.   Art called to wake me up for my doctor appointment.

1:30 p.m.   Told him the sheriff left card at door. They probably will call me in.

2:00 p.m.   Told him I need money in account to cover the checks I had written. (I didn't write any checks yet.) I said I needed money before everyone else since I've lost everything to help him. He needs to help me.

2:30 p.m.   Told him my jewelry pay off at the pawn shop is $20,000. They'll make a deal.

8:30 p.m.   Said he may not get Super Bowl tickets if he's going to jail.

Saturday, January 22, 2011

10:30 a.m.   I called him to see what his plan was. He may get Super Bowl tickets. Said I should have met him. He's going to be with his kids.

11:45 a.m.   Said we'll meet Sunday or Monday. I need cash and information. Will get Super Bowl tickets Tuesday.

He told Brad Johnson I was in the hospital. He asked when I'm going to the Grand Jury.

2:45 p.m.   He is mad at me for crying. *He should be crying; he's going to jail.* I wouldn't call my friends (to keep them calm) so they pressed charges and that's why we are going to jail. **It's all my fault.** I need to stop crying and pull together to make this turn out. It will be the last time to be with his kids. I didn't prolong putting people off to give him enough time to pay them off. He's screaming at me. "Stop your f**king crying and help me figure this out!"

3:30 p.m.   Buster Jurik called to say Art is going to call him on Monday and give him the details for Tuesday or Wednesday to go to Indy for Colts tickets. Cheer for the Jets; it could mean $1,000 more a ticket.

5:30 p.m.   John called to tell me they are doing handwriting samples on Art's mom. He said Art admitted to him about gambling. Don't let Art intimidate me. Stay strong to help convict him. *The Columbus Dispatch* will wait and (the reporter) will be good to me. Art told John he borrowed $300,000 to $400,000 from me.

Monday, January 24, 2011

** Art called to tell me about his mom. Said he'd get some money. I told him I must go before the Grand Jury on February 7.

** John called about my meeting with the Dublin Detective.

** Boris gave me $2,000 at a Shell gas station on Fishinger (Mill Run) Road.

** Art asked me to go with him tomorrow to talk to his attorney. My attorney said no.

Tuesday, January 25, 2011

8:45 a.m.   Wants me to tell Brad Johnson I'll call him in the afternoon. He's going back to sleep and wants me to wake him at 12:00. Going to his attorney at 1:00 p.m.

11:30 a.m.   Said, "I may have you meet me and my attorney." Will have money for me. Be ready to go at 3:00.

6:00 p.m.   Wants me to meet him Wednesday morning at Routes 36/71 to talk. I told him I need to be at OSU at 8:00 a.m. to have my ear worked on. He said, "I'll be there and we'll talk in the waiting room." I'm going to tell him Alan needs to drive me. I won't be able to drive, and I'll be sleeping all day. That should discourage him from meeting me at my doctor's office.

11:30 p.m.   Art was supposed to call me at 9:00 p.m. Then halftime of OSU-Purdue basketball game. No calls when he said he would call. He told me earlier he was just chillin'. I called him at 11:30 p.m. and told him I was tired of him lying to me about money, all his calls, and disrespecting me. I said goodbye and hung up.

Wednesday, January 26, 2011

12:15 a.m.   Art has been calling all three phones for forty-five minutes. I'm not going to talk to him. Voicemails are begging me to call him.

4:00 a.m.   Art is calling my cell.

4:15 a.m.   Twenty-seven calls. He's calling again now. He's still begging. I'm remembering all the times that I begged him not to make me call people or meet people. Also recalling the names he would call me and when he would tell me how dumb I was about doing certain things. I would tell him I was dumb

350

about certain things and didn't want to learn how to do illegal things (like how to kite checks to banks, etc.).

8:30 a.m.	He is still calling.
9:30 a.m.	Detective Davis came over and directed me as I called Art to ask him questions.
4:00 p.m.	John called me about Art. He said that Art admitted gambling in Vegas and overseas gambling. He has gambled all the money. John wants to call the police about him.
6:30 p.m.	I called Linda Scott and Art told me what to tell her. He says only he and his friend know where the money is.
7:00 p.m.	Art called me after he talked to Linda Scott and was ready to argue with me. I told him I couldn't talk. I had company. My neighbor and I were having a cocktail. He said he'd leave me alone tonight.

** Best Seat Tickets (Chip Greene) filed a civil case against me today to collect $18,400.

Thursday, January 27, 2011

6:30 p.m.	Art said he had a lot of Super Bowl tickets to pick up Monday in Indy. He will bring mine Tuesday morning.
	He told me Boris would bring me $3,000 Friday. I asked if he was giving me a lot of Super Bowl ticket money and he said, "I hope so." He wants to talk at 9:00 p.m. tonight.
9:00 p.m.	We didn't talk. He was tired.

Friday, January 28, 2011

10:30 a.m.	He was checking to see what was going on. I told him that Calder left a voicemail. Art told me not to

call him. He gave Calder part of his money and he wants tickets also.

12:30 p.m.   I told Art that (Special Agent) Terrence Brown left a voicemail. Art called John to see what was going on. John didn't know anything.

6:30 p.m.   Art said he may meet with John Saturday about how to make some money. They may have me join them.

Saturday, January 29, 2011

5:30 p.m.   Art says he's going to Marion to speak.

7:30 p.m.   He is speaking in Marion, Ohio, at a church. He said he talked to John today and John said he is going to prison for life for stealing from the elderly (me). He could confess and tell where all the money went, and where any money remains, and get less time. He wants to talk to me.

Sunday, January 30, 2011
Seven Days until the Super Bowl

10:30 a.m.   He said he spoke at a church last night and got a standing ovation before and after he spoke. *It's so sad he didn't stay on the right path to better his life.*

He says I'll get Super Bowl tickets Tuesday A.M. He wants to meet me and give them to me and talk about the Grand Jury. I remind him he hasn't given me any money for bills. I'm broke.

8:00 p.m.   I called Linda Scott to ask if Art had given her any money. He is supposed to put $1,200 in her account Monday.

***

Art Schlichter: Listen! Let me just explain this to you. OK? Let me just say what was said to me. Then you'll understand. I wanted to meet ya and tell ya this. OK? First of all, I don't want you to tell your lawyer I got any money.

Anita Barney: OK.

Schlichter: OK? 'Cause that brings heat on me. When he and Ron f**king O'Brien get together. OK?

Barney: OK. All right.

Schlichter: The second thing is, is that I have to go in and talk to him. OK?

Barney: O'Brien?

Schlichter: Yes. Sometime this week. I suppose. And let me just tell you what O'Brien said. He told John Amery, he said if Art comes in and tells me the truth, which I don't have any problem doing so much, but, O'Brien said I won't, I will take it easy on him. He said, but if he doesn't, if he comes in here and tells me one lie, I'm going to f**king bury his ass.

Barney: Oh, my gosh!

Schlichter: OK? So, let me just say something. So, when I go in there and he asks me if I've got any money put away and I've given you any money and this and that, if I don't tell him the truth and he finds out about it, I'll go down even worse. Right now, you know, I need just a few days. You just need to hang in there. The money's safe. It ain't going nowhere.

Barney: OK. All right. I didn't know all that. We never really talk, you know.

Schlichter: I'm just telling ya. We don't really talk because I don't even know what to talk about because I don't even know what you told them. Or what he is saying to them. You know. And then when you go back and say something to your attorney. And he automatically goes back and shares it to the Prosecutor.

Barney: Well, I should ask him about that. I don't know what he tells him.

Schlichter: You sh**ting me? And let me tell you something. If I tell them that I sent you $100,000 or $200,000 into your lawyer's account, which I'll have to do. If I don't do it, then they can get me for lying to them. And then I'll be f**ked. Completely. OK?

Barney: I understand.

Schlichter: But, listen, if I don't f**king do any of that, right now, I don't have to answer that question but emphatically, "NO!" You know $2,000 here, $1,000 here, $5,000, you know. But what they're going to do is, if they think there is any money there—and you've got it—they are going to make you pay all these people *they* want you to pay. OK? You won't be paying your bills with that. So, there's a lot that goes into this. And it's getting pretty ugly.

Barney: Well, that's why I wanted to talk to you about it. Because I don't know all that is going on.

Schlichter: That's what is going on.

***

Monday, January 31, 2011
Six Days until the Super Bowl

8:15 a.m.   Art called to ask me why Richard Head had such a large suit against me. He doesn't. *The pressure is really getting to Art and he's losing track of who is owed what.*

***

Art Schlichter: Why don't you tell me what's really going on, Anita?

Anita Barney: I don't know what's going on. What do you mean? I'm still in bed. I fell back to sleep.

Schlichter: How could you owe Richard Head $300,000?

Barney: I don't owe Richard Head $300,000. We gave him $20,000. He wanted $5,000 back. And he put a lien on my condo here, and Florida, and both my cars.

Schlichter: That's $20,000. Huh?

***

1:30 p.m.	Said he was on his way to get tickets. Buster Jurik said Art was going to Indy to get tickets without him. Art said a lot of pressure is on him.
3:00 p.m.	He said he would call me back on different phone in fifteen minutes. He asks if I really was at home.
5:30 p.m.	He's driving to Indy to get tickets. Says they are paid for and he got $4,000 apiece for them from a company in Indianapolis. Bad storm coming. John said that I must have talked to the people in Prosecutor O'Brien's office.

***

Art Schlichter: It's going to be a disaster.

Anita Barney: What's wrong?

Schlichter: There's already an inch of ice. It's already hitting and I'm not even to Indianapolis yet. I guess it's already hit Carmel. Any calls?

Barney: Just Perry on the corner, my neighbor.

Schlichter: Did you talk to your lawyer?

Barney: I have not talked to him yet.

Schlichter: You're hesitating every question I ask, what's going on?

Barney: No, I'm not. Just trying to hear you. Perry on the corner, they have to leave tomorrow night (for Dallas for the Super Bowl). I mean, Wednesday.

Schlichter: If I have to, I'll just drive them back myself. This is going to be a zoo. It's going to be crazy. I've got to pick up the tickets; I'm barely just getting them now. Let me just tell you something. My lawyer told me such bad stuff today. I don't even know how to even respond to it. I really don't. It's horrible . . . the RICO (Racketeer Influenced and Corrupt Organizations) Act. You know why it includes me? Because he said when Bill would come and pick up money from you, or Boris would come and I'd do their account or whatever, I mean these people are innocent. They didn't do anything. It's bullsh*t. I don't know if they are getting charged but it says I was using other people when I got money. That's crazy! These are just my friends. And John Amery told me today there's no way that you haven't talked to the f**king Ron O'Brien. They wouldn't be going after that unless you spoke to them.

Barney: I have not talked to Ron O'Brien!

Schlichter: Well then, he's talking to somebody, honey!

Barney: I haven't talked—I have not been down there and they have not been here! I'm telling you! I'm waiting for it every day. I'm waiting. I go to the Grand Jury when? On the seventh of February?

Schlichter: I've got to get this part done and I don't know what to do next. I'll talk to you later. I'll keep calling ya.

Barney: We'll see each other tomorrow then, I guess, and get these tickets to these people, and get this out of the way.

Schlichter: Well, I think you got a better shot of seeing me on Wednesday. If you see what's coming, you're going to understand. I didn't know the storm was coming like this. But if you want to drive it, you can drive it.

Barney: What do you mean, "drive it"?

Schlichter: I'M GOING TO TRY AND DRIVE BACK TOMORROW! OK? You might have to meet me somewhere because it's supposed to be horrible conditions. They made a statement that it could be the worst storm in history.

Barney: Oh, I hadn't heard that. OK . . . if I have to drive to meet you to get the tickets . . . Oh, this is horrible. You have a lot of tickets to deliver and a lot of people are going to be pissed at you.

Schlichter: —RICO Act or whatever that's called. I mean, it's disgusting. I hadn't heard of that before. It's like John Gotti and sh*t.

Barney: Have you already paid for the tickets that you're going after?

Schlichter: Mmm–hmm. Catch you later.

***

7:30 p.m.   Art calls to tell me he's in bad weather.

Oh, the irony of that last entry. He *was* in *bad weather*, both literally and figuratively. Unbeknownst to him at the time, there was no escaping the legal storm bearing down on him.

36 | THE STORY BREAKS
FEBRUARY 1-6, 2011

"Former Buckeye Schlichter suspect in probe: Money for tickets went to gambling, sources say."	*Headline in The Columbus Dispatch*

By the time February first rolled around, we were only five days out from the Super Bowl and Art had not come up with any tickets. I could feel the tension tightening. Art was still claiming he could deliver on the tickets, but it was getting down to the wire. I remained hopeful but unconvinced. Only time would tell if he was going out in a blaze of glory or the agony of defeat, and the clock was ticking down at an alarming rate.

Tuesday, February 1, 2011
Five Days Before the Super Bowl

11:15 a.m.   I called Art. He's nervous about tickets. Hopes I can postpone Grand Jury.

2:00 p.m.   John told Art he has three choices: kill himself, run, or turn himself in and confess. I called Art and told him neighbors are leaving tomorrow morning for Dallas. He will get me tickets and wire them to Dallas. He said Tim Baker messed him up with the

Colts and Art's guy is having trouble getting the tickets to him. *He had said the same about the OSU tickets.*

***

Anita Barney: Yanni Rivera's son just called me.

Art Schlichter: I know, he's such an a**hole.

Barney: Why do you say that? He's just wanting the tickets.

Schlichter: I WILL GET HIM HIS TICKETS! Jesus Christ! He's f**king—I talked to his dad and then he calls and threatens me.

Barney: Well, they are threatening me, as well. He said you are not coming through with them and they have to take care of those checks, and they want the money somehow, or the tickets. Since you've talked to them, I don't need to talk to you about it.

Schlichter: I'm going to call Yanni right now.

Barney: Talk to me first. Alan's coming over. I need to talk to you now before he comes over, OK?

Schlichter: These tickets, I may not have them until tomorrow. OK? And you're going to have to tell these people that they got their tickets and Indianapolis is in a f**king mess right now. And that if you have to, you will overnight them. But you will guarantee the tickets. They will have them. Tell them to go ahead and make their trip and you'll overnight them to wherever they are at, a hotel, anywhere.

Barney: They are not going to do that.

Schlichter: Well then they are going to have to—you know what they are going to do then? They are going to have to get their tickets on Thursday and then they are going to think that was really stupid. I got my tickets and I can go to the f**king game . . . you know what? I'll tell you the f**king problem, OK? The f**king problem is Tim Baker! Tim

Baker threw me under the bus with the Colts. People have called over there about these tickets and it's got me in a lot of trouble. My guy is scared to death; he's trying to get 'em out and bring them to me.

Barney: Did you already pay for them?

Schlichter: Yes, but I'm not allowed to have them. No one is allowed to get these tickets. The guy was doing me a favor trying to help me. It's f**king insanity. Listen! I'll call you back at four o'clock. I can't give you an answer right now on when I'm going to have them. I'll know about four.

Barney: I need to know. I need to tell these people because they are going to go to the Dublin Police.

Schlichter: HOW CAN THEY GO TO THE DUBLIN POLICE? SUPER BOWL HASN'T STARTED YET!

Barney: Art, you told me to tell them to go ahead and make their travel plans.

Schlichter: Tell them to go. You'll overnight the tickets.

Barney: I don't know how you're going to do that. How are you going to do that?

Schlichter: I'm going to bring them home and you're going to overnight them. Or I'll overnight them from wherever I'm at to wherever they are at. They do that, you know? Tell them it's a f**king quagmire in Indianapolis. F**king ice storm. Look at the f**king thing. We'll have them. They'll have them. And you'll overnight them to them. It will be fine. You've got to reassure them.

Barney: Well, you better protect me. I've protected you for a year and a half now.

Schlichter: I'm protecting you. You just have to reassure them. 'Bye.

***

5:30 p.m.   Art said he was picking up Super Bowl tickets tomorrow afternoon. Will wire tickets to people at their hotels.

***

Anita Barney: Floyd Rogers is having a fit because they are leaving in the morning.

Art Schlichter: Tell him you'll overnight the tickets to him. You wouldn't do him that way.

Barney: How are we going to do this—

Schlichter: Let me tell you something. If I were going to be there tonight to give them to ya, then you would just give them to him. Get a forwarding address and tell him they will be there by Friday, you'll overnight them.

Barney: By Friday!

Schlichter: Thursday or Friday. Tomorrow's Wednesday.

Barney: I know! They are going to go to Dallas without Super Bowl tickets and we promised them. We told them . . . I don't know, he'll have a fit . . . do you really have tickets or not? I'm getting really nervous about this, Art! I'm afraid we're in trouble.

Schlichter: (Sarcastically) Ha. Ha. Ha. Now, *that's* funny!

Barney: Why? People are threatening me, and you're not here with the tickets when you told me you should have had them last week. You said you would get them last week. And now you still don't have them. I'm getting nervous about this.

Schlichter: Well, it's just what I told you. I guess maybe I should talk to them.

Barney: Maybe so.

Schlichter: Then they can call me a piece of sh*t or whatever.

***

Anita Barney: Floyd Rogers called me. He's frantic. I don't know when to tell him I'll have the tickets.

Art Schlichter: That's a good question. It's pretty bad.

Barney: They leave for Dallas tomorrow morning. I don't know what to tell them.

Schlichter: I'll figure it out. I'll call you in a couple of hours when I figure out how I'm doing this.

Wednesday, February 2, 2011
Four Days Before the Super Bowl

9:30 a.m.   Art says he is getting tickets at 2:00 today. Will be home tomorrow to give me tickets. I'm very angry with him and told him so. No money to pay bills. I told him I need money. I cussed him out.

***

John Amery: OK. Well, I think the situation is all going to be explained on Monday. Because, they are going to indict Art after the Grand Jury, for sure. Is that when you're supposed to testify?

Anita Barney: So, when they indict him, what happens then?

Amery: Well, they'll issue an arrest warrant. That means he's not going to get any kind of bail or anything. He's done at that point. I mean, I talked to him yesterday, Anita, and he said to me, he goes, "Well, if you think there is a chance that if I came up with the money to pay everybody back, that they wouldn't indict me?" I said, "Art, I don't know the answer to that, but if you have the ability, you need to pay everybody back. You need to pay Anita back. If you've got that ability you've got to put your f**king freedom secondary here with all the people that you victimized." I mean, he's gotta pay people back. Honestly, I think he is full of crap. I don't know anybody that is going to give him a couple million dollars. I just don't see it. I don't see it

362

happening. I said, "Art, you have three choices: you kill yourself or you run. Or you tell the truth and you implicate all the other people that were involved in this thing. And to me option number three is the only and best option that you have. I don't think the other ones are for real." But you can't believe him so you don't know what he's saying. His answer to me was that he was going to—he knows now, his lawyer told him that they are going to indict him on these RICO charges. He knows that. There's no way out now . . . even if he pays.

Barney: I didn't know what that was. I've never heard of RICO.

Amery: Well, because what he did, is he got money from out of state, across state lines . . . it's not a good situation for him all the way around. I don't think he'll kill himself. I don't think he'll do that because I don't think he has that in him. I think he'll run and that will only make it worse.

Barney: Well, he is supposedly in Indiana getting those tickets. Who knows? But he knows that my neighbors, he told them to go and make plane reservations. They are all leaving tomorrow morning. He said he would have them. But now this weather may come up as an excuse to not have them. I don't know what he's going to do. He's supposed to call me back at twelve-thirty about what to do about these tickets but I haven't heard from him yet.

Amery: He told the people who think they are going to the Super Bowl, he told them—

Barney: To make plane reservations, yes!

Amery: Oh, my god! What happens if he doesn't have the tickets?

Barney: They will have to go to the police to file a report against him. I didn't do it. He did it.

Amery: Oh, my gosh!

Barney: My neighbor got six tickets. He's got his family from Atlanta; they are all going to meet him in Dallas. And then this other couple have eleven of them, brothers. They are all going to meet in Dallas, also. And they are supposed to have the tickets with them. Perry gave him $6,000 cash and Floyd gave $11,000 cash to him. Art said it was a done deal and tell them to go ahead and make plans. And now, actually, they are calling me. And I'm calling him.

Amery: Here's why I don't think that's real. Because he knows where he's going at this point.

Barney: Well, why did he do this? I thought maybe he would just go out and buy tickets for them or something. I didn't know.

Amery: No. No. I think he's lying.

Barney: Well, he probably is. I don't know what I'm going to say other than just go to the Dublin Police is what I'm going to tell them. I don't know what else to do.

Amery: Yeah, that's what you have to tell them. You don't have any choice. Because, remember, you've got to do everything you can to stay out of the fray on this thing. Make sure nobody thinks you're part of anything. The Prosecutor does. Bill Loveland and I, we both talk to him. So we won't have any issues there. Everybody knows. That's not a problem.

Barney: I was just crying a lot yesterday about my condo and where I'm going to live. But I'll figure it out someday; I can live anywhere. I said if I have to, maybe Alan will let me move in with him in that extra bedroom he has upstairs. Maybe I can move in with my son because I know I will be losing everything. I think about that all the time.

Amery: Well, I think, at the end of the day, it's going to be better than what you think it is. It's going to be tough but it's not going to be as bad as what you think because of exactly how this happened. That's the difference.

Barney: I hope . . . I didn't know how to get away from him. I didn't know what to do. Still don't know what to do, but I'm trying.

Amery: It is amazing . . . I don't get it.

Barney: Well, I was in fear. I didn't have any money. And if he didn't give me any money I couldn't pay my bills. So, he was paying my bills for me. That's how he had me. He said to me the other day that if he goes to jail now, he said he wouldn't be able to pay me back. He said, "Wouldn't it be better that I not be in jail? And I make $200,000 to $300,000 a year and start paying you back?" He just told me that on Monday.

Amery: I know. But it's all fantasy. It's crazy. Because as much money as he owes you, he owes that much to other people. That's why it's just not going to happen . . . Keep me posted.

***

1:30 p.m.   Detective Davis called Art and identified himself as Floyd Rogers (a friend of mine who gave me money for Super Bowl tickets).

Art Schlichter: Hello.

Anita Barney: Hello, one second. Hold on just a minute, hold on—

Detective Davis (posing as Floyd Rogers): Is this Art? . . . Art, Floyd Rogers, how are you? . . . Oh, not too bad. Hey, I stopped by Anita's to see if she had my tickets, yet . . . All right. Do you have the tickets? . . . OK . . . Well . . . Yeah, she didn't want to give me your number . . . OK . . . 740- -I'm sorry, you're breaking up . . . 8655, OK . . . I know, brother, but I—look, I've got eleven grand riding on this. I've got a lot of people depending on me here. I mean, if you're going to get the tickets, I need them today or tomorrow morning. I'm leaving tomorrow, but my flight got cancelled this morning because of weather, but it's clearing up . . . right now we are scheduled to leave at 11:35 . . . It's clearing up. It's cloudy but it's not too bad. The roads are clear, so it's not bad at all . . . Well, I'll tell you what, you tell me you got the tickets I'll jump in the car, I'll come get 'em. I don't care. I just need those tickets or I want my $11,000 . . . You'll have them today, right? . . . All right. Well, I'm going . . . All right. You want to talk to Anita?

Art was infuriated that I had revealed his involvement to Floyd Rogers and had put him on the phone with "Floyd" without warning.

***

5:30 p.m.   Art finally answered my calls and said something serious was happening to him. I told him that Tim Baker called me twice. Baker wants a meeting with me next week. Wants me to make my checks good. Art has the money, not me. Detective Davis (posing as Floyd Rogers) keeps calling Art about the tickets. Art said he would deliver them tonight or tomorrow morning at the airport.

7:30 p.m.   Art told Detective Davis that he would meet him halfway tomorrow to get tickets. Tim Baker and Buster Jurik said they have no tickets. Buster told me that Art told him yesterday that he was going to Texas to sell the tickets.

After Detective Davis concluded his calls with Art, he said he was amazed at the skill Art displayed in coming up with answers and explanations on the spur of the moment. Art had a credible response for any question thrown his way. Detective Davis said that even though he knew Art was lying when he said to go ahead and travel to Dallas and the tickets would be overnighted, Art sounded quite believable. Detective Davis was astonished at Art's ingenuity and said if he had not known differently, it would have been quite easy to buy into Art's story.

9:30 p.m.   Art said he would call me right back. He's talking to John.

10:15 p.m.   Art called to say he talked to John. John said Tim Baker and the Tree Surgeon (Gage Ratcliffe) have gone to Channel 6 and the police. It may be in the paper tomorrow. Art is going to confess on Monday. John told Art to give me any money he has. Art asked why I didn't tell him I talked to O'Brien's office. I denied it. Art wants me to meet him at his mom's home for about 20 minutes tomorrow morning. Art said John told him not to get any tickets. He said he will give Perry, Floyd, and Roy back their money. This is a nightmare!

Thursday, February 3, 2011
Three Days Before the Super Bowl

10:00 a.m.   Multiple calls throughout the day. He called and said he didn't get to sleep until 3:00 a.m. John is taking care of Tim Baker. Art is working on getting tickets for my people.

***

Art Schlichter: We need to meet tomorrow. You and I need to meet. All right? It's the last chance to meet. Comprehend?

Anita Barney: Are you OK?

Schlichter: Am I OK? No, I'm *not* OK. How can anybody be OK in this mess? . . . Well, keep your phone on. I may need to talk to ya. Those guys answer just tell them you'll have to reimburse the tickets . . . John told me not to give anybody tickets. He said all I do is create problems . . . he said to give the money to you and my mom.

Barney: All right, do whatever you think is best.

Schlichter: I'll see ya. 'Bye.

***

Art Schlichter: Hold on, let me get this. Hello? Listening to Bill (Hanners) . . . all right, what's going on, Anita?

Anita Barney: Not much of anything. Awful quiet.

Schlichter: Tim Baker just called my buddy and told him he's going to do twenty years with me . . . have you talked to the Prosecutor today yet?

Barney: I have not, the attorney, no, nothing . . . I don't know what's happened to Floyd Rogers, if he went on or what. Went on to Dallas? I have no idea.

Schlichter: All right. I will talk to you in a little bit. John and I are putting a game plan together.

***

Anita Barney: I'm sure my jewelry is not in your thoughts.

Art Schlichter: Actually, all your money is on my mind.

Barney: Well, I'm glad. I don't know how things are going to work out.

Schlichter: Well, they're not. But that's OK.

Barney: It's not going to work out?

Schlichter: Well, not for me. For you it will.

Barney: I hope you're right, Art. Because I'm scared to death. I don't know what's going to happen to me now if I don't have you there to depend on.

Schlichter: Don't be scared. You're going to be fine. I'm going to make sure that everybody's OK. OK?

Barney: But financially? And all this? You're not here to help me.

Schlichter: Well, financially I'm very here to help you. What are you talking about?

Barney: Well, you keep saying you're going to jail.

Schlichter: Oh. Well, that's no big deal. I'm going to take care of everything before that happens. When I go in and talk to them on Monday, I'm going to, you'll see when I'm done. I'll tell ya.

Barney: Well, I appreciate that. I tried to help you.

Schlichter: You need to, Anita, make sure on Monday night, you need to call John, OK? Not before then. On Monday night, OK? Everything will be cool. You got it? Be strong.

Barney: What is going to happen? How do we handle this when it all hits the press? What do we do about that? Just let it go?

Schlichter: I'm going to talk to the press. I'm going to do an interview with them on Monday evening. He's going to try to talk with you today. A guy named Mike Wagner. You do not answer your door today, all right? Or do not talk to the press today or tomorrow.

Barney: You know, someone was at my door a while ago and I didn't answer it. A red VW Beetle. I didn't know the guy. I didn't answer the door.

Schlichter: That's him. Tall, skinny guy? Do not talk to him. He wants to talk to you before he talks to me. I will talk to him on Monday evening. Do not talk to the press. I'm going to handle all this. Here is what I'm going to do. I'm going to take the complete burden off of you. I'm going to put it on me. So, there will be no legal implications to you. No financial burdens for you. They will all come on to me. You can't help me.

Barney: Whatever happens, happens.

Schlichter: You will be all right. Everyone else will be all right. It's OK. I created the mess. I'll end it.

***

Before anything can be resolved, I hear the rumble of what is certainly the beginning of my destruction when I listen to my voicemail.

"My name is Mike Wagner. I'm a reporter with The Columbus Dispatch *and I got your number and am calling you because I've talked with John Amery and some other people that have informed me about what is going on with Art Schlichter. I know Art extremely well. I did a huge profile on Art and spent months with him doing the story for* The Dispatch. *And I'm also scheduled to meet with Art on Monday night. To talk about everything that has happened. I'm not close to writing anything but I think it would be very, very important for me to sit down with you and talk about things that have gone on. I hope John got ahold of you because I asked him to give you a call before I would reach out and call you so . . . I have also come across some lawsuits filed in the last six or seven months or so by people that I know were involved in this who you borrowed money from on Art's behalf. I knew this was going to happen. I turned down the chance to write Art's book after I did the story, he wanted me to write his book a couple of years ago and I said, 'No.' And the reason for it is because I knew there was going to be something like this again some day and I guess I should say I'm very, very sorry you're caught up in this, but it's definitely going to come out. I'm definitely going to be writing about it. I just want to make sure that I'm accurate in everything that comes out of here. I've been a reporter for 20 years. I'm a projects reporter. I handle the bigger stories here at the paper. I just want to make sure, again, I'm fair to everyone, especially to you, being victimized in all of this. My cell phone number is ###-####. And it's Mike Wagner, and I hope to talk to you soon, Anita. Thanks."*

Listening to the message from Mike, I begin crying at the hopelessness of my situation and how, in a few hours, the entire world will be talking about Art's con and my involvement. I feel vulnerable and alone. I have no one to save me from the riptide that is threatening to drag me away.

And then Joel Chow calls and I can barely contain my panic:

"Anita, my name is Joel Chow and I'm calling from WBNS Channel 10, Columbus Ohio. We are working on a television news story about something that involves you and would like to talk to you. Please call my reporter, Paul Aker, back at 614-###-####, or his cell phone number at ###-####. Thank you."

I place a call to John Amery. He answers and says he will call me back before quickly disconnecting the call. The next call I receive is from Art.

***

Art Schlichter: Why are you calling John?

Anita Barney: I thought I was supposed to.

Schlichter: No!

Barney: Well, this reporter called and said I was supposed to talk to John before I talked to him. I wasn't going to talk to either one of them. I was just calling to see what my instructions were supposed to be. *The Columbus Dispatch* reporter. Wagner. Somebody Wagner.

Schlichter: Yeah. Who else has called you today?

Barney: Channel 10 called and left a message. It's on the recorder.

Schlichter: Channel 10? Who from Channel 10? Why did Channel 10 call you?

Barney: They are going to do something. A report. I don't know.

Schlichter: Who was that from?

Barney: I think his name is Joel something. I can go out and hit the recorder.

Schlichter: Channel 10 called you? I've got to call you back.

***

John called and instructed me not to talk to the press. He said Art could have avoided a lot of these problems with the press if he would have done what John told him to do which was to talk to the reporter, but not have him write anything until Art talked to Ron O'Brien. Art not following John's instruction is "causing all this crap." I told John that Mike Wagner was at my house earlier, knocking and ringing the doorbell, and then he left a voicemail message.

John wonders how all the people who went to Dallas for the Super Bowl are not losing their minds. "They've got to be going crazy." When I explained how I have been crying all the time and will be mortified when the story hits the paper, John attempts to calm me down by saying, "Art put you in that situation." Before we disconnect, John said he would call Mike Wagner and let me know if he finds out anything exciting.

A Channel 10 news van appeared at the end of my drive and the crew began taking pictures of my house. They knocked on my door and, when I didn't answer, they moved across the street and I watched as they talked with my neighbor. I was crying and shaking in fear. And as if things couldn't get any worse, Colleen Marshall called and left a voicemail message.

"Hi, Mrs. Barney, this is Colleen Marshall, Channel 4. I would really appreciate it if you could give me a call, the number here is ###-#### but I will also give you my cell phone which is ###-####. Thank you very much."

My phone begins ringing nonstop. A number appears on Caller ID that looks familiar and I answer the phone before I realize my mistake. Mike Wagner is on the other end of the line.

Mike Wagner: . . . last five years. I'm going to have to deal with this. I can't imagine what you've been through. I'm sure it's been awful. But, I just heard from John. I actually came out to your house, very early, about nine or nine-thirty a.m. I don't know if you were home and just didn't answer the door, but I was driving my wife's little red Bug, so it didn't look too tough. You didn't answer. But I understand. I didn't know Channel 10 had gotten wind of any of this. I've known about it for three for four weeks, but like everyone else, I've been waiting to see what happened with the whole Super Bowl thing. Could you at least take a few minutes with me? I would love to come over—

Anita Barney: I really can't right now. I have to, the Dublin Police are out here in my driveway, I want to see what is going on. So, when I'm able to talk or whatever we're going to do, I will keep in touch with John. OK?

Wagner: Was Channel 10 really out there?

Barney: Who told you that? I'm sorry.

Wagner: John told me that. Were they literally out there?

Barney: Oh, yeah.

Wagner: You didn't talk to them or anything, did you?

Barney: No, they were just taking pictures of the condo.

Wagner: They didn't knock on your door or anything like that?

Barney: Yes, they did.

Wagner: Oh, but you didn't answer?

Barney: No. No.

Wagner: If you would, just a couple of quick basics. All I want to do is confirm that you, indeed, were solicited for money and victimized. He, allegedly, is going to tell me this. Art is.

Barney: But I'm not allowed to say anything until I talk with my attorney. You know the procedure. In fact, my attorney is trying to call me as we speak. I can't go against his advice.

Wagner: That's OK. I left a message for him, as well. And I will respect that. But I just want to make sure all of this is accurate. From what I hear, Art used the contact with your son who survived that plane crash back in 1980 to somehow make a connection with you recently and, you know, make sure all that is accurate.

Barney: We will do all of that when the time is proper, OK?

Wagner: Thank you, ma'am.

Art called and informed me that John had spoken with Prosecutor Ron O'Brien, and I'm not supposed to talk with anyone. Art thinks Tim Baker is the one behind all of this mess. I told Art I didn't know what to do, that I've never had a life like this. He responded, "I haven't either. I've never been through anything like this."

My attorney, Bill Loveland, called Mike Wagner to attempt some damage control. Mike reviewed the article he had written and was scheduled to be published the next day, February 4, in *The Columbus Dispatch*. Bill reports the headline will read, "Former OSU star Schlichter investigated for alleged sports ticket scheme."

Art called and told me that the story is coming out at five o'clock today. I gasped when he said, "It's everywhere."

John called and confirmed Mike was writing the article and reminded me I was the victim. He said I would "come out of this thing pretty good." John said, "Get ready. Your name is going to be in the paper. Probably tomorrow. Don't panic. Mike actually went over a couple of things with me and I think he is going to try and do the best he can to take care of you. I think he will have me quoted in there as saying you were a good person that was taken advantage of. All things considered, I think he is the best guy to do this."

Was this good news? I couldn't make sense of anything and began crying. How did all of this break at once? I wasn't prepared and didn't know what to do. John tried to comfort me, "Listen, it could be a lot worse than it is. Art told me, I didn't know this, did Tim Baker get a judgment (against you)?" I didn't even know what "get a judgment," meant. Any paperwork that arrived I simply handed over to my attorney to process. Before we hung up, John advised me to lay low. "It will be OK."

**Hugh Buttke received a judgment lien against me today for $14,140 plus 4% interest.

Friday, February 4, 2011
Two Days Before the Super Bowl

There were no Super Bowl tickets. There never were any.

When the story broke in the paper and on the local news, my friends and associates finally received the confirmation they needed to validate their suspicions I was in big trouble and Art was at the center of everything.

All the local television stations ran the story about Art and me. Unlike Mike Wagner, who took the time to chase down those of us involved and attempted to get the facts, the broadcast stories were filled with speculation and innuendos. I looked bad.

Additional television crews arrived at my condo and people were coming and going and knocking at my door throughout the day. Bill advised me not to talk with anyone. I learned Detective Davis had been talking with the people who loaned me money or held worthless checks I had written.

Saturday, February 5, 2011
Day Before the Super Bowl

A second article by Mike Wagner, "Former Buckeye Schlichter suspect in probe: Money for tickets went to gambling, sources say," ran in *The Columbus Dispatch*. Some facts were true, but others were inaccurate. Wagner wrote that my friendship with Art was at the heart of the scheme. The Associated Press called, seeking an interview or, at the very least, a comment.

Sunday, February 6, 2011
Super Bowl Sunday

2:45 a.m.   Art called and woke me up. I answered out of habit, immediately wishing I had just let the phone ring.

***

Art Schlichter: I don't have anything to say. I heard the article was horrible for me and ridiculous for you. So, other than that, I don't really have anything to say.

Anita Barney: OK.

Schlichter: Everything going OK for you?

Barney: Things are not going OK for me. And they won't and I'm in a helluva hole. I really believed that you were going to take care of things. Jewelry and all this stuff. And my debts and my friends and all of those people were going to get paid. I can't believe how it hasn't happened. It didn't happen. I believed there were Super Bowl tickets and you lied to me about that.

Schlichter: OK, you believed in all those things! I believed in all those things, too.

Barney: You told me there would be tickets! And I got this money from my friends. And gave it to you. What did you do with it? WHAT DID YOU DO WITH IT??

Schlichter: How many people are there?

Barney: Nobody. I'm totally by myself.

Schlichter: You and I can't talk right now about this stuff on the telephone. All right? I've tried and tried and tried and tried to talk to you, you'll never talk to me. I can't talk about any of this stuff right now, but I do have a good lawyer. He may be able to help out in the end. Let's just see how it shakes out. I know I'm going to get astronomical years. I'll talk to you in a little bit.

Barney: Wait a minute. I just wonder how you could sit there the other day and when I asked if I should I have my neighbors make plane reservations say, "Absolutely!"

Schlichter: You can't understand. It's easy for me. It would have been easy for me to get those tickets for them.

Barney: Why didn't you get them?

Schlichter: Because I COULDN'T! I got blown up on Friday! I was getting blown up on Thursday and Wednesday. I couldn't get those tickets. I was told not to do anything. "Just let it go, 'cause it's coming."

Barney: OK.

Schlichter: Ask about last year. I had ten people I got Super Bowl tickets for. You act like I couldn't get these things. Bullsh*t! See ya later.

***

Art called later and told me he was going in and confessing everything on Monday morning. He told me to be safe, take care, and he loved me.

With everything else going on, I clung to the hope that Art *would* be arrested after confessing. His emotional abuse, calls at all hours, threats, plans that never panned out, schemes to get money, directives, scripts, checking up on me, and out-of-control crazy had pushed me to the brink. I couldn't take it any longer.

I force myself to remain calm with the thought that in less than twenty-four hours Art would be behind bars, and I would be safely beyond his reach.

37 | CONFESSION DAY

FEBRUARY 7, 2011

"I want to tell you something about Anita Barney. She deserves better. I hope nobody charges her with anything. If you want to place it on me you can. That's who deserves it."	*Art Schlichter to Authorities*

Monday morning arrived and while it was eerily calm at my house, my mind was racing. I had been anxiously waiting for this day and for Art to meet with the authorities. I assumed he would tell the truth, take responsibility, and be arrested. I would be exonerated and finally feel safe. The tension had been building for days, and everything was in place, but no one knew what would happen. I was nervous and on edge, wondering how events would play out.

Was Art actually going to follow through and confess? Or would he run? Would he implicate me, or vindicate me as he promised? Only time would tell.

At eleven o'clock, Art met with Franklin County Prosecutor Ron O'Brien before confessing everything to Detective Scott Davis and Assistant Prosecutor Steve Schierholt. Art answered every question posed to him and explained how he had taken advantage of me.

Authorities: When did you start collecting money for Super Bowl tickets?

Art Schlichter: Well, she (Anita) only had a couple of people she was involved with for Super Bowl tickets. These other people, Calder Fenwick, Tim Barnes, Yanni Rivera, she wrote some checks.

How did that come about?

I needed the money for a couple of weeks. She wrote the check, and I'll call and tell you when to cash it. She never called them back. In the end, a couple things that I did for Super Bowl tickets, I had her—and this is probably the worst thing and shows how desperate—I had them buy Super Bowl tickets and turn around and have her write a check to buy the tickets. When they didn't get their tickets or when they weren't satisfied, they went back to her and said, "You wrote me these checks for these tickets that you said you would help Art buy the tickets." They, in turn, sued her. And came after her. She was just an innocent bystander in the whole thing.

Give us an example.

This is very difficult for me to come in and talk to you. It's an addiction and eats you alive.

These Super Bowl tickets you sold. Did anyone get those tickets?

No, because at the end John (Amery) told me not to get any Super Bowl tickets. I was going to buy them and give them out.

Since Friday, we have come up with a number of people who have contacted us or we've heard about. Some of the people we've talked about but there are still a number of people.

Can I look at the list? You know, I've got to start all over. Got to come clean. Let's go through the list. I'll tell you the story.

Here's what I did: I would approach Yanni Rivera and tell him I could get Super Bowl tickets, because anyone can get

Super Bowl tickets. You pay out the butt to get them. But I needed the money right then. "Do you want to buy some? We can make some money on the deal." He said, "How many you got?" I said, "Ten." He would give me $11,000 ($1,100 for each ticket). Then I would go back to him and say I could buy ten or twenty more. "I got this lady (Anita) that'll buy some of these tickets and protect your money. So, we might as well get them all." I would have Anita write a check. She had no idea who these people were, unless she went and talked to them. I told her, "Hey, I'll get it handled. Just tell them it's OK." And she would. She had no idea what I was even doing. She met a couple of people, mostly after the fact.

Let's say, Calder. How much money did you get from him?

I got twenty-some-thousand dollars from him. And then I think Anita wrote him a couple checks to make him money. Immediately he turned on me and wanted his money. Obviously, I didn't have the money. So, I gave him some money back and told him I would get him the rest. He said he was going to do this and going to do that. I said, "Relax." And gave him some of the money back. He contacted Anita and wanted his money. I told him she didn't have anything to do with it. She can't afford to buy the tickets. She didn't get any tickets. She shouldn't have even been involved. I paid him back $14,000.

Initially, all these guys had a couple of checks from Anita. I told them she's not getting any tickets. She's not even involved. She wrote a check and decided not to do it. Well, they held firm. "She gave me this money! I'm going to get this money from her." And all along, they thought they could get this money from her because they thought she had money. That caused a lot of problems. In the end, all these people that I knew, but knew of her, they didn't know she was broke. So, they assumed here's a nice lady that has the money. I'll go to her. They beat her up. She was just basically an innocent bystander in all of this.

Maybe seven or eight people have checks from Anita. People I dealt with, not her, on Super Bowl tickets.

You ever had Super Bowl tickets?

No.

Ever deal with a guy named Rogers?

I think I talked to him on the phone this week. He only needed ten tickets or something like that. I told him to go ahead and go (to Dallas) and I would take care of him. But then all this hit.

Could you have taken care of it?

I could have borrowed (the money) and paid two or three times the amount.

You always had to borrow the money from someone?

Unless I had some. Gambled and won. But I didn't this time. Like forty tickets to Tim Baker. There was no way to do that.

Ever?

No way this week.

When you got the money from him, was there a reasonable way for you to get the tickets?

Someone says, "Is there a reasonable chance you can get 350 Ohio State tickets?" I did it. It killed me. But I did it. It buried me and it buried Anita. But I did it.

If it wouldn't have been for (Anita's) money, would this have hit the fan a year ago, or two years ago? Just from OSU tickets?

Oh, yeah. I don't know if it would have hit the fan. But I don't know how I would have gotten tickets.

Tim Baker? He paid up front?

Yes.

When he gave you the money, did you tell him that you were going to use that money to buy the tickets?

Yes.

Did you?

No.

Did you gamble it, some of it, or what?

Paid for some tickets.

Would he have given you some money if he knew the truth?

No.

Would any of these people have? Like Calder? Did he know you prior to this?

No. He wouldn't have given me the money.

When someone would prepay for tickets, was it their understanding from you that the money was to pre-buy the tickets?

Yes.

You had mentioned earlier some people gave you money to buy extra tickets other than what they wanted to use personally. Was it to make more money?

That's how the Super Bowl was. Tim Baker thing, part of it is his greed, too. A guy who thinks he's going to make $100,000 to $200,000.

If a guy is looking to buy 40 to 50 Super Bowl tickets, he is looking to sell them?

Yes.

Was he supposed to get them and he would sell them? Or you?

Either way. He did nothing but threaten me the whole time. And Anita.

Does he have any checks from her?

Yes.

How many?

*I think he has two for $20,000 or three for $30,000, maybe.
I gave him the checks.*

Has she ever met him?

*Yes, she has. After he started threatening. She just said, "Hey,
relax. I'll get the money for you." I told her she needed to
meet him because he was going crazy. I had her go to calm
him down.*

Of all the people who bought Super Bowl tickets, how many
thought they were going to make money?

*All of them. Well, maybe not the (Floyd) Rogers guy. I don't
know him.*

Did (Anita) have other neighbors that bought tickets?

*There was one other guy. I think he got four or six. I think he
lived right beside her. I don't know his name. Maybe it's him.
The Rogers guy, maybe ten or eleven.*

I got a call from another guy that actually went down there to the
game. Or thought he was going to the game. Did anyone get any
tickets?

*No. One guy that called. I told him to go on and I would get
his tickets. That was like on Monday or Tuesday. And this all
started brewing up and John (Amery) told me to just not
even worry about it. So, I didn't.*

"Don't worry about it?" You didn't have the tickets?

*I would have had to go and buy them. They would have been
pretty expensive. I would have to borrow money or if I had
won gambling money, I would have bought them. When
you're doing this stuff in October and November, February is*

a mile away. And you're crawling. You think, things will be better by then. I will win some money. At least give people back their money, or profit or whatever. You always have in your head you're going to make it right. Especially when you do it.

Going through the list: We've talked about Anita. You said you gave Calder $14,000 back, right?

Yes. I think he gave me $20,000. Let me tell you about Calder. He has threatened me as much or more than Tim Baker. He told me that he just wanted his money back. But he threatened to take Anita's checks to the police fifteen or twenty times. I have the voice mails. He still wanted me to give him all the tickets so he could sell them. Sell the tickets to get your money back and split the profits. I gave him ten Michigan (vs. OSU) tickets for free. He never gave me anything for them. That cost me $4,000. And I gave him $14,000 back.

Tim Baker?

Tim said he gave me $100,000. I don't know if that is true. I thought it was more like $60,000, until Wednesday of the Super Bowl week. He had a buyer for the tickets to sell them for $150,000 to $160,000. As long as I bought him the tickets he said we would be done and he would drop the lawsuit on Anita. His plan was to make $100,000 cash. (Had) a guy flying in to buy them. Anita didn't have anything to do with this except to write him a check and say she would buy some of the tickets. I told her I just needed her to write me two checks to get him to do whatever. He has held those checks against her like she had the tickets and was supposed to give them to her. She was an innocent bystander.

Boris and Sue Paveleski?

Friends of mine. Help me do a lot of different favors. When I need them to pick up money, send money to their account. Whatever it is. Bystanders. They don't have anything to do with any of this. Both retired. Good people. Would do anything for me if they could. They are like Anita. They never received any money for their sake. Never put a con in to get money from her. They knew I was borrowing money from Anita. But no idea how much, when, where, or how. But they met Anita. They like her. She likes them. She doesn't owe them anything. Live in Pickerington. Good friends of mine.

Bill Hanners?

Same thing. Runner. Bill just would pick up money if I needed him. If I wasn't in town. Or run an errand for me. Put money in someone's account. Getting divorced. Doesn't have a pot to piss in. Never called Anita for money. Wasn't involved with anyone actually. If I needed money and Anita was in Florida, she would fax over a thing that said Bill Hanners is going to come in and get $8,000. And he would go and get if for me. He might bring it to me.

You didn't want Anita contacting her bank to say Art Schlichter is coming in to get money?

Correct.

So, you might just be out in the car?

Mostly not. But that could be the case. He was my friend for a long time. Someone I could trust to go pick up money for me. He lives here in Columbus. His wife is a little mad at him. I guess him running money for me could be part of it. I don't know.

Douglas DeLarge?

Douglas is a good friend of mine. Back and forth with him and tickets. Started out with Douglas just selling OSU tickets. But then he's tried to help me. That's kind of a complicated relationship. He's got some checks of Anita's. He cashed some of them to cover my debt when she had money.

Phil Evans?

I think he and Ben Roberts were partners. They lent her the money thinking they were going to get $10,000 profit. I don't know these people.

Rod Cheetham?

Don't know him. Same thing. I know she borrowed $30,000 from him. Didn't pay him back any. Think he sued her.

Richard Head?

Same way. I think she had to get season tickets for him for football. He got every ticket he asked for. Great seats. I think she owes him $4,000.

Yanni Rivera?

A guy I went to and sold Super Bowl tickets to him and gave (Anita's) checks to him as someone who was buying Super Bowl tickets. For profit. I think he got twenty-some tickets. He bought it, he and his son. His son has threatened me a thousand times. He's been paid back $3,000. I gave him Anita's checks.

How do you keep all these numbers straight in your head?

I don't know. I just know these people. After a while you just remember.

Chester Meeks?

A guy that helped me buy tickets early last year. Used his credit cards. And he may have some of Anita's checks. I think he sent those back to her. I probably owe him $150,000. I probably paid $50,000 back. He lives in Columbus. He's from Wooster, or past (Route) 23. Met him through a gentleman at a golf tournament.

Brad Johnson?

Has checks I gave him from Anita. I owe personal money, also. Never paid him back.

Have you ever borrowed money from anyone, telling them you were going to gamble with it?

Never. Never. Most of the people I borrow money from, if I have some debts or I'm in trouble or need to buy some tickets, I just tell them. It wasn't like I was—some of the money I might gamble with, but most of the money was to pay back those things. Probably some of the money I would gamble with, but most of the money I would need to buy tickets and I'm in trouble, "Will you help me?"

Linda Scott?

A girl I knew in prison. You must have gone through Anita's checkbook and that's how you got these names. Because I know Linda wouldn't have called you. She holds some checks from Anita, but Anita never had any dealings with her. Except for those checks.

You still owe her quite a bit of money, don't you?

Well, she had a weird way of doing it. When I started out with Linda, I met her in prison. I've known her for a little bit. She was young and I was young. But she wrote me a letter while I was in prison. She sent me commissary. I talked to her on the phone all the time. When I got out of prison, I didn't like her. I couldn't see myself with her. So I broke up with her, which didn't work out very well. And she decided she was going back and tabulate anything she gave me while I was in prison, and I went and borrowed more money from her. But a lot of that money is fluff with her. A lot of that is what I didn't owe her. I didn't get it from her. She kept adding on. There was a time where I would go to her and get $10,000 or $20,000 at a time. I would tell her the truth. I was in trouble and needed help. She might have two or three of Anita's checks.

Last person you borrowed money from?

I borrowed money from a guy named Lance Sellars, who you talked to on the phone the other day. $4,400 the other day to *pay back The Tree Surgeon. He got four tickets. He and Tim Baker are the ones that . . . in the newspaper.*

Who before Lance Sellars?

My gambling buddies. Hagan Reddy. Guys I gambled with. He's taken a lot of money from me in the last six months. Lots of money. Where did the money go? Tickets and to him. For the most part.

Any other women besides Anita?

Linda Scott. A woman from Baltimore I was getting money from. $20,000 from a lady that's not local. I don't want to bring her name up. But, not really. Many men. But Anita was the one who helped me the most.

Anyone else you got one million dollars from?

No. There's a girl in Washington who helped me out a lot when I first got out. She was an alcoholic/gambler. Gave a lot of money to my foundation and gave me loans early on. This was before I got started into gambling.

Anita always gave me pre-written checks. I don't think I touched any. I don't remember, but maybe she has given me some blank checks with her signature on them. Wait. One time, about one and a half months ago, she gave me a check. I don't remember who I gave it to. She had not signed it. I signed it. I don't even know if I used it. I may have. But that was the only time.

One of the things I was hoping, if I have to report, I don't have to report to Franklin County. I heard it's bad. Am I being charged in Dublin?

It would be Franklin.

I came in here today because of Anita Barney. I don't want to see her get charged. She doesn't deserve to get charged. She's done nothing wrong except try to help me. My friends were just trying to help me. They weren't involved in schemes. No one was involved except for me.

There may be people out there you don't remember?

Could be. But mostly I deal with them every day.

I was getting a little paranoid so I bought a couple TracFones in case someone was going to tap my phone. Up until these people started suing Anita Barney, it was just really between Anita and I. It got to the point that we were desperate. And others got involved. A lot of money went through her to me. There wasn't a point that I can't make this right some way with her. Now, I'm probably going to prison for who knows how long. I always thought that I would make it right with her. Speaking, a movie, or whatever. It's very abnormal. You think you're going to win but it gets worse and worse and worse.

As part of your contact with friends and family in the next few days, are you heading to Indy?

I'm trying to set it right. I don't do this on a daily basis for anyone. I've told you more today than I have ever told anyone. This is the majority of it. If you have more questions, I'll be glad to answer them. All you have to do is tell me when to come.

We've got your numbers and probably Scott (Davis) will be the person to call you.

You know, I want to tell you something about Anita Barney. I love Anita Barney. She did more to help me than any person in the whole world would ever do, times ten. She's a great woman. She deserves better. I hope nobody don't charge her with anything. If you want to place it on me you can. That's who deserves it.

I hope this helps, my coming in today. I want to have a life in the future. If it's possible.

I probably have bigger problems with the Feds than I do with the State. And I have problems with the State.

***

After Art left the station, Detective Davis called and provided a very brief recap of Art's interrogation. He told me Art confessed to his crimes and said I was the victim. I was quite surprised to learn Art was allowed to leave and didn't have to report until the following Monday, February 14, at 10:00 a.m., when he would be arrested. The idea of Art roaming freely on the street terrified me. Certainly he had figured out that I had been working with the authorities. I didn't even want to think about what might happen between now and his arrest in seven days.

By the time John Amery called me around 3:00 p.m., all the adrenalin that had brought me through the morning had been replaced with confusion and despair.

***

John Amery: I've got to see what Ron's position is. So, don't say anything or talk to anybody until I get some more word from O'Brien.

Anita Barney: I'm not going to talk to any press or anything. No, no. I'm not doing anything right now. No. It's going to be a long time. Whenever anybody says I can, if they want me to. You know what I'm saying? We'll all work on this together. 'Cause I'm not going to be talking to the Associated Press or Channel 6 or anything like that.

Amery: I hate that, when those people just show up like that. That's just so ridiculous.

Barney: Well, I said, I'll be kicked out of this neighborhood within the week, probably. I might start packing.

Amery: (Laughing)

Barney: I'll tell you. I'm so embarrassed and mortified. But that's all right.

Amery: Listen. Today was a big day.

Barney: Yes, it was.

Amery: Today was a big day. One step at a time, Anita. You listen to Corby at three. I think you're going to really like what he has to say.

Barney: The only thing is that is a call-in radio show. I'm afraid to hear the calls about me. I'll need to put my amour suit on for that, I think.

Amery: Well, that's probably true . . . you can't please everybody.

38 | PUBLIC REACTION

"A great athlete, a sick man, Woody Hayes' golden child, a charmer, an addict, a criminal: Art Schlichter was many things to many people, evidenced by the variety of comments spilling out of the radio that day."	Anita Barney

Later that afternoon I did as John Amery instructed, and listened to the *John Corby Show* on 610 WTVN. As the host greeted his listeners, I quickly grabbed the recorder Investigator Davis had given me and pressed the red button.

During his nearly 20-minute monologue, Corby explained what he knew. Art was accused of selling tickets he failed to deliver, and was involved in another con which allegedly ran into the millions of dollars. *I gasped. Was he referring to me?* Corby also revealed Art was supposed to have reported to Prosecutor Ron O'Brien's officer earlier in the day. Few other details had been confirmed.

I sat on my sofa, glued to the radio. I was mesmerized by Corby's serious tone and the fact that he appeared to be taking the situation so personally. He stated how likeable Art was—at least on the surface—and how he had been pulling for his former colleague to "get it together." *Yes! That was what I had seen in Art months ago. He was a likeable guy whose life was a bit messy and I had the resources and willingness to help him get it together.*

Corby also shared he had introduced Art to his agent, John Amery, when Art had mentioned the possibility that his book, *Busted*, might be turned into a movie. Corby now felt terrible he had made the connection and said he had apologized to John for the introduction.

Corby reminisced about the former star quarterback's fantastic job as a co-host on the radio. Art had been one of the greatest football analysts around, always came prepared, and didn't miss a show. But Corby found it peculiar that Art carried two cell phones and he was constantly placing and receiving calls during commercial breaks. *Oh, boy! I knew a thing or two about Art and his phones!* When asked about it, Art explained one phone was for personal use and the other for his foundation. He elaborated he was constantly taking calls from compulsive gamblers who needed guidance. Corby recalled Art's response seemed to make sense at the time.

At one point, Corby shared how Art had approached him to purchase Ohio State season basketball tickets. Later when Corby mentioned the opportunity to his wife, Jodi reminded him that selling season tickets was one of the cons Art detailed in his book. *I couldn't believe what I was hearing. Art must have viewed everyone as a mark.*

The radio program began to fade into the background as my mind started wandering down a rabbit trail, focusing on how crazy everything had become. *Why did I fall for Art's cons? How could I have failed to see what was obvious to others?* I could feel the darkness closing in as anxiety consumed me. My thoughts raced uncontrollably, obsessing about the future and considering one eventuality after another until I heard Corby say my name.

I listened as Corby told his listeners I had been bilked out of a lot of money. That *Anita Barney was a victim* and Channel 10 had treated me unconscionably by running a story portraying me as operating the scam in conjunction with Art. Corby was emphatic that not only was I victim, but that I might have been the biggest victim of all. When he said I deserved a big-time apology, tears filled my eyes.

Corby detailed how charismatic and charming Art could be. He described how long ago Art had been a tremendous athlete with a bright future—a number one draft pick who pissed it all away. That no one could imagine he was gambling again until people started calling the radio station with claims Art was up to his old schemes. Corby questioned how could Art could do ten years in prison and then turn around and do it all again?

While I sat in my living room alone, I heard a statement that has stayed with me. Corby wondered if Art working at the station and being on the radio made it easier for him to get into the mess he, apparently, was in. I wanted to shout: *I can't speak for everyone, but seeing Art accepted by the general public and hearing him on the radio made it easier for him to get into* my bank accounts.

As Corby's monologue came to a close, I could identify with the sorrow and weariness I heard in his voice. Art had played him, the station, and the public for fools. Deception was Art's specialty and he had once again expertly spread his nets far and wide to claim the largest possible number of victims.

It was a sad day. Everyone, it seemed, had been conned.

***

After a break, Corby took calls from the public. A steady stream of people were waiting to express their opinion, and there were as many perspectives as there were callers. One lady said she had suspicions about Art's intentions for a while. Others recalled Art as a college athlete at the Scioto Downs racetrack, illegally racing on Route 315, or engaging in other wrongdoing. Another caller stated that he would miss Art on the radio when the next football season rolled around. It was surprising to hear Art had recently approached one caller about buying OSU tickets. The man was glad he had declined to take the deal. Yet another caller mentioned he had fallen prey to Art and his lies—there were so many lies—and lost money to Art's ticket scheme.

One guy suggested Art may have been trying to start a legitimate business and I was a greedy investor who blamed Art when things didn't work out the way I wanted. The caller was hoping this was an honest effort by Art that just went terribly wrong. I had no way to defend myself against this stranger's claims. His comments left me unnerved, as I couldn't imagine how many more people felt the same way. *Were my friends listening to this? What did they think about my involvement? Did they understand I was a victim, and had been victimized for months?*

The next caller said he was in the audience when Art gave a speech just the week before. The man recounted Art had arrived to the venue an hour late. It looked like he had slept in his clothes for a couple of days, and there was a sadness about him. The caller said it didn't look like the convicted felon had conquered anything from his past, and wondered if Art knew a meeting with the authorities had been lurking just around the corner. *I recalled Art mentioning that speaking engagement. He had been sick and, from the sounds of it, should have cancelled but I'm sure he desperately needed the honorarium.*

Yet another caller took Corby and the radio station to task for bringing Art on as a host. This guy, Mike, understood giving people a second chance, but when someone like Art had been in forty–four prisons or jails and devastated lives for more than thirty years, perhaps the time for second chances was long past. He said he felt bad for people like me, who had been swindled. The caller accused Art's supporters of being responsible for creating an environment that allowed him to continue to rip people off. What Mike couldn't understand was the motivation for welcoming Art time and again into the community. He wondered if it was because Art had four good years playing football at Ohio State.

After a commercial break another caller suggested Art suffered from an anti-social disorder while the next said Art didn't have a disease, he had a weakness and was morally flawed. Before hanging up the man called Art a jerk. A retired psychologist called and diagnosed Art with a psychopathic personality disorder: Art was a sociopath.

Some people blamed Art's upbringing or his DNA, while others called out the media, Ohio State University, and the fervent devotion of Buckeye Nation. A great athlete, a sick man, Woody Hayes' golden child, a charmer, an addict, a criminal: Art Schlichter was many things to many people, evidenced by the variety of comments spilling out of the radio that day. My emotions ebbed and flowed, each new caller like a spin of the gun barrel in a game of Russian Roulette. I never knew what I was going to hear: the click of the hammer or the explosion of the bullet, understanding or accusations. Nonetheless, I was compelled to listen until Corby's program ended at 6:00 p.m.

Exhausted, I finally turned off the radio.

39 | ANOTHER VICTIM COMES FORWARD
FEBRUARY 2011

"Art needs to be isolated from people who are vulnerable. With Art, everyone is vulnerable."	*Vernon P. Stanforth, Sheriff* *Fayette County, Ohio*

Facebook

Karin sent you a message.

Karin Kennedy Brooks
February 9, 2011 at 8:44 pm

Anita, you don't know me but I wanted to tell you I understand how your life has become a tragedy because this man did the exact same thing to me beginning in 2007. Please know that you are not alone. I read the article by Mike Wagner from *The Columbus Dispatch* just minutes ago and could not believe how our stories are hauntingly identical. I am praying for you to find strength to rise above this and I offer my friendship to you if you so desire.

Karin Kennedy Brooks
February 9, 2011 at 9:10 pm

> I tell my story to the federal grand jury in Cincinnati next week... Anita, before reading this article regarding you, I felt ashamed. Now through sharing your own experience I am stronger... For this, I thank you. It is a difficult struggle as "one," but together we can get through this. I will help you if I can in any way.

Karin Kennedy Brooks
February 11, 2011 at 7:40 pm

> Hi Anita. I've been thinking much about you... Are you doing OK? I sure hope so. Best to you, Karin

Karin Kennedy Brooks commented on her wall post.

February 13, 2011 at 11:24 am

> Karin wrote: "I would love to speak to you as well...however, am not sure phone lines are secure. I will be in Cincinnati this Wednesday for a 1:00 appointment and my flight does not leave until 7:00 that evening. Any chance of meeting in person?

***

I wish Karin or any of Art's victims had been strong enough to expose him before he and I crossed paths in November 2009. I understand how shame and fear gag our voices, but if we don't speak up loudly and often, who will warn future victims?

I will. I am willing to bear the responsibility of serving as a cautionary tale. To reveal my faults and expose my actions in order to bring down a predatory gambling addict.

Karin, did you know Art pled guilty to being a habitual offender in 2004? That he was on probation when he targeted both of us? Who was watching to ensure he didn't reoffend? Who was responsible for supervising his actions and subverting his plans so he would be unable to destroy additional lives?

How did he slip through the cracks of justice and continue his crime spree? He said when he left prison in 2006 that he simply picked up where he left off.

As much as I would love to hold someone accountable, there is no power in pointing fingers or placing blame. It's too late for all of that, and there were too many of us complicit in creating the perfect storm for Art to do as he pleased: community leaders, talking heads, the media, pastors, business leaders, greedy "investors," innocent bystanders, gullible victims, football experts, enthusiastic fans, and myself, a mother with a need to pay an unsatisfied debt. The frenzy of college football can scoop up everyone in its path, and this time it left a trail of destruction that will be felt across generations.

For as long as I have a voice, I will sound a clarion call to all who will listen. I am no longer concerned with what's popular or politically correct. Justice may be blind, but she can also be messy. When someone's life is on the line because of the lies of an obsessive gambler and our court system is incapable of stopping a criminal from reoffending, we must shout out a warning.

I will do what I can so that not one more unsuspecting person becomes a victim of Art Schlichter. Damn political correctness and public opinion; full speed ahead!

Be warned!
Art Schlichter is addicted to gambling.
Do not trust him in your pulpits.
Do not invite him on your radio programs.
Do not celebrate him with magazine covers.
Do not invite him to participate in any
sports-related conversation.
He will convince you.
He will lie to you.
He will harass you.
If you show him kindness
he will ruin your lives,
destroy your families,
and scar your communities.

He will trash your reputation without remorse.
Does he need help? Without a doubt.
But the help he requires will not come
from the bank accounts of friends and acquaintances.
Forgive? Yes.
Forget? Never!

40 | ART IS ARRESTED
FEBRUARY 8–14, 2011

"Thank you, Mrs. Barney, we couldn't have done this without you."	*Ron O'Brien* *Franklin County* *Prosecutor*

Tuesday, February 8, 2011
The Day After Art Confessed

While I received numerous phone messages all day from media personnel including friends and acquaintances Dom Tiberi, John Corby, Dimitrious Stanley and even from someone with the Associated Press, I didn't return any calls.

Art called me mid-afternoon and we talked for about forty-five minutes. He wanted me to tell him the truth about my involvement with the authorities. He promised he wouldn't be angry with me if I would just tell him the truth. He accused and speculated and assumed. I was too fearful to reveal anything and avoided answering his questions.

Because both John and my attorney, Bill Loveland, had spoken with Mike Wagner about his first story, I felt comfortable working with him on a second story to set the record straight about my involvement and how Art conned me. Surprisingly, this caused a lot of anxiety for Bill and Prosecutor Steve Schierholt. Bill interrupted his vacation in Mexico to contact me and find out exactly what was going on. He was worried that I might sabotage any plea agreement he was working toward. Steve was concerned about information I might share in the article compromising the case, especially since Art had not been arrested.

I called Mike in a panic, explaining the circumstances and asking him not to reveal certain details. He was gracious and agreed to make changes to protect the integrity of the case. Bill, John, and Steve all made additional comments and requests throughout the day. Mike came out to the condo and, along with Alan, we combed through the article. Later in the evening, I made a final call to Mike. I told him there was one additional item that needed changed. He told me it was too late; the article had already been submitted and was to be published the next morning. I hoped that in my desire to correct details with a new article, I had not done more damage than good.

Wednesday, February 9, 2011

I felt better about things when I read Mike's article the next morning, "Woman says she considered suicide after involvement in Schlichter scheme: Anita Barney met Art Schlichter 30 years ago, amid tragedy. Now, after placing her trust and money in him, she says her life has become a tragedy." Art called twice in the morning, but I didn't answer. I also received calls from Terry Sullivan at Channel 6, a Channel 10 reporter, and Mike Wagner from *The Dispatch*.

My cousin Connie called and wanted to give me $100. My cousin Rock brought groceries over. I was touched by their kindness and generosity and devastated that I had been reduced to accepting handouts.

When Art called in the afternoon, I didn't answer.

Friday, February 11, 2011
Three Days Before Art Is Arrested

Art called and sounded arrogant. He told me he had spoken with Special Agent Terrence Brown and suggested Terrence should have called *him* first, before interviewing all of his friends. As he relayed the advice he gave to the Federal Agent on how to conduct an investigation against him, I shook my head. *Art will never get it!*

He proceeded to tell me all he wanted to do was take care of me and his mom. *He was delusional. He couldn't even see that he was unable to take care of himself, much less anyone else.*

He asked if I could find someone to loan him some money so he wouldn't go to jail. He guaranteed it would be a legitimate transaction and he would even have his attorney call to verify the agreement. *Seriously? Isn't that the story he told me at the very beginning? After everything he had done to me, how could he think for one minute that I would help him get even more money?*

I was shocked at his inability to understand the seriousness of what he had done and the penalty he was facing. *What was wrong with him and how did I not see it before?*

Saturday, February 12, 2011
Two Days Before Art Is Arrested

Art called me around 10:30 a.m. and asked if I found anyone to loan him money. The truth was I had not even attempted to find anyone, but I only said I couldn't *find* anyone. He told me about the difficult meeting he had with his daughters, telling them about turning himself in on Monday and returning to prison. "We were all crying very hard," he said.

During our conversation I told him about Karin Kennedy Brooks and the Facebook messages she had sent me. He responded that Karin was a drug addict he met in rehab. He took her to rehab two times, and paid her $1,000 a week for three years. Karin had loaned him $150,000. He said I should ask Karin for my money back, because Art was using my money to pay her. He wasn't making a lot of sense and I didn't understand his logic. He also said I should sue Chip Greene of Best Seat Tickets because Chip got a lot of my money and I didn't get anything in return from him.

Monday, February 14, 2011
Art Turns Himself In

Art called me around 1:45 a.m. and we talked for forty-five minutes. We discussed the situations we both were in and what he anticipated would happen when he turned himself in—which he planned to do in less than ten hours—at 11:00 a.m. It was a depressing call. A tragic bookend to what started as a promising friendship less than sixteen months before. I was sad for him. Yes, he had ruined a lot of lives, mine included, but I still believed people deserved a second chance. Was he getting what he deserved? Definitely! But I sincerely hoped he could find a way to overcome his gambling addiction and stop destroying lives.

Art called unexpectedly again at 2:55 a.m. This time he was crying. He lamented how he messed up our lives, and said he knew how much I tried to help him. He promised this would be his final call. Before he said good-bye he told me to be safe, be good, and that he loved me. I suppose his tears were mostly for his own loss, but I would like to believe his sorrow was partially triggered by empathy for the disaster he had created of my life and the lives of my friends.

***

Later that morning, Detective Davis filed a warrant for Art's arrest in Franklin County Municipal Court, and Art was charged with a first-degree felony for theft. The warrant was checked and approved by Ron O'Brien.

At 11:00 a.m. Art voluntarily turned himself in to the Franklin County Prosecutor's Office. His attorney, Samuel Shamansky, accompanied him. Art was read his rights before waiving them. An interview was conducted by Special Agent Terrence Brown from the IRS. Detective Davis and Sergeant Bill Krayer served as witnesses. During the interview, Art clarified several points covered in his first interview the week before:

1. Schlichter stated he had no idea of exactly how much money Barney had collected from friends and family that she gave to him in the past year.

2. He met Barney for lunch in November 2009 and asked for a loan of $100,000 under the pretense that the money was to be used for his gambling program he was starting. He, in turn, used the money to live on and to gamble.

3. Calder Fenwick gave him $20,000 in cash for the purchase of Super Bowl tickets. He still owes Fenwick about $14,000.

4. Tim Baker gave him $100,000 and he still owes Baker $60,000.

5. Boris and Sue Paveleski are old friends that have helped him over the years with collecting money and picking up tickets.

6. Douglas DeLarge is a friend who has delivered OSU tickets and helped collect monies to buy tickets that Art would use to gamble.

After the interview was concluded, Art was taken to the Franklin County Jail. That evening, all of the local stations were broadcasting the story about Art's scams and my involvement. It was a very bad day.

Tuesday, February 15, 2011

The day following Art's arrest, my grandson Sean Martin and his fiancée Monica Day accompanied me to the Franklin County Court House to attend Art's hearing. Art came into the courtroom from a side door in an orange jail jumpsuit and I silently gasped at seeing my tormenter reduced to a prisoner in handcuffs. I watched as he made visual contact with a woman seated in the gallery and later learned this was Maci Paskell, the woman who oversaw his foundation. John Amery, Art's former attorney, was seated nearby. My assigned Victim Advocate, Jane Mackenzie, and Attorney Bill Loveland were seated in the row with me. Art was standing at the defendant's table with his attorney when the judge asked if he had anything to say. Art turned around, looked me in the eye, and said he was sorry. He said he didn't plan for anything to happen this way. I was beyond the point of being able to believe him.

When the brief proceeding concluded, Bill exited the courtroom before me in order to speak to my friend and local newscaster Carol Luper, whom we had spied in the hall earlier.

After Bill left the courtroom, Ron O'Brien approached me and expressed his appreciation for my efforts. A safe distance away from the media, with just Sean and Monica by my side, he shook my hand and said, "Thank you, Mrs. Barney, we couldn't have done this without you."

41 | DAMAGED GOODS
SPRING 2011

"Anita, either you are one of the dumbest people on earth or you were in love with the guy."	*Anonymous*

After Art was arrested, my house became silent. The only person calling with any consistency was my attorney, keeping me updated on legal events concerning Art, as well as details concerning my own case.

My friends were confused and hurt and angry. After watching breaking news reports and reading newspaper articles about Art Schlichter and the "Dublin Socialite, Anita Barney," they quickly came to understand why I had been avoiding their calls. There was no money to satisfy the promises I had made. Their outrage could not be contained and they were vocal in expressing their disgust toward me.

They left phone messages and sent letters—both anonymous and signed—asking questions, placing blame, and voicing their opinions. I would prefer to believe that the one signed by Chris P. Critter, with its interesting use of clip art, was sent by one of Art's associates, but it was most likely sent by a former friend of mine.

Anita, what were you thinking?

Either you are one of the dumbest people on earth or you were in love with the guy.

Those are the only two reasons that you would give money to a crook like Art Schlichter.

I don't think that you are dumb, so it must be love!

How could have involved friends and family without telling them that the money was for Art.

You knew that if you told them that the money was for Art that they would have said no way.

You scammed your friends & family, so you should go to jail along with Art!

<u>We are coming to get you Art</u>

Best regards,
Chris P. Critter
Dublin. Oh

Detective Davis would occasionally check in, but he was busy tying up lose ends associated with the numerous cases he had been investigating simultaneously related to Art and me. I willingly provided the names and contact information for all of the friends Art forced me to call and who still were owed money. Detective Davis systematically contacted every victim of the scams to determine how the individual had been defrauded and if they wished to make a formal complaint. Several individuals declined to press charges. Perhaps their reluctance was out of humiliation of being associated with Art Schlichter. Others were adamant about their desire to see me brought to justice.

- Farley Daft told Detective Davis that I had lied to him and he wanted to see me put in jail. He didn't understand why I had not been arrested and charged along with Art. Farley had given me $20,000 that had not been repaid and had filed a complaint with the Franklin County Sheriff's Office.

- Sam and Joyce Nelson were also very vocal about their desire for me to pay for my crime and were, in fact, interviewed by the local ABC station for a broadcast news segment. They were still owed $85,000 and had filed a complaint with the Franklin County Sheriff's Office.

- Cruz Hill advised that he wanted to pursue charges against Art and me for theft of the $30,000 he had given me. He was included in a Dublin Police Case with twenty–five additional victims.

Steve Schierholt kept in touch, but he moved out of the Prosecutor's Office and on to a new job as Assistant Director of the Ohio Bureau of Criminal Investigation a couple of days after he interviewed Art on February 7. Assistant Prosecutor Jay Moore stepped in to fill the vacancy.

Calls from John Amery were fairly regular at the beginning as he would encourage me and offer advice, but over time they, too, became less and less frequent.

Art's "friends," many of whom I had talked to regularly and exchanged large sums of money, scattered like rats. If they weren't already identified by the authorities or charged with a crime, they weren't willing to take a chance by being associated with me.

I was in default on all of my loans, and barely able to pay my utilities or purchase groceries.

I was estranged from my extended family and shunned by former friends.

I was damaged goods.

42 | I AM A VICTIM

Around the middle of May, 2011, I received a letter from Ron O'Brien, Franklin County Prosecuting Attorney.

May 17, 2011

Dear Ms. Barney:

We understand that you have been a victim of a crime and that you have experienced a traumatic incident. We want to offer our assistance to you during this difficult period. As a victim in a criminal case, you are entitled certain rights under Chapter 2930 of the Ohio Revised Code. As Prosecuting Attorney I want to assure you that members of my staff and I will do our best to assist you.

I didn't need to read any further. Here, in writing, was the proof that validated my claims. The Franklin County Prosecutor stated I was a victim. If only Mr. O'Brien's words had the power to change the hearts and minds of my former friends and family members.

43 | MY LETTER TO ART
JUNE 2011

"When Art was charged, I was left holding my own bag of trouble."	*Anita Barney*

After nearly sixteen months of non-stop communication from Art, his menacing phone calls abruptly stopped. I was eager for that day to arrive, anticipating I would finally feel a measure of relief and safety. And I did, in a small way. But the wounds Art had inflicted were deep and infected and would take time and care to heal; there wouldn't be a fast or easy remedy.

I continued to deal with so many emotions and I was stressed beyond belief; I was in pain and I was angry. I wanted an opportunity to call out my abuser, scream, throw things, rant and rave, and force Art to truly acknowledge the path of destruction he had caused.

I wanted him to feel sorrow and pain and remorse for someone other than himself. I needed proof that he understood his actions had far-reaching consequences. I desperately craved explanations. I needed him to take responsibility for this awful nightmare I had been living.

But it was not to be and when Art was charged, I was left holding my own bag of trouble. The accusations continued.

Demands for payment arrived. New lawsuits were filed and made their way through the courts. Victims still required answers. Former friends turned away.

I was still alone, but in a different way than ever before.

One day, feeling especially depressed over the course my life had taken, I sat down in the lonely quiet of my home and, as tears fell from my eyes, put my thoughts on paper. It was a letter to Art that he would never receive; words I never had the strength to say to him in person.

Hello, Art –

All that stress is gone now—your health must be very good now. You get three proper meals a day and a roof over your head. Now you don't need to be watching over your shoulder all the time and worrying about phone taps.

I always believed you would pay me back, and my friends. You came out of John's office with the signed promissory note, plus you had your attorney call me twice to confirm that the book money would be coming and for me to loan you the money and I would get paid. Was he an attorney or someone you had call me and pretend?

I'm so sorry I was willing to ever help you—you destroyed my life and reputation—you drove a wedge between my children, my family and me. I've lost the friends you made me call and get money from, and people I didn't get money from tend to stay away, as well. I'm living a very lonely and sad life now. Your life is better than mine—that must make you happy to know that.

You have girlfriends and male friends coming to see you. I have no one. All of this because I was helping you to straighten your life out because you helped my ten-year-old son thirty years ago after he was in the plane crash. I was blessed he lived and you brought him out of his depression with your visit to him, and the gifts. I never got to thank you after you left our house, and to let you know how well Alan came out of his depression after your visit. I never forgot that you did that and I told many people over the years about it when I would see you in the news.

I was just being a thankful mom who wanted to help you. After I saw you speak at church, I believed you. Well, I helped you, and then you took advantage of me and my friends in the community.

I'll never trust again and my shame will never go away.

I'm just one of many that you've been conning—I didn't know that God made people like you who could lie to people so easily and live with themselves.

Remember how you would hang up on me when I would cry to you about all that was going on? Well I cry now more than I thought I could ever cry.

I'm losing everything because I wanted to help you. I didn't realize that you wouldn't care what happened to me or my children—so sad—they are good people and I've embarrassed them because of my contact with you. I'm more embarrassed and ashamed than anyone.

Why did I ever agree to go to listen to you? The minister said you conned him as well.

I'm so sick of sitting in the front row of the pity bus and crying all the time. You are not worth it. I'll soon be able to start to change my life around and I'm going to fight like hell.

Enjoy your new friends in prison—

Anita

44 | STATE OF OHIO VS. ARTHUR SCHLICHTER
CASE NO. 11–CR–000931

In part, Art was sentenced to a total of 468 months of imprisonment and ordered to pay restitution in the amount of $680,000 to Anita.	*Franklin County Municipal Court Records*

On September 15, 2011, in Franklin County Municipal Court, Art pled guilty to one count of Engaging in a Pattern of Corrupt Activity (a first–degree felony, considered the most serious) and twelve counts of Felony Theft and was sentenced to a total of 468 months (thirty-nine years) of imprisonment, five years of mandatory post-release control (probation), and ordered to pay $680,000 in restitution to me, along with various amounts to other victims.

According to the plea agreement, the prosecution and defense jointly recommended to the court a sentence of eleven years and six months to be served concurrently with the sentence received for federal offenses.

Restitution was stayed until after Art served his sentence, which would not commence until he reported to the Federal Bureau of Prisons in 2012. The court also found that Art had 214 days of jail credit.

45 | UNITED STATES V ARTHUR SCHLICHTER
CASE NO. 2:11–CR–00223–MHW–TPK1

"We couldn't have developed the case against Art to the extent we did without Anita. She recorded conversations and introduced us to others."	*Official assigned to the 2010 investigation of Art Schlichter*

In September 2011, after Art had pled guilty in Franklin County, I traveled to the Federal Courthouse for his sentencing on three counts of fraud. When I arrived, I saw that Lew and Annabelle Sanchez, Cruz Hill, and several other people I knew had already arrived. The proceeding felt more casual compared to the earlier one I attended in Franklin County when Art was wearing an orange jumpsuit.

Art was dressed in street clothes, and already seated in the front of the Gallery. The bailiff called his case and Art walked up front with his attorney. Special Agent Terrence Brown addressed the court regarding federal charges being filed. A bond hearing and Art's arraignment were scheduled for early October.

After the proceeding ended, Art was released and I watched as he walked out of the building and up North High Street, accompanied by his attorney. It didn't seem right that he was walking free, enjoying the day like any other law-abiding person. I noticed all the other people walking around the courthouse and wondered how many just had federal charges filed against them.

Later, at Art's bond hearing, both Bill Loveland and my daughter Angela accompanied me. Art was wearing khaki pants and a white shirt. His hands were cuffed to his waist and he had shackles on his ankles. There was only a single entrance into the room, and Art was escorted right by my seat on his way in and out. Immediately after the proceeding ended, Bill escorted us to a small side room and out of the path of the Federal Agents who were transporting Art out of the courtroom.

The final time I saw Art was on October 11, 2011, when he appeared in the United States District Court for the Southern District of Ohio, Columbus and entered a guilty plea to Wire Fraud, Bank Fraud, and Making and Subscribing a False Tax Return.

Former friends Sam and Joyce Nelson were in the gallery, but, of course, we didn't speak. Art's mother was seated behind us. The judge asked Art if he had anything to say to anyone. He looked toward his mother and said, "I'm sorry." I do believe he was sincere and I felt sympathy for him and his broken life. I could now see he was a compulsive gambler who had destroyed a lot of people, but I still felt compassion for him as a human being who, when all hope was gone, had worked a miracle in my son's life thirty years ago. As a mother, I also felt a great deal of sorrow for Art's mother.

At the end of the proceeding, Art was released on house arrest. As he walked right by me, he kept his gaze straight ahead and didn't even glance my way. He left the courthouse that day wearing an ankle bracelet and carrying a trash bag full of his personal belongs. It was a tragic sight to watch a formerly celebrated athlete who had the talent to win in the big leagues, reduced to carrying his life around in a garbage bag. I couldn't understand how a person could fall to such depths time after time.

46 | CANCER

FALL 2011

"After everything that had happened, I was convinced cancer was supposed to be my punishment for the role I played in Art's schemes."	*Anita Barney*

The summer of 2011 had dragged on endlessly, as I had nowhere to go and no one to visit. I was relieved when cool fall days finally arrived because I had been looking forward to Art's state and federal cases making their way through the courts.

It didn't really matter that I was regularly stranded at home; I didn't have any funds and did my best to avoid running into old friends or people to whom I still owed money. Authorities remained concerned about my safety so I tended to stay indoors with the blinds closed as much as possible. I assisted Bill as he prepared for my case by gathering information, recording details, and answering questions. There were still a large number of lawsuits and liens and demands for payments making their way to me and some days I avoided the mailbox altogether. To say I was emotionally damaged was an understatement. I had been abandoned by my friends, estranged from my family, abused by Art and his associates, and shamed by my own actions. Even friends who had not given me any money believed the worst about me. I continued my therapy appointments with Dr. Jayson, the one safe place where I could talk about anything.

With everything else vying for my attention, I had neglected my annual mammogram the previous few years. I didn't find this especially troubling as my family did not have a history of breast cancer and I had never had a mammogram that revealed anything suspicious, but that was about to change.

On November 24, 2011, I had just disrobed in preparation for a shower when my cousin Carol Jean called. As I answered the phone I flopped across my bed and immediately noticed a rather large lump pushing up through my breast. I was shocked at what I saw. Even though it was Thanksgiving, I called Dr. Ron Gutheil at home. Years before I had dated Ron when he was an intern. Later, after I married Dick and he married Jimilea (who now manages his practice), the four of us became good friends; my friendship with the couple has endured to this day.

Dr. Ron told me to come in the next day. After an examination, he said the large protrusion I had seen was not the urgent problem. He had discovered other tumors that were much deeper in my breast, and those really concerned him. Dr. Ron referred me to a specialist across the street from his office and made an appointment for me the following Monday. I didn't know this new doctor, but I immediately liked him. I underwent a mammogram and then a breast biopsy at Doctors Hospital. As we were sitting in his office after the procedure, he asked if I had been under a lot of stress. His kind, sweet nature caught me by surprise and before I could stop myself I started crying. I gave him a brief recap of the stress I had been suffering through for two years. He gently responded, "OK, let me contact you as soon as I get the results."

Within a week I received a call from the specialist. He said, "I know you have a lot on your plate right now, but I want you to come in and bring another set of ears with you. I really hate to have to tell you this, but you have cancer." I took Carol Jean with me to the appointment where we learned I had so much cancer that, in his opinion, a lumpectomy was out of the question. Before we left I had a confirmed date at Grant Hospital for a mastectomy and an appointment to meet with a plastic surgeon immediately after surgery for a reconstructive breast implant.

When I returned home I placed a call to Dr. Mike Caligiuri, CEO of The James Cancer Center. I knew Dr. Mike from the Buckeye Cruise for Cancer. We had enjoyed dinner together several times on the ship and a professional friendship had developed. Dr. Mike's secretary answered the phone and before long Dr. Mike was on the line. After exchanging a brief greeting, he asked what was going on. I explained I had just been diagnosed with breast cancer and was going to be treated at Grant Hospital. He encouraged me to come to The James instead. I told him my insurance didn't include coverage at his hospital. Dr. Mike wouldn't hear of my going anywhere else. "No, Anita," he said. "I will work something out and call you tomorrow. You've got to come here!"

Dr. Mike came through on his promise and made it possible for me to receive treatment at The James. Even though the facility was out of my insurance network, they agreed to accept my in-network provider benefits. He got me right in to see Dr. Bill Farrar, a highly respected surgeon who usually had a twelve-month waiting list. In all, during my treatment for cancer, I endured thirteen biopsies, which were quite painful.

My self-worth had plummeted to the point that I thought I deserved to get breast cancer. After everything that had happened, I was convinced cancer was supposed to be my punishment for the role I played in Art's schemes. I wouldn't allow myself to indulge in one moment of self-pity about my condition. There was no, "Why, me?" I knew exactly why.

What really bothered me, however, was sitting in waiting rooms alone and watching couples seated around me. Nearly every other patient had a companion—a husband or partner, mother, sister or daughter—holding her, offering comfort, compassion, and strength. I had no one. And every time I walked into another doctor's office or waiting room alone, I was mocked by the isolation I felt. The most difficult aspect of battling my cancer wasn't the cancer; it was facing it alone.

In an attempt to save my breast, I underwent three lumpectomies on three different dates. After the last procedure, Dr. Bill decided there was still too much cancer remaining and suggested a mastectomy. After he removed my breast, I had a skin expander installed to make room for an appropriately sized implant. However, when the plastic surgeon inserted the implant several weeks later, it was much too small and I looked unbalanced. I inquired about seeing another doctor and was referred to a plastic surgeon, Dr. Miller.

Dr. Miller suggested the TRAM Flap procedure to reconstruct my breast. This is when the abdomen muscle is used to carry abdominal skin and fat up to the chest wall, so a breast shape can be created or a pocket can be built for an implant. It is a quite complicated procedure and I was in surgery for twenty-two hours, followed by two emergency surgeries. It seemed that everything that could go wrong went wrong. My blood pressure plummeted to thirty-six. I needed thirty-five pounds of fluid pumped into my arteries in order to expand them to the size the surgical team required. The implant was inserted and then removed because it wasn't right. Finally, they took me to recovery where another problem was discovered and I was wheeled back into surgery. I remember talking to the doctor before the second procedure started and telling him to stop. I didn't want anything else done. Dr. Miller assured me he could fix the problem, and I agreed to let him continue. There was another trip to recovery and then back to surgery again one last time. I was fortunate that due to the type of cancer I had and the surgeon's ability to remove it all, I didn't require radiation or chemotherapy afterward. Instead, I was put on a daily pill regimen, which my doctor anticipated I would need to take for five years.

Unfortunately, the procedures resulted in so many staples, sutures, and drains, the pain was nearly unbearable. I spent a week in the hospital before transferring to The Convalarium of Dublin—a skilled nursing facility—for more than a week.

After eight days, Alan brought me home and then Carol Jean stayed with me for a few days to assist with the drainage tubes, help me take showers, and prepare meals. Unfortunately, I developed an infection, which required a return trip to the hospital and an additional surgery. The pain was constant and severe for weeks.

When I returned home the second time I was so appreciative to learn that my neighbor, Gloria Beadell, had organized a schedule for neighbors to bring me meals. Most everyone she contacted signed up for a night. It broke my heart that glaringly absent from the list was my former good friend, Camilla Cox.

For the next month, I had a home visiting nurse come twice a day to change my dressings. After my insurance benefits were exhausted, I had to let the nurses go and attempted to tend to my incisions myself. I couldn't always see what I was doing and it was nearly impossible to change the bandages on my own. I became frustrated and angry at my dilemma. Even though I didn't want Alan to help care for my breast wounds, I eventually pushed my pride aside and asked for his assistance. When Gloria heard about my predicament, she offered to come over and help me.

This was a very dark time for me; probably the lowest time in my life. I was physically damaged, mentally discouraged, emotionally drained, and spiritually disheartened. If not for Gloria's kindhearted compassion and positive encouragement, I'm not sure I would have survived.

47 | BANKRUPTCY

FALL 2011

"I can't explain exactly what happened that day or why it occurred, but I do know I was undeserving of their kindness and the compassionate forgiveness I experienced."	*Anita Barney*

As my creditors began taking more aggressive action to collect the monies they had loaned me for Art, and with no resources or income to repay my debts, my decision to file for bankruptcy was forced when Rod Cheetham filed legal action for a sheriff's auction on my condo. The auction was scheduled for November 2011. I was distraught at the thought of becoming homeless but even more upset about filing bankruptcy. There was never a reprieve; although I was scraping bottom, every day brought terror and was worse than the day before.

On Friday, October 28, 2011, less than two years since I had heard Art speak at Genoa Church, I filed for bankruptcy. I was crying in the car as I drove to meet my bankruptcy attorney, Judith McInturff. On the way home I was sobbing so hard I had to pull off the road and compose myself. I called Bill who explained (again) this was the right decision, as I had no way to pay the massive debts I had incurred for Art. I wanted to scream and was intent on killing myself to end the relentless pressure bearing down on me. Thankfully, Bill talked me down from the edge.

Every day I could feel my stress building. I could barely sleep more than a few hours at a time, and I woke exhausted. In early December I was speaking to Dr. Jayson on the phone when blood began pouring out of my nose. I promptly ended the call and began trying to stop the flow of blood, but it was so heavy I began having difficulty breathing. As I made my way to a chair, it felt like I was drowning. I willed myself not to panic. My grandson, Scott, happened to call at that moment and when I explained what was going on, he called his stepmother in Dublin who called 911 for me. By the time the squad arrived, the blood had soaked through several towels. Paramedics registered my blood pressure at 220 and immediately transported me to the hospital. After the emergency room physician was able to stabilize my condition, he said that with a blood pressure reading that high, if I hadn't had a nose bleed it was likely I would have suffered a stroke. My body would have needed to release the pressure one way or another. They were able to eventually stop the bleeding at the hospital and send me home. But later that night, my nose started bleeding heavily again and I returned to the ER.

On Thursday, December 8, 2011, I was scheduled to attend my 341 Bankruptcy Hearing—The Meeting of Creditors—at three o'clock. As I was backing out of my garage to drive to the United States Bankruptcy Court downtown, I experienced another frightening nosebleed. I didn't have many tissues with me so I opened the door of my car and leaned over the driveway. In no time there was so much blood on the concrete it looked like a murder victim had bled out. I made my way across the street to Gloria Beadell's condo to ask for assistance. Gloria helped stop the bleeding, and exclaimed that she had never seen anyone bleed so heavily. I had blood all over my sweater, and she helped me clean up as best as we could. Seeing I was in no condition to drive, Gloria offered to take me to court. I called Bill and explained the situation and told him I was on my way but running late. He said he would notify Judy McInturff and agreed to bring me home after the proceeding. I entered the courtroom with disheveled hair, smeared makeup, and blood clearly visible on my clothing; nonetheless, I looked better on the outside than I felt on the inside.

And when I looked around, I saw the source of my night terrors and the reason uncontrollable stress caused my blood pressure to skyrocket: my former friends—people whom I had loved and respected and now owed hundreds of thousands of dollars—were seated around the room. Eric Turner, Farley Daft, Phil Evans, Cruz Hill, Sam and Joyce Nelson, Joy Blanco, Eric and Diane Turner, and Lew and Annabelle Sanchez were prepared to make statements regarding the money they loaned me in good faith simply because I had asked. I couldn't reconcile how I had reached a point where I had to ask the same court to relieve me of these debts to my friends. But I had no choice. There were no resources to pay what I owed.

One by one my creditors would raise their hand to be acknowledged before they were given the floor. My friends just wanted to be heard, and I respected that. I suffered through the hearing, listening to the testimony, and reliving the awful circumstances surrounding each transaction. Emotions were running high and at one point, the judge reminded Farley to keep quiet or he would be removed from the court. I instantly recalled the details of every request as Art's threats and screaming, his random targeting of people, dialing numbers, and handing me the phone, flooded my consciousness. Tears filled my eyes as I witnessed the reality of what Art had orchestrated and I couldn't stop.

After everyone else was given a chance to speak, it was my turn. Even though my voice was wavering, I told my friends how devastated I was about what had happened. That this—my owing them money and being unable to repay it—was not what I had intended. I also revealed I had cancer and I was so distraught over my diagnosis that I didn't want to take my medication and would rather let cancer end my life than fight through it. Before I could continue the judge threw down her papers and interrupted me. "What do you mean you don't want to fight? I had Stage 4 cancer and fought it, and I'm still alive." I quickly set the record straight saying that *before*, when I was first diagnosed, I had felt that way. But now, I realized I had to fight for my life or I would never have the opportunity to find a way to pay everyone back. Full restitution was my goal.

By the time the hearing concluded, I was a sobbing mess. Judy and her assistant escorted me to the restroom, allowing me time to compose myself while everyone exited the area. Joy Blanco (to whom I still owed $10,000), had seen my distress and came in to check on me. We hugged and I gained strength from the embrace of a dear friend. Then Joyce Nelson (to whom I still owed $85,000), Annabelle Sanchez (I still owed more than $29,000 to her and her husband), and Diane Turner (who, with her husband Eric, held an unpaid note for $10,000) came in and we started hugging. Through our tears, the five of us began talking about how much we missed each other and reminiscing about better times.

And right there, in a ladies room in Bankruptcy Court, God granted me peace through the forgiveness of friends. Joyce left and called to her husband, Sam. As she explained what was happening, the grace of God washed over Sam and he also felt compelled to extend love and forgiveness to me. By this time, everyone was in tears, even Judy's assistant! Now, I can't explain exactly what happened that day or why it occurred, but I do know I was undeserving of their kindness and the compassionate forgiveness I experienced. It had been more than a year since I had enjoyed the casual conversation or warm embrace of any of these friends. But in an instant I witnessed God's love for me as He restored relationships. It was miraculous.

Weeks later, when I had to return to sign the final bankruptcy papers, I went alone. Having created this mess myself, I didn't want to burden anyone with a request to accompany me. After the emotional high of the last time I was at Bankruptcy Court, my health and financial situation had continued to deteriorate and things were looking worse. My mind was in overdrive, convincing me there was no way out of my disastrous life. I was just kicking the financial can down the road until the next emergency revealed I had even fewer resources available to address the problems I faced. I was out of hope. I cried the entire drive home.

Exhausted by discouragement and desperate for some peace, I grabbed sleeping pills from the medicine cabinet and swallowed a few. I was tapping out the next handful when the phone rang. It was John Amery. He wanted to talk; I was distracted and wanted to get him off the phone. We chatted for a while about my lack of money and my bankruptcy, but he knew something wasn't right and asked, "What are you doing?" I didn't answer. He said, "You sound sleepy." I still didn't answer. He became alarmed by my unusual behavior and kept questioning me. Eventually, I told him I was just trying to sleep. Realizing something was amiss he kept prodding me for answers. Finally, I told him I had taken some sleeping pills because I was so depressed I didn't know what else to do.

"Anita! You must stop it right now!" John demanded. "I'm not a religious man, but I think God had me call to interrupt you. STOP IT! Art is not worth it. Do not do this to yourself!"

While little else would have sliced through the cloud of depression hanging over me, John mentioning that God was looking out for me grabbed my attention and reminded me there was still hope, regardless how the circumstances appeared. John and I talked a while longer before, convinced I wasn't going to harm myself, he said goodbye. I put the cap back on the pills and didn't take any more.

I slept soundly that night, and felt a little better about life when I woke in the morning.

48 | GUILT, SORROW, FORGIVENESS

"She better pray that God forgives her, because I'm not going to forgive her."	Former friend at Anita's sentencing

What is this delicate dance of seeking and offering forgiveness?

It's not making an excuse. It's getting to the bottom of it. Wondering why. Taking the time to look at things from a different perspective. Inspecting the pieces individually instead of simply judging the entire picture. Asking questions. And listening for the answers.

It's not being content to assume your perspective is their view, too. The truth is, it's always different for each one of us. Good? Bad? Can we be content with only one bucket or the other? What happens when the unexplained causes a life to take a detour? Are we willing to give the benefit of the doubt?

And what should we do when the accused is also a victim? When harmful actions have been perpetrated as a result of the abusive attacks of a predator? And whom should we hold accountable for failing to give proper warning, hiding past bad acts, and neglecting to protect the innocents so they aren't caught up in the schemes?

It takes effort to pull back the curtains and look at the facts, to listen to both sides instead of agreeing with the headlines produced by someone on deadline. To consider that sometimes it's the multi-hued colors of life that push us beyond the easy choice of *this* or *that*. Life is rarely confined to a clear Choice A or Choice B. Guilty or Not Guilty.

What would happen if we would step closer? Take time to listen? Return a phone call or extend kindness, warranted or not? Are we concerned that our own "friends" will brand us guilty by association? Are we worried that by offering charity we condone actions or decisions? Are we fearful that by looking honestly at our friend in need, we disclose our own weakness or indiscretion?

And frankly, who is to say if kindness is unwarranted? If the offense was too great and the pain too deep, is it permissible to be cruel? What if forgiveness has been requested? Even then, are we willing to allow bitterness to poison our lives in order to prove we were the wounded party? Just because we shout from the rooftops that we are a victim, doesn't prove we were an innocent bystander. Is our testimony and public scorn an attempt to divert attention from the role we played?

Each of us makes decisions, whether privately or publicly, that we would rather forget. We have all taken action that seemed acceptable or correct at the time, but is later proven to be regrettable. Sometimes our poor judgment is insignificant and quickly forgotten. Other times, our blunders leave permanent scars on the hearts of those we love and care for deeply. And while time does heal all wounds, our memories often take longer to recover.

When it comes down to it, who we are is revealed in how we conduct ourselves in private, when we think no one is watching. It is not the bright shiny self we reveal to the world. We can host the biggest benefits to support the most worthy causes, but what does it say about our character when we privately shun the outstretched hand of one asking forgiveness?

What if, instead of being introduced with accolades of wins on the field or our efforts of money raised for charity or feats equally prestigious, we were introduced by how many people's lives we touched through our kindness, forgiveness, and patience?

See, all those times we refuse to include someone who has "wronged" us, walk out of a room because we spotted *that person* in attendance, or choose not to answer a request for mercy, we are revealing our own hurt and pain. Hurting people naturally respond in ways that hurt others. Healthy people instinctively find ways to bring healing and show kindness to those around them, even if it is difficult to do so.

Are we pleased with ourselves when we respond to requests for reconciliation with ugly comments or, sometimes, with no response at all? If we believe in karma or the golden rule, or whatever we want to call it, then we must realize that we're traveling around on a carousel of unhappiness and what goes around will surely come back around.

So, what if the person requesting forgiveness does not deserve it? Does that matter? If we wish for others to extend forgiveness to us when we don't deserve it, if one day we find ourselves in a position where we're hoping for unwarranted mercy instead of deserved justice, then we better be willing to plant some of the good things we want now in order to be able to harvest good things later.

Sometimes the unforgiveness we hold onto is personal. While we are able to forgive others, we struggle to find a way to extend mercy to ourselves. Too often we are unable to move beyond the distress, loss, or grief we have caused. We brand ourselves unworthy and join in the chorus of those demanding relief.

But how do we find relief from the destruction that bears our name? When it stares back at us from our mirror? When talking with the therapist brings only fleeting relief? When our first waking moment and last conscious thought are crushing torments you cannot escape? What then?

I had such a good reputation that people didn't question me when I approached them about money; they were more than happy to give me money to make more money. Now, they despise me, even though I'm still a good person. I made a mistake. A personal crisis. A public failure. Should eighteen months of poor decisions erase a lifetime of good work? If I could go back, I would go back 100 times and do it differently, but I cannot. I can only move forward.

Does it make any difference that I helped bring the predator—everyone's predator—to justice?

I can't force people to forgive me. I can only forgive myself and accept the forgiveness God has extended. Some days it's more difficult to forgive myself than others, because I carry a heavy burden of the knowledge that I was the catalyst that caused my treasured relationships to break. What choice do I have?

Refusing to forgive myself would be a death sentence of my own creation.

Every day I think about those I have wronged. I understand the questions and anger. I put myself in their place and I can't blame them for their response. I realize full restoration might not be forthcoming, but I desperately crave their forgiveness.

When our paths cross, I celebrate when former friends—including those to whom my husband and I loaned money, often times never being repaid—no longer turn around and leave the room. I'm aware of every fleeting interaction. The comfort of a hand on my shoulder. Of eye contact. Of a polite greeting. Of a warm farewell.

I know they are working through this, too.

At their own pace.

On their own terms.

It will take time.

49 | ART GOES TO PRISON
MAY 2012

"You (Mr. Schlichter) have caused Mrs. Barney's financial ruin . . . Your word is bankrupt . . . Restitution will never get paid. . . . The guidelines for sentencing in this case are, frankly, insufficient."	*Honorable Michael H. Watson*

Before Art's sentencing in Federal Court on May 4, 2012, Bill prepared and submitted a Declaration of Victim Losses on my behalf for the judge to consider when handing down his sentence. The estimated amount of my loss directly related to the fraud and theft perpetrated by Art included exhausting investment and retirement accounts, losing my Saturn Sky, jewelry, and condo in Florida, racking up enormous credit card balances, incurring a reverse mortgage on my Dublin condo, and incurring more than $500,000 in personal debts and $225,000 in unpaid taxes.

Art pled guilty and was sentenced to 290 months (twenty-four years) imprisonment for three counts of fraud (Fraud by Wire, Radio or Television; Bank Fraud; Fraud and False Statements). Interestingly enough, Judge Michael H. Watson assessed points to Art's sentencing guidelines based upon his past criminal history:

- Burglary
- Fraud/theft/receipt of stolen property (April 1995)
- Unlawful Gambling conviction (Indiana)
- Crime(s) committed under federally supervised release (2006-2011)
- Case No. 11CRO-2931: 9/15/11 Conviction (Judge Horton in Franklin County Common Pleas Court)
  - F2 Theft, F4 Count, F5 Count – Pattern of Corrupt Activity
  - (11 Victims totaling $841,000)
  - Substance Abuse (positive test for cocaine)

Because Art was permitted to serve his time on each federal count concurrently, his punishment on the three counts of which he was convicted was diluted to about ten years and six months of real time behind bars. While he was serving his federal sentence, his state sentence was being satisfied at the same time, even further reducing his actual time in prison. It didn't seem fair that for a habitual offender like Art, the judge would consider him eligible for any reduction in sentencing.

During sentencing, Judge Watson had this to say:

"You (Mr. Schlichter) have caused Mrs. Barney's financial ruin . . . you have played on the emotions of a number of women, and have taken advantage of them both financially and in other ways . . . Your word is bankrupt . . . Restitution will never get paid . . . The guidelines for sentencing in this case are, frankly, insufficient."

***

Society is conflicted when it comes to obsessive gambling, and there are multiple opportunities to share an opinion, especially when the person involved is high profile.

After the news of Art's federal sentence flooded social media, I stumbled upon the "Latest News & Rumors" section on the ProFootballTalk.NBCSports.com site. Several comments posted in response to the headline "Art Schlichter to spend the next decade in prison" reveal the diverse opinions people have toward gambling addiction.

seanx40 says:
May 4, 2012 1:45PM

There has to be some better way. Now taxpayers have to take care of him for the next decade at the cost of several hundred thousand dollars. He hasn't actually physically hurt anyone. But there has to be something better than locking up non-violent offenders. Perhaps 10 yrs of public service under strict supervision. Cleaning bedpans at nursing homes perhaps. Shoveling snow. Something. The NFL should make him speak at the rookie meetings every year.

hawkforlife says:
May 4, 2012 2:55PM

To seanx40, so Bernie Madoff should walk free too? How many people that have been swindled are physically hurt, who knows but in some cases they lose everything and commit suicide. Throw the book at him.

hawaiifunfnull says:
May 4, 2012 3:05PM

He hasn't actually physically hurt anyone. But there has to be something better than locking up non-violent offenders.

Schlichter estimated that he had stolen around $1.5 million total by 2007. Add the million from this ticket debacle and you're 25% of the way to eight digits in fraud. His crimes may not involve violence, but they are hardly victimless. He belongs behind bars.

TheWizard says:
May 4, 2012 4:17PM

All this guy is addicted to is "too lazy for honest work."

nickswearsky says:
May 4, 2012 5:13PM

I've never seen such an intractable case of gambling addiction.

***

Perhaps obsessive gambling remains a "victimless crime" because too few victims are willing to come forward. Shamed. Embarrassed to tell family. Fearful to go public or enlist the help of authorities. After all, the money wasn't handed over to the swindler while staring down the barrel of a gun. No, the threat is more subtle. It's a loan. A favor. A promise of repayment. Until—in a heartbeat—it isn't.

Unless the victims speak out, how will the perception change? Who will warn the next target?

50 | MY DAY IN COURT
JULY 2012

"I can't help but wonder if Judge Horton, as an elected official, was more influenced by the facts of the case or the by the camera crew that lined the back wall of his court."	*Anita Barney*

Since December 20, 2010, when my attorney had called Detective Davis, he had been working diligently on my behalf. Bill negotiated my full cooperation and silence in exchange for a guilty plea and a conviction that would not include jail time. The records and documents I had turned over, the introductions I had made, and the conversations I had recorded expedited the investigation, revealed details that might not otherwise have been discovered, and were the catalysts for Art's convictions. Because I had contacted the police and agreed to cooperate without any restrictions, and my actions had resulted in federal and state convictions against Art, Bill had been able to work out a plea deal on my behalf consisting of Community Service and Community Control (probation) along with restitution and a fine.

My date with destiny arrived and everyone associated with the case felt it would be a routine hearing. Both Bill and Assistant Prosecutor Jay Moore would address the court. Plea deal recommendations would be made. The judge would read his comments before signing the paperwork and concluding the hearing. But they had badly misjudged how Judge Timothy S. Horton would play to the media. In the blink of an eye, everything was in jeopardy.

In stark contrast to the nominal media presence at Art's proceedings, I was shocked to see the large number of reporters and cameras waiting to record the details of my appearance in Courtroom 3F. Among others, I spotted Kathy Gray with *The Columbus Dispatch*, Carol Luper with WSYX/WTTE, and Paul Aker with WBNS. Bill had his hands full keeping my anxiety under control. I could feel my heart speed up and found it difficult to catch my breath. Detective Davis approached and I asked if I could hug him. He said I could and that calmed me down a little, but my hands were visibly shaking as I walked through the gate separating the Defendant's Table from the Gallery.

I was surprised to see so many former friends had come. When they were permitted to address the court, they hurled ugly things my way. This was the first time my victims were able to confront me in person, and there was no stopping them. Months of pent-up frustration were unleashed. That I had been referred to as a "victim" in the press and by the Prosecutor had created resentment and fanned the flames of their hostility. I sat immobilized in horrified silence as the accusations rained down on me. I could feel hatred permeating the room, and watched the unblinking lenses of the cameras as they documented every word.

One person said he didn't blame Art; he only blamed me and stated that I had made decisions based on my flawed moral character. Another stated I was a crook who belonged behind bars and that I would never be forgiven. Someone else said I gambled with all their lives. I was a victim who was being victimized all over again. I felt small and beaten down.

Facing my accusers was the most difficult thing I have ever done in my life. To see friends I had hosted and celebrated and generously included in my life stand mere inches away and spit vehement comments about me in open court was humiliating. I watched the anger flash across faces and heard the pain of betrayal in their voices.

Then Judge Horton asked if I had anything to say.

Confident of the terms of the plea agreement, I had not prepared any comments. Now that I was given an opportunity to speak, I was woefully unprepared. I turned toward Bill, seeking guidance. He advised against speaking extemporaneously. His overriding goal throughout the entire process was to keep me out of prison. He could see things were going badly, and the agreement we had with the Prosecutor was unraveling under the judge's scrutiny. My emotions were high and Bill feared I might blurt out something that would negatively affect the agreement he had worked out on my behalf.

Against Bill's advice I stood and faced the judge, prepared to speak from my heart. I wanted to share my side of the story, and how I had just wanted to help Art, but that he had threatened and abused me. I wanted them to know he was a career criminal who had taken advantage of a financially naïve woman. That I was so very sorry, and I would do my best to pay everyone back. "I didn't mean for this to happen," I said to the judge before he harshly interrupted me, pointed to my victims and commanded, "Tell them!"

I turned around and started again, but it came out wrong and sounded more like an excuse than an explanation. "Nobody really knows what happened. I was coerced." I hesitated for a second, trying to formulate my next sentence. Before I could begin, my former friends—now accusers—turned their backs on me and walked out of the courtroom. Stunned, I returned to my chair.

After listening to my accusers, and not being bound by the terms of the plea agreement, Judge Horton shook his head and commented he had changed his mind about my culpability in the matter. "What has moved me the most," he said, "is her lack of remorse. I gave her an opportunity to apologize today. A simple apology would go a long way." Even though Prosecutor Ron O'Brien had stated that I had cooperated with investigators in building their case against Art by allowing phone conversations to be recorded and those taped calls were a substantial force in their ability to arrest, charge, and obtain a conviction against Art, it seemed to matter little to Judge Horton.

People say justice is blind, and that might have been true at one time. But when news cameras are present in the courtroom and reporters are recording details about the actions of a judge who serves at the pleasure of voters, it can be difficult to differentiate between what is right and fair, and what amounts to political posturing. I can't help but wonder if Judge Horton, as an elected official, was more influenced by the facts of the case or the by the camera crews that lined the back wall of his court. Was he playing to Lady Justice or an electorate who would decide his fate at the polls?

Those closest to the case, the investigators and Prosecutors, knew I was a victim. In fact, Steve Schierholt, the Assistant Prosecutor who had been part of the investigation from the beginning and was aware of the plea deal, was present in the courtroom that day. He said he was concerned about what was happening and what action the Judge might take.

In the end, I pled guilty and was sentenced to three years of community control (probation), 100 hours of community service, a $5,000 fine, and ordered to pay restitution in the amount of $426,800 to nineteen victims.

Several months later Judge Horton approved my request for freedom to travel while I was still on probation. I wondered if he ever had second thoughts about the merits of the case when the lights were dimmed and the cameras were off, or when he faced his own accusers several years later? If his grandstanding against the seventy-year-old victim became unnecessary when public interest had waned and the voters were less likely to be influenced by a judge who otherwise might be considered "soft on crime."

My sentence of community service involved working at the Franklin County Courthouse each Saturday from 8:00 a.m. to 2:00 p.m. I wanted to fulfill my sentence of 100 hours as quickly as possible and started right away. There were a number of offenders, many with DUI convictions, that showed up on Saturday mornings. Based on our abilities, we were given different assignments throughout the building. I was tasked with destroying documents. I would sit in a room with six or seven others and the officers would bring in big bins of old files that were to be shredded. We were instructed to tear up papers and pictures in a certain way, without looking at the content, to prepare them to be mechanically shredded. The officers would generally assign me the easiest duties because I was still healing from breast surgery and couldn't do any reaching or lifting.

The first day I reported for community service was a terrible experience. Once I arrived I was instructed to wait in a line with the other offenders until we were called. No purses! No cell phones! If you brought a cell phone you were sent home. No talking! I had never had restrictions like that. There were so many rules and the officers were so strict and mean. The reality of being punished in such a tangible and visible way was repulsive.

I was so ashamed. I had always considered myself to be a good person and couldn't understand why I was in this place. I thought it was a frightening miscarriage of justice that I had received a penalty for simply trying to help someone. I was upset with God for allowing this to happen. I was angry at Art. It didn't make any sense. I cried the entire way home and tried to reach Bill. I was a wreck.

For anyone who hasn't had to perform community service, my hysterics might seem a bit over the top for someone who was tasked with shredding paper. The issue I had wasn't with the work, it was the idea that what had started as kind generosity to the man who saved my little boy's life had resulted in my paying a publicly humiliating penalty. I had already been disgraced in the press and sentenced in court to pay restitution to my victims; was the indignity of community service really necessary?

Once I arrived home and calmed myself down that first day, I realized there was nothing I could do to change reality. I had to complete 100 hours of community service and I was determined to make the best of it. The next week I went in and forced a smile. "OK, Larry," I said. "What's on the agenda for today?" And that's how Larry Shaw, who was the Community Service Director, and I became friends. He and I and the others assigned to the shredding room would share our stories and, before long, we were all enjoying lunch together. Even the guard, Ken Bethea, noticed my change in attitude and we developed a close rapport.

I started looking forward to Saturday mornings and community service. I think it was because for the first time in a long time I was among people who weren't judging me. They didn't care where I lived or who I was or what I had done. They simply enjoyed my company. They would tell me about their lives and families. And when I heard they were taking the bus to and from the courthouse, I recalled my own humble beginnings and the inconvenience of public transportation and would often take them home at the conclusion of our assignments—even though I barely had money for gas.

EPILOGUE
OCTOBER 2015

When I was a young woman, I often would question God, "Why me?"

Although my grandmother founded a church, my parents rarely attended, except on the big holidays: Easter, Christmas, and Mother's Day. Mother's Day was a pretty big deal with all the moms boasting about their children and proudly displaying their corsages. But I think my mom's aversion to regularly attending church was a result of all the time she was forced to spend there as a child.

So, while I had an awareness of God, The Creator, I had never been introduced to Him on a personal level. Yet even as a child, I was aware of the good things in my life and struggled with the reasons that I should be so blessed. I had always enjoyed supernatural favor with my instructors and friends, and doors of opportunity opened to me before I even had a chance to knock. Teachers selected me for special assignments and my peers elected me to various offices whether or not I was on the ballot. On the days voting would take place for Class President or Homecoming Queen, I would stay home feigning illness and hoping my absence would allow someone else to win. I was uncomfortable being in the spotlight. No matter what I did to discourage my popularity, it grew in spades.

As an adult it seemed like I was always in the right place at the right time. I was offered good jobs without interviewing. My employers were always generous, extending bonuses and offering to co-sign a loan when I needed a car. I went to a concert with my mother and grandmother and one of the artists jumped off the stage and asked for my phone number. I was always aware of how I was the recipient of so many good things that seemed to bypass others, and I regularly wondered why.

To be sure, life has taken me through some exceptionally dark valleys, but I never questioned God about these times. I accepted them, attended to the details, and worked through the consequences. Whether or not the undesirable condition was of my making, I always felt it was my responsibility to fix it. Alone. I simply didn't involve my parents or others for support or assistance. For the good or the bad, I harbored an unspoken burden to address my own problems.

On the other hand, the good times—and there were plenty of good times—were something that I never took for granted. I didn't necessarily credit God for blessing me, but I was aware that He was responsible. And while I freely shared my good fortune with those around me, I always wondered why God was generous toward me. I couldn't figure it out. I hadn't accomplished anything worthwhile or impacted humanity in a meaningful way that would warrant His kindness. Why me?

These days I've been asking "Why?" for different reasons.

Why didn't I change my phone number? Obtain a restraining order? Seek assistance from my family and friends or contact the authorities earlier? How could I allow Art to steal hundreds of thousands of dollars from me personally, and then coerce me to request money from my friends on his behalf?

I wish there was a simple answer.

Like all the previous times in my life, I thought it was my obligation to fix this mess I had caused. I didn't realize I was being victimized. I didn't recognize a gambler in the throes of his addiction. I couldn't identify the individuals surrounding Art as either criminals or victims; I mistakenly thought the people he instructed to collect money and return payments were his friends. Art isolated me and, eventually, I was convinced I was utterly alone with no escape.

Looking back over the events that transpired, I cannot believe how blinded I was to Art's schemes. *How could I have been so foolish? Why me, God? What have I done to deserve this?*

Even now there are times that a flood of disappointment washes over me with such force that the thought of suicide is the only "life-saving" option I can consider. It's not the disaster of losing it all or of friends forsaking me and family alienating me, or the absence of wealth and position that drags me through the darkness.

What haunts me at night and terrorizes the corner of my conscience is the unintentional harm my actions have caused others. Unwittingly taking advantage of their kindness and generosity. Abusing their trust. Causing their lives to be more difficult simply because they agreed to help me: draining life savings, severing lifelong relationships, casting shadows on memories that used to brighten their days. Compelling them to write hateful letters to me—or about me—instead of giving them a reason to pen lovely thank you notes as they had in the past in response to my hospitality and generosity.

But I realize that ending my life would be the final selfish decision in a recent string of poor choices. Sure, I could stop *my* pain and memories but with that final act, I would open the door to new pain and sadness for my children and grandchildren, while permanently closing the door on any hope of repaying those I had victimized or reconciling with those who have turned away.

When the moments of despair threaten to drown me, I must consciously take control of mind and turn my thoughts toward God. I realize the worst of my life is behind me. And although I have enjoyed the benefits of wealth and position in the past, I am confident that now I have a purpose and the best of my life lies ahead.

Yes, my life will look different than before. But that's OK, because I'm a different person. No one can go through what I have *barely* survived and come out on the other side the same person. The core of who I am, a generous, fun-loving, people-focused woman, is the same. But since I have turned my life over to a merciful and gracious Heavenly Father, my focus—how I see things and determine their importance—has vastly shifted.

And now, when the question of "Why me?" surfaces, I finally have an answer. My life has been infused with a purpose to share this amazing grace that God has shown me. To proclaim there is hope for those who are searching for redemption, and the comfort of forgiveness offered by a loving Heavenly Father is only a prayer away.

Although my recovery is a work in progress, I can honestly say that I'm glad God was willing to accept me at my worst and turn this terrible situation into a message of promise for others. It is only because of Him that I am able to awaken each day with an expectation of what the future holds. Now that everything has been stripped away, I can clearly see Christ without distraction. And I'm able to point others to Him.

To be sure, I've had an incredibly interesting life. Now, I have a reason to share it.

That's why.

AFTER THE DUST SETTLED
NOVEMBER 2015

After everything, we've learned that life goes on.

My daughter Angela Genereux is a designer and sales representative in Florida. Her older son, Scott Martin, stays busy in the remodeling business. His son, Landon, is interested in all kinds of sports. Scott is married to Yessie, who is a pediatric nurse anesthetist, and they also live in Florida.

Angela's younger son, Sean Martin, is a successful financial planner. He lives in the Columbus area with his wife Monica Day, a television reporter.

My son Alan Valko owns a sealcoating company in the Columbus area.

I've been blessed by the companionship of caring friends— many who never knew me when my bank accounts were full—and I'm growing stronger and healing more every day. Recently, a friend who has known me for years commented that my new friends are much nicer than many of my former friends.

And Art? Well, he's in prison in Indiana.

SECOND CHANCES
DEANNA C. STEVENS

There are individuals in society who have committed such egregious crimes that society has deemed them unworthy of a second chance. They are identified by sentences of life without parole and titles of murderer or sexual predator. Some are permanently banned from working in education, others are forbidden to practice medicine. Law licenses are stripped away. Preachers are removed from churches.

Within our homes we often struggle to extend second chances. A brother battles drug addiction, unable to stay clean. A partner chooses infidelity over sacred commitments. Friends who have accepted our generosity exploit our weakness. Those who have promised to protect us discover they can destroy us in ways we didn't even know we were vulnerable.

What is it about forgiveness and extending second chances that is so complicated? Is it because we're thrust again into a reactionary position toward our offender? How is it that some people are able to live life with neat lists of rules and consequences and then effortlessly wrap their actions around them?

If the light is red, you stop your car and wait.
If someone violates trust, you forgive them.
Simple as that.

Others struggle to even identify what forgiveness looks like. Certainly, the broken relationship cannot be restored to what it had been. Can it? A wrong has been perpetuated. A memory has been created. Even if the wound heals, a scar has formed.

What are we to do with the scar? Of course it fades over time and with luck, becomes nearly invisible. But can the memory itself fade into nothingness? What happens when it does not?

Does forgiveness depend on the ability to forget?

What happens when the offender repeats? Can we trust someone who has "done this before"? God says we are to forgive a person seventy times seven, or 490 times. That doesn't make sense. Is it even possible? Isn't that irresponsible? Does this crazy level of forgiveness provide free rein for the person to offend again without accountability?

And, what if the offender is found guilty and completes the sentence levied upon her by the justice system? Is that *enough* justice when a record remains, loans are unpaid, and relationships still lie in ruin? After the police reports are completed, the Prosecutors have reviewed the evidence and filed charges, and the court has rendered a verdict, there is still the matter of forgiveness.

Some people forgive because it is the mandate of their religion. Following this law relieves them of having to think it through, wrestle with the facts, or look at the scar. Similar to the way they don't have to think about stopping the car when they see a red light, their foot automatically moves toward the brake pedal. They forgive out of the habit because it is the right thing to do.

Others may seek to forgive so that they have peace of mind or to restore a broken relationship they once enjoyed. Motivated by their emotions, they forgive with their soul.

Others can completely erase the offense and step back into relationship as if nothing had ever happened. These superheroes are able to forgive *and* forget for both of their sakes. They forgive with their heart.

Others, knowing they are unable to return to exactly what had been, look at forgiveness as a philosophical concept impossible to achieve.

Sometimes the damage that has been inflicted is terrifying. With recovery appearing as nothing more than a mirage in the future, these victims are too weak to extend forgiveness.

Others choose unforgiveness so the offender *gets what she deserves.*

For most of us, we are in some process of working toward forgiveness. We know it's the right thing to do on a number of levels. But we also recognize it isn't always easy. Forgiveness is often a journey starting with, "I *want* to forgive," and after traveling through peaks and valleys, hopefully culminates in, "I forgive you."

Forgiveness doesn't wash away the intent or the pain. It doesn't clear the slate or give approval of the action. It simply gives the forgiver permission to move on, without carrying the negative burden of the betrayal.

Is it OK to think about forgiveness as an attitude? A destination? Knowing we are human, can we give ourselves the time and space we need to forgive others without succumbing to condemnation in the process?

I don't have all the answers, but I have watched Anita work through the forgiveness process. With God's help she is committed to finding the strength to forgive Art so *she* is no longer a victim.

***

Some might call it fate, but just before Anita went to see Art speak at Genoa Church in November 2009, she heard both Dr. Phil and Oprah talk about the importance of giving people second chances. At the time, their messages resonated with her and she recalled thinking how fortunate she was to be in a position to give Art a second chance.

The irony is not lost on her, as she is now the one seeking a second chance of her own.

Made in the USA
San Bernardino, CA
30 August 2016